MW00989571

WORKFORCE EDUCATION

Dr Johnson—

Nature creates few men brave,
industry and training makes many
The Prince

All the best
Brian Jackson

WORKFORCE EDUCATION

A New Roadmap

William B. Bonvillian and Sanjay E. Sarma

The MIT Press
Cambridge, Massachusetts
London, England

This book was set in ITC Stone Serif Std and Pangram by New Best-set Typesetters Ltd. Printed and bound in the United States of America.

Library of Congress Cataloging-in-Publication Data

Names: Bonvillian, William, author. | Sarma, Sanjay E., 1948- author.
Title: Workforce education : a roadmap / William B. Bonvillian and Sanjay E. Sarma.
Description: Cambridge, Massachusetts : The MIT Press, [2021] | Includes bibliographical references and index.
Identifiers: LCCN 2020007620 | ISBN 9780262044882 (hardcover)
Subjects: LCSH: Working class—United States. | Employees—Training of—United States. | Labor market—United States. | Technological innovations—Economic aspects—United States.
Classification: LCC HD8072.5 .B66 2021 | DDC 374/.0130973—dc23
LC record available at https://lccn.loc.gov/2020007620

10 9 8 7 6 5 4 3 2 1

CONTENTS

AUTHORS' NOTE

Most of this book was researched and drafted before the COVID-19 pandemic, so the content was written to speak of a world before the pandemic's dramatic economic and social blows that have followed. Then massive protests over historic racial inequality broke out during the pandemic. As we write this note, we cannot be certain of the situation by the time the book is published and available for you to read. This note is a snapshot in time as well as a glimpse into the future.

We, of course, updated the book with considerations about the virus's effects on the economy and the implications of both the virus and the protests for workforce education. It turned out that in reexamining the work, we found that it actually speaks effectively to the new set of problems the pandemic and protests have raised.

This work describes the nation's growing economic inequality, including its effects on the working class and minorities, and suggests that a new system of workforce education is one remedy. The coronavirus has called out this inequality problem because, as we write, it is hitting the poor and minorities particularly hard at one end of the economic spectrum, while the wealthier in our society have been able to exit urban congested conditions to protect themselves and maintain income by working at home. The protests have been even more directly on point. If the nation is to grow out of this inequality and its consequences, these issues have made the subject of the book even more significant.

The coronavirus will transform a number of sectors. Overall, the virus is showing what thin margins much of the economy has been operating on, and therefore how fragile it is. In particular, in-person retail is suffering massive cutbacks and job losses. Some critical manufacturing sectors have been hard-hit, particularly the aircraft industry. Manufacturing overall has been oriented to large lots and automation, and it will need to become more flexible and resilient, with more carefully controlled supply chains. Education has gone online in a remarkably short period, which may alter the way it develops and is delivered. Health has shifted toward new kinds of telemedicine and delivery. Together, these sectors dominate the economy, and each is a particular focus of this work.

The internet has also become even more of a societal mainstay during the virus, both in some of these sectors and in daily life. In Albert Camus's 1947 novel *The Plague*, the diseased society he portrays lives by hearsay and rumor because the communication system has broken down. In this pandemic, in sharp contrast, the level of communication and connectedness has been remarkable. While retail and travel have crashed, the internet is soaring. Online education, including workforce education, may be a beneficiary. Some of these shifts had already been evolving, but the coronavirus has sharply accelerated them.

An underlying policy that will affect this inequality is to address new sets of workforce skills that will be required because of the changes in each. While other public policy areas are also relevant to enabling and retaining quality jobs, workforce education has, arguably, been driven much higher on the priority list by the messages of the pandemic and the protests.

August 2020

ACKNOWLEDGMENTS

This book grew out of the Workforce Education Project, a research effort begun in 2018 at the Massachusetts Institute of Technology (MIT) Office of Open Learning program. As MIT's implementation of online courses and programs has developed over the past several years, there has been a growing focus on meeting workforce needs through our massive open online courses (MOOCs), MicroMasters certificates, boot camps, and professional education. Given this focus, we felt a need to understand the landscape of workforce education in much more depth. We also felt a strong need, in light of the social disruption of recent years, to try to contribute to understanding and meeting the nation's growing workforce needs.

This work deals with problems in the current US workforce education system and in our accompanying labor market information system; the roles employers, community colleges, high schools, and universities could play in workforce education; new education technologies that could help us reach the scale required to meet workforce needs; new apprenticeship programs; a range of new models that could help in delivering workforce content; and a detailed series of policy recommendations.

There are many to thank for assisting us in the development of this book. First, we thank Schmidt Futures for the foundation grant that made the research behind this study possible; we have benefitted from the foundation's deep concern about these workforce issues.

Our two able research assistants were very important to the project: Meghan Perdue, digital learning fellow at MIT Open Learning, and Jenna Myers, MIT Sloan School doctoral candidate. Each tackled major parts of the workforce puzzle. We were also assisted by an early travel grant from the MIT International Policy Lab led by Chap Lawson and Dan Pomeroy, which got the project started; we thank Dan for his assistance on a series of early meetings and briefings that helped shape the overall project.

Our MIT colleagues played an important advisory role. Tom Kochan and Paul Osterman, the MIT Sloan School's able experts and leaders on workforce issues, helped us in many ways, from their writings to reviewing their ideas with us. We particularly appreciate Tom's close read and suggestions on an earlier draft. David Autor, David Mindell, Elizabeth Reynolds, co-chairs, and the members of MIT's interdisciplinary task force on Work of the Future, helped us better understand an important context for our study—the effects on the workforce of evolving new technology advances. Political scientist Suzanne Berger contributed insights at many stages, helped review the draft, and has been a great sounding board, as has George Westerman of MIT Open Learning's Jameel World Education Lab (WEL) Workforce Learning project. Zenep Ton of the MIT Sloan School advised on retail sector developments. Kim Kimerling and Julie Diop, leaders of the AIM Photonics Academy located at MIT, helped us see the practical demands of developing workforce education in an advanced technology sector. MIT's WEL supports ongoing research on education and workforce issues and has contributed insights to this study. At MIT Open Learning, we have appreciated the assistance of Lana Cook, Tom Smith, Yvonne Ng, Patricia Gao, and Cindy Sambataro.

We were also greatly helped by many experts and leaders who showed us new models for workforce education firsthand. Particular thanks go to Sandy Shugart, Kathleen Plinske, and Joe Baptista at Valencia College in Orlando and Oceola, Florida; Captains Wes Naylor and Erik Etz at the Naval Air Warfare Center Training Systems Division in Orlando; Marilyn Barger of Florida Advanced Technological Education and Kevin Carr of FloridaMakes; Mitchell Harp and Melissa Stowasser of Trident Technical College in Charleston; Vince Lombardy of VTL in Charleston; Mark Johnson, Josh Summers, and Kapil Chalil Madathil of Clemson University; Ira Moskowitz of the Mass Tech Collaborative; Frank Gulluni, James Lombella, and Jose Marcelino of Asnuntuck Community College in Enfield, Connecticut; David Cruise and Larry Martin of MassHire Hampden County Workforce Board in Springfield, Massachusetts; Michael Valario, Anne Marie Zenni, and Elvio Ferreira of Diman Regional Vocational Technical High School in Fall River, Massachusetts; Brad Markel of the AFL-CIO; Tom Kirger of NABTU; and Amy Firestone, formerly of the US Department of Labor Office of Apprenticeship and now with Apprenticeship Carolina. Other practitioners who contributed to our thinking include Judith Glassgold of Rutgers University; Wilma Liebman, former chair of the National Labor Relations Board; Paul Lewis of King's College London; Andrew Reamer of George Washington University; Celeste Carter of NSF's Advanced Technological

Education Program; Michael Britt-Cane, David Heckman, and Emily DeRocco of Mantech in the office of the U.S. Secretary of Defense; and Phillip Singerman of NIST.

We have relied on studies from experts at many schools and organizations and specifically cite their contributions in endnotes. Here we must mention, in addition to those noted previously, some to whom we are particularly indebted: David Autor; Anthony Carnevale and colleagues at the Georgetown Center on Education and the Workforce; Richard B. Freeman; Claudia Goldin; Kenneth Gray; Edwin Herr; Harry Holzer; Lawrence Katz; Robert Lerman; Frank Levy; Mark Muro, Jonathan Rothwell, and colleagues from the Brookings Institution; Merrilea Mayo; William Symonds, Amy Loyd, and Robert Schwartz from the Pathways to Prosperity Project; and Kathleen Thelen.

We also thank Susan Buckley, associate acquisitions editor at the MIT Press, for her early understanding of the need for this work and for guiding us through the publication review process. We thank, too, our editor Scott Cooper for his steady guidance in helping us transform this work from an academic report into (hopefully) a more accessible book. (And we thank Jeff Burdett of MIT's Information Systems & Technology service desk, who saved Scott's computer at a crucial moment.)

Last, but by no means least, we thank our families for their support throughout this project.

William B. Bonvillian and Sanjay E. Sarma
Cambridge, Massachusetts
August 2020

1 INTRODUCTION

American democracy was built around an ever-expanding middle class, but it is starting to fray as that middle class declines. Our society faces growing income inequality and too many dead-end jobs. Technological advances are placing quality jobs out of reach for too many precisely because those workers are unprepared for these jobs.

What are we going to do about it? A much better educated workforce seems to be one critical answer.

We begin with the possible: brief previews of three new types of workforce education programs, all in Florida, that might make a difference and that illustrate major themes of this book. The first shows how short community college skill courses could reach underemployed workers; the second illustrates the potential of new education technologies; and the third shows how disparate federal programs could be integrated at the state level.

PREVIEW #1: A SHORT, INTENSIVE PROGRAM IN ADVANCED MANUFACTURING

Valencia College, based in Orlando, has some seventy-five thousand students in Orange and Osceola Counties in Central Florida's Orlando area. With Sandy Shugart, the college's president, we visited Valencia's Advanced Technology Manufacturing Center—a small, new, never-opened factory in Osceola County, clean and bright, with the building loads and power access to handle heavy manufacturing equipment and infrastructure. Valencia took over the factory after the 2008 economic crash and turned it into a working campus.

At our first stop, the welding center, a group of some twenty men in their twenties or thirties—Hispanic, Black and white, mostly tattooed—operated a dozen large, glass-enclosed advanced welding machines. Next, we watched another group at work in the large space for computer numerical control

(CNC) machining and milling equipment. Then we sat down in the mechatronics class, where an instructor in a shop apron guided a group of students on computers as they followed a circuit design above them on a large screen and built circuit boards for operating advanced equipment. Even more races worked here, of many ages, and half the workers were women.

Valencia was running short, intensive, ten- to twenty-two-week courses in advanced manufacturing fields to achieve certificates meeting Manufacturing Skill Standards Council (MSSC) standards and Veterans Affairs Department's requirements and provide credits toward a Valencia associate's degree. The Orlando area has a growing manufacturing sector, including in its Space Coast and defense industries, and graduates with these new Valencia certificates were being snapped up immediately by area manufacturers into full-year jobs paying twenty dollars per hour or more, with benefits—putting these students squarely on the first step of working careers that could support families.

Beginning as a community college, Valencia—like others in Florida—was elevated to four-year-college status in response to swelling population growth. The college today offers a number of bachelor's degrees, as well as associate degrees and a range of certificates, and in recent years accelerated its training focus with short-term certificates in the region's expanding job sectors. But while one-third of the region's workforce is well placed in the area's strong knowledge economy—technology and healthcare—Shugart says "the caboose has been left off":

> Roughly one-third of the area's urban population, over three hundred thousand, are poor, often Black and Hispanic, often immigrant, and in lower-end, low-skill, low-pay services jobs that are often not full year or full time, offer no benefits, and can end abruptly. In the education world of talent, strategy leaders want to talk about a "pipeline," but it's the wrong metaphor. There are many who never enter the pipeline. As technology changes work, we need to train people much more quickly while they're already working. It's not the pipeline that gets them into the ecosystem—they're not in the pipeline. They can't take two years off to get into an associate's degree program and then into the pipeline. The timing doesn't work. Most degree programs don't fit these skills.[1]

Part of what Valencia is doing is gearing its two-year associate degree programs to high-skill areas and professions. But as work changes, what professions and skills are going to be required? Healthcare is growing, and Valencia has a nursing school that offers eleven professional degrees in advanced skill areas. Software development is a large new focus. Valencia may be doubling or tripling its hospitality education; skilled chefs are in high demand at nearby Disney World. The University of Central Florida

(UCF)—the area state university—has asked Valencia to develop bachelor's programs in business; adding a business degree to these other skill areas enables students to move ahead into management in the area's strong tourism economy. Still, the bottom one-third Shugart described remains, and two-year programs don't fit. "It doesn't matter how high the minimum wage is set," he says. "The bottom is too sticky and the employment is too easily interrupted."

Valencia Provost Kathleen Plinske argues for another pathway into the job pipeline other than two-year and four-year degrees. "There's a huge labor force," she says, "that can't even get to the bottom rungs of the ladder. How can you get them on the ladder?"[2] So Valencia's new goal is to create that new pathway by educating for good jobs, to get people on that ladder that can lead to the middle class and jobs that offer year-round work with increasing benefits. And because there are very real shortages of skilled workers in the area, the college's short, intense certificate programs aim at getting participants hired in six to nine weeks. "Imagine if, in five years, twenty-five thousand families made that leap," Plinske adds. "That is Valencia's education acceleration goal. It could make a real difference."

Accordingly, Valencia is unbundling the specific skills for its accelerated training programs that lead to industry-recognized certificates. It now offers certificates in advanced manufacturing, construction, heavy equipment, logistics, transportation, and healthcare. There is a risk here that short programs don't provide enough depth: Participants may be job-ready, but will they be career-ready? Valencia understands this, so complementary skills can be stacked for multiple certificates, and they count as credits toward a Valencia associate degree. But the key is to get students rapidly into a work/learn environment and then into the workplace with the skills to earn a good wage—and with a path for follow-on career readiness.

Because Valencia receives no state aid for this program, there is no state oversight, which means Valencia has been able to move quickly. Federal Pell Grants go to enrolled college degree students, so the accelerated workforce program is funded entirely by tuition. Valencia does, however, offer tuition subsidies, and it used a $2.5 million US Labor Department grant to set up the first program in manufacturing. Area employers provide much of the training equipment.

Valencia's six campuses share four Centers for Accelerated Training, with nearly seven hundred students in their short programs. The college aims to grow enrollment to five thousand a year, hoping twenty-five thousand students can complete these certificates by 2025. The certificate program has even been extended to area prisons, with one hundred newly released prisoners entering the program and finding jobs—and with a recidivism rate far lower than usual.

Achieving the objective, argues Shugart, "would change Orlando."

PREVIEW #2: PUTTING NEW EDUCATION TECHNOLOGIES TO USE

A team of sailors, each wearing an augmented reality (AR) headset, stood in front of an eighty-four-inch touch screen portraying a mobile cart—a *huffer*—that is used to start jet aircraft engines on carrier decks. The cart's control panel doors were open, and a member of the team was flipping the master switch by hand and then the start switch on the touch screen to warm it up.

The huffer is a small auxiliary turbine engine that generates high-pressure exhaust using the same fuel as the real engine. A hose led to the F/A-18 Hornet aircraft's engine, and exhaust air began pushing through its big turbine. Jet engines need substantial airflow before they're started; if turbine blades aren't pushing enough air through the engine to get the revolutions per minute (RPMs) up to the right level, the "hot start" causes overheating and damage. With a $70 million aircraft at stake, the huffer team has to get it right every time.

We watched them flip the next set of switches, first in the correct order, and then in reaction to incorrect sequences to test their ability to make rapid corrections. Then we saw the huffer fault out and watched the operators use the screen to go through protocols—in the form of instructional videos and equipment system designs that can be cued to pop up for each piece of the equipment—to repair it and make it operational again. This is how the navy now teaches sailors to start jet aircraft engines without equipment, and without the safety risks and costs of actual practice.

Also using AR, another team at the Naval Air Warfare Center Training Systems Division in Orlando walked through the cramped quarters of a Virginia-class nuclear submarine. We watched on the screen. The crew has to live around the massive equipment—the nuclear reactor and cruise missile tubes—that take up most of the sub's space. Some sailors have to *hot bunk*—using a bunk when off watch and turning it over to another when on watch.

The team entered the engine room spaces and halted in front of the backup diesel engine used in emergencies if the reactor shuts down. They threw switches on the screen to get it operating, then shut it down, and went through a troubleshooting exercise to make repairs, with video pop-ups guiding them through the touch screen. Then the team entered the forward torpedo room and went through launch drills. This is how the navy now teaches sailors to operate a nuclear submarine, one of the world's most sophisticated technology platforms.

Increasingly, the United States Navy uses immersive VR (virtual reality) and AR simulations as its core training tool. Its Multiple Reconfigurable Training System (MRTS), developed for aviation training at the Training Systems Division in Orlando, is now used at the other major Navy schools, including the submarine school at Groton, Connecticut, and the aviation mechanics school in Pensacola, Florida. The navy made a deliberate choice to build MRTS on commercially available technology to save costs, enable rapid scale-up, and avoid depending on a single contractor. MRTS uses a high-end gaming computer with a widely available gaming platform, the license for which cost only $1,500—because the navy qualifies as a non-profit organization. All told, each MRTS unit cost approximately $20,000, with the gaming computers, flat screens, VR/AR sets, and so on. Developing the software, of course, costs far more, but it is a one-time cost and can be spread over thousands of training sessions.

The training tool is also becoming the operating tool. The navy is moving scaled-down, smaller-screen variants of these simulation systems to the points of need on ships and bases so training can be tied to actual equipment operation, using the online system in non-VR mode as the operating guide. The navy is also developing a standard and simplified software development kit so that simulations can be developed for the many different types of equipment and variants the navy uses. MRTS simulations produced equivalent results to hands-on training with actual equipment and far exceeded classroom instruction.

Captain Wes Naylor, a retired navy pilot, former squadron commander, and former commander of the training division, says MRTS took advantage of the billions in venture capital support that developed VR and AR technology in recent years. It was developed by contractors for the training division, is owned by the navy, and as of the time of writing was in fifty navy sites.[3] He cites tremendous benefits. For example, the contractor for electromagnetic catapults (replacing the old steam ones) for launching jet aircraft from aircraft carriers proposed a $100 million plus training system, but the MRTS system developed training software implemented across the navy for $12 million. A toolkit under development will allow anyone in the navy to make simulations for the MRTS system. Like real equipment, any student trainee can use the simulated equipment in an individual, nonproscribed way. Intelligent agent features are on the way that will enable individualized evaluation of each student using MRTS. This is *learning by doing*—with extensive instruction features built in.

Captain Erik Etz, a Stanford-trained electrical engineer, flew F/A-18s and helped lead the development team for sensors and software on the new F-35 fighter. He's the commanding officer of the training division and notes that its location is no accident.[4] The Orlando region has become the Silicon Valley of simulation and modeling technology. All the armed services are developing comparable simulation training systems at centers next to each other and adjacent to the UCF campus, which in turn is becoming the academic center and a major talent provider for this technology. More than three hundred firms, from major defense contractors to computer gaming companies to simulation start-ups, belong to the National Center for Simulation, the active area trade association. The cluster was built around the $4.8 billion annual defense budget spent locally for training simulations, but is expanding beyond it, including into medical simulations. The Veterans Affairs Department is building a new medical simulation training center nearby.

Will the military's new education technologies eventually transfer into the civilian sector? The prospects for learning by doing in immersive learning environments is truly startling from an education perspective. Imagine learning about ancient Egypt by participating in building the pyramids; it could be transformative. But the first adopters may be in workforce education, where learning by doing is paramount and where the risk, cost, and safety challenges of using actual equipment are often high. It will require moving simulation and modeling technology from the military into mainstream workforce education.

PREVIEW #3: COLLABORATION BETWEEN FEDERALLY SUPPORTED PROGRAMS

Someone once called interagency cooperation a contradiction in terms, but we found an exception at the state level when we spoke with Marilyn Barger and Richard Gilbert, the founders of Florida Advanced Technological Education (FLATE); Andra Cornelius, senior vice president, and Dehryl McCall, workforce development director, for CareerSource Florida; and CEO Kevin Carr of FloridaMakes—who convened the discussion.

FLATE is a National Science Foundation (NSF)-supported Advanced Technological Education (ATE) program working with Florida's community and state colleges. CareerSource Florida is the state's nonprofit workforce policy and investment organization; its business and government leaders and professional staff guide and support workforce development in Florida, backed by US Labor Department funding.[5] FloridaMakes is the

Manufacturing Extension Partnership funded by the National Institute of Standards and Technology (NIST, part of the US Department of Commerce) and the state of Florida to provide technical outreach to the state's 20,600 small manufacturers.

Why were these three programs, sponsored by very different federal agencies, talking? The answer can be found in a few more details of what they do and in the example that connecting their dots might provide for collaboration elsewhere.

FLATE has received recognition for creating an industry-defined and industry-endorsed two-year engineering technology degree that integrates national skill standards and is now offered in twenty-three of Florida's twenty-eight state colleges and community colleges; enrollment in the degree reached two thousand in 2018. It has developed frameworks for twenty different certificates within the engineering technology associate degree and ten specializations in manufacturing skill areas offered at these schools. All this was done in collaboration with manufacturing companies, trade associations, and government agencies across Florida.[6] FLATE's industry and community college partners leveraged more than $80 million in state and local workforce funding for its programs.

Here's how the engineering technology associate degree works. The program prepares students for skilled jobs in manufacturing and other high-technology industries. Students in the first year take classes in introductory computer-aided drafting, electronics, instrumentation and testing, process control and materials, production quality, and safety—core skills that align with the national MSSC's portable production technician certification that many Florida manufacturers recognize. In the second year, students focus on a technical specialization. A valid MSSC credential also translates to fifteen credit hours for the engineering technology technical core in any of the schools offering the degree in the state. So the credentialing works both ways: having the MSSC certification translates to credit at the state's community and state colleges, and the degree translates into recognized MSSC job qualifications.

FLATE also runs a training program supported by CareerSource Florida's Quick Response Training grants; since the 1990s, these have assisted seven hundred plus Florida employers train more than 120,000 employees in specialized fields.

FloridaMakes, as the state's Manufacturing Extension Partnership (a program funded throughout the country by the US Department of Commerce's NIST), works to bring technology and process advances to Florida's small and midsize manufacturing firms and, with the state's fourteen regional manufacturing associations, is developing an overall strategy for the state's growing manufacturing sector. A major goal is to significantly increase the productivity of that sector; the state ranks thirtieth in productivity in the United States.

Part of all this involves connecting the dots with FLATE through a merger that will link the manufacturing certificate programs at the state's community colleges much more directly to manufacturing industry workforce needs and employment. Workforce education is at the center of a strategy to raise manufacturing productivity: a talented workforce ready to work with the latest technology advances is the best way Kevin Carr sees to grow productivity, and the much more direct link between the state's small manufacturers and the community and state college programs initiated by FLATE is the way, he believes, to achieve this. FLATE is already one of the most well-regarded state ATE programs.

Together, they will expand their mission to include a big new area—apprenticeships. Carr contrasts what FLATE can do with the multiyear, time-based German model that he says is hard to adopt in the United States: "Manufacturers here aren't that patient. They don't want to wait three or four years for employees; they don't have the resources to sustain this timeframe. They want highly adaptable programs for shorter periods designed in a custom way to meet their needs. . . . FLATE is already piloting approaches in Polk County, in addition to what they're already doing with certificates, where they're using a mix of some community college classroom courses, tooling, and some on-site courses at manufacturers. We need a new apprenticeship approach that works in Florida."[7] An alliance between FLATE and FloridaMakes, with its links to manufacturers and the regional manufacturing associations, makes possible a new synergy and way to scale FLATE's education programs. To Carr, that's the logic behind connecting the dots.

CareerSource Florida is the third dot. It can use a modest part of the state's share of Workforce Innovation and Opportunity Act (WIOA) funding, the federal government's primary workforce development legislation, to reimburse employers for a substantial portion of their training costs—up to 75 percent for small companies to increase skill levels. That would enable small manufacturers with limited resources and trainees to afford the new kind of apprenticeship and workforce training FloridaMakes and FLATE envision. CareerSource's existing manufacturer leadership council would serve as a common advisory mechanism for the effort across the three organizations.

Federal-level funders tend to be siloed. In Florida, they're being brought together. The week before we spoke with this group, their three organizations had brought employers (including manufacturers), state program officials, federal agency representatives, and community and state college administrators together for Florida's first-ever summit on apprenticeships.[8] The trio is clearly off to a start. Could this kind of collaboration work in other states?

THE PROBLEM

We have previewed three examples of emerging approaches to workforce education. Valencia College is implementing short, intense training programs with industry-accepted certificates tied to industry needs. The aim is big: help move a region's underclass onto a ladder toward the middle class. The navy is experimenting with a suite of new technologies that could enable a new type of immersive learning by doing, a key to workforce education. Also in Florida, three entities supported by three different federal agencies are attempting to join programs. FLATE's technical training courses, developed with industry players and taught in community colleges, will join FloridaMakes in 2020, using its connections to bring new talent to small and midsize manufacturers to improve their efficiency, with CareerSource contributing a funding mechanism to help both put new designs from a new linked system in place. Ultimately, these three approaches—short-term skill certificates, new immersive technologies, and tying community colleges more closely to employers with funding support—could even be combined.

All three new programs are working, with promising initial results, but none is fully tested. All three represent hypotheses, not full theories backed by all the needed evidence. All three confront deep problems in workforce education: Valencia's short program could reach displaced workers and the underemployed; the navy's development at its Orlando training division of new VR and AR technologies could move training closer to learning by doing; and efforts in Florida to strengthen the connections among federal workforce programs could deliver better training. Results from these programs need fuller examination before scaling up to broad application; we need to show more clearly that they move participants into better, higher-paying jobs with longer-term prospects and that the new training experiences better prepare workers for jobs.

Like many other experiments this report highlights, these three programs are aspirational. But hypotheses remain quite important: without ideas, there are no solutions. And these programs are not just policy notions; they are working models being tested. Reform of workforce education is only now being recognized as a need, but new working models—new hypotheses—are coming to bear. We don't have many proven theories yet, but the hypotheses deserve illumination. Social policy proceeds through replicating demonstrated models. This work aims to collect new models.

Florida is not alone in experimenting. New kinds of workforce education are beginning in many states; we highlight many other examples in the chapters that follow. All these efforts are aimed at solving a big social disruption. Manufacturing was once a critical route to the middle class for those with high school educations or less,[9] but the United States lost one-third of our manufacturing jobs—5.8 million—between 2000 and 2010. By 2018, only about 18 percent had come back.[10] The largest manufacturing job losses are those lost to international trade,[11] coupled with a general hollowing out; some sixty thousand factories were closed from 2000 to 2010.[12] Automation hasn't been the major factor thus far.[13]

Retail is another sector in decline. Its underlying problem is that the nation has overbuilt retail space, but online commerce has also reshaped the flow of goods, replacing store jobs with warehouse jobs. In warehouses, meanwhile, robots and automation are taking on significant roles.

Because manufacturing is the largest job multiplier—manufacturing jobs create many more jobs compared to service jobs—the effects of these job losses rolled through other sectors of the economy. They were not geographically uniform; some communities suffered more than others. Nationwide, the median income of men who never graduated from high school dropped precipitously, as did income for men with high school diplomas or some college.[14] Women without a high school diploma also experienced a serious median income decline, while the median income of women with a high school diploma stagnated. The numbers of workers without a college education who dropped out of the workforce during this period hit historic highs. Only slightly more than half of prime working-age men without high school diplomas worked in full-year, full-time jobs, and more than a quarter did not work at all.[15] The economic disruption from the coronavirus may exacerbate all these problems.

In sum, a significant part of the workforce is being left behind. Healthcare services are a growing sector offsetting declines in other sectors, but it needs more trained technicians to field new medical technologies at scale and is hindered by various barriers to entry. Meanwhile, our workforce is increasingly polarized, income inequality is growing, and the middle class has been in decline. Even with unemployment at the beginning of 2020 at below 4 percent, many workers faced a job *quality* problem: they tend to be stuck in lower-end service work lacking benefits. The coronavirus recession has worsened both job availability and job quality.

Upskilling

Manufacturing is a particularly good marker for what is going on because of its historic role in leading productivity gains. It is no longer dark and dirty; factories look more and more like clean labs. New production jobs involve upskilling.

In essence, US manufacturing workers fall into three categories.[16] *Lower-skill* assemblers and basic production workers once dominated, but we have had two decades of significant growth in the *high-skill* category (often called *middle-skill*) that includes machinists, technicians, welders, and other skilled workers; there's also a *very high-skilled* category of engineers, researchers, and scientists. Middle-skill jobs are generally defined by the educational level required: some postsecondary education, including an associate's degree or certificate, or, alternatively, significant certified training—an imperfect but workable measure used as a proxy for actual skill.[17] All this illustrates part of a remarkably swift shift in US labor markets: required skills are moving steadily upscale in the overall economy.[18]

The Education Divide

People with the right skills can command a wage premium when advancing technology creates rising demand for those skills. It is the absence of those skills that best explains the growing income inequality in the United States. How real is this income inequality? As table 1.1 shows, real median income was stagnant between 2000 and 2016.

Both wealth and income in 2016 were highly concentrated in the top 1 percent and top 10 percent of the US population, as table 1.2 shows.

The upper class and upper middle class are thriving; the rest are not. These trends are accelerating: the share of wealth owned by the bottom 80 percent fell from 18.7 percent in 1983 to 11.1 percent in 2010.[19]

The clearest sorting mechanism for understanding these differences is a college education. The thriving upper middle class has it and captures the

TABLE 1.1
US real median family income

1955	2000	2016
$35,442	$72,417	$72,277

Source: US Census Bureau, "Real Median Family Income in the United States" [MEFAINUSA672N], FRED, Federal Reserve Bank of St. Louis, August 5, 2019, https://fred.stlouisfed.org/series/MEFAINUSA672N.

TABLE 1.2
Distribution of income and wealth in the United States (2016)

	Top 1%	Next 9%	Bottom 90%
Before-tax income:	24%	27%	50%
Wealth:	39%	39%	23%

Source: Chad Stone, Danilo Trisi, Arloc Sherman, and Roderick Taylor, *A Guide to Statistics on Historical Trends in Income Inequality*, Center on Budget and Policy Priorities, December 11, 2018, figure 4 (numbers rounded).

increasingly sophisticated tech jobs; the rest of Americans do not.[20] The lifetime earning differential for those with college educations is dramatic, exacerbated by the increase in lower-end, lower-pay service jobs that many with lower skills who lost middle-income jobs have been forced to take.[21] Those without the education and higher skills will continue to fall far even further behind the advancing technological curve.

The Training Problem

A strong system of workforce skills training could make up for this college education divide. But US labor markets generally invest in suboptimal levels of broad skills training[22] because after one company trains people, competitor companies often acquire those trained employees, and thus the first company fails to recapture its training investment. So employers who do provide training have tended to build their programs around very specific skills needed only by their firms and that are more valuable for them than for their competitors. This is a clear market failure. Reflecting this, data suggest corporate investment in workforce training has declined since the 1990s[23]—a significant problem for American workers. Government investment in workforce education has also been in decline.[24] No one is throwing American workers a lifeline; they are increasingly stuck in place.

Automation

Is automation and the productivity gains it enables causing all these problems? While predictions grow of the imminent end of jobs and corresponding societal dystopia stemming from the combination of robotics, artificial intelligence (AI), machine learning, the Internet of Things, and so on,[25] they seem premature.

US productivity—in the 1 percent range—and capital investment rates reported in 2017 were at very low levels.[26] Even if major new automation got us to a sustained 3 percent productivity rate (which we haven't seen since the information technology (IT) innovation wave in the 1990s), it would take a quarter century to realize a 75 percent improvement in productivity.[27] Work will not end tomorrow; we have some time to adjust our workforce. The sky is not falling, but change is coming. Workplaces will continue to shift to higher levels of digital technology, and too many workers lack the associated skills. But because key parts of the workforce have already been disrupted, largely by trade displacement, an upskilling is now underway. Over time, the new technologies will eliminate jobs, but more jobs will likely change and new jobs will be created.[28]

In other words, upcoming technology challenges don't make improved workforce education hopeless. They make it a necessity.

Taking Up the Workforce Challenge

A consensus around the need for improved workforce education is growing. We're not going to send displaced steel workers or incumbent retail workers to four-year colleges, but we can build systems to give them and others the skills they need to move toward quality jobs and back onto middle-class pathways. Workforce education may well be the best alternative to solving the country's growing income inequality. The public policy landscape for "good job" creation and, therefore, tackling inequality—as Dani Rodrik has discussed—falls essentially in three areas: preproduction (of a good or service), production, and postproduction.[29] There is a long history of industrial policy that in the United States has focused on two areas: early-stage innovation (through R&D support), which has been preproduction, and industry support justified primarily around a defense technology mission, which has been at the production and postproduction stages, although it has not focused on the production process itself. This has provided new technologies that historically have created jobs. But there is another dimension of governmental policy that operates in a complementary way: the workforce side. In the preproduction area, policies historically have been in the areas of support of higher education and workforce development programs. In the production area, policies have ranged from minimum wages to labor laws to protections in trade agreements. In the postproduction area, policies have included income transfers (though the Earned Income Tax Credit), safety net programs (such as unemployment insurance), and wealth taxes. The policy focus here is on one of those areas—workforce development. It is not the only policy option, but is likely one for which the most political support can be nurtured and where policy, because the current system is highly problematic, can have a substantial impact. Various forms of income redistribution have lately been under discussion (such as a universal basic income), but those alternatives seem highly unlikely and don't get to the root skills imbalance.

The signs of that growing consensus around workforce education include bipartisan congressional passage in 2018 of a major reauthorization of the Perkins Act, which supports federal training programs.[30] The president in 2018 issued an executive order promoting apprenticeships.[31] The US Chamber of Commerce has launched a new workforce education program built around regional consortia of employers.[32] Community colleges are developing new certificate programs, new online training programs are evolving, and the US secretary of labor's Workforce Information Advisory Council in early 2018 proposed a major revamping of the information systems behind our problematic labor markets.[33] In a period of profound political divide, workforce education is an exception. The disruption from the coronavirus as well as antiracism protests could be a further incentive. The public, the private sector, and even the political system appear ready for change.

This book focuses on the American *working class*—a term many stopped using beginning in the 1960s, when we began pretending we were all "middle class." Part of the American dream was that each succeeding generation would be better off, more economically successful, than the last. The middle class was the bulwark of our democracy, the basis for a consensus-based political system. But the erosion of the middle class accelerated after the turn to a new century, paralleling in significant part the decline of manufacturing. We now have growing economic inequality, not economic convergence, with the upper middle class thriving and most everyone else falling behind economically.

Who is in the working class today? One practical definition, based on Census Bureau data, suggests it is the forty-four million adults who lack an associate degree level of education and earn less than $35,000 per year.[34] This gives us a rough sorting mechanism for those who lack the education, skills, and credentials to earn adequate income to support themselves and their families. Half of these people are likely to live in poverty.[35] Only 11 percent of these working-class Americans earn a bachelor's degree by age twenty-four.[36] Only two of every twenty-five children born in lower-income households ever reach the top quintile of the economic ladder.[37] They are of all races and ethnic groups.

They are being left behind. They need a new workforce education system. Without action, their situations will deteriorate. The jobs of the future—indeed, more and more jobs of today—require significantly more education and training than they have.

THE STORY AHEAD

This book addresses all the issues you've just read about and related ones, from the decline of manufacturing (as well as trade and productivity issues) to retail change—including how this happened and what lies ahead. We address quality job growth, workforce education challenges, and new approaches like those in Florida.

First is the story of a disrupted working class. Chapters 1–6 confront the societal challenges our nation faces. We look more closely at who gets ahead and who gets left behind in the current system and elaborate on the extent of the *social disruption*, growing income inequality, low rate of workforce participation, upskilling of the workforce, rise of educated workers (including the protected role held by the college educated), upper middle class and working class divergence, and public attitudes toward all this.

The *breakdowns in today's workforce education* are a focus. We examine all the major actors in the current problematic system and review the disconnects and gaps between the actors and the problems they have in scaling up their efforts to make an overall impact. Beyond that, we take up *technological change in the workplace*. How will the current workforce cope with new digital technologies and robotics? How must the workforce education system respond?

Three major sectors—*manufacturing, healthcare, and retail*—amount to about one-third of the American economy, and we examine them in part because our general well-being will largely be determined by evolutions in each. We already know manufacturing requires a renewed focus; an important part of its renewal will be improved productivity and efficiency to compete, and a more productive workforce will be crucial to that story. As suggested earlier, the massive US retail sector has been in decline in recent years. We delve into what will happen to workers in this retail sector, what opportunities may arise in the healthcare sector, and the challenges facing both.

This first part of the book closes with a discussion of our *broken labor market information system*, which makes for a weak and poorly functioning labor market with limited information available to participants and employers. A new navigation system is needed.

Beginning with chapter 7, we pivot to exploring solutions to the workforce dilemma that may be on the horizon and develop a model for a new, more connected system for workforce education. In its six chapters, we examine *the role of colleges and universities in workforce education*, including the declining support for higher education in business and political circles and the sector's own resistance to disruptive change of the sort needed to educate for the workplace and provide career skills. We explore *new education technologies* and the many new education-delivery systems—including online education, virtual reality, augmented reality, artificial intelligence, digital tutors, and computer gaming—that present dramatic new learning opportunities. How could they contribute to workforce education, with its requirement for learning by doing? How do they fit into new learning models and into established education and training institutions?

In our discussion of *education content*, we shift the current focus on education for the skills needed in the workplace to the five training competency categories defined by the US Department of Labor: personal skills, academic competencies, workplace competencies, industry-wide technical competencies, and occupation-specific technical competencies. We also set out the possibility of a *new apprenticeship model*, comparing the limited apprenticeship history in the United States (primarily in the construction trades) with Germany's well-known system and its intricate collaboration among employers, educators, and government, which has cut youth unemployment and largely ensured a solid transition to work. We also look at interesting new apprentice models emerging in this country.

When we confront the *content-delivery challenge*, we scrutinize emerging models and explore what would be the new mechanisms for meeting the challenge with displaced, out-of-work workers or underemployed workers in lower-end services jobs; existing workers wanting to upskill; and new job entrants, just out of high schools or community colleges, who are seeking work. What partnerships among community colleges, universities, employers, apprenticeship offerings, and manufacturing institutes could reach each community? How can we create a new workforce education system? Policy advance requires demonstrated models that can be scaled up to affect society. Of the models we identify, many have been well tested while others require further evaluation. But all are operating.

Our book ultimately aims to pull together all these strands and form them into a coherent policy approach. We close in the final chapter with a roadmap to a new system of workforce education we believe is critical if our nation is to successfully tackle the many adverse societal challenges we analyze.

2 THE AMERICAN WORKING CLASS: ECONOMIC DECLINE AND GROWING INEQUALITY

Southeast Chicago was once among the world's largest steel-making regions. Beginning late in the nineteenth century, steel mills lined Lake Michigan, employing hundreds of thousands of workers. The mills and surrounding community pulled in immigrants from across the globe, looking for better lives.

That all began to change in the 1980s. One by one, the mills closed, and tens of thousands of jobs were lost, leaving the local economy in ruins. As plants were torn down, the land they sat on became a toxic dead zone from industrial pollutants. Eventually, the area was forgotten, as if its former residents had become invisible. The exit ramp off the interstate is numbered zero.

Christine Walley, an MIT anthropology professor, grew up in the neighborhood. In 2017, she and her filmmaker husband Chris Boebel made a documentary film, *Exit Zero*,[1] that tells the story of Southeast Chicago from its nineteenth-century origins to the unionization battles during the Depression and through the shutdowns, weaving in her family's story. It's an epitaph for a lost order.

The film opens with footage of nighttime cargo ships on Lake Michigan and Christine's voice-over:

> Early one morning when I was fourteen, my mother stepped into my bedroom and shook me awake. "Don't worry," she whispered to me, "It'll be ok. They called the ore boat back. It'll be alright."
>
> I had no idea what she was talking about or why a boat with oars would be called somewhere. Later, I found out she was talking about a giant freighter on Lake Michigan that carried iron ore to the steel mill in Southeast Chicago where my father worked as a shear operator. The Coast Guard had been sent out to stop the ship from delivering its cargo because the banks were about to foreclose on the mill, throwing my father and thousands of others out of their jobs. I didn't know it then, but that moment in March 1980 was a crucial moment,

> dividing our lives into the moment before the mill shutdown and after the mill shutdown.

Christine's father never found full-time work again; her mother took a part-time job as a bookkeeper at a toxic waste site to pull the family through. Like a soldier unable to talk about a war, her father—interviewed throughout the film—is never able to talk about his lost job.

Janesville tells a similar story.[2] The small Wisconsin city lost its General Motors (GM) plant and its seven thousand jobs two days before Christmas in 2008. It hit all of Janesville. The plant closing reverberated deep into the entire social fabric of the once thriving community. Companies that supplied the GM plant gradually failed, taking their jobs with them. Roofing companies closed because families couldn't afford to get roofs fixed. With a declining tax base, social services were cut back just when they were most needed. School funding was slashed. Private charity fell off.

The local community college was awash with former GM workers looking for retraining; it had to battle to provide services needed for the flood of older students. Most had limited education and struggled to adapt to being full-time students. Job-retraining programs helped some but frustrated others; too often, workers went through training only to find there weren't enough quality jobs left in the area to go around. Of 1,800 students in Janesville's high school, two hundred were using a teacher's secret food closet to stave off hunger. By 2017, unemployment in Janesville was down from 13 percent to 4 percent, but at the cost of a new normal. A new Dollar General distribution center opened, but union jobs were gone. Service jobs typically paid half the salary of the old GM jobs.

Amy Goldstein, *Janesville*'s author and a Pulitzer Prize–winning reporter for the *Washington Post*, began covering what was happening to Janesville families in 2011. She had to take leave from her job to keep covering the painful saga of wrenching economic and social disruption; otherwise, it would be invisible.

The Southeast Chicago and Janesville stories are largely about white working-class Americans. Production decline, though, is not only a story of white working-class decline; it also blocked what had been a crucial pathway into the middle class for minorities.

In the 1940s, with the World War II mobilization, growing numbers of industrial jobs became available for men with high school diplomas or less in many Midwest and Northeast cities. These jobs spurred a massive, thirty-year emigration of poor Blacks from the South for jobs in auto, rubber, steel, and other heavy industries, which enabled a significant number of

Black families to gain a foothold in the lower middle class. These were often union jobs with benefits and employment protections. When a global shift in the manufacturing sector began in the 1970s and these jobs declined, many lost that foothold and slid into what became a social underclass.[3]

Today, African Americans hold some 10 percent of manufacturing jobs and Hispanics some 16 percent. Although Hispanics held a larger share of manufacturing jobs in 2016 than they did in 1991, reflecting an overall population rise, Blacks lost 30 percent of their manufacturing jobs in the same period.[4] The effects of manufacturing job losses on both these communities were dramatic.

Writing in 1987, noted sociologist William Julius Wilson found that the obstacles poor African American workers faced in their neighborhoods were particularly difficult because they were a mix of race- and class-based. He saw class growing in importance, strengthening economic and educational disadvantages and inequalities and often paired with industrial decline to create what he termed a *spatial mismatch* that led to the development of a ghetto underclass.

The disappearance of industrial jobs from large cities in the 1970s and 1980s increased unemployment and created a host of social problems. There was, for example, a disincentive for marriage because fathers faced limits on their ability to become breadwinners—which multiplied single-parent households. Wilson was advocating a broad public policy agenda to improve the life chances for this community, including comprehensive educational, community, and human service interventions—and particularly training and retraining to address essential skill development.

WHAT THE US CLASS AND POLITICAL DIVIDE TELLS US

The work from 2005 of noted US political economist Benjamin M. Friedman provides a key rationale today for workforce education. He argues that conventional economic thinking about growth has been too narrow because it fails to consider its moral and political dimensions. A rising living standard, he contends, not only improves how individuals live, but also shapes "the social, political and ultimately the moral character of a people."[a] He identified a clear pattern in the historical relationship between economic growth and social values: During periods of rising economic prosperity, people tend to be more tolerant, optimistic, egalitarian, willing to settle disputes peacefully, and inclined toward democracy. By contrast, periods of stagnation and recession tend to breed pessimism, nostalgia, xenophobia, and violence, and lead to a search for demagogues and intolerance for pluralistic democracy.

Growth, then, carries with it a critical and massive positive externality—the political and social dimensions that drive the basic fabric of a society. While economists, with their dependence on metrics, can't plot these landscapes as they can markets, Friedman shows that this moral and political dimension of growth or decline is every bit as real.

While America's upper middle class is thriving in twenty-first-century America and has an expansive, optimistic view, the working class feels economically cornered and is unwilling to risk competition from minorities and immigrants. This makes Friedman's concern a critical pursuit. The 2016 US presidential election brought this home; some 90 percent of communities most affected by jobs lost through trade voted for Donald Trump.[b]

[a]Benjamin Friedman, *The Moral Consequences of Economic Growth* (New York: Knopf, 2005), 4.

[b]Joseph Parilla and Mark Muro, "Where Global Trade Has the Biggest Impact on Workers," Brookings Institution, December 14, 2018, https://www.brookings.edu/blog/the-avenue/2016/12/14/where-global-trade-has-the-biggest-impact-on-workers/. See also David Autor, David Dorn, and Gordon Hanson, *A Note on the Effect of Rising Trade Exposure on the 2016 President Election*, paper, March 2, 2017, http://economics.mit.edu/files/12418.

THE OVERALL ECONOMIC BACKDROP

The growth in US gross domestic product (GDP) since the end of World War II can be divided into three periods.[5] From 1945 to 1975, the United States dominated world technology development and correspondingly had the world's highest productivity economy; GDP growth was close to 4 percent. But that declined to 3 percent during the next three decades, with some periods in the 2 percent range, as Japan and Germany implemented strong manufacturing economies and as global competition grew. In the decade following the 2007 recession, GDP growth fell to 2.1 percent—a decline of nearly half from that postwar period economists sometimes refer to as the "thirty glorious years." Although the 2020 coronavirus pandemic has created additional disruption, that's roughly the overall range where the US Federal Reserve has been projecting it will remain for some time.

Household income is a component of GDP, so it comes as no surprise that the US real median household income since the 2007 recession has been stagnant. At the same time, overall wage growth has been anemic.

What's behind these developments? It is axiomatic from growth economics that economic growth is driven predominantly by technological and related innovation.[6] Despite sharply increased global competition,

TABLE 2.1
Federal unemployment data for October 2019

Category	Description	Unemployment rate
U3	Unemployed, actively seeking full-time work	3.6%
U6	Unemployed (U3) plus underemployed and recent dropouts from labor market	7.0%

Source: Macrotrends, U6 Unemployment Rate, October 2019 (citing US Bureau of Labor Statistics data), Bureau of Labor Statistics, Economic News Release, "Employment Situation Summary," October 2019, released November 1, 2019, https://www.bls.gov/news.release/empsit.nr0.htm.

federal growth-inducing investments in research, technology, and the innovation system have been neglected for two decades.[7] Instead, policymakers have relied almost entirely on low interest rates and stimulating demand through fiscal policy, with the effect of multiplying borrowing and speculation in real estate and stocks. That's what led to a nearly disastrous Great Recession of 2008 from which we seem not to have learned. Fiscal tools are important but are not the only ones. A lack of productivity-enhancing investment takes a toll on growth.

Current growth policies are unlikely to change this wage and household income situation significantly; 2 percent growth can't overcome stagnation in wages or the standard of living for the bulk of the population, and stagnation jeopardizes the ability of the federal government to meet expanding Social Security and Medicare commitments.[8] It seems US policymakers have forgotten growth economics.

Then there's the question of unemployment. Table 2.1 shows the federal government's figures at the end of 2018.

That low 3.9 percent figure (although it has been disrupted by the coronavirus) had not been seen since 1969. But it was the U6 rate, twice the U3 rate, that was of the most interest.[9] It includes as unemployed those who had recently given up looking for work and those working part time but wanting to work full time. The differential suggests a continuing level of underemployment. There is also likely higher unemployment in the "shadow" economy of undocumented immigrants, which is not counted. Youth employment has improved in recent years but is still three times higher than the general joblessness rate and more severe for racial and ethnic minorities. In other words, there is a lot of nuance in the employment story.

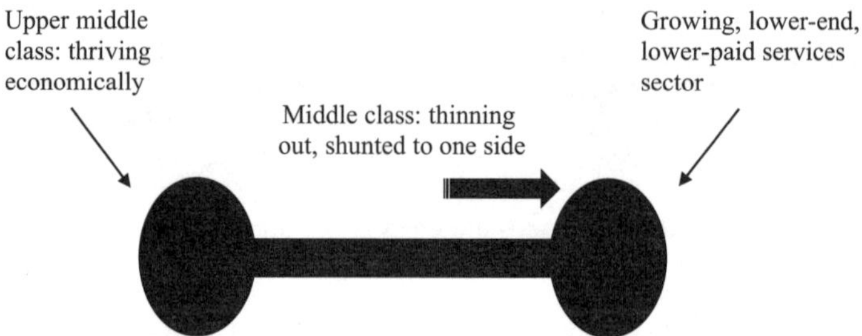

FIGURE 2.1
The impact of occupational employment. *Source:* Authors' rendering, after David H. Autor, "Polanyi's Paradox and the Shape of Employment Growth," *Proceedings of the Federal Reserve of Kansas City*, August 2014, 142.

THE BARBELL

When economist David Autor, our MIT colleague, graphed occupational employment in a series of charts, he found the data took on what he called a barbell shape. Using an actual barbell image (figure 2.1) shows quite vividly what has been happening in American labor markets.[10] At one end, the upper middle class has been thriving. Across the bar, the middle class is thinning out. A significant portion of the middle class is losing its place and being shunted toward the other end, which represents a growing lower-paid, lower-end services sector.

The income numbers bear out Autor's barbell shape, as table 2.2 shows.

While the lowest quintile received a gain comparable to the upper middle class, it was largely because of increases in government-provided health care benefits. Access to more healthcare services may count as income, but it's not money in people's pockets. And despite this, life expectancy has been declining in the United States, particularly among those with lower incomes.[11]

What declined were middle skill jobs. Examining a third of a century, Autor identified ten broad occupational categories and found that four core middle-skill occupations—production worker, sales, office worker, and machine operator—accounted for 60 percent of American jobs in 1979.[12] By 2012, these categories had fallen to 46 percent. Meanwhile, in three services areas—personal care, food and cleaning service, and protective service, all jobs that involve caring for or assisting others—jobs have grown rapidly in the past thirty years, growing by double digits in the 1990s and in the prerecession period of 1999–2000. These jobs, which have low education requirements (no postsecondary education) and offer low pay, grew even

TABLE 2.2
Increases in income, by quintile of population

Income level	Increase in income, 1979–2015
Top 1%	242%
Top quintile, minus the top 1% (eighty-first to ninety-ninth percentile)	78%
Bottom quintile of income (first to twentieth percentile)	46%

Source: Richard V. Reeves, "Restoring Middle-Class Incomes: Redistribution Won't Do," Brookings Institution, November 20, 2018, https://www.brookings.edu/blog/up-front/2018/11/20/restoring-middle-class-incomes-redistribution-wont-do/?utm_campaign=Economic%20Studies&utm_source=hs_email&utm_medium=email&utm_content=67840211; Congressional Budget Office, "The Distribution of Household Income, 2015," November 8, 2018, https://www.cbo.gov/publication/54646.

during the recession and immediately thereafter (2007–2012). Meanwhile, at the high end—managerial, professional, and technical occupations—most workers had four-year college degrees and were highly paid. This, too, has been an expanding sector, with robust growth between 1979 and 2012. Even during the Great Recession and its aftermath, these categories experienced almost no decline in employment.

The coronavirus has introduced an additional problem. The middle-skill workers who have lost their skilled jobs and find themselves in lower-skilled service jobs may find themselves with no jobs at all, given the massive layoffs in the services sector. The low-end services bell of the employment barbell has begun to break up during the pandemic.

These statistics paint a picture of wage polarization, of a middle class thinning out. The United States faces a jobs crisis because far too many jobs fall below a standard that most Americans would view as good and decent work. A quarter of working adults are stuck in jobs that don't provide living wages, health insurance, or expectations for upward economic mobility, a status that crosses all races and ethnic groups, including native-born and immigrants.[13] These are the jobs on the right side of the barbell in figure 2.1, and too many along the bar are moving in that direction.

WAGE STAGNATION AND DECLINE

The United States has had *minimal growth in median hourly wages* since 1980—stagnation with very real implications for the US economy, both in

TABLE 2.3
US real hourly compensation (nonfarm business sector) and median income

Date	Annual increase in real compensation per hour
1950–1980	2.8%
1981–2005	1.3%
2006–2016	0.6%
	Median income
1999	$58,665
2016	$59,035

Source: Gregory Tassey, "Make America Great Again: Investing in Research, Technology Development, Worker Training, and Modern Technological Infrastructure Is the Only Prescription That Will Maintain the Health of the US Economy," *Issues in Science and Technology*, Winter 2018.

terms of individual living standards and the country's overall macroeconomic growth. As table 2.3 shows, since 1950 we have had lower increases in compensation, and median household income has been stagnant for two decades. Wages have gone up for the top level of income distribution but have fallen for those in the bottom. So between 1979 and 2016, real wages in the top fifth of income grew 27 percent, the next fifth grew 12 percent, and the bottom fifth fell slightly over the same period.[14]

The widening inequality between top and bottom was not the way the US economy worked in the first thirty-five years of the postwar period. Overall income growth (including both labor and capital income) benefitted the lower end of the distribution from 1946 through 1980.[15] Incomes rose faster in the bottom half of the income distribution than in the top 10 percent or top 1 percent. Since 1980, that process reversed. This is reflected in the share of US economic output received by workers, which declined between 1974 and 2017, from 64.5 percent to 56.8 percent. And, as the barbell image suggests and table 2.4 details, less educated male workers have faced a particularly troubled earnings picture: more of them worked during that period in lower-paying jobs, and their earnings fell in every occupational category except technician. Could it be an echo of some of those earlier concerns about an *underclass*?

To understand all this, we also need to look at the different *wage effects for men and women*; both groups face significant wage problems. Table 2.4 shows the decline in median income for less educated men between 1990

TABLE 2.4

Changes in median income and type of work for less educated men, 1990—2013

By education level	Change in median income
Men without high school diplomas	20% decline ($31,900 to $25,500)
Men with high school diplomas or some college	13% decline ($47,100 to $40,700)
By education *and* middle- and lower-paying jobs	Share of middle- and lower-paying jobs
Working men without high school diplomas in middle-paying jobs (machine operators, construction workers, etc.)	15% decline (from 40% to 34%) of these men in middle paying jobs
Working men without high school diplomas in lower-paying jobs (food, cleaning, groundskeeping, etc.)	47% increase (from 11% to 21%) of these men in lower-paying jobs

Source: Melissa S. Kearney, Brad Hershbein, and Elisa Jacome, "Profiles of Change: Employment, Earnings and Occupations from 1990–2013," Hamilton Project report, April 20, 2015, http://www.hamiltonproject.org/assets/legacy/files/downloads_and_links/Employment_Earnings_Occupations_Changes_1990-2013_FINAL_1.pdf.

and 2013; women without a high school diploma or with a high school diploma and some college also had a drop in median income, although at considerably lower rates than men. Over a longer period, between 1979 and 2016, the wages of white, Hispanic, and African American men were stagnant or fell over time, while women appear to have gained ground during the same time. But underlying problems offset those gains. White women have seen a wage increase of 34 percent, while Black and Hispanic women experienced lower growth at around 17 percent. However, although the gap has been narrowing—in part due to growing educational attainment for women—their wage levels remain significantly below those of men. The remaining gap is more related to the fact that women are still being paid less, and promoted less, than men.[16]

Displaced workers who lose their jobs because of plant closings or cutbacks face particularly serious problems: their lost earnings tend to be large and continuing. Studies indicate that, in recent decades, displaced US workers see their earnings decline by 25 percent or more after they lose their jobs. A decade later, their earnings remain depressed by 10 percent or more compared to their wages at their prior job.[17]

TABLE 2.5
The college education income premium

Year	Education level (ages 25–54)	Income level (compared to high school education)
1979	Bachelor's degree	134%
	Advanced degree	154%
2016	Bachelor's degree	168%
	Advanced degree	213%

Source: Jay Shambaugh, Ryan Nunn, Patrick Liu, and Greg Nantz, "Thirteen Facts about Wage Growth," Hamilton Project report, September 24, 2017, https://www.hamiltonproject.org/assets/files/thirteen_facts_wage_growth.pdf.

Several factors spur this growing wage inequality. *Education differences* are an important part of the story; there is a clear wage premium for college education, which has been growing.[18] The wage benefit for college and postcollege degrees increased dramatically during the last three decades, as table 2.5 shows.

Although this difference leveled off around the year 2000, it was at a historically high level. During the same period as in table 2.5, the percent of workers with at least a four-year college degree also rose dramatically—from 23 percent in 1979 to 40 percent in 2016. Some studies suggest that encouraging more workers to complete college could significantly offset declining median annual earnings,[19] although increasing those education levels requires an extended period of time.

Researchers have tied increases in US wage inequality to *globalization* and trade imbalances.[20] China's entry into the world economy has been a significant factor in the loss of US manufacturing jobs, particularly the steep job declines of 2000–2010.[21] Harry Holzer, a leading workforce scholar, suggests that because US employers faced high costs and organizational challenges for training middle-skill workers, they may have opted to offshore or outsource their work.[22]

Economists recognize that the *wage growth is tied historically to the growth in labor productivity* (the output per hour of workers), which in turn depends on the human and physical capital used in the production process and how efficiently labor and capital are used. The combination of technological advances, the expansion of human and physical capital, and improved business processes allows for much more efficient uses of human labor over time.[23] Wages can rise as a result. However, the extent to which

TABLE 2.6
Compensation and labor productivity

Time period	Factor	Level of increase
1979–2017	Labor productivity	2% per year
	Real *average* compensation	Less than 1% per year
1979–2017	Labor productivity	97% over full period
	Real *median* compensation	14% over full period

Source: Jay Shambaugh and Patrick Ryan, "Introduction," in *Revitalizing Wage Growth: Policies to Get American Workers a Raise,* ed. Jay Shambaugh and Patrick Ryan (Washington, DC: Brookings Institution, 2018), 3–7.

workers benefit from productivity growth depends on how that growth is distributed—how much, for example, is allocated to compensation versus profits or capital income.[24]

For living standards to rise over any significant period, economists have long held that labor productivity must also rise; that is, for workers to be paid more per hour, the value of their economic output must increase. Rising productivity enabling rising wages has been a long-standing US economic story. However, productivity and labor compensation have diverged in recent years. While workers as a whole might benefit from productivity growth over some period, those benefits can sometimes be shared unequally. When labor's gains disproportionately go to those with high incomes, as we've seen with real wages since 1979, gains for the typical worker will lag even farther behind productivity growth.

Table 2.6 compares productivity and labor compensation, which tracked together relatively closely from the late 1940s through the 1970s, until compensation growth began to slow compared to productivity growth. Part of this historic divergence between median wages and productivity can be explained by shifts in how productivity gains are split up—as compensation, increases in nonwage benefits, gaps between average and median pay, or shifts from workers to firms.

While benefits have been a rising portion of overall compensation for US employees, due in significant part to rising health costs, they explain only a small percentage of the difference between wages and productivity. A modest part of the difference is attributable to a decline in the labor share of income, since total compensation to labor has fallen and the share going to capital has increased. A much larger portion of the gap is due to inequality: the difference between median compensation and average compensation (which reflects the growing income of the upper middle and upper classes). Productivity gains, then, have gone to the higher levels of income distribution, so the middle—the median income—has been falling short in the gains from productivity growth. A series of more technical pricing and depreciation factors make up the remainder.

Despite the divergence between wages and productivity, productivity growth is still a prerequisite for an American worker to get a larger pay raise. The next step is that any notable productivity gains must be shared between firms and labor. But the decline of unions, which now represent around 6 percent of US private-sector workers, has greatly diminished workers' bargaining position in this regard.[25] Pervasive noncompete agreements, "no poaching" agreements between employers, and the decline in the value of the minimum wage standard for low-income employees[26] also affect employee bargaining power.

Productivity gains also must be shared between lower- and higher-income workers; otherwise there is increasing wage inequality. But the data now show an imbalance. Understanding the long-run divergence between productivity and wages is essential to understanding wage stagnation in the United States. Underlying all this, however, is labor productivity growth and the factors that have limited it in recent years.

Between the Great Recession and 2017, the United States experienced some of its weakest labor productivity growth for any post–World War II period: 1.1 percent annually.[27] The trend, though, predates the recession. Productivity growth began to slow in 2004, after the 1990–2001 information technology innovation wave, and then slowed even more during the recovery from the Great Recession.[28] Behind this was weak investment growth; growth in capital intensity (the ratio of capital services to labor hours) has been below historical levels and actually fell in 2010–2014.[29] The low level of capital investment affects productivity advances and, correspondingly, wages.[30] And in turn, the reduction in capital investment growth in the economy is related to that low level of GDP growth in the post–Great Recession period discussed earlier.[31]

The productivity slowdown is a global phenomenon, affecting developed nations, emerging markets, and developing economies. The slump has continued despite a host of new computer and information technologies expanding their reach into the economy. There is an important ongoing debate about causes and remedies for low productivity growth,[32] but what matters here are not the results of that debate but the fact of productivity's decline.

LABOR MARKET NONPARTICIPATION

In 2013, more than one-quarter of working-age men lacking high school degrees (excluding those in prison) were not working, and only 55 percent worked full time for the full year.[33] In the next education category up were also troubling, trending numbers. Men with a high school degree or some college (who account for more than half of men ages thirty to forty-five) who were working full-time for the full year fell from 76 percent in 1990 to 68 percent in 2013. The share of these men who did not work at all went from 11 percent to 18 percent over the same period. In 1950, 14 percent of men were out of the workforce. That number was 31 percent in 2018.[34]

These increasing problems of less educated workers falling out of labor markets for extended periods, or even permanently, can be set against complex overall data on labor market participation. This labor participation rate, which concerns those not in jobs or actively looking for jobs, is a significant indicator of overall economic well-being and household living standards. However, since 2000, the participation rate has continued to fall: in 2016, more than one-third (37.2 percent) of adults in the United States, including nearly one-fifth (18.7 percent) of prime working-age adults (between twenty-five and fifty-four years old), were not in the workforce.[35] This sizable number cannot be accounted for fully by factors such as baby boomers aging out of the workforce, women engaged in caregiving, or recent college graduates delaying work entry.

There are many reasons people of working age do not participate in the labor market. Women with high school diplomas or less, primarily because of the high number of them that serve in caregiver roles, are overwhelmingly the largest group of Americans out of the labor force. Beyond caregivers (some 43 percent of nonparticipants), though, a 2017 study found that men and women report the same reasons, at similar levels, for nonparticipation in the labor force: almost 30 percent reported being ill or disabled, while 8 percent were students, and 5 percent were early retirees.

More important to the issue of workforce education is the most important driver: that the decline in the workforce participation rate is related to declining opportunities for those with lower levels of education.[36] This stems from trade, especially with China, and its effect on manufacturing jobs, along with the rise in skills required by continuing workplace advances in technology. Labor participation factors also include increases in the use of disability benefits and other safety net programs, the support provided to a growing number of unemployed young men by living with parents, and, although it is less clear in the data, increased opioid use. Here, however, the causality goes both ways: the opioid epidemic may be a symptom of social problems as well as a cause: opioid deaths may directly correspond with unemployment,[37] or, as one report stated: "Local wellbeing losses associated with job and wage reductions from local manufacturing decline led to greater opioid use and increased drug and opioid deaths at the local level."[38] The coronavirus may also have an effect, since knowledge workers working online have tended to retain jobs while lower-end service workers have lost jobs.

Labor market nonparticipation in the United States, then, affects disparate groups with different backgrounds, but the recurring story is that less educated, lower-skilled male workers are particularly affected. Their numbers are rising more sharply than other groups. The United States now has the third-worst prime-age (twenty-five to fifty-four) labor force participation rate in the Organisation for Economic Co-operation and Developmet (OECD), behind thirty-one other nations.[39] A significant portion of this trend is due to declining demand for low-skilled workers.[40] This is a particular problem group for which workforce education could be targeted.

The consequences are quite serious. Falling out of the labor market tends to drive families toward poverty. Some 45 percent of households (3.3 million) with a male prime-age nonparticipant and 28 percent of households (4.6 million) with a female prime-age nonparticipant are in the bottom quintile of income.[41]

Has the "gig economy" contributed to job insecurity? Except in the area of personal transport, with the rise of Uber and Lyft, the increase in "gig" work (where the worker is not paid a wage or salary and lacks a predictable work schedule or earnings) appears minimal.[42] Instead, the great bulk of work is still in traditional jobs, with a relatively stable number of contract workers.[43]

HEIGHTENED EFFECTS ON MINORITY COMMUNITIES

The problems less skilled workers face are more problematic for minority workers because they occur against a long-standing higher unemployment rate. The racial unemployment gap is an enduring feature of US labor markets, with Black unemployment averaging, over an extended period, about twice that for whites. The gap was at its worst during the late 1980s; since then, it has improved slightly on average, but the white unemployment

TABLE 2.7
Likelihood of education success for white and minority students

Grade ten students[a]	Degree attained	Earn degree within ten years
White	Associate	8%
	Bachelor	54%
African American	Associate	5%
	Bachelor	46%
Hispanic	Associate	9%
	Bachelor	37%

Source: Anthony P. Carnevale, Megan L. Fasules, Michael C. Quinn, and Kathryn Peltier Campbell, *Born to Win, Schooled to Lose: Why Equally Talented Students Don't Get Equal Chances to Be All They Can Be* (Washington, DC: Georgetown Center on Education and the Workforce, 2019), 30, https://1gyhoq479ufd3yna29x7ubjn-wpengine.netdna-ssl.com/wp-content/uploads/FR-Born_to_win-schooled_to_lose.pdf.
[a]With above-average scores on standardized tests.

is still only 54 percent of the Black rate. While white unemployment in 2018 was 3.7 percent, Black unemployment was 6.8 percent.[44] Hispanic men face a comparable problem: in 2017, their unemployment was 5.1 percent.[45]

There is also a large gap in student success for African Americans and Hispanics. Black and Hispanic tenth graders with above-median math scores in standardized tests are significantly less likely to earn a college degree within ten years than their white and Asian counterparts (table 2.7).

THESE PROBLEMS PREDATE THE GREAT RECESSION

Many blame the Great Recession for initiating these labor market developments, but they actually predate them as structural problems in the economy, not just problems driven by business cycles. For instance, median income for nonelderly US households fell five years in a row, from 2000 through 2005—just *before* the Great Recession.[46] And while US productivity and wages have historically risen in parallel, the "decoupling" of productivity growth and wages noted earlier was also in full force before the Great Recession: between 2001 and 2007, worker productivity rose 15 percent, but wages barely changed.[47] Median wages for women between 1979 and 2006 rose by 24 percent, reflecting the growing entry of women into the workplace, but remained 23 percent below men's median income. Real wages for men in the bottom 60 percent of income in the same period remained stuck below their 1979 levels. For those without a high school diploma, real wages declined 18 percent.[48]

These problems of working-class wage stagnation and decline have become enduring.

REGIONAL LOCK-IN

"Distressed communities" with high poverty levels are highly regional, with major pockets in certain urban and rural areas.[49] More than fifty million people live in districts stuck in the equivalent of an ongoing recession, with a falling number of businesses and in which the local population has low median income, poor labor force participation, high levels of poverty, and low educational achievement. These distressed areas suffer high housing vacancy rates and saw a 6 percent average fall in employment from 2011 to 2015, compared with a near 25 percent surge in the country's most prosperous areas. All this underscores the uneven aspects of US economic "recovery" since the Great Recession.

For much of the twentieth century, a robust American economy reduced the job, wage, investment, and business formation disparities between more heavily developed and less developed areas.[50] This enabled more of a convergence between communities. In the 1980s, however, that began to break down with the decline of the Rust Belt's manufacturing economy. The growing information technology sector also tended to reward regions that led in IT skills and firms. Convergence shifted to divergence, as the top 2 percent of US communities (based on growth and wages measurements) began to grow faster than midsize and less prosperous cities. And in many small towns and rural areas with populations of less than fifty thousand people, employment is stuck at prerecession levels.

Minorities, particularly African Americans, disproportionately tend to get stuck in these less prosperous areas.[51] Demographic analysis shows stark racial divides. Blacks and Native Americans are three times more likely to live in a distressed community than a prosperous one. The new economic geography "has brought economic and social cleavages that have spawned problematic externalities: entrenched poverty, 'deaths of despair,' and deepening small-town resentment of coastal cosmopolitan elites."[52] In the poorest-performing areas, economic stability continues to erode.

The problems in distressed communities have been developing over an extended period: most have seen zero net gains in employment and business creation since at least 2000. Prosperous communities added 188,000 business establishments from 2011 to 2015; distressed areas saw a net loss of 17,000. The best-off areas of the United States captured more than half of the rise in business establishments over that period—twice their share in 2011. Those prosperous localities, home to 84.8 million people, host nearly half of the country's advanced degree holders.

There are complementary findings concerning the manufacturing sector: the dramatic decline in manufacturing since 2000 is tied to a large decline in the rate of employment and hours worked among prime-age US workers and particularly affects less educated workers.[53] These declines are localized to areas particularly affected by manufacturing decline: a 10 percent drop in local manufacturing employment cut employment overall by 3.7 and 2.7 percent for prime-working-age men and women, respectively. These local impacts translate nationally into an estimate that between one-third and one-half of the decline in employment rates and annual hours for prime working age workers is tied to manufacturing decline between 2000 and 2017. The local declines have been of such a scale, then, that they drove overall national impacts.

Deindustrialization has led to record-setting joblessness in historic manufacturing centers, with widespread effects in the overall economy.[54] This raises the question of whether the US labor market could still produce enough jobs with good pay and benefits for most workers without a change in the character and location of jobs and new economic strategies.

The dichotomy between economically strong and weak regions was further illustrated in a study by Jeffrey Lin.[55] He found that new kinds of work, as illustrated by new employment categories, tend to originate and concentrate in metropolitan areas with a variety of industries and a high density of college graduates. This finding suggests that geographic areas with these characteristics may be better able to weather globalization and to benefit from technology advances that may disrupt labor markets.

There's an important caveat to the idea that urban metropolitan areas are the location for rising incomes.[56] The better-educated workers in these major urban centers, which have a high density of talent and ideas, pay a premium in living costs to take advantage of rising incomes; companies tolerate paying the wage premium, in turn, to take advantage of the educated talent. For the less educated, clerical and production work is down and white-collar work is harder to reach because the rungs are further apart now when less educated workers try to climb occupational ladders in these urban areas.[57] The hollowing out of middle-skill work reflected in Autor's barbell, then, has affected those with less than a college education in urban areas as well.[58]

RURAL EFFECTS

Rural residents form another large category of those affected. In 2015, one of the present authors attended a conference at the University of Nebraska, part of which involved traveling by bus through some of the richest farmland in the world to a town about an hour from Omaha to discuss rural issues. The town was classic Midwest: white wooden stores and homes, occasional brick ones, churches, and a crossroads Main Street. Many storefronts, however, were neat but closed; one had been repurposed into the community center where we met. We learned that residents went to Omaha to shop. As the bus pulled to a stop, I asked the organizer about the big crowd of people in a long line of aging pickup trucks, many with families in the truck bed. It was for the food bank.

Later, we wandered around a show of the latest tractors, combines, cultivators, and fertilizer spreaders at a nearby county fair. The vehicles, which cost hundreds of thousands of dollars, dwarfed the people looking at them. A friendly conversation began with an elderly farmer who said that when he returned home after the Korean War, he assembled one of the largest farms in the county—five thousand acres—that was now one of the smallest. The monster equipment was scaled to serve larger farms than his.

The scale of industrial agriculture has become massive and capital intensive. A farm is now a factory with a dirt floor that needs far fewer workers than ever before. With far fewer farm laborers, and with the major acreage now required, fewer *own* farms. The children in farm families leave for cities in large numbers. But many people from farm country don't have the education to secure jobs in metropolitan areas that increasingly require specialized skills.

The data bear out these pictures of an increasing "ruralization of distress."[59] Rural areas not adjacent to a metropolitan area are losing population.[60] The median age in rural counties was forty-three in 2016, seven years older than in cities; median incomes are lower; and there's the matter of the businesses lost during the "recovery" from the Great Recession.[61] By 2017, large metropolitan areas had 10 percent more jobs than when the recession began, but rural areas had fewer—and with the opioid epidemic, drug addiction, once primarily an urban problem, has become a rural one.

According to the Department of Agriculture, almost a quarter of the children growing up in rural America in 2016 were being raised in poverty—and the situation is becoming more pervasive.[62]

STUCK IN PLACE

Given this emerging economic geography, one option is for families to move to regions with stronger economies—which in the past has helped bind the United States into a common economy and democracy and increase economic opportunities, in turn increasing productivity and wage growth and reducing regional economic shocks. But families from poorer regions today tend to be stuck in place.[63] Movement from lower- to higher-income areas has decreased in parallel with declining economic convergence between states.[64] Workers are now less likely to move to a new job or to a new state; geographic mobility is less of a response to problematic labor markets than it has been in the past.[65] This may be in part because education is the key dividing line, and opportunities may not improve without it despite a location change.

From 2015 to 2016, more than half the migration out of the least-successful US counties was to other counties only marginally more successful; nearly two-thirds of migration out of the most-successful counties was into other relatively successful counties. Only 13 percent of those leaving the least successful counties moved to the most successful counties. Education was the best predictor of geographical mobility: highly educated individuals are more mobile than the less educated. Overall, geographic mobility is not helping to close economic gaps. On top of this, there is far less migration among children born to lower-income families. "Diminished mobility is often caused by limited means: young adults from low-income families may have less of a family safety net to fall back on in the event of employment setbacks, less information about opportunities in distant locations, or simply fewer resources to fund a move," write Brookings researchers.[66]

There's also the matter of confronting similar quality employment problems in the big city, where living costs are also higher. Young people have long tended to move from less dense areas to urban areas for college; increasingly, they now tend to stay after graduation, also affecting the net migration rate.[67] But while it has been assumed that a number of large metropolitan areas have been enabling all income segments to do better, these "success" areas turn out to be suffering from the same barbell effects on noncollege, middle-skilled workers as rural or failing industrial areas.[68]

From a policy perspective, this means it's not enough to focus on workers. Policies also will need to address affected regions in new ways.[69]

THE COLLEGE DIVIDING LINE: UPSKILLING

In 2017, the average income of the top 20 percent of Americans was more than sixteen times the average income of the bottom 20 percent, a disparity that continues to grow.[70] This provides a vivid picture of US income inequality. Again, a college education has become a great dividing line, and there is an ever-rising curve in the American economy of technological advance.[71] Work today is ever more technical and complex. An 1890 factory worker would be lost in today's automobile or semiconductor plant. Office workers from most of the twentieth century would be shocked by smartphone videoconferencing with colleagues across the globe. The curve of technological advance requires a parallel, rising curve of workforce educational attainment.

The United States was the first nation to create public mass higher education through the Land Grant College Act of 1862. We dramatically expanded higher education through the GI Bill following World War II. These were likely the most successful social policies in US history. They kept the education curve out ahead of the technology, so the curves could be mutually reinforcing: the ever-growing talent pool enabled ever-growing technology advances and vice versa, with corresponding growth and wage gains. But when the US college graduation rate leveled off in the early 1970s, as Claudia Goldin and Lawrence Katz have discussed, the technology curve kept rising with the advent of the information revolution.[72] Those with the skills to manage the technology advance could command a wage premium, while others faced wage decline or wage stagnation.

The college diploma has become a dividing line. Of the 7.2 million jobs lost in the Great Recession, 5.6 million were held by those with high school diplomas or less. And during the slow recovery between 2010 and 2016:

- Workers with a college degree gained 8.4 million jobs, those with associate degrees or some college gained 3.1 million, but those with a high school diploma added only eighty thousand—in effect, no job recovery.
- Some 11.5 million of the 11.6 million jobs created went to workers with at least some postsecondary education (73 percent to those with college degrees). Workers with a college degree or higher took almost all the jobs in high-skill (5.8 million) and middle-skill occupations (1.9 million).
- Workers with at least some postsecondary education captured the vast majority of good jobs paying more than $53,000 for full-time, full-year work with benefits (e.g., healthcare, retirement).

- Those with no postsecondary education increasingly settled for low-skill, low-wage jobs; they lost 181,000 high-skill jobs and 951,000 middle-skill jobs, but gained 1.2 million low-skill jobs.
- With declining quality employment for the less educated, those workers with a college degree or higher by 2016 made up a larger share of the workforce (36 percent) than those with a high school diploma or less (34 percent).[73]

Wage levels show what has been happening. In 1979, those ages twenty-five to fifty-four with bachelor's degrees could expect to earn 134 percent of the wages of those with only a high school education, and advanced degree holders could expect to earn 154 percent. By 2016, those wage premiums had risen to 168 and 213 percent, respectively.[74]

The first job matters.[75] Those who start out well employed rarely slide into underemployment; the great majority of college-educated workers who in their first job secure quality positions matched to their education continued to hold such quality positions five years later (87 percent), and nearly all of those were still at that level ten years later (91 percent). But those who start out behind tend to stay behind. Four in ten college graduates studied were underemployed in their first job; two-thirds of these graduates were still underemployed five years later; and of those, three-quarters were still underemployed at the ten-year mark. This persisting underemployment has major lifetime earnings impacts—and for women, who are more likely to be underemployed than men, it has very real implications for the gender pay gap.

Overall, there has been a massive demand for an upskilled workforce—and the upskilling shift is now being implemented. The accepted indicator of those skills is college education, and it matters what you study: a degree in most STEM fields (science, technology, engineering, and mathematics) means less likelihood of initial underemployment. Those without college face being left behind, shunted down the barbell toward lower-end, lower-skill, lower-paid service jobs.

Are we trying to turn this problem around? US spending on programs for job training, job search assistance, community college work-related education, and apprenticeships is lower as a share of GDP than nearly any other developed (OECD) country. Public expenditures for what are known as *active labor market policies* were only 0.12 percent of GDP in 2014, which is only slightly above levels in Mexico and Chile. The public sector now spends less than half what it did thirty years ago on such programs.[76]

TABLE 2.8
Percentage of employees receiving employer-provided training

Year	On-the-job training	Training assistance
1996	20%	13%
2008	11%	8%

Source: Council of Economic Advisors, "Active Labor Market Policies: Theory and Evidence of What Works," issue brief, White House, December 2016, 4, https://obamawhitehouse.archives.gov/sites/default/files/page/files/20161220_active_labor_market_policies_issue_brief_cea.pdf. See also Jeffrey Waddoups, "Did Employers in the United States Back Away from Skills Training during the Early 2000s?," *Industrial and Labor Relations Review* 69, no. 2, December 2015, https://journals.sagepub.com/doi/10.1177/0019793915619904.

Raising educational attainment over time can improve the wage differential between workers who have completed different levels of education, but that pace is gradual. The part of the workforce being left behind needs new, shorter-term job-training programs to help them adapt to technological changes by building skills that will be more in demand, which will raise earnings.

Despite this need, the problem is not only with governmental expenditures—and studies through 2008 and 2009 show decreased on-the-job training and training assistance from employers (table 2.8). This apparent parallel decline occurred at a time of growing income inequality and as employers increasingly hired on the basis of education credentials, making alternative education approaches much needed.

College education is increasingly the hiring default, and there really is no substitute system in place for evaluating skills. This means an individual's expectations for future work and wages are being set at the point they leave school.[77] What students in high school decide about education now largely determines their work future and economic success. Is the public ready for a change to this system?

A COMPLICATING CHALLENGE: OLDER WORKERS

Meanwhile, in a major demographic shift, the American workforce is aging. In a 2017 study, the Bureau of Labor Statistics (BLS) projected that by 2024 some 25 percent of the workforce—about forty-one million people—will be over fifty-five. Although not as large as other segments, workers age sixty-five and older—some thirteen million people—are projected to have faster

TABLE 2.9
The aging US workforce (projections, 2014—2024)

Age of workers	Growth rate in labor force
Sixty-five to seventy-four	55%
Seventy-five plus	86%

Source: Mitra Toossi and Elka Torpey, "Career Outlook, Older Workers: Labor Force Trends and Career Options," Bureau of Labor Statistics, May 2017, https://www.bls.gov/careeroutlook/2017/article/older-workers.htm.

rates of labor force growth annually than any other age groups (see table 2.9). For the labor force as a whole, that rate is 5 percent.

From 1970 until 2000, workers fifty-five and older comprised the smallest segment of the labor force. In the 1990s, however, these older workers began to increase their share of the labor force, while the share of younger workers began to decline. By 2003, the older age group no longer had the smallest share.

People have been working later in life for a number of reasons.[78] In general, they are healthier and have, until recently, had a longer life expectancy than previous generations. They are better educated, which increases their likelihood of remaining in the labor force. And changes to Social Security and employee retirement plans, along with the need to save more for retirement, created incentives to keep working (but not necessarily full time). In 2016, some 27 percent of workers fifty-five and older, and 18 percent of workers ages twenty-five to fifty-four, worked part time (from one to thirty-four hours per week). For those sixty-five and older, the rate of part-time employment was considerably higher, at 40 percent.

With a quarter of working Americans likely to be over fifty-five by 2024, this is a major workforce opportunity space that can offset demographic declines in other age groups.[79] But aging workers face many challenges. Displaced workers often tend to be older workers; mass layoffs based on age have allegedly occurred in some large companies.[80] At the technician level, this group tends to have lower or more outdated skills than the emerging technology economy requires and so is less ready for new positions.

Retraining could be vital for assisting this fast-growing workforce segment. Even an economist who envisions an automation doomsday has argued that these older workers need to be working in new roles to help the economy.[81] The reality is that labor force participation among older workers has been rising since the 1980s, and surveys indicate that most retirees would return to the workplace if given the opportunity.[82] This segment is a major upskilling challenge, but also an opportunity.

THE BARBELL DILEMMA

All these data help substantiate what Autor found. But if middle-skill jobs are declining or stagnating while upper-middle-class jobs and lower-end services sector jobs are growing, why bother to educate and train for the middle-skill jobs? Autor, of course, is characterizing the labor market, not proposing we lock in its imperfections.

The middle of the labor market is still enormous—some twenty-five million middle-skill jobs were created between 2010 and 2020.[83] It will continue to generate strong hiring demand, particularly if one considers gross hiring, especially replacements for retiring employees—with potentially 45 percent of job openings in one period studied by Harry Holzer and Robert Lerman in the middle-skill sector.[84] Middle-skill demand requires new education pathways for those who cannot enroll in four-year degree programs. Given that there will still be a great number of quality job openings in middle-skill fields, particularly because of retirements, we should better organize our workforce development efforts around this category. Part of that task will be moving many more people from limited opportunities in lower-end services sectors into middle-skill categories—the very goal of the Valencia College short program noted in chapter 1.

But we should also better characterize and understand the dynamism within the middle skills. It is not a stagnant category. The National Academies of Sciences, Engineering, and Medicine's 2017 *Building America's Skilled Technical Workforce* report urged dropping *middle skills*—which it noted can be a pejorative term to many—in favor of *skilled technical workforce* in recognition of major ongoing upskilling.[85] Why steer workers to the "middle" in a nation that historically aims for the top?

The middle skills are becoming ever more technically oriented, with "old" categories involving less training and lower skill levels declining (such as in construction and clerical work) and "new," more technical skills (such as those of medical technicians) growing.[86] As of 2011, some twenty-six million jobs—part of a "hidden STEM economy"—required a high degree of knowledge in particular STEM fields, with half of them available to workers without bachelor's degrees.[87] It is not too much to hope that those who acquire strong technical skills don't simply remain in place but begin to capture skills currently associated with the growing numbers of jobs held by the upper middle class.

Developments in the information technology sector, which is creating a new opportunity space for the technically skilled in many occupational areas, illustrate the point. These are the "new-collar" workers former IBM CEO Ginni Rometty[88] describes as those with the skills needed in areas such as cybersecurity analysis, app development, and cloud computing implementation. They are a far cry from blue-collar workers doing rote assembly in Henry Ford's River Rouge Ford plant, but they don't require four-year degrees.

The new-collar workforce doesn't just have to be limited to IT jobs. A host of increasingly technical jobs will be needed in workplaces in many sectors (see chapter 5).

JOB TRAINING VERSUS JOB CREATION

Some analysts have attacked politicians for pretending that job training is a substitute for economic development.[89] They're right that job training is not a panacea. Job training is not a replacement for job *creation*: a region losing jobs cannot train its way out of the problem. Nevertheless, the need for improved job training has been increasing because job markets have been changing:

First, the technological demands of the workplace are growing, shortages are emerging in a number of higher-skill areas, and workers who can't keep up with these advances face declining job opportunities. Training is a key part of the answer to this problem.

Second, because of worker demographics, demand for trained workers will be growing in the future. There will be significant job openings in areas such as manufacturing and utilities, but only if workers have the skills that match needs in these sectors. Training is a key part of the answer to this problem, too.

Third, a well-trained workforce in an era of technological advances may be a prerequisite for economic development. Data suggests that job creation is stronger in areas richer in educated talent. Workers with skills seem to attract employers needing skills. Training, then, may be a part of the answer to this aspect of economic development as well.

Finally, data strongly indicates that the overall workforce is upskilling and that incomes for the less skilled are too often stagnating or in decline. Further education increasingly appears to be a prerequisite to entry into the middle class.

So given all these ongoing developments, the training that some analysts once attacked as counterproductive appears to be an important answer.

THE PUBLIC'S PERSPECTIVE

The public seems to understand the shift in the workforce and supports the education needed, as a major survey in 2016 of public attitudes shows. The great majority of workers see new skills and training as the key to future job success.[90] More than half believe it will be essential for them to get training and develop new skills throughout their work lives to keep up with changes in the workplace. The most highly educated workers, it turns out, are the ones who feel most strongly about the need for continuing workforce education, perhaps because their current jobs already tend to rely on higher levels of skills.

What drives this new perception is that the public sees threats to jobs coming from a host of directions: increased outsourcing of jobs to other countries, more foreign-made products being sold in the United States, increased use of contract or temporary workers, and declines in union membership. At the same time, most see global markets for US-made products as helpful for workers and jobs. People are split over whether workplace technology advances, particularly automation, hurt or help workers.

What are the specific skills these surveyed workers believe they need? Large majorities rank a mix of technical (including a detailed understanding of how to use computers) and soft skills as critical. Among the latter, mentioned by more than eight in ten workers, are the ability to work with those from diverse backgrounds, writing, and communication—also mentioned as important skills on which they rely in their current jobs. To that, many add critical thinking.

Workers are quite clear that acquiring new skills will be largely their responsibility, supported by public schools, but less clear on how the skills-upgrading task will be executed. There are many different views regarding the roles of companies and the government.

The survey suggests that the American public is on track with what is happening. While the 2020 coronavirus pandemic has added to economic disruptions, it may have buttressed the case for workforce education. So this 2016 survey remains an accurate gauge of public views. They see workplace change and job threats ahead—and the need to counter that with ongoing upskilling, both for themselves and generally for the workforce. They even have some sense about the range of skills they will need. That public readiness is a promising start for our task of reconsidering workforce education.

3 BREAKDOWNS IN TODAY'S WORKFORCE EDUCATION

Ask most Americans to describe what middle school and high school are like, and they will. Ask them to describe a four-year college program, they also likely can. They also have a good idea of what community colleges are all about. But ask what the workforce education system looks like and you will most likely draw a blank stare. The system is not a unified one, and the elements that exist are not well understood. While many European nations have systems that effectively prepare young people and transition them from school to workplace, arming them with the skills needed for well-paid careers, in the United States there is a disconnect between the worlds of school and work. Incumbent workers also need access to workforce training to keep up with technology advances, including lifelong learning opportunities.

Our nation has the most decentralized labor market in the developed world, and the government creates only limited active labor market policies. A European-like system, with career paths locked in at very early ages, would not work well here. Our system's complexity—many entry points, allowing workers to change their minds about careers and restart—may well be an advantage.[1]

Such is the backdrop to the intense international competition the United States has been facing, particularly since 2000 and particularly in manufacturing (as discussed in chapter 2). The coronavirus has applied additional economic pressure. The resulting social dislocation from job loss, hitting more routine jobs especially hard, has also jarred our political system. At the same time, our education system is not ready to prepare the workforce for the rapid rate of technology advancement led by information technologies, with a suite of robotic, artificial intelligence, machine learning, and data analytics technologies looming on the horizon. Our social program networks are not prepared for the workforce transitions that may be needed.

That does not mean no one is paying attention, and it's not that there aren't high-functioning parts of the system. There are some outstanding efforts at numerous community colleges, among numerous employers, and in creative new programs—but there is still a system problem. Reformers are present in force in numerous institutions, but their combined weight has not yet led to the scope of improvements needed. The actors and programs are often not well connected, funding can be problematic, and too many fall into the gaps. Despite valiant efforts overall, there are still system breakdowns at many stages.

It has been more than two decades since publication of the last overall study of workforce education in the United States,[2] and much has changed in US labor markets. Today's task is to elevate some of the best new elements to show what a new system could include. That means also highlighting areas and gaps that need attention.

There are a number of breaking points among the numerous institutional actors in the workforce field.

UNDERINVESTMENT BY GOVERNMENT AND EMPLOYERS

Following economic theory on interventions in labor markets, *governments* often make significant investments in active labor market policies; they invest in identifying job opportunities, in job training, and in employment services. The OECD country average is to invest 0.5 percent of GDP in such policies, whereas the United States invests only 0.1 percent, ranking it twenty-ninth among all thirty-one OECD nations.[3] And that US investment is less than half of what it was three decades ago. It's a basic breakdown in workforce development policy: in a period in which skills are more important than ever in setting earnings in labor markets, we are spending ever-declining amounts.[4] One analyst notes that after a high point in 1979, federal funding in actual dollars for the various workforce education programs fell by 70 percent by 2008, and 87 percent in terms of percentage of GDP.[5] These cutbacks seem to have been falsely justified based on a perception of program ineffectiveness: the same analyst found overall positive and cost-effective impacts from the investment, with more positive impacts for women than men and for adults than youth.[6] Why, then, with significant evidence of private and social returns for education and training, would training for disadvantaged adults or youth be considered less effective?[7] The answer seems to lie not in the facts but in the politics around poverty.[8]

Labor market intermediary organizations play a particularly significant role in helping connect the actors and programs, better linking workers and jobs.[9] These intermediaries can range from workforce development boards to internet job services, and overall, high-quality intermediaries can play a significant role in supporting job placement and related training. But with the decline in federal support, many of these institutions have trouble playing their roles.[10] A wild west of new, unregulated, and often transitory organizations—from computer coding academies to hair dressing schools—have stepped in to fill the gap, attempting to provide training services. This reflects the lack of resources available to more established institutions, such as community colleges.[11]

This decline can be seen on the *employer* side, too. Employers provide the bulk of the training, but workers who reported they received employer-provided training dropped from close to 20 percent to approximately 11 percent between 1996 and 2008—that is, prior to the disruption of the Great Recession.[12] US census surveys indicate a troubling 28 percent decline in employer training between 2001 and 2009, widespread across industries, occupations, ages, education levels, job tenure, and demographic groups—with the decline particularly affecting workers in the middle of the education spectrum.[13] Companies, particularly small companies with limited resources, have often been reluctant to invest in workforce education, and the economic effects of the coronavirus are likely to make them even more reluctant. Workers with higher levels of education tend to be the focus of more employer training attention. There is, though, wide variation among US employers:[14] some employers historically adopt what Tom Kochan and others have called *high road* policies—including higher wages, incentives, teaming, and training coupled to opportunities for promotion—and others the opposite *low road* approaches, reflecting different attitudes to the role of employees.[15] In part because of the great variety of employers and sectors, definitive data has not been collected on this issue.[16] US employers tend to play a weak role in educating the under-twenty-five workforce compared to their European counterparts, and there is a problematic disconnect in the United States between employer-based training and school-based career and technical (vocational) education.[17]

While government and firms appear to be disinvesting—and we need better data on employer developments—the workforce needs to upgrade its skills. As noted in chapter 2, quality jobs are going to the better educated; those with high school educations or less face stagnating or declining incomes, while those with a college education are receiving a significant wage premium. The falling demand for less skilled workers seeking middle-income wages means a substantial percentage are no longer in the workforce, which can be largely attributed to declining demand for lower-skilled workers as upskilling evolves.[18] Clearly, the need for training is out of sync with investment levels.

What is the employer role? There is a long and varied history. Skilled workers are a key driver of productivity gains for their employers and the economy; overall, improving workforce learning is a key driver of growth.[19] The division of labor of the nineteenth century paralleled the industrial revolution, enabling low-skilled employees in an assembly system to replace skilled artisans to scale up production. Replacing labor with capital equipment developed at that time and remains a long-standing tradition in American production. Larger employers had the revenue base to train employees, smaller employers less so. But as global competition soared in the 1970s, a financial model drove employers to cut costs to go "asset light" (discussed further in chapter 5), and training too often fell by the wayside. Further, as larger firms were driven by the financial sector and global competition to thin out to pursue their core competencies, they also often outsourced noncore activities. Outsourcing to US-based contractors often meant low-margin firms. Between 1997 and 2012, larger firms (with more than 500 employees) reduced manufacturing employment by 44 percent.[20] There simply aren't incentives to encourage larger firms to switch strategies and go more labor intensive, which means many have fewer workers and less incentive to train. In turn, the low-margin outsourcing firms have limited resources and therefore limited interest in training.

Employers still need skilled workers and may well have hoped public programs and institutions could provide them. This is even more the case given the economic shifts caused by the coronavirus. However, when public institutions become the training providers, that means employees have to act on their own initiative, responsible for their own education and bearing the costs, and can get out of sync with employer needs. Tighter labor markets in recent years are forcing some employers—particularly larger ones in more economically stable sectors—to rethink their training roles. Workforce education has become a priority for business organizations, including the Business Roundtable, the U.S. Chamber of Commerce, and National Association of Manufacturers.[21] However, the many different employer approaches to workforce education have become a maze, and there is an era of disengaged employers and economic cutbacks, and now coronavirus cutbacks, to overcome. Employers typically try to make their own arrangements with training providers and education institutions, rarely acting in concert with other area employers to pool resources and make a significant dent in mutual training problems. Individual firms acting alone simply cannot operate at the scale needed to solve the workforce development challenge. There are few incentives to collaborate, and this gap in collective activity amounts to a market failure. What is lacking is a *system*.

THE ROLE OF UNIONS

Historically, labor organizations have played an important role in American training and workforce development. Yet the percentage of workers belonging to a union went from 20.1 percent in 1983 to 10.3 percent in 2019, with union members making up only 6.2 percent of private sector workers.[22] However, unions still play a significant role in the workforce in some key sectors, including construction, aerospace, automotive, utility, and healthcare fields.

There are union-industry joint training funds, and union collaborations with companies still dominate apprenticeships, particularly in the construction trades, with efforts underway to expand and improve them. There are also joint union-management training programs in a number of industries apart from apprenticeships, including in services sectors such as healthcare, hospitality, and culinary skills. While union influence on the workforce has been in decline, unions remain a source for potential workforce collaborations in some key sectors.

BACKGROUND ON WORKFORCE LAWS

The US Labor Department's training and employment programs arose in significant part out of Lyndon Johnson's 1964 War on Poverty. As Harry Holzer has detailed, they evolved in successive laws and reflect shifts in the priorities of both the executive branch and Congress.[23] The Manpower Training Act, in place from 1962 to 1973, provided direct grants to employment and training service providers, and in parallel in 1965, the Job Corps began to provide a year of training and education at residential centers for disadvantaged youth. The focus of both programs was on the disadvantaged.

With the Comprehensive Employment and Training Act (CETA), in place from 1974 to 1985, the federal government began to shift responsibility for employment and training to state and local advisory committees. Funding for training rose dramatically in the late 1970s recession as employment fell for low-income, minority, and youth populations. Public sector employment was provided to 750,000 individuals in 1978 because of the conclusion that they couldn't obtain employment elsewhere.

The Job Training Partnership Act (JTPA), in place between 1984 and 1999, altered these programs. The Reagan administration opposed public sector service employment as a wasteful substitute for private sector employment, so its funding was sharply reduced. JTPA funding was dispersed through private industry councils (PICs) in an attempt to match local labor demand. The remnants of public service employment were ended when funding for summer youth employment programs was curtailed.

The concept of a "demand-driven" system further developed with the 1999 passage of the Workforce Investment Act (WIA), under which locally-based "workforce investment boards" (WIBs) were established—with a voting majority from local industry—to implement training for the labor needs of local businesses. The concept behind the WIA was empowering local employers and workers to cooperate in the job search process. To end any welfare stigma, assistance for adults was no longer for the disadvantaged only. The Job Corps continued to be funded, and the WIA funded job training and employment for adults, youth (largely in school), and dislocated workers (regardless of skill level or income) who had lost jobs through plant closings or downsizings. The WIA created *one-stop* offices where workers could access all Labor Department services, including unemployment insurance and the labor exchange job openings posted by private employers.

WIA services fell into three key areas: *core services* included use of the employment search system, with staff assistance as needed; *intensive services* included job skill assessments and job counseling; and *training* included any education that qualified workers for specific jobs.[24] Workers acquired more control over how their training funds were spent through "individual training account" vouchers. But the WIA emphasis was on work first—that is, getting adults into jobs as soon as possible, with or without specific training. By the mid-2000s, the goal of broadening services had been met; only one-fifth of those receiving employment services and half of those receiving training were low income.

LIMITED FOCUS ON HIGHER SKILLS AND INCUMBENT WORKERS

The Workforce Investment Act was succeeded by the Workforce Innovation and Opportunity Act (WIOA), which went into effect in 2015 and is today one of the Labor Department's two major programs with training features. The WIOA continues to authorize the core federal programs for workforce development, including employment and training services for unemployed and underemployed adults and dislocated workers. The WIOA also supports adult education and literacy programs and assists individuals with disabilities. Under the act, state and regional workforce development boards (WDBs), with members drawn mostly from area employers, set regional employment strategies and funding priorities for worker training, registered apprenticeships, transition jobs, on-the-job training, and customized training. They also support one-stop career centers for job search and counseling assistance.

The WIOA continues the WIA's demand-driven focus, emphasizing serving the needs of local labor markets and responsiveness to local employers. Most funding is distributed through formula grants to states,[25] which constitute 60 percent of total WIOA funding for job search education and training programs and are allocated primarily to local WDBs to determine the mix of service providers and programs and the types of training programs. The WIOA requires the alignment of workforce development services through unified state plans for providing core programs, a common set of performance indicators, and regional planning across regions. Like its predecessor, the WIA, the WIOA provides universal access to workers at one-stop job service centers, but for career and training services priority is given to low-income and low-skill workers. The WIOA emphasizes career pathways for workforce development and industry sector partnerships with employers; the WDBs are directed to develop strategies around these concepts. Program participants retain a significant degree of consumer choice on the training they receive through their individual training accounts. Other parts of the WIOA continue programs for adult education and literacy, the employment service program (linked to the one-stop centers), and vocational services for the disabled.

There are indications that training programs for low-income and unemployed adults can help increase these workers' pay by as much as 10 to 25 percent within three years. Sectoral training programs for particular industries may raise incomes up to 30 percent within two years.[26] But funding is simply not approaching the scale of the problem. The National Skills Alliance projects that there are thirty-six million working-age adults with low levels of skills, yet the annual formula funds to the states for a range of the WIOA programs declined by 40 percent from 2001 ($4.6 billion) to 2018 ($2.7 billion).[27]

The decline of routine jobs and the need to upskill workers for the technology challenges ahead demand a new focus. But under the WIOA, there is limited flexibility available to states and the WDBs to make a shift. David Cruise, a highly experienced educator, organizer of precision manufacturing training programs and president of the MassHires workforce development board in the Springfield, Massachusetts, area, knows the problem well. He knows that the workforce in Springfield's network of small and midsize industrial firms is going to have to upskill in major ways to meet the challenge of advanced manufacturing technologies. But he can't repurpose his board's WIOA funding to reach those workers. "I know what's headed our way," he says, "and we must get onto this problem or we're going to leave many behind. But I don't have support I need to really reach the incumbent workers."[28]

Overall, the local nature of these boards can be a strength: it puts them in touch with local employers and job needs. But neither the boards nor the employers they work with are in a position to be the first to see new technologies and get ahead of the implementation curve. That challenge may require some centralization and additional mechanisms to supplement the current WIOA programs and boards.

Trade Adjustment Assistance (TAA), originally proposed by President Kennedy in 1962, is the other major Labor Department program. It assists workers, firms, and farmers damaged by import competition from trade. Workers can receive a trade readjustment allowance that supplements state unemployment insurance if they participate in training programs. Workers over fifty with limited income can get job search assistance and income subsidies. Funding in 2018 for training and employment assistance was $387 million.[29]

TAA efforts, though, are too small, too narrow and piecemeal, and too difficult to access at scale.[30] China trade dislocation in the manufacturing sector in the 2000s swamped the program's funding, and most trade-displaced workers ended up relying on Social Security and disability benefits.[31] The programs for trade adjustment tend to focus on narrow, individualized causes of disruption. It seems help arrives only after a plant closes and layoffs hit a community hard. And because it's only about trade, TAA can't be used to upskill workers for the entry of new technologies. A broader, proactive, multipurpose adjustment program that anticipates training needs is necessary.

The Labor Department also leads the country's registered apprenticeship programs. Although growing in the last few years, there were only 585,000 apprentices in these programs in 2018, up from 420,000 a decade earlier. There were still only 282,000 workers who completed apprenticeships in the previous five years.[32] These apprenticeships are still largely tied to the construction trades, reflecting trade unions that dominated the organized part of the sector. The program, which needs further reach, is just beginning to branch out in significant ways to other sectors.

EDUCATION DEPARTMENT PROGRAMS FILL ONLY SOME GAPS

Two programs of the US Department of Education—carried out both from Washington and on the ground in regions and states through different organizational silos tied to the federal programs—are highly relevant to this discussion. They are neither connected nor complementary to those of the Labor Department, although these programs end up helping to fill some gaps.

First, and most significant, is the Education Department's Pell Grants of up to $6,195 annually (for the 2019–2020 school year),[33] which go to students enrolled full time in undergraduate programs at colleges or community colleges who show clear financial need. Pell Grants are for degree programs, not workforce programs. Stand-alone, short-term certificate programs can qualify, but have in the past required extensive data showing the student's subsequent "gainful employment."[34] Unlike student loans, these do not need to be repaid. For the 2017–2018 academic year, some seven million students received Pell Grants totaling $28.2 billion—a figure that dwarfs all explicit federal workforce education expenditures combined.[35]

Of Pell Grant recipients in 2015 in two- and four-year college and related programs, 2.4 million attended community colleges and 1.3 million went to for-profits; the remainder went to public and private colleges.[36] Community colleges and the for-profits alike offer what is largely workforce education, but they are often shaped as college programs so their students can qualify for the Pell Grants. Nevertheless, the Pell program is mismatched with actual workforce education needs and labor market demands. Undergraduate degree education may not overlap directly with workforce training, and the grants have not been available to students seeking shorter-term certificates in workforce skills unless, as noted, the sponsoring educational institution collects additional subsequent employment data. This barrier excludes many who cannot make the time commitments required for undergraduate degree programs or extended certificate programs, or who need particular job skills.

Opening up Pell Grants for workforce education programs more generally outside of degree programs has been a major topic of discussion, but there's a problem. For-profit schools that are funded largely by Pell tuition money—so-called Pell mills—have low college student completion rates.[37] Efforts by the Education Department to crackdown on poor performers have had limited results. Opening up Pell further to workforce education not only faces a major additional federal cost but also creates serious program quality vulnerability.

Paralleling Pell is the student loan system for loans available either directly from the Department of Education or indirectly through private lenders.[38] These go to students in accredited two- or four-year programs or certificate programs attending at least half time and play a major role in funding workforce education.[39] However, as of 2018 student debt had climbed to $1.46 trillion, reflecting rising college costs, with $166 billion of these loans in "serious delinquency" status, reflecting problematic program completion rates, as well as the often stagnant wage growth of recent years (outside of the top income tiers) that limits the ability to repay.[40]

The other relevant Education Department program, career technical education (CTE; the term has replaced *vocational education*), is funded through the Perkins Act and is explicitly for workforce education. It includes high school and community college CTE for a wide range of middle-skill occupations, with both certificate and noncertificate programs eligible. Funding is allocated by formula grant to states, with some two-thirds going to secondary institutions and the remainder to postsecondary. States have flexibility to shift a portion of their formula funding to meet state workforce priorities. While a bipartisan reauthorization of the program was passed in 2018,[41] funding has been stagnant for many years, hovering around $1.2 billion.[42] Frankly, Perkins Act funding, which is dispersed in small amounts across all the states, is minimal given the need. And because the Education Department's programs don't connect or mesh with the Labor Department's programs, these federal program disconnects are replicated at the state level as well.[43]

STEEP DECLINE IN SECONDARY SCHOOL VOCATIONAL EDUCATION

Public high schools resulted from a major reform movement in the late nineteenth and early twentieth centuries; students were often taught vocational skills such as woodworking and metalworking along with more academic subjects. In the 1950s and accelerated by the Sputnik crisis, systematic tracking increased, separating college-bound students from those in "shop"[44]—too often weak, low-quality vocational programs that missed emerging technical fields and ended up directing students into dead-ends. The civil rights movement confronted tracking's class and racial biases, and the emphasis in high schools shifted to preparing all students for college. In the end, many vocational schools and tracks were dropped in many states. Many students, however, still did not go on to college.

Strong CTE continues in some states; Massachusetts, for instance, strengthened rather than dropped its programs, and its technical high schools now often have long student waiting lists.[45] But economic pressures continue to buttress vocational education in other states. The six-hundred-thousand-student Los Angeles Unified School District, for example, had planned to eliminate all its career technical education courses by 2013 to reduce costs; after protests, the program was saved, but cut by half.[46] The disconnect between secondary school and work has created a significant gap in the workforce education system.

FOR-PROFIT HIGHER EDUCATION: A PROBLEMATIC MODEL

The for-profits mentioned earlier require some further attention, in particular because they provide a very large proportion of workforce education, particularly for poorer students and minorities—which they have clearly identified as an underserved niche. But they also have some deep problems that affect overall workforce education.

Today, there are some 1,300 for-profit institutions engaged in postsecondary education in the United States, offering a wide range of programs, from associate degrees to graduate degrees, as well as certificates in skill areas. The largest of these emphasize technology and business courses, but across all programs they've tended to focus on certificates in emerging fields (such as allied health fields) with growing demand, which they market quickly to students and scale up rapidly to meet demand.[47] For-profits enroll a majority of all US students in non-degree-granting programs of this sort.[48]

They were early adopters of online education, which has been a key enabler of their rapid expansion. Several large chains of these for-profit schools have grown into sizable public corporations.

Along with community colleges, for-profits are now the major education institutions offering workforce education. They have become heavily dependent on Pell Grants and student loans to fund their programs, even shaping them to fit Pell college requirements.

Table 3.1 shows enrollment levels in these for-profit institutions, which climbed dramatically through 2010 and have begun to slip in recent years. In 2015, for-profits constituted some 7 percent of the enrollment of degree-granting institutions, public and private.[49] Their student bodies overall are disproportionately older, female, African American, Hispanic, and lower income compared to nonprofits.[50]

These schools have definite strengths: they provide flexible schedules to accommodate students, reach low-income and underserved minorities, provide very efficient enrollment and better career services than their public

TABLE 3.1
Students enrolled in for-profit higher education

Year	Enrollment in for-profit institutions
1970	18,000
2000	400,000
2010	2,000,000
2015	1,300,000

Source: David J. Deming, Claudia Goldin, and Lawrence F. Katz, "The For-Profit Postsecondary School Sector: Nimble Critters or Agile Predators?," *Journal of Economic Perspectives* 26, no. 1 (Winter 2012): 139, https://pubs.aeaweb.org/doi/pdfplus/10.1257/jep.26.1.139; Department of Education, National Center for Education Statistics, "Total fall enrollment in private for-profit degree-granting post-secondary institutions, 2014–2015," table 304.50, https://nces.ed.gov/programs/digest/d16/tables/dt16_304.50.asp.

counterparts, support online and stackable credentials, and conduct market research on new fields.[51] By being market-driven, they tend to innovate around user needs, with a particular focus on online education. For example, Industrial Training International (ITI) was formed in 1986 for rigging, crane, and equipment training and now has a series of training centers for teams from employers in the United States, Canada, Britain, and Brazil, serving additional industrial missions.[52] It was an early experimenter in online education and has moved into virtual reality training simulations, including the first mobile crane simulator.

But the weaknesses in the for-profit model are often substantial.[53] Tuition is, on average, nearly 20 percent higher than public, nonprofit options, making them less affordable and therefore less financially sustainable for their low-income student base.[54] Their curricula are generally proprietary and neither transparent nor accessible to employers. This disconnect with specific employer needs creates difficulties in working with industries that tend to prefer more trusted nonprofits. Their completion rates are low, particularly for longer-duration college programs, to the detriment of many students.[55] Poor performance for students in obtaining improved employment is another problem.[56] In turn, for-profit student default rates on federal aid programs greatly exceed those at other institutions of higher education. Because for-profits rely on federal student aid for more than two-thirds of their revenue, this—coupled with significantly higher tuition rates—has particularly adverse consequences for federal taxpayers.[57] A number of major chains have gone bankrupt, stranding students, and in some cases there has been significant evidence of fraud.[58]

While there certainly are quality for-profit programs, too many of these institutions are problems, not solutions.

COMMUNITY COLLEGES ARE UNDERFUNDED AND DISCONNECTED FROM UPCOMING WORKFORCE NEEDS

Public institutions of higher education are major providers of workforce education. But while community colleges are overwhelmingly state institutions and 74 percent of four-year college enrollment is at state universities,[59] funding for higher education has been in decline for decades. Since 1980, state and local appropriations went from 50 percent of the revenue for public higher education to 37 percent by 2000, and from 2008 to 2016, all but four states cut per-student higher education spending—some by as much as half.[60]

Community colleges, which are highly engaged with workforce education and where much of the country's lower-income and working-class students go, have had a particularly difficult time. Poor completion rates, often linked to low per-pupil spending, are a major problem.[61] Private colleges and universities spend five times more and public universities three times more per student than community colleges, where spending has been declining.[62] This reflects an unwillingness to invest in workforce education for the lower economic levels of society.

Yet to the extent that there is a pathway to workforce education, community colleges are a critical part. Studies suggest that because of the additional remedial help they need, education for disadvantaged students may require 40 percent more funding—but there is no such additional funding available to community colleges.[63] The fact that transferability of community college credits and associate degrees to four-year state universities is not assured in at least twenty states is a further problem.[64]

On top of all this, community colleges are not necessarily educating students the in the *new technologies* critical to succeed in the workforce. For instance, although computer science skills are increasingly necessary in many careers, less than 0.2 percent of the 1.8 million first-time college students who entered a community college in fall 2007 went on to earn a bachelor's degree in computer science by 2014. It's just one example of where the system is failing: an industry projection indicates that current college graduation rates in computer science will only meet one-third of job demand,[65] and community college students continuing on to four-year institutions would help improve that number. New energy technologies represent another skill opportunity not being met.[66]

Community colleges are also ideal for providing the *lifelong education* that will be important to keep improving workforce skills as new technologies are introduced, as well as help workers in a number of licensed professions (e.g., accounting, nursing, engineering) meet the continuing education requirements to retain licenses. But while these institutions do reach older students, they have limited funding to keep up with new advances, such as the suites of new equipment to teach advanced manufacturing.

Meanwhile, four-year colleges and universities, despite their stronger resources, are largely disengaged from workforce education. Most still think this is a problem for high schools and community colleges.

ADVANCED TECHNICAL EDUCATION PROGRAMS REMAIN SMALL

The workforce education need lies not simply in teaching current skills for routine jobs, which are declining, but in upskilling workers to fill jobs in the production and services sectors—with the new and emerging technologies. *That* workforce education, though, is very limited.

Today's leaders in advanced technical education are the National Science Foundation's Advanced Technological Education (ATE) program and the advanced manufacturing institutes program begun in 2012. ATE focuses on community colleges to promote the education of technicians for high-technology fields, with thirty-one centers and 278 active projects.[67] The centers and projects develop curricula and supporting materials, including online resources, for teaching key advanced skill areas from advanced manufacturing to micro- and nanotechnologies. For example, ATE has made available extensive materials in fields such as computer system engineering and programmable logic control hardware for use in community college courses.[68] It is a critical resource for community colleges in terms of their new curricula and online materials for emerging technical fields. But ATE's FY 2020 budget was only $75 million to provide new course materials and programs for the 5.7 million community college students that year.[69]

The advanced manufacturing institutes, part of the Manufacturing USA network, began in 2012 with the aim of boosting the robustness and innovative capacity of the US manufacturing sector and improve its global economic competitiveness.[70] Each of its fourteen institutes are regional collaborations of small and large manufacturing firms, regional universities and community colleges, and state and regional governments. The institutes each focus on a specific new technology—from 3-D printing to

TABLE 3.2
Manufacturing USA's advanced manufacturing institutes' education programs (2018)

Program type	Completions
Internship, training, or education	200,169 students
Certificate, apprenticeship or training	2,630 incumbent workers
Teacher and trainer training	2,455 teachers/trainers

Source: Manufacturing USA and the National Institute of Standards and Technology (NIST), 2018 Annual Report, NIST AMS 600-5, September 2019, 14, 20, https://nvlpubs.nist.gov/nistpubs/ams/NIST.AMS.600-5.pdf.

advanced composites, digital production, photonics, and biofabrication—with programs that reach nearly every state. Seed funding is competitive and comes from the Departments of Defense, Energy, and Commerce; this in turn leverages larger amounts of industry and state funding for each institute. Overall, the federal share is matched two to one by industry and state governments.

Beyond each institute's central technology development task, workforce development in the institute's advanced technology field is also critical. Some of the institutes are beginning to understand that workforce education is their most important way to disseminate their new technologies to achieve actual implementation in firms; without an educated workforce, the technology simply will not scale.[71] Each has its own workforce education program, some larger than others. Table 3.2 shows the reach of workforce programs from the advanced manufacturing institutes.

Innovative programs have been evolving. For example, DOD's Mantech, which funds the DOD-backed institutes, is supporting them to develop advanced manufacturing technology courses and an online platform to host them. The photonics institute's workforce program has developed new online MOOCs for optics and photonics fabrication, is introducing virtual and augmented reality into its courses, and has collaborative programs for photonics education with state, private and community colleges.[72] Along with ATE, the manufacturing institutes could fill a major gap in workforce education: educating for next-generation skills.

In a $2 trillion manufacturing sector,[73] expenditures in 2018 for the fourteen institutes were only about $500 million (including federal plus state and industry matching funds) for all institute activities, from technology development to capital equipment for demonstration centers; workforce education was only a modest portion of that total.[74] Put starkly, neither ATE nor Manufacturing USA is operating at the scale required for a workforce transformation—despite their many creative program elements.

A BROKEN INFORMATION SYSTEM

On top of all these problems in what needs to be a true workforce education system, there is a broken information system. A sound labor market must be based on sound information shared by the participants (discussed further in chapter 6). But workers and job seekers lack good information about jobs they could qualify for or complementary skills they could acquire. Employers lack tools to evaluate worker qualifications. Education institutions offer more than three hundred thousand different certificates and degrees[75] but lack the data to match them to actual job qualifications. Government agencies provide basic job market data but need to assemble more and package this into a system. In short, everyone is missing information about the relevance of education and its relation to actual qualifications.

THE DIFFICULTY OF INSTITUTIONAL CHANGE

Existing workforce education mechanisms and institutions are a complex, established legacy sector[76] that has, over time, "locked in" to technical, economic, social, and political systems that are resistant to change. Higher education, government workforce support programs, and employer training all operate in different spheres, with different missions and within their own established paradigms. They use established technologies and processes, from textbooks to funding formulas, and established delivery models. They have established economic models, from "seat time," semesters, and degrees for higher education to worker productivity tests for industry. Their social systems support teaching and training, from tenured faculties in higher education to training instructors in larger companies, as well as students and workers with different kinds and levels of status. And there are political supports for the current delivery models, such as state and federal support of existing community colleges, universities, student aid allocation, and worker assistance. None of these delivery mechanisms are easy to alter; making transformative changes across them is harder still.

The problem points in current workforce education are myriad. Labor Department programs are underfunded and have only a limited focus on advanced technical skills and incumbent and new entrant workers. Education Department programs are not aimed at workforce education and are not linked or complementary to the Labor Department programs. Vocational and career technical education programs in secondary schools have largely been dismantled. Publicly supported community colleges are underfunded and lack the resources to provide advanced training in emerging fields. For-profits have a problematic completion rate. Colleges and universities are disconnected from workforce education. And there are vital missing links. Lifelong learning, advanced technical education, labor market information systems, and connections between school and work are all missing in action.

Models for change are needed, along with change agents to implement them. Within what is a maze of largely disconnected actors lurks a potential workforce education system that can emerge only with much better connections and pathways among the actors and can eventually be leveraged into a larger overall system that could move toward the needed scale.

4 TECHNOLOGY VERSUS JOBS

Like a number of major automakers, Toyota—through its US-based Toyota Research Institute (TRI)—is pursuing a project to develop a fully autonomous vehicle, which it calls Chauffeur. In parallel, TRI has its Guardian project to develop next-generation driver-assist safety systems. At the 2019 Consumer Electronics Show in Las Vegas, TRI showed a vivid 3-D video reenactment of a three-car crash on a California freeway.[1] Although no one was injured in the crash, the video was jarring.

The video was shown to demonstrate how new technologies could have avoided the crash. TRI researchers developed a precise simulation that was then translated into a learning tool for the car to figure out its options, in a split second. They recreated the scenario on a test track, using real vehicles and a guided, soft target, dummy vehicle. TRI believes Guardian now has the technology to avoid that three-way collision situation.

Unlike Chauffeur, Guardian is being developed not to replace human control of a vehicle, but rather to enhance it significantly by foreseeing pending accidents and implementing corrective responses in coordination with driver input. With Guardian, TRI is "doubling down on humans,"[2] working on blended envelope control that combines and coordinates the skills and strengths of the human and the machine.[3]

In an age of tremendous concern about machines replacing humans, particularly in the workplace, Guardian is being developed as an automated safety system to enhance a human driver (of course, it could also be used with an autonomous driving system). In this case, the machine does not replace but *complements* the person. TRI's safety project is on a much faster track than its autonomous vehicle project, where it has found that the complexities of urban driving create major implementation barriers.[4] Gill Pratt, TRI's leader, says about autonomous vehicles, "Americans tend to completely overestimate what can be done in five years and completely underestimate what can be done in fifty." But the complementary role is on a different timeline.

While our society periodically panics about automation, economists have long argued that the introduction of new, productivity-enhancing technologies always increase overall employment, net and over time—even if they disrupt this or that established sectors. Since the advent of the Industrial Revolution in the eighteenth century, they have always been right. But the panic is pervasive today.

In February 1961, *Time* carried a story expressing concerns identical to those of today: "The number of jobs lost to more efficient machines is only part of the problem. What worries many job experts more is that automation may prevent the economy from creating enough new jobs . . . Throughout industry, the trend has been to bigger production with a smaller work force . . . In the past, new industries hired far more people than those they put out of business. But this is not true of many of today's new industries."[5]

Automation concerns led President Kennedy to create a US Labor Department Office on Automation and Manpower that same year.[6] President Johnson followed with a Commission on Technology, Automation, and Economic Progress in 1964. Then strong economic growth and wage growth set the concerns aside. But a severe recession in the 1980s led to new panic. One economist predicted that artificial intelligence would idle 20 percent of the workforce in a generation; another wrote that "what happened to horses will happen to people."[7]

Earlier in this century, futurist Ray Kurzweil wrote of a coming machine intelligence infinitely more powerful than all human intelligence combined.[8] More recently, researchers have predicted information technology–driven shifts more dramatic than those of the Industrial Revolution,[9] and a "fourth Industrial Revolution" that will dwarf "anything humankind has experienced before," potentially disrupting labor markets and increasing inequality.[10]

What might be the most widely-known *specific* projection is that machine and deep learning, robotics, and computerization put 47 percent of both blue- and white-collar jobs in the United States at high risk of being automated.[11] Toyota's Guardian, however, suggests that complementarity, not displacement, could be how robots enter the economy at scale.

COMPLEMENTARITY OR DISPLACEMENT?

The debate over complementarity or displacement has been raging, particularly since around 2010. Through print and online articles, books, podcasts, and public presentations, researchers, businesspeople, and social activists have been lining up, usually firmly on one side or the other.

On the displacement side, the arguments often confront the standard view of economists that technology-driven productivity over time increases jobs—essentially arguing that increases in computing power and the expanded capabilities of information technology make lower-skill work and even white-collar jobs in finance and other areas vulnerable to displacement. This leads to a higher rate of economic inequality and a continued thinning out of the middle class—even, potentially, creating a kind of neofeudalism in which unemployment increases, further exacerbating class competition and driving down wages until the consumption-based US economy falters.[12] Some have proposed solutions for managing rising inequality that seem politically unlikely: redistribute wealth through Pigovian and other taxes[13] or establish a guaranteed basic income.

That's the displacement side of the argument. Those on the complementarity side sometimes begin by pointing out that the occupations predicted to lose the most jobs are those that have seen limited productivity growth in recent years. If machines were entering the workplace at scale, goes the argument, reducing workers and making work much more efficient, as projected, this would be signaled in the productivity data. Instead, we're in a productivity slump. And further, were IT-based automation and corresponding large-scale technological displacement imminent, we would also expect to see a sharp increase in related investment levels—but even five years after the end of the Great Recession, in 2014, computing and software investment as a share of GDP was still at only 3.5 percent and has continued at this lower level ever since.[14] Another argument on the complementarity side concerns the so-called lump-of-labor fallacy, the idea that there is a fixed amount of work to do with no new work appearing when it's done.[15]

However, data shows that new technologies have created their own employment, meaning they often offset the amount of work "lost" to automation.[16] And when the number of jobs at risk of automation is analyzed based on a more targeted job content approach—that is, what a worker actually *does* as opposed to what a job description suggests might be automated—workers usually turn out to be doing more than the tasks that can be automated. This means the share of jobs potentially at risk of automation is much lower than that 47 percent projection.[17] This is buttressed by data on the ratio of jobs to workers, which actually increased from 1980 to 2016 *despite* the advent of IT during that period—suggesting that while up to a quarter of today's jobs could be significantly affected by automation, dystopian warnings are not in order.[18] Of course, since automation does affect more routine jobs the most, the disruption that does occur could most affect those with the lowest education and therefore least prepared for it, including Latinos and African Americans.[19]

Economist David Autor—we introduced his barbell model in chapter 2—comes down on the complementarity side. He argues that most commentators tend to overestimate the amount of automation that will substitute for labor and goes further, noting that automation, overall, can change work content and thus increase the opportunity to create quality employment.[20] So it can also *augment* work, improving its productivity and removing rote tasks. He notes that people's desire for new products and services appears insatiable—another reason we won't run out of job opportunities. A 2019 MIT task force he co-chaired on "Work of the Future" reported that slow labor force growth, a rising proportion of retirees to workers, and more restrictive immigration mean that industrialized nations may be facing more job openings than their workforces can fill.[21] Incremental advances in e-commerce, internet services, and online and mobile delivery have been ongoing; they tend to require new skills but have not been creating large-scale job disruption.[22]

While studies indicate robotics has, over a quite extended period, created modest job losses in the United States, there has been no net job loss in Germany—which has much a higher level of industrial robots per worker—over a decade-long period.[23] Overall, the picture to date is more of a symbiosis between people and machines than outright displacement. The symbiosis line of thought was first articulated by J. C. R. Licklider, a psychologist and computing visionary, who argued that what became personal computing would enable human enhancement, not replacement, with computers doing what they do best (calculations, storing and retrieving data, accessing information, etc.) and people what they do best (insights, seeing patterns, identifying new ideas, etc.).[24] More recently, David Mindell updated this view, finding underwater and aerial drones, planetary robot rovers, and semiautonomous vehicles are extenders of human reach, not replacements.[25]

This debate—and, more importantly, what actually transpires—clearly matters in the context of workforce education. If massive technological displacement lies ahead, one could argue we should just forget about workforce education. But if the complementarity argument is the right one, and work content is just shifting—even if the shift is massive—we need to understand how to adjust the education content.

Meanwhile, we cannot ignore other causes of workforce polarization and income inequality—particularly what has been happening in manufacturing more generally. Historically, the manufacturing sector has always led productivity advances, based on the introduction of new technologies. The service sector typically lags well behind.

As discussed in chapter 3, US manufacturing output has made a slow and still incomplete recovery since the Great Recession (lower output, again, does not signal a rise in automation). US manufacturing productivity growth has also shifted sharply downward, to historically low levels.[26] If automation is not responsible for the massive losses in US manufacturing jobs, they *can* be largely explained by trade pressure and the faltering US competitiveness that resulted, affecting some two-thirds of the 5.8 million manufacturing jobs lost between 2000 and 2010.[27] While the manufacturing sector could have mitigated trade effects by accelerating technology advances to make it more productive, instead manufacturing productivity rates dropped.[28]

It's worth noting briefly that until the early part of this century, there was a general consensus among economists that trade could affect national wages in modest ways, but had no effect on employment.[29] But what some economists have called the *China shock*—beginning with China's entry into the World Trade Organization—seems to have changed that: the resulting disruption led to significant reductions in jobs, numbers of plants, and employment per plant.[30]

AN ECONOMIST WARNS ABOUT TRADE

Harvard economist Dani Rodrik has attacked economics orthodoxy for its failure to alert the public that global trade had distributional effects in developed nations, creating gaps between the well educated who do well in global trade and the less educated who tend to do badly.[a] The economics mainstream, he argues, understood that the long-standing view that trade would not affect employment was full of questionable assumptions and contingent conclusions. Still, in public they discounted the domestic costs of free trade and greatly overestimated the gains, despite mounting evidence that their consensus view was wrong.

Although job offshoring, a decline in routine jobs, a hollowing out of the manufacturing sector, and advancing technologies were also causes, trade appears to be have been the largest disrupting factor.

A more integrated global economy offers major economic benefits, raising GDP among trading nations, but the process of integration requires offsetting approaches to assist those affected.[b] Economic optimism allowed those approaches to be neglected.

[a]Dani Rodrik, *Straight Talk on Trade* (Princeton, NJ: Princeton University Press, 2017), x–xii.

[b]David Autor, "Trade and Labor Markets: Lessons from China's Rise," *IZA World of Labor* 431 (February 2018): 1, https://wol.iza.org/articles/trade-and-labor-makets-lessons-from-chinas-rise/long.

If trade has been the largest disruptor, which makes even clearer that productivity advances have not been the cause of the job shifts, it confirms that an automation revolution simply has not yet occurred.[31] But knowing that doesn't solve the workforce education problem—especially because the fact that a full-blown IT-driven automation revolution has not yet occurred doesn't mean it won't. We can only be certain, given the trends of slow productivity growth and low capital investment, that it's not going to be tomorrow.

That means there will be some time to prepare and adjust the workforce to reduce the disruption that technological change could cause. The coronavirus has put additional economic pressure on many firms, which will further slow the introduction of new process technologies and automation until after a fuller recovery takes hold.

Where are the robots? A 2019 MIT survey of forty-four successful small and midsized manufacturers in three states found only a handful of operating robots.[32] Why so few? Firms stated that the cost of a robot itself was only a quarter of the cost of getting it up and running on a production line, making them costly, and firms were reluctant to trust integrator companies with the competitive secrets of their production systems. Firms with a mix of high and low volumes and different production jobs were reluctant to adopt robots that are most cost-efficient for high-volume, stable production. Some supplier firms complained that if they could be alerted by their larger customers of more assured volumes of parts orders, they would be more willing to install robots, but the traditional information disconnect between larger US firms and their suppliers apparently remains. Robots were proving useful, however, for unsafe, heavy, and unhealthy work, protecting workers from the dangerous side of production. The study suggested a robot invasion would take time.

We can explore what the shift might look like and uncover in advance some of the effects that will be felt in the workplace over time that could help us ensure that the workforce can be ready.

COMPLEMENTARITY AND AUGMENTATION

We can say up front that work *will* drop in areas that can easily be automated. But in other areas, where more human input is required, jobs may even grow and new occupations may even arise, offsetting automation on overall employment. Our MIT colleague David Autor refers to three simultaneous labor force developments when new technologies arrive; they provide a good way to categorize what needs to be done. With *labor enhancement*, workers will get new tools and new productivity; *task displacement* means technology will displace tasks within jobs, or the jobs themselves; and there will be *new tasks* created by the new technology.[33] In other words, there will be real substitution of technology for workers, but there will also be complementarity—new jobs and job tasks creating and enabling the new technology—as well as worker *augmentation*, giving workers new tools to better handle their jobs.

We can see these factors playing out in the following three snapshots.

Snapshot 1: A Modern Industrial Plant

Let's look first in a typical modern industrial plant setting: Steelcase, based in Grand Rapids, Michigan, best known for its office furniture. Largely due to international competition, Steelcase shut seven of its nine US plants and shifted production abroad, including to China, Mexico, and India. To keep its two remaining plants in Grand Rapids competitive, it cut back on the number of workers and adopted automation technologies, including industrial robotics. There are automated assembly lines. Robotic arms lift tabletops once hauled by laborers. Computerized controls run equipment and workstations that detail production steps for workers, control parts access, and help assure that each production step is followed correctly.

Steelcase's current Michigan workforce is able to work much longer before retiring because there is far less heavy lifting for them in the workplace. Safety has also been enhanced significantly, and workers have a cleaner, less noisy, and more productive factory than in the past. When a production problem develops, they can troubleshoot it quickly by reviewing the computerized data. There are also more college-educated engineers involved, evaluating tasks and ensuring an efficient, "lean" production model.

Workers have generally welcomed being rotated through a range of different positions, rather than doing the same thing for years at a time. As one worker commented, "It's just getting to be a much more comfortable atmosphere around here. The technology is really helping that kind of thing, too. Instead of taking responsibility away from you, it's a big aid. It's definitely the wave of the future here."[34]

That's what work augmentation can feel like. While the computerized process controls mean there is quite routinized work under computerized directives, there are also new jobs for workers with the technology skills to maintain and operate the new computer-driven machinery. And while sophisticated new technologies have to be understood, programmed, and maintained at complex new levels, computerized controls also mean the technologies themselves may become more straightforward to operate. Just as personal computers have become easier to use over time thanks to a better human-machine interface, so too do the computerized controls on new technologies, over time, become simpler. It is a manageable mix of complexity and routine.

Snapshot 2: White-Collar Jobs and Artificial Intelligence

We have entered a new period in which new cognitive technologies and artificial intelligence are already automating some work involving basic decision-making in areas such as medical diagnosis and stock selection.[35] This is causing alarm—but it is also an opportunity for complementarity. As a popular cartoon caption reads: "You're not being replaced by a robot, you're being replaced by someone who understands robots."[36]

The algorithms that drive AI still must be created by manual human labor—which makes machine learning still largely human work. Figuring out how to optimize something is a computer problem, but what to optimize remains a human decision. AI is not autonomy. It is *augmented* intelligence, not a replacement for humans.

So although AI may not replace humans, it may replace jobs and tasks within jobs, as well as enhance job performance. But even if the effects on employment of AI and machine learning are more complex than the simplistic "end of work" story emphasized by journalists, the implications for the workforce going forward are still quite significant.[37] AI can get better and better, but it will remain behind human capabilities for a long time, including those capabilities that make up much of work: judgement, tacit skills, and common sense.[38]

AI offers an opportunity for complementary jobs. There is a shortage of AI software designers and data scientists, to be sure, but some experts are recognizing that organizations also need full cross-sector teams that include data engineers, data architects, data visualization experts, and, perhaps most important, a new employment category—translators.[39] These are needed to ensure organizations achieve real results from their AI and analytics initiatives. Translators are not necessarily analytics professionals and may not have deep technical expertise in programming or modeling, but they can bridge the technical expertise of data engineers and data scientists with the operational expertise of marketing, supply chain, manufacturing, risk, and other frontline management functions. Their role is to translate AI and analytics to enable impacts that can be scaled up. One estimate states that demand for translators in the United States alone may reach two to four million by 2026.[40] Even if the low estimate is off by half, that's a lot of complementary jobs.

Snapshot 3: An Advanced Manufacturing Digital Factory

MxD (the digital manufacturing institute) focused on digital production technologies and processes and related workforce education, is one of fourteen new advanced manufacturing institutes. Working with the Manpower Group, MxD explored what digital production would actually look like in a factory setting and what new complementary jobs and skills would be required to accomplish digital production at scale. It found that a series of new work domains will establish the patterns of work, tools, and technologies needed for digital manufacturing and design.[41] These are worth describing because of the large number of complementary jobs, as well as job or task substitution, they clearly imply:

- *Digital enterprise*, the overarching digital model organization, is built on information systems and work relationship connectivity, as well as research partnerships and engagement with external technology communities.
- *Digital thread* includes the guidance, integration, and security of data across the product lifecycle, which must be both interoperable and secure.
- *Digital design* includes the digital tools to design, simulate, and plan a product through development.
- *Digital manufacturing and processing* includes digital-enabled tools, technologies, and work that produce and assemble a product line.
- *Digital product* involves a product's digital data and connectivity to the production enterprise so that product feedback can be incorporated into subsequent design and production.
- *Supply network* includes the technologies and work that supply the components and materials for production and move a product to customers.

The MxD report estimates that 165 new digital tasks will be required in an advanced manufacturing enterprise to meet domain needs. Each will incorporate new domain-relevant digital technologies and processes and will need workers trained in new skills to fill new technician, specialist, professional, engineer, and management roles both inside and outside an enterprise.

It was an ambitious effort to think through what a new production facility must actually look like to take advantage of the productivity gains offered by digital technologies. It is a picture of what might genuinely be needed in terms of a new workforce for digital production. But it cannot be implemented unless the workforce is ready.

THE REEMPLOYMENT PROBLEM

Of course, augmentation and complementary jobs will not be the only story. To date, the culprits in the loss of jobs have largely been trade and globalization, but the coronavirus has created job disruptions and additional problems lie ahead as technological displacement increases over time.[42] There will be those who lose jobs and must be assisted, not ignored.

Workers who are displaced can—depending on their skill level—have trouble being rehired (especially older workers) and face pay cuts if reemployed. Sometimes, the problem of getting a new job persists for years—even when unemployment generally is at a relatively low rate.[43] The pay cuts can be sizable,[44] and those with less education, older workers, and those with longer tenures at the job they lost all faced heightened problems.[45] Most of those who exhaust unemployment benefits have had to change industries or occupations, and wage declines can last for two decades.[46]

When the loss of a job turns into longer-term unemployment, the effects on health can be serious. Stress is a particular problem, and stress-related problems often include loss of sleep, weight gain, and increased use of alcohol or drugs. Despite a need to seek medical help for stress, many displaced workers put off healthcare for themselves and their families.[47]

Older workers face a harder time finding jobs and greater earnings losses than younger workers who lose their jobs, and they can often face longer periods of unemployment.[48]

Just as we've already seen in the reemployment effects from globalization, we can project that technologically displaced workers with less education, older workers, and those with longer work tenures will face the greatest problems in finding new employment. It will take them longer to find work that will likely pay less than their old jobs. They'll suffer from health problems. The current supporting infrastructure is no more ready now than it has been as it has failed to mend the socially disruptive experience of globalization over nearly two decades. Job polarization is a reality now upon us.[49]

The bottom line is that the emerging complementary jobs and augmented work, as well as assisting the displaced, largely depend on creating a new and better workforce education system.

A FRAMEWORK FOR UNDERSTANDING SKILLS

Snapshots such as those earlier in this chapter are useful illustrations, but they are not enough. Are there general frameworks that will give us a better idea of what kinds of jobs will face technology disruption so that mitigating policies can be developed? Some labor and education economists have been working to define the categories of work that technologies will absorb and what they leave for people to dominate.[50]

Technology can reshape work faster than skills and training can keep up; the major technology thrust now reshaping work is, of course, computing.[51] Because computers perform some tasks faster and cheaper than people, but are inferior to people in others, we're seeing a new division of labor between human and machine. With a fuller understanding of which kinds of tasks computers will do better than people, and vice versa, we can begin to reshape our skills acquisition landscape accordingly. In other words, we can consider the skills required for the work that will be led by people and the ways computers can assist that work.

Labor economist Frank Levy classifies all labor force tasks into five broad categories that provide a framework to understand better the kinds of work that could be affected by the growth of digital technologies. On one side are *routine manual tasks* and *routine cognitive tasks*, which can be computerized; on the other are *nonroutine manual tasks*, *complex communications tasks*, and *expert thinking tasks*, which are harder to computerize.[52]

We've already seen reductions in jobs in the routine task categories, especially jobs in the lower middle of the earnings distribution held by clerks, assembly-line workers, low-level accountants, and customer service representatives, while tasks involving complex communication and expert thinking are increasingly significantly.[53] The trends point to a hollowing out of the job system. As computerization increases, labor markets will increasingly reflect these trends, with continuing strong growth of well-paying jobs in technology-rich workplaces for higher-end tasks involving expert thinking and complex communication.

How do we need to think about training for advanced skills such as expert thinking and complex communication? Levy argues that a computing-rich workplace will require foundational skills, including numeracy and literacy, that go beyond the basic: basic math is not sufficient for managing the abstraction of computerized systems or operations, and basic reading skills are not sufficient to enable mastery of computer-based designs and processes. The problem-solving skills needed compare in many ways to the expert thinking category because the problems go beyond the rules-based solutions with which computing can help. Workers will need capabilities in case-based reasoning that can draw on the experience and knowledge of others. Technology can be complementary here, and workers will need a knowledge of how to use digital tools and a knowledge of how to structure problems, set goals, measure progress, reflect on one's thinking process, and make decisions about continuing with or adopting a particular approach to a problem.[54]

Put simply, "many middle-skill *tasks* are susceptible to automation [while] many middle-skill jobs demand a mixture of tasks from across the skill spectrum."[55] A medical technician, for instance, enjoys relatively well-paid middle-skill employment, doing tasks that combine technology with interpretation. It is a good example of a future in which routine and non-routine tasks will increasingly coexist within an occupation to the extent that they complement each other, and the quality of the service performed will improve when the worker combines technical expertise and human flexibility.

Because of this required mix, we cannot draw absolute lines in defining routine and nonroutine tasks or in deciding which will stay or go. "Many of the middle-skill jobs that persist in the future will combine routine technical tasks with the set of non-routine tasks in which workers hold comparative advantage—interpersonal interaction, flexibility, adaptability and problem-solving," writes economist David Autor.[56] The heart of his point is that much of the gain from new workplace technologies will both require and accrue to people.

A number of the conclusions of a National Academies study of information technology and the workforce track with what we've reported here. It notes that people remain better than computers at numerous tasks, including those that require "creative reasoning, non-routine dexterity, and interpersonal empathy."[57] A major part of the upcoming workforce story will involve complementarity—new tasks and jobs formed to complement the opportunities new information technologies create. Advances in these technologies will, over time, automate some jobs, as well as create new jobs; importantly, they will also augment the ability of workers to perform many jobs better. Admittedly, as further IT advances emerge, they could play a role in exacerbating the social disruption and growing economic inequality (to date, largely from globalization) in the United States. But the demand for workers with skills that "emphasize creativity, adaptability, and interpersonal" capabilities, as well as new technical skills, will increase as more routine information and manual tasks decline.[58]

New technology advances accelerate the need for new kinds of workforce education, so more people can ride these IT-based innovation waves rather than be submerged by them. The middle ground of complementary work, where the new technologies augment human potential, will need particular attention because this will entail the creation of new tasks and occupations.

Our society largely ignored the dramatic social effects of globalization. We cannot make the same mistake with how technology is affecting employment. As new technology advances take hold in the future—and this likely will be incremental—we have time to develop new labor market assistance programs for those most affected.[59] Most important, the workforce education system must change to meet the needs of this changing labor market.

5 THE THREE SECTORS: MANUFACTURING, HEALTHCARE, AND RETAIL

Developments in the workplace cannot be understood solely at the national level; the American economy is also sectoral. Each economic sector, while connected, is different and needs to be understood in its context. Here we take a close look at what has been evolving in three major sectors—manufacturing, retail, and healthcare—and draw some lessons about what workforce education needs will be. These three sectors account for nearly fifty million members of the US workforce, which is well more than 30 percent: 12.8 million manufacturing workers, 15.8 million retail workers, and 20.1 million healthcare workers.[1] Our economic well-being will be determined, in significant part, by what will evolve in these sectors. Two of the sectors are classified as services, while manufacturing is considered a goods-producing sector. Before we dive into each sector, though, let's step back for a broader look.

While mid- and longer-term job projection is difficult, the periodic projections from the Bureau of Labor Statistics about where the workforce is headed are the best we have, and the BLS attempts to accommodate many variables. Its key projections from the Fall 2019 report—which relate to the 2018–2028 period—are worth reviewing.[2] Obviously, this projection from late 2019 could not have foreseen the economic disruption caused by the coronavirus in 2020. Yet because it made decade-long estimates, it still merits a close look.

- Total employment will grow by 8.4 million jobs over that period, reaching 169 million jobs in 2028.
- As the labor force continues to age, the overall labor force participation rate will decrease to 61 percent, down from a peak of 67 percent in 2000 (well before the 2007–2009 recession).

- As the baby boomers age, the share of workers over fifty-five (a group at a low level of participation in the labor force) will grow to 25 percent of the workforce—up from 22.4 percent in 2016 and 16.8 percent in 2006.
- Industry employment will grow at a rate of 0.5 percent per year from 2018 to 2028—slower than the 0.8 percent annual rate from the preceding ten years and much slower than the historic rates seen during the decades leading up to the 2007–2009 recession.
- New jobs will overwhelmingly be in the service sector (some nine in ten), resulting in more than 7.6 million new jobs, or 0.6 percent annual growth.
- What the BLS terms the *manufacturing sector* is a major part of the goods-producing sector. The manufacturing category will decline at an annual rate of 0.5 percent, while the goods-producing sector overall will decrease by a rate of 0.3 percent per year over that same period.
- Retail trade is expected to decline by 0.1 percent annually, largely because of e-commerce entry, although there will be a parallel increase in transportation and warehousing employment.
- In contrast, jobs for healthcare practitioners and technicians and in healthcare support will grow by almost two million, approaching one-third of all new jobs; this growth will make healthcare the largest employment sector by 2028.
- Healthcare and related occupations will account for eighteen of the thirty fastest-growing occupations. (Of those thirty fastest-growing occupations, entry to 60 percent of them will typically require some level of postsecondary education.[3])

There is another overall trend that will affect these sectors and needs to be accounted for: the percentage of routine jobs has been in sharp decline since 1990:[4] 34 percent then and only 25 percent by 2014. These jobs include both routine manual jobs that involve repetitive work, such as assemblers and packers, and routine cognitive jobs, such as bank tellers. The overall trends, then, are as follows:

- Modest overall job growth, constrained by an aging workforce
- Service sector jobs continuing to dominate new job creation
- Healthcare becoming the largest job sector
- Postsecondary education increasingly required for the fastest-growing occupations
- A significant decline in routine jobs

MANUFACTURING

Donald Trump's 2016 election was in significant part based on his appeal to working-class voters in states most affected by the loss of one-third of US manufacturing jobs between 2000 and 2010.[5] While this has led to extended discussions of manufacturing's role, debates over manufacturing support are not new.[6]

In summer 1791 in Philadelphia, Alexander Hamilton drafted his "Report on Manufacturers," probably his most innovative report to Congress. Opposing the exclusively agrarian orientation of Jefferson and Madison, he found that "manufacturing establishments not only occasion a positive augmentation of the produce and revenue of the society . . . they contribute essentially to rendering them greater than they could possibly be, without such establishments."[7] As Hamilton proposed, "Manufactures, and particularly the means of promoting such . . . will tend to render the United States independent of foreign nations."[8]

Hamilton was arguing that American independence from the era's contending great powers, and ultimately its liberty, would depend on building a strong manufacturing sector. Because "it is the interest of a community, with a view to eventual and permanent economy, to encourage the growth of manufactures," Hamilton made a series of what we would call *market failure* points; opposed laissez-faire, noninterventionist arguments; and advocated government support and "bounties" to foster manufacturing.[9] And applying innovation to manufacturing was one of his ideas; he advocated federal encouragement of "new inventions . . . particularly those, which relate to machinery."[10] A few months later, he concluded that "a spirit of manufacturing . . . will serve to promote essentially the industry, the wealth, the strength and the independence and the substantial prosperity of the country."[11]

Acting on his ideas, Hamilton backed what we would today call a public-private partnership with Paterson, New Jersey, and its Passaic Falls, a seventy-seven-foot water drop, to found what became a cluster of factories now considered the birthplace of America's industrial revolution.[12]

Hamilton's arguments still echo in a 2018 Department of Defense (DOD) report, which found a series of macrofactors to be creating challenges to the nation's industrial strength. These included the "decline of U.S. manufacturing base capabilities and capacity" in the form of "reductions across the U.S. manufacturing and defense industrial base [that] affect the viability of suppliers, overall capacity, and capabilities available domestically."[13] This problem was exacerbated by "domestic industrial and international trade policies of competitor nations [that] directly or indirectly degrade the viability, capabilities, and capacity" of the US industrial base.[14] These industrial base problems were made even worse, the DOD found, by "diminishing U.S. STEM and trade skills" and "gaps in American human capital, including a lack of STEM talent and declining trade skills, diminish domestic capabilities to innovate, manufacture, and sustain."[15]

As the DOD stated, "The roots of America's defense industrial base are planted in the broader manufacturing ecosystem" and "the manufacturing sector is the backbone of U.S. military technical advantage."[16] The 2017 US National Security Strategy concurred, stating, "The erosion of American manufacturing over the last two decades, however, has had a negative impact on these capabilities and threatens to undermine the ability of U.S. manufacturers to meet national security requirements."[17] The report called for a series of governmental steps, including development of an advanced manufacturing strategy, pursuit of advanced manufacturing opportunities, direct investments to support suppliers, and workforce development efforts.[18]

American manufacturing has indeed been in decline. While most Americans believe the United States has lost manufacturing to low-cost producers in Asia because of high US wages, Germany—where manufacturing wages are much higher—tells a different story. Manufacturing accounts for almost twice as large a share of GDP in Germany as in the United States, and the country runs a massive manufacturing trade surplus, including with Asian nations. Germany has maintained a strong manufacturing ecosystem for its manufacturers that closely ties innovation and production, undertakes collaborative research and development (R&D) between small and large firms and university engineering, and has a skilled manufacturing workforce of world renown.[19] Its system of more than seventy Fraunhofer Institutes is a public-private partnership that effectively pursues each of these tasks.[20]

In contrast, the United States faces a series of gaps in its manufacturing innovation system, beginning with the *hollowing out of the manufacturing sector*. Between 2000 and 2010, the United States lost some one-third of its manufacturing jobs, driven largely by international competition.[21] Only 18 percent came back by 2017, and by 2018 US manufacturing output was still 4.7 percent below its prerecession 2007 level.[22] The output problem is reflected in productivity levels. While US manufacturing productivity was increasing by an average of 2 percent per year from 1992 to 2004, it declined by an average of 0.3 percent per year from 2004 to 2016.[23] Manufacturing productivity grew at less than 1 percent from 2011 to 2018[24] and stood at 1.2 percent in 2019. In turn, investment in capital plants, equipment, and

IT is also at historically low levels, and the United States has been running a massive trade deficit in overall manufactured goods that rose to $868 billion in 2016[25] and a 2018 deficit of more than $120 billion in advanced technology goods.[26] The job loss data is a signal of a hollowing sector, with sixty-four thousand plants closing from 2001 to 2013.[27] The low productivity level signals an underlying innovation system problem.

While the United States once had firms and supply chains organized in a more vertically integrated system, a financial model of short-term returns with a focus on "core competency" led to firms going "asset light" and to a *thinning out of the manufacturing ecosystem*, including its shared best practices in production and training across supply chains—especially for small and midsize manufacturers.[28]

There is also a *scale-up problem*. While there are many industrial sectors, there tend to be three kinds of manufacturing firms—multinationals, small- and midsize firms, and start-ups. Large multinationals are generally strong, but they are global, need to be in international markets, and increasingly have been producing abroad. Small and midsize manufacturers (those under five hundred employees) produce 46 percent of US output[29] but have trouble obtaining the financing to scale innovation; to survive, they tend to be risk averse, thinly capitalized, and perform little R&D.[30] While the United States relies on entrepreneurial start-ups with venture capital financing to bring innovation into the economy, venture capital is focused increasingly on returns from software, services, and biotech. "Hardtech" firms that planned to manufacture received only 5 percent of venture funding investments in 2015 and thus are effectively being blocked from scaling their innovations.[31]

Another problem stems from *the disconnect between innovation and production*. In the United States, it's R&D and not manufacturing that is considered the source of innovation. But innovation is a *system*, from R&D through production stages, and the failure to understand production as a key part of that system is a fragmented view. Production, especially initial production of a new technology, requires very creative engineering and typically reconsideration of the underlying science in dense feedback loops leading to final design and production.

In the post–World War II period, the United States had an "innovate here/produce here" system and reaped the full spectrum of gains from every stage. This has increasingly shifted to a distributed system of "innovate here/produce there," aided by information technology advances.[32] Because production is part of the innovation system and most products require a close connection between production and innovation, a "produce there" system increasingly risks morphing into "produce there/innovate there." Because there is a now a close link between production processes and the R&D efforts they require, losing manufacturing capacity in various products means the United States losing the R&D capability behind them as well.[33]

Manufacturing still generates two-thirds of US R&D and company patents, but there is already evidence that firms are losing market share to trade cut innovation activities and investments.[34] If the United States wants to keep pioneering new technologies, we will also need manufacturing strength. A strong innovation system is crucial to the US advanced economy; a technology strategy disconnected from manufacturing advances leads to a broken innovation system.

In the context of these gaps, the *weak workforce education* in the United States becomes an exacerbated problem. After shedding 5.8 million jobs in the 2000s, it became increasingly difficult for US manufacturing to attract workers, even with baby boomer retirements and tight labor markets creating regional shortages in manufacturing skills. The entire system is upskilling; the jobs lost in manufacturing in the 2000s were largely in lower-skill fields, and skilled workers are now needed. Sound markets, however, require access to sound information; the broken US labor market lacks both an information system to help employers and employees navigate it and a system for effective skills training.[35] If the United States is to move into advanced manufacturing, there is no effective system at present for educating the workforce in the advanced skills it requires.

If the innovation system for production has significant gaps, can the United States apply its still strong innovation system to fill them?

Reviving Manufacturing-Led Innovation

The United States has R&D-led innovation, but other countries—Germany, Japan, Korea, Taiwan, and now China—have manufacturing-led innovation. Because of its remarkable mass-production capability, the United States led world production output after World War II. No other nation was close. The United States assumed this would continue and focused on the R&D stage.[36] Japan's leadership of the quality production paradigm led the United States to try to catch up on quality in the 1970s and 1980s, but not to adopt a manufacturing-led innovation capability along with its R&D-led innovation. Some policy leaders now suggest, in effect, that it's time to do both by pursuing policies for advanced manufacturing.[37]

Scientists and engineers tell us that a series of new advanced manufacturing paradigms may be in range that could transform manufacturing efficiency, productivity, and returns. These new production paradigms will include the following:

- *Digital production:* a mix of advanced information technologies, radio-frequency identification (RFID), sensors, and the Internet of Things applied in every stage and element; new decision-making from machine learning and big data analytics; advanced robotics; supercomputing; simulation and modeling
- *Advanced materials:* a "materials genome" capability, applying supercomputing to design all possible materials with designer features to fit specialized needs for strength, plus light weight and resilience
- *Biofabrication:* including synthetic biology
- *Nanomanufacturing:* fabrication at the nano-scale that enables new precision and capabilities
- *Mass customization:* production of single products or small lots at the cost of mass production, to allow for highly customized goods, enabled by 3-D printing and new computerized processes
- *New distribution efficiency:* information system advances that yield efficiencies in distribution, supply chains, and connecting with customers
- *Energy efficiency:* technologies that reduce the use of energy (which is, in effect, waste) in production to cut costs and raise efficiency

There are also specific new technology areas such as photonics, new chemical and biopharma processes, power electronics, and advanced composites that can translate into both production efficiency and innovative products. The core idea behind advanced manufacturing, then, is to bring the still strong US innovation system more directly into manufacturing. This, in turn, will require new advanced workforce skills and corresponding training. The economic slowdown from the coronavirus pandemic will slow down firm interest in adopting new production paradigms, but over time this will require attention.

The innovation system gaps we have discussed are structural problems in the manufacturing system and require systems solutions. Manufacturing, of course, is overwhelmingly in the private sector, as will be advanced manufacturing. Even Defense Department procurement, while sizeable, supports only some 8 percent of manufacturing output.[38] A government-only effort won't work; an approach that engages the private sector more thoroughly to address system needs is required if it is to scale. The advanced manufacturing institutes model, a collaboration that brings together industry, universities, and state and federal governments, began in 2012 and now includes fourteen institutes, with programs that reach companies in nearly every state in most of the new technology areas listed previously. It attempts to deal with the gaps in the system by

- connecting small and large firms to restore the thinned-out ecosystem;
- relinking innovation and production in collaboration between firms, universities, and governments;
- pursuing production innovations to grow efficiencies and productivity;
- providing shared facilities for scale-up; and
- building a skilled workforce to implement and disseminate advanced production technologies into companies.

These features address key structural issues, but the institutes face a limited timetable of federal support because they currently have five-year terms. The structural problems, though, are longer-term problems and require longer-term leveraging from federal investments. There are signs that these terms will be extended for successful institutes.[39] The industrial base needed if the United States is to have sustained technology leadership is at stake.

America's key trading partners and competitors spend much more at the governmental level on their manufacturing bases and invest more in advanced manufacturing than does the United States.[40] The leading example is China. Its share of world manufacturing output grew from 5.7 percent in 2000 to 22.4 percent in 2012, while the US share fell to 17.4 percent.[41] In 2016, China established a $3 billion fund for advanced manufacturing, and in 2019 it created a $29 billion fund for semiconductor advances alone, which far exceed US investments.[42] There is growing recognition, however, of the importance of maintaining this base in the United States.[43] No one actor, including the government through its contracting role, can generate all the new manufacturing technologies and skilled workers and suppliers on which it depends. Instead, a system is needed in which a connected network of firms, universities, labor, governments, and national and corporate labs together nurture the next generation of production technologies, processes, and education infrastructure. The market alone does not support efficient levels of investment in these networks, often called a *manufacturing ecosystem* or the *industrial commons*. The institute model is designed for the problem of getting to advanced manufacturing.

A National Academy of Engineering 2015 study, "Making Value for America," noted that manufacturers serve and depend on complex networks of activities that "span multiple locations, companies, and economic sectors" and include services and software.[44] These networks create complex value chains, and those that rely on manufactured goods either as a part or as a delivery mechanism "account [in the United States] for 25% of employment, over 40% of gross domestic product, and almost 80 percent of R&D spending."[45] And while the sector producing information and communications technologies has been growing much faster than manufacturing since 2008, it still accounts for well below half of the value added from the private goods-producing sector.[46]

Manufacturing is indeed a critical area. The report found that "the greatest threat to American prosperity is not that other countries will get better and catch up to—or surpass—the United States; it is that the United States will fail to keep improving itself and thus fall behind as other countries continue to improve."[47] Advanced manufacturing, then, appears to be a priority task—one that will require new technologies and therefore new training.

Restoring American leadership in production innovation may prove crucial to our continued innovation leadership, which the nation has viewed as our core competitive advantage. The public-private manufacturing institute partnership model, because it addresses structural problems in the manufacturing innovation system, appears to be an important route for the federal government to continue to pursue. In parallel, it mandates new training systems to implement the new technologies.

Coronavirus Effects

How will the coronavirus pandemic affect these developments? Obviously, a number of significant services sectors have been badly hit. And it will be difficult to restore companies, particularly small companies, that have failed. But for manufactured goods, theory suggests much demand will remain. If you needed a car before the coronavirus, that demand will remain. However, aerospace, a leading high-end manufacturing sector, has been hit hard by airline cutbacks, leading to canceled orders. The broader economic effects of the pandemic will limit overall buying power for a time, including for manufactured goods. However, the political system seems to have learned, and then tried to practice, the Keynesian lesson of governmental intervention in both the 2008 and 2020 downturns.

Firms with vulnerable global supply chains appear to be particularly vulnerable from the pandemic. COVID-19 will not be the last "black swan" event for the economy; climate effects may offer more. And calling these black swans misstates their predictability—infectious disease experts have tracked the successive SARS, MERS, and Ebola outbreaks and have long noted the likelihood of a global pandemic. Further, predictive efforts are well underway for climate effects. But resilience, previously not a major factor, could be a new value in looking at the strength and value of firms. This will mean companies will want more direct control over supply chains. The financial model of requiring firms to pursue only their core competency and go "asset light" may be shown by the pandemic to be a problematic model, at least in some sectors. A rethinking of the extent of global supply chains may occur. If so, this could force some reintegration of tasks within firms, as opposed to the distributed sourcing model many had been following. This could mean less offshoring.

For example, Apple's distributed production model, with its manufacturing in China, came about in part because of the short product development cycle of its product lines. The model was more labor intensive because more automation requires longer product cycles. But what happens to the Apple model? Will firms with globalized production have to produce more in their home market areas to assure these home markets?

Much depends on whether the financial sector adopts a reintegration lesson. Firms initially will be tempted to get back on their feet quickly by contracting out and distributing production because financial pressure may have cut resources for internal investments. But the value of a more integrated model and the additional control and resilience this provides may be appealing over time. Even if the financial sector remains oriented to the short-term advantages of wholesale distributed production, government may want to consider requirements for secure domestic supply chains in critical industries. This seems to be the case particularly in medical products, devices, and therapies, given the shortages underscored by the pandemic. But there may be broader pressure for strengthening and controlling supply chains that could reach other critical areas of manufacturing, including defense-related sectors, forcing some rethinking of the distributed production approach. The need for more flexible manufacturing so that firms can shift quickly between production lines to meet new production demands rapidly may become apparent, with corresponding new production technologies and processes. The pandemic will weaken firm resources and so reduce the ability to shift to new production technologies and the productivity gains that go with them. But over time this should revive. All of these production changes will require new kinds of skills.

Manufacturing Workforce Trends

To summarize points made thus far, the United States has been trading places on manufacturing output share with China, which now leads world output. Because its innovation leadership is at stake, key analysts believe the United States needs a way to restore its production leadership.[48] Many see advanced manufacturing as a way for the United States to compete with lower-cost, lower-wage nations by raising efficiency and lowering production costs, enabling it to better compete. Innovation also brings its own rewards: it can bring about new and often unforeseen economic opportunities. There may also be pressure from the coronavirus pandemic for more secure supply chains and less distributed production, which may relocate some production in the United States in critical sectors. While the economic fallout from the virus may reduce initial pressure to raise productivity through new technologies, over time this should return. New technologies are not the only means to productivity gains; a more productive workforce also can be the source of new efficiencies. New training efforts will be needed to implement the opportunities presented by advanced manufacturing.

But are there production-sector job openings that would require training? The United States has created more than a million new manufacturing jobs since the lowest point of the Great Recession,[49] although manufacturing is still a long way from its employment level in 2000. The Bureau of Labor Statistics projects a decline between 2016 and 2026 in its production workers category,[50] but that is largely composed of the more traditional manufacturing jobs, where the numbers of lower-skilled employees have long been declining, and doesn't necessarily reflect the higher-skilled jobs the sector is moving toward. For example, manufacturing conducts more than two-thirds of US R&D, and industrial firms employ over 60 percent of STEM workers.[51] STEM-based jobs are projected to grow by 10.9 percent or over a million jobs by 2026,[52] but those dynamics are not captured in existing production categories, nor are many computing and software positions that manufacturing will likely require. It's important to note that manufacturing also has a rapidly aging workforce, with 3.8 million workers over fifty-five; these positions will need filling as well.[53] So while manufacturing may have a declining share of overall US jobs, there will clearly be many jobs to fill in the sector.

The manufacturing workforce is already upskilling. Workers with high school educations or less by 2016 made up only 43 percent of the manufacturing workforce; some college education is increasingly required.[54] But if the United States adopts advanced manufacturing, it will need a suite of even higher skills in manufacturing.

Senior manufacturing executives, according to a 2018 Deloitte survey, overwhelmingly believe there is a skills shortage for what may be 2.4 million jobs to fill between 2018 and 2028.[55] A 2014 report by Accenture for the Manufacturing Institute asserted most manufacturing employers contemplated increasing their employee numbers, but said they were experiencing a skills shortage, that these shortages were starting to affect earnings, and that companies were investing in training, spending $3,000 annually for new hires and $1,500 for incumbent employees.[56] Given the decade of manufacturing layoffs, others find this projection problematic.[57] But one economist suggests a nuanced analysis: there likely are particular shortages for workers with the skills to manage the latest technologies.[58] We don't measure the skills they require, making a shortage hard to pin down. But manufacturing will require new skills due to technological advances, which suggests there will be openings for more skilled workers.

In general, manufacturing workers continue to be quite well paid. In 2017, the average manufacturing worker earned $84,832 annually, which includes pay and benefits and an average wage of twenty-seven dollars per hour.[59] This is $18,000 more than the average worker in other, nonfarm industries.

Manufacturing has long been understood as the economy's largest job multiplier: manufacturing processes raise demand for raw materials, energy, construction, and services from a wide range of supplier industries,[60] and many tasks manufacturing companies used to do themselves—from back-office operations and accounting to some logistics—are now contracted out. Contracting out is an example of backward linkage among major economic sectors; manufacturing's is the highest. Growth in manufacturing output encourages additional output and growth in other sectors, both directly and indirectly, in terms of jobs, investment, and innovation.

These are quite dynamic factors. One standard estimating process indicates that for every dollar spent in manufacturing, another $1.89 is added to the economy—the highest multiplier effect among economic sectors.[61] Manufacturing's effects on the economy are even greater when the entire manufacturing value chain plus manufacturing for other industries' supply chains are taken into account; manufacturing could account for one-third of GDP and employment. That taken into consideration, the Manufacturers Alliance for Productivity and Innovation (MAPI) estimates the total manufacturing multiplier effect at $3.60 for every dollar of value-added output, with one manufacturing job generating another 3.4 workers elsewhere.[62]

Another underlying issue that affects the manufacturing workforce and the viability of new training efforts has to do with the tendency of US manufacturing employers to treat their workforces as a variable cost that can be readily cut whenever downturns threaten. But what may have worked when workers were predominantly low-skilled and readily replaceable may be problematic as manufacturing becomes more technologically advanced. As economic and political sociologist Fred L. Block has noted, US manufacturers' "employment strategy simply won't suffice in the technologically sophisticated context of advanced manufacturing, where employees have a significant level of skill and management is dependent on their judgment to manage and supervise the production process to get the best possible results. Such employees cannot be treated as throwaway people; they need to be recognized as a vital and important part of the enterprise."[63]

Germany, which is also moving to implement advanced manufacturing, has figured this out. It sees its workforce, not just capital investments, as key to the production productivity gains needed for what it calls Industry 4.0. Its manufacturing workers are paid much higher wages and benefits, are highly trained, have job protections, and have a voice in management through work councils and often company boards.

HEALTHCARE

Healthcare, as noted at the outset, is a rapidly growing employment sector. Driven in large part by the nation's aging demographics, it is on its way to becoming the nation's largest job sector.

There is a big economic inequality in the community of healthcare workers. Well-off doctors are at the top of the chain; a very large group of lower-end, low-paying service jobs providing direct personal care are at the bottom. The sector seems to have a limited middle class providing technical and middle skills, which likely will grow in complexity and need as additional technologies enter the sector. Those at the bottom have very limited pathways for advancement; there is not a good road ahead for them to move to higher skills and better wages. Yet there appears to be a significant need to encourage a stronger healthcare middle class.

The sector already faces two particular workforce shortages. First, there is a growing shortage of primary care physicians, and the system is struggling with using nurse practitioners, physician assistants, and primary care technicians to fill that gap—which creates significant training needs. One cause of the primary care physician shortage is the lower wages these workers earn compared to specialists—even though basic medical school training costs the same for both. Physician associations have also played a role in supporting specialist versus general medical residencies.[64] While one approach to offset the shortage is increasing general medical residencies and subsidizing primary care practice through forgiveness of student loans and increasing Medicare compensation for primary care,[65] the other, training more nurse practitioners and physician assistants for primary care, is more comprehensive. Concerning the second shortage, new mandatory mental health coverage requirements and an opioid epidemic are putting heavy demands on the behavioral health workforce for mental health and substance use treatment. These fields have an aging demographic and acute shortages in pediatric and adolescent mental health. There is also a growing training need in this area, including for specialty mental health. In both primary care and behavioral health, pay for professionals through public payer reimbursement rates and fee-for-service practices tends to be higher in wealthier urban areas, which exacerbates shortages in other areas.[66] Meanwhile, new healthcare technologies are driving up the need for skilled medical assistants. Professional licensing and scope-of-work requirements, however, create entry barriers to the healthcare workforce, especially for many of the newer "allied health professions."[67]

A tangled web of health policy, economics, education, and established professional cultures make for a tangled web of healthcare workforce issues. Nurses, psychologists, and pharmacists all must have professional licenses that are more restrictive than physician licenses, and these workers are often required to work under doctor supervision. Many analysts now identify licensing laws as limiting the effective use of nonphysicians. Shortages of healthcare professionals also keep prices high for existing providers.

Mental health is a growing field, but the expert workforce is aging, limited in size, not diverse, and facing growing demands.[68] The opioid epidemic highlights policy failures and treatment shortages, in part due to a lack of research on treatment modalities and a lack of trained providers. Some states and localities are developing ways to reimburse paraprofessionals through state Medicaid policies, such as in substance abuse treatment, as a way to increase capacity across the spectrum of care, which includes prevention, intensive treatment, and rehabilitation.[69]

Let's look at some of the key healthcare workforce issues in more detail. First, there are the *limiting effects of state laws and regulations*, which define the legal scope of practice for healthcare practitioners under a system that increasingly cannot support the workforce innovations needed for an evolving healthcare system, including requirements of the Affordable Care Act. These rules are blocking efficient use of the health workforce by creating mismatches between professional competence and legal scope-of-practice laws. The lack of uniformity in these laws and regulations across states limits workforce deployment, and overall, these laws limit needed overlap in scopes of practice among professions that often share some tasks and responsibilities. The process for changing the laws is slow and contentious.

There's a strong argument that what's needed is a new alignment process for existing and emerging professional categories, regulatory flexibility in recognizing new health professional fields, and a national clearinghouse for scope-of-practice information.[70]

These limitations are curtailing the emergence of *allied health*, the mix of health practitioners, both established and new, needed to meet growing healthcare needs. It is a field that lacks definition, and clarity is need.[71] Although these professions have overlapping skill sets, scope-of-practice laws are limiting application of these skills to patients. Kaiser Permanente and Geisinger Health Systems have provided respected health-delivery systems organized around collaborative, team-based care; medical homes, accountable care organizations, and bundled payment arrangements are emulating this model.[72] Yet scope-of-practice regulations limit the ability to implement the lean, team-based, and information technology–enhanced approach. Nurse practitioners, physician assistants, and allied health professions have growing numbers and could help offset the shortage. However, as of 2013, only seventeen states allowed nurse practitioners more independence from doctor supervision, despite particularly serious care shortages in rural areas.

Another issue concerns *new delivery mechanisms*. New approaches are evolving that call for additional skill sets in the medical workforce: the expanding team-based approach is one example.[73] Another is the patient-centered medical home, where newly skilled technicians and assistants, in addition to doctors, are needed to encompass the use of more evidence-based medicine drawn from sound research findings, use of clinical decision-support tools, better chronic medical care delivery approaches, better and more convenient access to care, use of quantitative indicators of quality care, more health information technology, and ongoing feedback on performance.[74] Yet another example is the now widespread retail clinic that offers convenient access to basic health services. These are frequently staffed by nurse practitioners, where allowed by scope-of-practice rules, and research suggests that nurse practitioners can provide significantly lower costs per medical episode if care begins with a clinic visit.[75] These clinics also open the door for new kinds of nondoctor practitioners.

Accountable care organizations (ACOs) are at the center of a new model that ties payments to meeting quality metrics. They are formed by coordinated groups of health care practitioners, including participating hospitals, doctors, and other health workers, with Medicare as the primary payer. They require new groups of technical workers, including those with information technology, data analysis, and other skills.

New technology advances will also drive new training requirements. For example, artificial intelligence, after many years of discussion and experiment, is now beginning to move into the healthcare sector. Early applications have been in imaging—X-rays, CT scans, MRIs, echocardiograms—because of the large volume of data they provide for analysis.[76] We are still a ways from AI diagnoses,[77] but risk stratification is a key mission in which it could assist.[78] Thus, AI could help predict the likelihood that patients with particular conditions and various characteristics will need to be readmitted to hospitals, which could lead to improving their care after discharge to avoid readmission.[79] There is a significant new workforce opportunity here that could significantly enhance team-based healthcare, but the technology also creates a significant new training demand.

There are, then, new *training needs* for the healthcare workforce. While team-based delivery mechanisms likely offer better care, health professionals are not trained in collaborative skills, doctors are often noted for non-collaborative tendencies, and doctors are also burdened by many tasks for which they are not trained, including computer data entry and analysis, patient education, and insurance inquiries and management.[80] These tasks could be better delegated to other qualified personnel, which creates new training needs.

Increasing the numbers of nurse practitioners, physician assistants, allied health practitioners, and community health workers appears to be one key to meeting America's healthcare needs. Taking advantage of modern health information technology could enable this group of providers to improve the effectiveness and reach of patient-centered medical homes significantly by providing basic preventive, minor illness, and stable chronic disease care, including in rural and other communities with limited medical resources.[81] This will require new kinds of professionals and corresponding training.

The coronavirus will create some new kinds of demands and therefore new skill requirements. The vaccine development and production process has been exposed as painfully slow given the potential speed of a contagion. Gaps in supply chains for key medical products, tests, equipment, and therapies will require closing. More flexible and rapid production systems for these goods will be needed to fill shortages. Concerning care delivery, the large-scale advent of online telemedicine has put new flexibility into the system and requires medical information system managers. Online disease and infection tracking capabilities first developed in South Korea and other countries are proving to be useful tools in managing the coronavirus; given appropriate privacy protections, some may also be applied to other medical and disease areas in the United States. Capabilities for robotic room disinfection, high-speed health surveys by robocall, remote temperature taking, and robotic supply delivery are all being experimented with during the pandemic. All these new technology priorities will carry with them new skill needs.

The *aging population* has needs both for more general practitioners and for particular kinds of specialists. Demand for adult primary care services will grow by approximately 14 percent between 2013 and 2025, but the supply of specialists in the greatest areas of demand growth—vascular surgery, cardiology and neurological surgery, and radiology and general surgery—may be inadequate.[82] This will require more training in these areas, including in related allied health fields, as well as moving existing specialists from lower- to higher-priority areas.

It's not only specialists that are needed. There is an oncoming problem, for example, with the size of the overall treatment workforce for Alzheimer's disease and dementia patients as these patient populations grow. The demographics of the baby boomers will create a major policy problem in upcoming decades for quality long-term care, but underinvestment in the training and compensation for the direct care workforce represents a significant barrier.[83] We need to change direct care jobs to include a broader range of tasks and roles, with additional training and advancement opportunities to enable this higher-quality care, in what has been a neglected but quickly growing occupation category.

There are also needs within the *mental health and addiction workforce*, which has long faced shortages, high turnover, diversity problems, and concerns about its performance.[84] The Mental Health Parity and Addiction Equity Act of 2008 required group health plans and health insurers to provide mental health or substance abuse disorder benefits on a similar basis as medical and surgical benefits, which has driven an expansion of services to meet these long-standing needs. The Substance Abuse and Mental Health Services Administration (SAMHSA) in the Department of Health and Human Services has estimated that more than half of US counties have no practicing behavioral health worker, and more than 70 percent report unmet behavioral health needs.[85] It has been working to integrate mental health care into primary care settings; implement a workforce training strategic plan; develop training for community health workers on public health screening, brief intervention, and treatment referral approaches using community settings for intervention; and work with historically Black colleges and universities on behavioral health services and workforce training to diversify the workforce in this field.[86] We also need to train other kinds of healthcare providers to address behavioral health needs, as well as train and use individuals in recovery.

On top of all these healthcare workforce needs, *students seeking education in allied health fields face difficulties*. Skilled technical training is supported by complex and uncoordinated programs at a mix of federal agencies, as well as at the state level, which tend to reflect the unconnected federal programs. While medical school and nursing training are understood, there is limited information available about allied health fields, including on the quality of education programs for training and of job opportunities. Students have a great deal of trouble choosing programs of study that will fit them, and the cost is a problem. "Moving from low-paying, lower-skilled occupations (such as personal care assistants) to higher-paying, higher-skilled occupations (such as registered nurses) requires educational investments that may be a barrier to many potential workers," writes one economist,[87] with funding uncertain and difficult to secure. Career pathways are also not clear; beyond the cost of obtaining credentials, there are issues around scope-of-practice limits, as well as exam and licensing requirements. Mentors and counselors can be important in leading potential workers through the varied mix of training and job opportunities,[88] but they are largely missing in this sector. Low completion rates in community college programs that provide the training remain a problem.[89]

The healthcare sector, like others dominated by professionals, has a clear preference for skills validated by a four-year college degree. But the more than forty healthcare occupations that fall into the allied health category have no such requirement, and of nearly four million new jobs in the healthcare sector and related areas, 40 percent may go to allied health professions.[90] In fact, healthcare professions dominate the BLS's list of fastest-growing occupations.[91] Creation of a strong allied health base could go a long way toward creating the middle class that healthcare arguably needs to offer more efficient, better quality, and more affordable care.

RETAIL

More than fifteen million people in the United States worked in retail trades in 2019. But by all indications, traditional retail is in deep trouble. Often a first job *and* a job of last refuge, retail jobs are in trouble as stores, malls, and entire chains close. This all has a domino effect: first the department store closes in a town center or mall, customer traffic falls, and then the stationary store closes, and then the clothing boutique. A nail salon may unshutter some windows, but over time foot traffic drops again, and eventually the ice cream shop, the coffee shop, the restaurant, and the bakery close. Downtown and mall closings spiral, municipal taxes drop, and dereliction becomes inevitable. The coronavirus social distancing rules have greatly exacerbated the situation, shuttering tens of thousands of retail establishments.

The impact on the American worker has been profound. There may be a way out of this tailspin, but it requires some understanding of recent history and trends in retail.

The United States saw an extraordinary expansion of the mall over the fifty-year period from its inception in the mid-1950s—more than 1,200 new malls opened, with growth peaking in the 1980s and 1990s. To a large extent, this coincided with the growth of suburban developments after World War II. Department stores and shopping centers grew too, resulting in a saturation of retail.[92] In the United States today, there are nearly twenty-four square feet of retail per capita, which is about half again as much as in Canada, which ranks as the next-highest nation.[93] Retail was overbuilt.

Innovation was never a priority in retail, but it did occur. The barcode, introduced in 1974, transformed the cash register and checkout processes. IT enabled better coordination in the supply chain, and warehousing innovations such as cross-docking (directly shifting loads between trucks without storage) improved just-in-time delivery. But the pace of innovation was slow as growth and other factors were prioritized. Much of manufacturing moved to Asia, and cheaper and cheaper goods from overseas spurred the culture of consumption. But there were underlying issues negatively affecting retail: inventory inaccuracies created significant costs; sales were lost because of out-of-stock items; and there were high levels of retail theft, euphemistically termed *shrinkage*—much of it from employees.[94] RFID was developed for inventory tracking; leading retailers were interested, but broad recognition of retail's operational issues was to come later. Retail labor, meanwhile, suffered from high turnover, at least in part because workers were not considered partners in improving operations.[95]

So while retail was an unhealthy industry by the mid-2000s, the portentous signs were mostly invisible from the outside. Then two things, one more sudden and another that had been unfolding for some time, changed retail forever.

The sudden event was the 2008 recession, which was an existential shock for retail. As consumer confidence dropped, retail sales also dropped to thirty-five-year lows.[96] By December 2008, US retailers were saddled with massive inventories, and liquidating became a priority—to consumers, other retailers, or even to other countries.[97] By March 2009, average same-store sales in malls were down 6.5 percent; mall closures peaked in 2008 and 2009, and more than one hundred had closed by the end of the year.[98] More than six thousand stores closed in 2008, a number to be surpassed only in 2017.[99] The traditional brick-and-mortar retail bubble had popped.

The coronavirus has been a further shock, with hundreds of thousands of employees laid off and tens of thousands of establishments closed, a large number of which lack the resources and depth to reemerge.

Beyond the recessions, though, retail was suffering from a *long slide propelled by online commerce* that began, essentially, in 1995, when Jeff Bezos launched Amazon and Pierre Omidyar launched what was to become eBay. By Q1 2009, online retail sales were already $34 billion; in Q1 2019, they were $137 billion.[100]

Traditional retailers who thought the end of the Great Recession would portend a brighter future were sadly mistaken. The inexorable force of online commerce has created a long and endless slide. In 2017, there were more than eight thousand store closures. Toys"R"Us and RadioShack are among the well-known brands that have disappeared. Between 2006 and 2016, department store sales were down nearly 30 percent, but square footage decreased by barely over 10 percent.[101] Retail debt, real estate costs, and, of course, sales will keep the downward slide going.

This story of brick-and-mortar retail does not mean that overall retail is in trouble. In fact, according to the Census Bureau in 2019, overall retail sales as a whole have grown, driven mostly by online commerce.[102] As for retail jobs, growth recovered somewhat after the Great Recession, but became anemic more recently: in 2016 and 2017, retail jobs did not keep pace with the economy's job growth,[103] and the 2020 pandemic has been a jobs disaster. Retail job growth is also lopsided: department stores employed three times fewer people in 2017 than in 2001, and department stores have lost eighteen times more workers than even coal mining.[104] Women tend to be more deeply affected by retail job loss than men because they usually work in the fronts of stores, whereas men typically hold the transportation and warehousing jobs, which have grown at a remarkable 12 percent during the same period.[105] In fact, as of March 2019, the United States had a shortage of truck drivers.[106]

Automation in Retail

What about robots and automation taking retail workers' jobs? Storefront jobs are shrinking, and that trend will continue with self-checkout stores (such as Amazon Go),[107] automatic checkout at stores using RFID,

RFID-based inventory-taking within stores, AI to scan and sort deliveries for store departments, and even robot-based planogram analysis with robots roving aisles scanning inventory.[108] But retail shipping, warehousing, and delivery jobs are increasing. That growth, though, is not a panacea. The jobs may be higher paying, but they are more geographically concentrated.[109] Furthermore, many of those jobs are also automatable, and will likely dwindle over time. Kiva Systems, a robotics company, was acquired by Amazon to automate aspects of order picking, and self-driving trucks will someday likely automate aspects of trucking.

The Rethinking of Retail

Omnichanneling is a new direction in retail that takes advantage of digital technologies, social media, and mobile devices to redesign marketing for customers, who seek product information and offers in the physical store and from mobile devices. Firms can better allocate and integrate inventory and improve service to customers across physical stores and online channels and can include features such as easy returns and same-day delivery. These links between the physical store and online support must be seamless and mutually reinforcing. Another element, *beaconing*, uses Bluetooth to send in-store alerts to customers' smartphones about discounts, promotions, and availability as they peruse particular products. These developments require new IT skills from the retail workforce.

What does the new retail model look like? To a large degree, it is an outgrowth of what has been called the *experience economy* and the *experience age*, in which customers overwhelmingly favor experiences over transactional product purchases.[110] This has serious jobs implications. The future of retail may look much more like Apple's highly committed and trained sales staff, a Genius Bar, no checkouts, Bluetooth beacons, low tables, open displays, and an inviting ambience; these factors have helped propel Apple to have the highest sales per square foot in retail today by far.[111] Like at Starbucks, retail will include more online ordering with store pickup (omnichanneling) and smartphone payments at the cash register; like Macy's, RFID will likely turn more stores into virtual warehouses that enable omnichanneling. And as Walmart is already doing, more retailers will enable shopping online for pickup at stores, with geofencing linked to your store loyalty card so the store gets your order ready as you drive in.

Retail Jobs of the Future

Brick-and-mortar retailers, although hard-hit, are innovating. At the heart of all this innovation are technology and, more than anything else, people.

Each new technology and process requires people who are trained, innovative and, in particular, cocreating. Unfortunately, retail workers have been treated as expendable in much of the industry. Staff numbers have dropped 10 percent, salaries have been reduced by about 4 percent, and training budgets have diminished in the decade before 2019.[112] Retail pursued lowering staff pay and experience levels following the 2008 collapse, hoping that combined with discounting it would offset the decline. Research, though, shows that it is a store's staff that drives sales, and training definitively improves staff performance in retail.[113] By cutting customer service, much of the retail industry seems to be moving in exactly the wrong direction.

If people are at the heart of future retail, then training is essential. Customers, awash in a sea of online and in-store product information, want store staff to be their expert guides to products. This will require product knowledge training and process training. Omnichanneling means staff will also need technology know-how to operate across channels.

There appear to be clear benefits to sales training. At Dillard's department stores, for example, the average hourly sales of associates who participated in voluntary training through online modules were 46 percent higher than for those who didn't.[114]

Understaffing stores and undertraining workers remove the advantage traditional stores have over e-commerce: a live person a customer can talk to customers about products. The more expert the staff, the larger the potential advantage; training turns out to be critical.

Our colleague at MIT, Zeynep Ton, has written extensively about treating retail workers like partners; she makes an apt connection between a "good jobs system" and manufacturing's noted Toyota Production System.[115] The successful physical retail operation, she argues, will be more staff-centric, with a focus on enhanced process training. Retail's focus in recent years on reducing wages does not lead to better performance; retailers that focus on staff training and satisfaction achieve better staff performance. Trained staff can simplify operations by reducing product lines and promotions so staff can focus, perform multiple tasks, eliminate waste, and improve decisions by participating in those in which they are directly involved.

In fact, opening education opportunities has become a key strategy to retain employees at some large retail companies. Employee turnover is a major problem for many retailers; staff training can increase worker job commitment, and many large companies are turning to college tuition reimbursements as a way to keep loyal, committed employees—including, for example, Starbucks, Amazon, Walmart, and Peet's Coffee.[116]

In short, retail is shifting to a new survival model that seeks to merge online and brick-and-mortar shopping seamlessly. It aims to give traditional retail the advantage over online shopping that comes with face-to-face contact. If store staff are experts, fluent with products, costs, and online channels, they will be sought out for that expertise, which is difficult to replicate online. The new people-centric retail model means upgrading retail staff. But the model requires new training initiatives in a sector that historically has been weak on training. The coronavirus has hit small and large retailers hard, so it will be difficult for them to move to a new model. Innovation, accelerated by the coronavirus, will continue to affect the sector. While online and warehousing jobs are growing and offsetting retail clerk job losses, automation will affect these jobs over time. New technologies, though, as in other sectors, have the potential to create jobs as well—which also will require new training programs.

6 THE BROKEN LABOR MARKET INFORMATION SYSTEM

Adam Smith explained that market economies operate through an "invisible hand,"[1] but what was that hand? In 1945, Friedrich Hayek argued that a market is an *information system*.[2] Economies seeking to allocate resources and goods efficiently through societies with millions of market participants (both people and firms) had what Hayek called a "problem of the utilization of knowledge which is not given to anyone in its totality." Pricing in a market, he wrote, is "a mechanism for communicating information." Markets work, then, through the aggregation and transmission of information among the participants, and the better the underlying information, the sounder the market. Markets with good information systems could be far more efficient than, for example, groups of central planners who inevitably have only partial information.

Is the US labor market an efficient one? Harvard University labor economist Richard Freeman sets out the basic issues: "The United States has an exceptional labor market. With less institutional regulation than is found in any other major advanced country, it relies on decentralized wage setting to determine pay and provides workers with lower safety nets to deal with unemployment, disability and health problems. It gives managers great rewards and power."[3]

The United States has the most decentralized workforce management of any developed nation. Its labor market is highly individualized and localized, and so is fragmented with relatively few information connections between participants. The information disconnects are affecting managers as well as workers. But at least one expert argues that we have "dysfunctional" information systems behind our labor and education markets.[4]

Efficient labor markets, like all other markets, require good information flow and widespread participation—which we lack. On the supply side, younger workers face difficult education decisions, especially at ages seventeen or eighteen, that will largely determine their work futures; they must act with limited understanding about their options and therefore on limited information. It's even worse for displaced workers, who lack the tools to understand job openings and education and training options. And managers are increasingly frustrated in their ability to hire and retain the talent they need in an ever more complex technological society.

There is a highly complex array of disconnected actors:

- Recognized *occupations* grew from 269 categories in 1950 to 840 in 2010.[5]
- Among *employers*, we have more than 251,000 manufacturing firms alone.[6]
- The number of *colleges and universities* more than doubled between 1950 and 2015, from 1,851 to 4,627.[7]
- The number of *college students* grew almost nine-fold from 2.28 million in 1950 to 20.2 million in 2014.[8]
- *Postsecondary programs of study* quintupled between 1985 and 2010, from 410 to 2,260,[9] and today there are more than 300,000 different certificates and degrees offered.[10]
- The nation has some 39,600 *public and private secondary schools.*[11]
- *Unions* today represent only 6.5 percent of the private sector workforce.[12]

The disconnects among all these actors exacerbate the information problem. On the supply side, the certificate and degree programs lack the data to match them to actual job qualifications. Therefore, employers lack information about the relevance of education and of actual qualifications. On the demand side, job seekers face great challenges knowing their employment options, where those jobs might be, the skills they require, and how those skills could best be acquired. The sharp decline of unions figures into the equation because they once played a significant employee aggregator and information transmission role.

Our labor market information system is broken. Workers and employers alike are largely flying blind.

All of this is complicated by the vast array of agencies that collect relevant data. Workforce and labor market information has primarily been provided by a few federal agencies: the Bureau of Labor Statistics and the Employment and Training Administration in the Department of Labor, the Census Bureau in the Commerce Department, and the National Center for Education Statistics in the Department of Education are the primary data collectors.[13] But a large number of others also collect relevant data: the National Agricultural Statistics Service in the Department of Agriculture, the National Center for Health Workforce Analysis in the Department of

Health and Human Services, the National Center for Science and Engineering Statistics in the National Science Foundation (NSF), the Office of Research, Evaluation and Statistics in the Social Security Administration, the Bureau of Economic Analysis of the Department of Commerce, the Statistics of Income program for the Internal Revenue Service in the Treasury Department, and the National Center for Veterans Analysis and Statistics in the Department of Veterans Affairs.

A JOB NAVIGATOR

It's a mess—but suppose we had a work navigation system. There could be online-delivered interventions to help workers facing job dead ends find work opportunities requiring skills adjacent to their own that they could master. The navigator could be an online guardian that collects and scans occupation shifts and alerts employees, finds relevant job openings, and identifies the skills needed on new jobs—from soft teamwork skills to basic education skills to technical skills. The system could be finely grained and nuanced around jobs, skills, and openings. Government job displacement data and training support information could also be delivered.

Such a navigator could also link workers to training interventions, including training opportunities from colleges and community colleges. Schools are increasingly developing online education programs. Online accredited degree programs are growing, offered both by individual schools and consortia; digital technology firms offer online programs in topics related to their software; and certificate programs—many of which are open to anyone who wants to complete the courses, even without obtaining the certificate—are extensive. Other microcredential programs are growing. Could increasingly available online education and training content be linked to job opportunity and qualification information? An online navigator that delivers information on job shifts and job openings could also find and deliver the training that fits a worker's opportunities.

The navigator would be multipurpose. It could alert clerical retail workers to what's happening to retail jobs in their area, to retail job sectors holding firm and those that are fading as online warehousing expands. It could alert these workers to complementary service fields that are expanding, such as restaurants, hotels, or office work. Healthcare is an expanding sector in most communities, but applicants often require new skills. The navigator could link health, manufacturing, or retail workers to job training courses, link to online education for new skills sets, and link to new job opportunities—and it could alert employers to newly trained workers that fit their needs. In other words, we could build an efficient labor market.

Countries like Germany, Austria and Switzerland have famous apprenticeship-based workforce education systems.[14] There is a rich information system behind them, based largely on shared personal knowledge and face-to-face education and exchanges that worker and employer participants understand. The United States is unlikely to replicate those kinds of workforce education systems, but we could build an online information navigation system that substitutes for a person-to-person system.

THE NAVIGATOR'S ROLE

What would a navigator look like? Think about how Netflix sends you movie recommendations based on the kinds of movies you have been viewing, or the way Amazon makes book recommendations. In 2010, LinkedIn created a job recommendation engine that uses what are called *content and collaborative filtering systems* to compare job profiles with job applicant profiles.[15] For example, it enables companies posting jobs to sort and connect to the most relevant talent potentially interested in the job; similarly, it can aid job seekers with information on relevant job openings. More advances are on the way. University of Arizona and LinkedIn researchers are working to predict career paths that could help guide job seekers.[16] They are using large digital datasets on employees, skills, and companies to look at job profiles and employment, and then performing data mining to map and predict subsequent career paths. While LinkedIn is focused largely on professionals, the quality job problem is in middle- and lower-skill areas.

The US Labor Department's Employment and Training Administration already provides valuable data through its O*NET system.[17] If you want to become, say, an electrician, O*NET can answer many questions you might have. It tells you the number of electricians employed nationwide and regionally and that electricians work in a number of sectors, including building/construction and mechanical (with industrial machines, equipment, and tools). It lists the skill requirements, including those on the horizon as the content of an electrician's job expands. O*NET indicates median wages for the profession and shows projected job growth. There are also state-by-state job trends. O*NET also provides information on job education preparation among the current electrician workforce and explains that vocational school and/or community college for one or two years, plus on-the-job experience, are typically required. In addition, O*NET lists some of the available training offerings.

O*NET can provide building blocks for more expansive systems. Noting the problems of increased job polarization and declines in income mobility, an MIT Media Lab team is pursuing, for example, more closely defined skill categories, relying on detailed Department of Labor O*NET occupational skill surveys. Their system can identify sets of skills that are highly complementary to produce a larger network of jobs that workers in a specific region could pursue, from pump operator to claims examiner. Their network, called Skillscape, can identify bottlenecks that limit career mobility and help locate pathways through them.[18] Overall, it shows that workers with social and cognitive skills versus physical and sensory skills are doing better and that regions with higher numbers of workers with these skills are thriving, and it connects this information to occupations and areas to further help workers consider repositioning themselves.

Burning Glass Technologies tracks numerous sources for labor market data, from government information to want ads. It applies data analytics and skill mapping, and it presents businesses with a strategic view on skills they will need and where to get them. For government officials, its data can show evolving labor market skill supplies and skill needs to guide workforce training programs and economic development efforts.

Headai, a Finnish company, is developing a microcompetencies system that maps regions, cities, and organizations, showing in real time the skills most in demand and where they are needed.[19] It is working on a way to map online an individual's skills, identify employment fields that fit that personal map, ascertain additional skill areas that would help the individual meet job demands in other fields, and show the kinds of skills the individual has or is missing for particular types of jobs.[20] It will also link the individual to programs to acquire missing skills.

Another example comes from the Strada Institute for the Future of Work.[21] Recognizing a new imperative that workers must adapt and advance their skills throughout their careers because jobs and tasks are changing with new skills required, it has attempted to build a new way of collecting job market and skill data in close to real time. It seeks to understand better just what skills employers are seeking and how these match the skills held by the regional workforce. Its "skill shapes" approach aims to help not only employers and employees but also educators and policymakers to pursue education and economic development strategies that fit their region's skills.

The Workforce Investment and Opportunity Act, passed on a bipartisan basis in 2014, called on the US Secretary of Labor to create a new and much larger workforce and labor market information system. The act also provides a full framework for organizing this system,[22] and the Secretary of Labor's advisory council on the legislation developed detailed implementation recommendations in 2018 to form this system.[23] Meanwhile, the Census Bureau in 2016 began creating a jobkit site that compiles government job information sources and, since 2018, has been developing more in-depth data on postsecondary school employment outcomes;[24] NSF in 2019 began undertaking a new National Training, Education, and Workforce Survey;[25] and the Commerce Department and the White House formed an American Workforce Policy Advisory Board that began meeting in 2019.[26] The Internal Revenue Service and the Social Security Administration hold vast data on income and employment trends that, if made available, could provide important information for an strong database, as could Commerce Department data on companies.

This rich lode of government data could provide a base for an operating information system that potentially could be complemented by employer and educator data. The example of the US National Weather Service may be relevant. It compiles extensive weather data collected from its nationwide systems, which, augmented by algorithms, forms a strong weather prediction system. It makes that data available to the private sector. This is the source for the Weather Channel and for apps on your smartphone, but also for many specialized companies serving diverse needs in agriculture, insurance, and other weather-sensitive industries. These specialized firms would not have evolved without the government data; in turn, the government itself, if it just held on to the data, would not have developed these specialized capabilities in areas such as insurance or agriculture. Data sharing has worked well for all participants. Evolving something similar for labor market data, with the government sharing its databases and the private sector adding to it, could be key to a new labor information system.

All these critical elements could evolve into a system that links workers, along with an appraisal of their skill sets, in real time to employers with jobs and the actual skills required. The navigator must help workers not only move laterally to other jobs for their existing skill sets but upward to new and better opportunities; to do this it must suggest additional competencies within range of the worker's capabilities that the worker could acquire, then directly link the worker to education programs, online and blended, to acquire the actual skills required. As part of that, it must be predictive of where promising employment opportunities lie, helping workers avoid dead ends. And it must guide educational institutions toward offering better programs more realistically tuned to actual skills that will be needed and that carry accepted credentials.

Overall, to be an efficient information system—for the invisible hand to work—this system must operate at a large scale.

INTEGRATING EDUCATION AND LABOR MARKETS

The integration of education with the labor market system we need is a particular challenge. A high school education no longer assures a solid career.[27] While some college education is increasingly important to career success, simply showing college attendance and solid grades won't be enough. Increasingly, systems will be needed to unpack credentials and show their value in actual job settings. There is a maze of pathways through college education and training systems that now require measurable outcomes that can translate into workplace needs. Increasingly, states and municipalities that once offered tax incentives to attract employers will need to supply employers with workers that possess sought-after skills acquired through postsecondary education and training. Talent will be the new economic development strategy. Alliances among employers, postsecondary institutions, and states will be key.

Higher education administrators will need to do a better job aligning their education offerings to promising career fields, which will require them to track the job and career data better and also become much better at getting it to their students. Community and four-year colleges also will have to get better at career counseling. Most students, particularly those with limited workforce experience, make decisions that will dramatically affect their career opportunities and economic well-being with little understanding of how their college choices will affect their employment outcomes. Greater use of predictive analytics and having trained career coaches doing the advising could help avoid these problems. And postsecondary schools should start supporting and developing online information systems in their career services to better match their students with career fields and required education and training. Industry advisory groups could help.

INTEGRATION OF ONLINE EDUCATION INTO A NAVIGATOR

Online education for particular skills can be an important tool for four-year and community colleges as they embark on this integration. One advantage is that online courses can be readily accessed and delivered from a navigation system as *part* of such a system.

Online offerings specifically for workforce education are expanding and could be linked into a navigation system. Relevant examples include the following, for example:

- *NSF's Advanced Technological Education* program, which supports groups of cooperating community colleges, often with regional universities, is already involved in developing online, classroom, and onsite training, often in blended approaches in a series of industry sectors.[28]
- *The Manufacturing Skills Standards Council*, which supports the skills certification system for the manufacturing sector, offers thirty-five- to forty-five-hour online skills courses in manufacturing and logistics, organized in modules and available to high schools, community colleges, technical colleges, and workforce investment boards.
- *NIST's Manufacturing Extension Partnership* programs offer online skills training in many states; and firms such as *180 Skills*, *Tooling U-SME*, and *THORS* offer hundreds of online, on-demand courses in a wide range of technical skills, from foundational skills to robotics to welding.[29]
- The fourteen *advanced manufacturing institutes* supported by the Defense, Energy, and Commerce Departments are developing workforce education programs for the new manufacturing technologies they support;[30] and *AIM Photonics*, through its workforce academy, is already developing a suite of online courses for technicians and for engineers in photonics and optics.[31]

Based on what kinds of jobs they want, workers and students need to be able to use a job navigator system to find these kinds of online and blended skills certificate programs. Once they start moving through the programs, they can use the navigator to locate initial and subsequent jobs and get advice on adding to their skills. Bringing new technologies into online learning linked to a navigator—from digital tutors to virtual reality—may help too. The navigator can be a common ground for students, community colleges, and industry to find each other. It can be an education delivery system, tied to specific job search needs.

INTEROPERABLE LEARNING RECORDS

If the navigator could link workers to online and other education materials related to their job searches, how could the resulting credentials or other experiences be validated and made meaningful to employers?

A working group of companies, educators, and government officials from the president's American Workforce Policy Advisory Board issued a report in September 2019 calling for interoperable learning records (ILR), which are digital records that can document and communicate educational attainments and credentials as well as learning from experience, training, and professional affiliations.[32] Were the steps it advocates taken, an ILR could go a long way toward forming a critical element in a job navigator. Job seekers today rely on resumes, job applications, and formal credentials to tell employers about their skills, experience, and job qualifications. However, this traditional method does not convey enough information. It doesn't effectively capture the depth of skills workers have acquired on the job or show how current the cited skills are. It tells nothing about the knowledge behind degrees, and it doesn't verify that workers have the credentials they claim without third-party confirmations.

The advisory board report noted that it takes an employer forty-two days, on average, to fill a position, at an average cost of $4,129.[33] An ILR could be key to making that process much less cumbersome, helping both workers and employers. It could establish common definitions and terms for occupations, skills, and credentials, as well as show and validate all the information about a worker—including the integrity of credential data and the content behind a specific credential—without requiring further validation from education institutions or prior employers. It could be sharable, portable, secure, verifiable, transparent, and interoperable—and controlled by the worker. The worker's qualifications could link to employer job criteria, showing how they match.

Getting thousands of education institutions and employers literally onto the same wavelength to create an ILR system will not be easy. But the report sets a timetable for creating an inventory of participants from education organizations and employers, for identifying existing pilots that could be built on, for forming a development group, and for launching a prototype. As the report states, "American learners deserve a way to translate education, training and work experience into records of transferable skills that will provide them opportunities at higher wage occupations. Employers deserve to have a way to communicate to potential applications what skills and abilities they require to fill a position. ILRs that use open standards can bridge education, training and employment."[34]

MOVING FORWARD TO FIX THE BROKEN SYSTEM

Of course, unless an information system—the job skill and job opening data tied to rich data on training options and links to the training systems themselves—is made available, no online navigator will work. But there are signs this could be improving. A series of organizations are moving to gather those data. In 2014, in a rare moment of bipartisanship, Congress required the Labor Department to build a better system of workforce information and the data behind it. As the Labor Department's 2018 advisory panel recommended, better identification "of in-demand occupations and industries" to "fill a career awareness gap" for workers would benefit from new databases from unemployment wage records; expanded information collection on occupations, skills, and credentials; a new career awareness education framework; and better information on the changing nature of work—along with improved data sharing, new involvement by states and other agencies, and new analytics.[35]

Labor information systems are receiving increasing attention. For example, the US Chamber of Commerce Foundation is encouraging employers to develop a much deeper skills identification system for jobs they need to fill, tying it to a new, more dynamic job registry through its T3 skills credential and standards innovation network[36] and Clearer Signals job registry.[37] Some 160 education and training institutions have collaborated to build a common online Credential Engine registry, with a search system to help both employers and workers understand the skills behind their certificates and degrees.[38]

With such data systems, education providers would be better able to tailor education to actual skill needs. Online education could be a way such a navigation system scales, potentially creating a common ground for the triangle of workers, employers, and educators. With this data, a genuinely needed job navigator to help guide American workers and employers through the maze of our dysfunctional labor markets could be enabled.

If we can build the information, we can build this crucial workforce tool and rebuild the market.

7 THE UNIVERSITY ROLE IN WORKFORCE EDUCATION

The United States was the first to develop mass higher education.[1] Its development paralleled the rise of American industrial and then technological leadership that moved toward ascendancy beginning in the closing decades of the nineteenth century. Public universities began with Thomas Jefferson's state-supported University of Virginia in 1819 and multiplied through the passage and implementation of the Morrill Land Grant College Act in 1862, which created a nationwide system of public institutions of higher education supported at the state level. It was supplemented by the GI Bill following World War II, which in turn played a key role in moving a growing portion of the population through higher education. At its peak in 1949, nearly half of all students admitted to college were veterans, and many institutions nearly doubled their student bodies.[2] The GI Bill played a key role in democratizing higher education.

Today, public institutions provide some three-quarters of American higher education. Together, the Morrill Act and the GI Bill may constitute the most important social legislation ever passed in the United States because of the remarkable economic well-being that has reached such a large number of higher education participants. Federal student aid programs and federal research programs that fund science and engineering student researchers have supplemented the earlier legislation. Expenditures on higher education amount to 2.6 percent of US GDP, still the highest percentage in the world.[3]

HIGHER EDUCATION AS AN ENGINE OF ECONOMIC MOBILITY

Harvard economists Claudia Goldin and Lawrence Katz have portrayed the societal advantages—indeed, the necessity—of continually raising the college graduation rate. They argue that the continuing technological advances in industry since the Industrial Revolution require an ever-increasing level of technological skill in the workforce.[4] In effect, there are two curves: an ever-growing curve of the technological advance implemented by industry, and a corresponding curve of the technological skill base in the workforce needed to support this technological advance. In a successful, technologically advanced economy, the societal skill base curve must stay parallel to and ahead of the technology implementation curve because the two curves interact and are mutually interdependent.

In this context, we can see how higher education has become increasingly tied to *societal* economic well-being. In particular, mass higher education was a critical step in ensuring that the skill base of the US workforce stayed ahead of the curve while new technologies were implemented.

For a hundred years, the United States kept the education curve ahead of the technology implementation curve, but beginning in the late 1970s we allowed the higher education graduation rate to stagnate. Goldin and Katz argue that this stagnation is a major cause of the growing income disparity in the United States, highlighted in chapter 2.[5] While the US upper middle class kept ahead of the technological skill curve, increasing its graduation rate, the lower middle and lower classes did not.[6] The resulting gap in the skill base created a wage premium for the upper middle class and left the other classes behind. The income gap continues to grow, and there is a close correlation between these income disparities and college graduation rates.[7]

Clearly, higher education has societal importance. While the college graduation rate has grown in more recent years, there is still much room for progress (table 7.1).

Beginning during World War II, the amount of federally funded research was multiplied twenty-fold, and many universities added significant research to their roles as education providers. This research led universities to play a growing economic role in their regions, which expanded further with passage of the Bayh-Dole Act of 1980, which enabled universities and their researchers to retain the intellectual property value of their federally funded research. In more recent years, a growing number of universities have become important generators of entrepreneurial start-up companies based on their research.[8]

Universities are now seen as critical actors in regional innovation clusters and ecosystems, often linked with small and large businesses and providing talent and research to cluster capabilities.[9] A 2017 Brookings report found, for example, that communities in the Great Lakes–Rustbelt region with strong area universities have been able to leverage these as economic assets to help get through the area's overall economic challenges of recent decades.[10] The region has twenty of the world's two hundred top-rated

TABLE 7.1
US college attainment (2018)

Level of attainment (postsecondary)	Percentage reaching attainment
Graduate or professional degree	12.2
Bachelor's degree	21.1
Associate degree	9.2
Postsecondary certificate	5.2
Total, with postsecondary credentials	**47.6%**
Some college (no credential)	15.4
High school graduate (or GED)	26.0
9th–12th grade (no diploma)	6.7
Less than 9th grade	4.3
Total, some college, high school, or less	**52.4%**

Source: Lumina Foundation, "A Stronger Nation: Learning beyond High School Builds American Talent," Lumina Foundation (report), February 12, 2018, https://www.luminafoundation.org/resources/a-stronger-nation-report.

universities, nearly all state-supported public institutions. Satellite campuses of these leading state university systems are also central to attracting and preparing talent and serve as anchors for new business growth and economic development in many of the region's historic industrial and trading cities. In turn, these college and university towns boast among the highest educational attainment levels across the Midwest, which contributes to high and rising incomes in the local communities. The report found that higher education anchors many of the Rust Belt counties that boast above-average incomes. The Midwest's colleges and top-tier public universities generated a disproportionate share of the nation's research, innovation, and talent. With 31 percent of the nation's population, Rust Belt states produced 35 percent of the country's bachelor's degree holders, 33 percent of its STEM graduates, and 32 percent of higher education degrees awarded.

THE CRITICAL ROLE OF HIGHER EDUCATION IN WORKFORCE CREDENTIALING

Research at universities is not their only or most significant economic role. Increasingly, institutions of higher education across the board—public colleges and universities, four-year private nonprofits, and two-year community colleges—are central to providing the critical credentials required in the workforce.

Growth in Colleges and College Programs

A high school education is no longer enough for a good job future; entering the middle class requires some post–high school education.[11] That's the new economic reality—reflected in a quintupling of the number of postsecondary programs of study (for-credit degree and certificate programs)[12] between 1985 and 2010, from 410 to 2,260; between 1950 and 2014, the number of colleges, universities, and community colleges more than doubled, from 1,851 to 4,724, outpacing population growth.[13] All this has transpired as complexity and specialization in the workforce have continued to rise: the number of identified occupations grew from 270 in 1950 to 840 in 2010.[14]

ALTERNATIVES TO COLLEGE?

In their book *Other Ways to Win*, Kenneth Gray and Edwin Herr of Penn State's College of Education decried this situation of college as "the one way to win." While some 30 percent of high school students are academically strong and most of these can readily shift into four-year schools, the rest have been told that going to a four-year college is the only accepted course. In general, they have to absorb the idea that if they don't go this route, they are "losers":

> Some (30%) of these teens go to work full time though few will have been prepared to do so by their high school. And the rest? They go to college not really knowing why except they do not know what else to do, and despite being somewhat unprepared to handle college studies. And of course, most [in this middle group] fail with mathematical predictable certainty . . . There are, of course, many reasons why teens in the academic middle lose out in high school, [including] that they are somehow less important than the academically blessed . . . This is not however the central problem. The core is that virtually everyone has come to believe in the "one way to win" paradigm.[a]

Although Gray and Herr go on to delineate alternative routes to success for those who don't get to college, they fully acknowledge the ascendency of the college degree.

[a]Kenneth Gray and Edwin Herr, *Other Ways to Win*, 3rd edition (Thousand Oaks, CA: Corwin Press, 2006), 5.

Importance of the College Degree

These signs of demand growth for college reflect the growing centrality of college education in the workforce. Workers with a college degree during the slow economic recovery between 2010 and 2016 added 8.4 million jobs, while workers with only a high school diploma added only eighty thousand jobs in the same period; these workers, in effect, experienced no job recovery.[15] In that same period, those with associate degrees or some college gained 3.1 million jobs. To state it another way, nearly all the jobs created during the recovery between 2010 and 2016—some 11.5 of 11.6 million—went to workers with at least some postsecondary education, with those with college degrees taking 73 percent.

Other data shows that workers with a college degree or higher took almost all the jobs in high- and middle-skill occupations: 5.8 million high-skill and 1.9 million middle-skill jobs between 2010 and 2016.[16] Workers with at least some postsecondary education captured the vast majority of good jobs that pay more than $53,000 for full-time, full-year work with benefits, such as for healthcare and retirement. Those without any postsecondary education are increasingly facing low-skill, low-wage jobs. These workers lost 181,000 high-skill jobs and 951,000 middle-skill jobs since the recovery began in 2010. With declining quality employment for the less educated, workers with a college degree or higher by 2016 made up a larger share of the workforce (36 percent) than workers with a high school diploma or less (34 percent). These trends are not just post–Great Recession, but have been developing since the 1970s, with the percentage of the workforce with higher education assuming an ever-growing share.[17] Obviously, this is a historic shift.

But four-year higher education is not a monolith automatically delivering uniform economic gains. There are key variables that affect its economic role that we need to understand:

- *The earnings premium for a college degree* is substantial and continues to grow.[18] Millennials with a high school diploma earned only 62 percent of what the typical college graduate earned in 2016. The median income of recent graduates that year reached the highest level in more than a decade—greater than 50 percent higher than high school graduates.
- *Place* is assuming a growing role for higher education students, with the majority of incoming freshmen attending public, four-year colleges within fifty miles of their homes.[19] For community colleges, the median distance is only eight miles. Upper-middle-class students tend to be more mobile; working-class students are less mobile. So place matters: zip code is a key determinant of life outcomes, affecting whether higher education can deliver economic gains.
- *The field of college study affects earnings.* The disconnect between college and the workplace is illustrated by data showing that only a little over

a quarter of college graduates work in a field directly related to their college major.[20] College graduates have much lower levels of unemployment, enjoy better health, and have lower mortality rates, but not all college degrees are equal.[21] At the higher end of the earnings distribution were graduates who majored in fields emphasizing quantitative skills, such as engineering, computer science, economics, and finance. But there is another variable: while there is a high economic return initially for STEM degrees, these returns decline significantly after a decade as technological change introduces new job tasks and makes skills in older tasks less valuable.[22] The message here, then, is two-fold: it matters what you major in, and you need to keep upgrading your education and skills in technical areas.

HIGHER EDUCATION AS A LEGACY SECTOR

It must be remembered that college education was not initially organized in the United States to provide what we would term *career training*; historically, it provided a liberal arts education emphasizing foundational skills. While early colleges educated ministers, the development of professional schools accelerated in the second half of the nineteenth century, typically to supplement a college education; these more career-oriented schools taught law, medicine, education, and later engineering and business, and even separate schools for religion. Of course, the land grant college movement that created state universities began to scale after the passage of the Morrill Act in 1862 and emphasized undergraduate practical education in agricultural science and engineering to augment liberal arts and professional education. This was supplemented by graduate education, based on the German university model, in the natural sciences, social sciences, and humanities, developed primarily to train faculty for the higher education system. So with the exception of engineering and agriculture, undergraduate education was not initially designed or intended to provide job skills; that was more a high school or graduate education task.

After a long emergence, community colleges reached large-scale prominence in the 1960s, in significant part as a way to fill this gap.[23] They enroll some 35 percent of all undergraduate students.[24] Of course, there is not a single model in US higher education and four-year institutions vary, but as general trends the points noted earlier tend to hold.

With the shift in labor markets, today's employers are being forced to reorganize their businesses around computing and information technologies and are understandably anxious about adopting them. They appear particularly concerned that college graduates lack training in these technologies. Computer science is not taught in three-quarters of elementary and secondary schools,[25] and universities have trouble hiring and retaining computer science faculty because their salary scales cannot compete with growing job opportunities in the private sector. Colleges and universities often feel they are fighting a losing battle on the computer education front, unable to meet the growing demand. Meanwhile, for-profit coding academies have been sprouting up to fill the void.[26]

But even if universities wanted to adapt, change at universities is difficult. Higher education fits the characteristics of a complex, established, legacy economic sector that resists change, including with respect to its cost, price, and demand structures.[27] Higher education's established infrastructure and institutional architecture, coupled with its powerful vested interests—particularly faculties and the academic departments they control—make it averse to innovation. The public perspective on higher education only amplifies the resistance to change.

Higher education is largely unable to organize collective efforts around reform of learning or curriculum because the system is highly decentralized, scattered among thousands of institutions. Even university systems that join public colleges and universities together within a particular state remain quite decentralized, and many states have not organized such systems. The decentralized nature of higher education institutions means that reforms adopted in one or even some are hard to spread to the others at scale. Bringing change to the sector with these kinds of legacy characteristics in play is particularly challenging.

In the context of the workforce education needed today, a question is posed: Are universities to convey marketable skills and information, to educate an informed and conscientious citizenry, to develop in their graduates lifelong intellectual and cultural interests on which they can construct more rewarding lives, all of the above, or something else?

HIGHER EDUCATION CREDENTIALS ARE NOT A SUBSTITUTE FOR ACTUAL SKILLS

The absence of an effective US labor market information system (see chapter 6) means job credentials, to the extent they exist, are generally not tied to actual competencies and lack recognition across fragmented labor markets. Although universities are now providing critical credentials to the workforce, they are stuck in these credentialing problems. Because employers provide only limited training themselves and their training investments appear to have been in long-term decline, they seek credential substitutes—especially education attainment as a signal of skills.[28] Employers believe educational attainment signals potential (if not job competencies) and hire more and pay more to four-year college graduates.[29]

Changing federal regulations helped drive this. Prior to 1978, employers often used cognitive tests to evaluate applicants, but these tests were found to discriminate against minorities and were frequently not related to actual job performance. That year, the Equal Employment Opportunity Commission restricted their use.[30] Most employers dropped them, some substituting psychological personality tests (also minimally useful for predicting job performance). After 1978, many employers simply shifted to using college degrees as a substitute for cognitive testing. One study explained it this way:

> For many employers, the solution to the shortage of soft skills among their middle-skills applicant pool is to "upskill" the position or to add credential requirements, such as a Bachelor's degree or more work experience. In other words, companies use credentials like advanced degrees as proxies for soft skills . . . Employers have increasingly come to rely on a Bachelor's degree as an employment screen, even if it may not be related to actual job duties. This "short-cut" to ensuring soft skills in employees very often comes back to haunt employers. By using overly restrictive screening procedures, employers effectively choke off viable talent from applying to their organization—and lengthen the hiring process.[31]

Despite being largely disconnected from actual job skills, higher education credentials have come to be a critical employment signal, in significant part because there is no alternative set of accepted actual skill credentials.

EROSION OF BIPARTISAN POLITICAL AND BUSINESS SUPPORT

The strong support higher education long enjoyed from both political parties now seems to be breaking down, particularly among conservatives.[32] This is a major problem because public higher education depends on solid government support for funding and student aid.[33]

Some of this concern about public support for higher education may be related to concerns in the business community. A 2018 study by the Association of American Colleges and Universities (AACU) found solid overall support for college education among business executives and hiring managers, but there were some significant gaps. Table 7.2 shows limited support in the business community for how well colleges do in two areas considered critical.

Some employers point to a growing "skills gap" against the backdrop of a generally tightening labor market, with a disconnect between education

TABLE 7.2

Do colleges train effectively in critical skills?

Critical skills	Business executives agree	Hiring managers agree
Applying knowledge and skills to real-world settings	33%	39%
Communication skills	40%	47%

Source: Association of American Colleges and Universities (AACU), "Liberal Education and the Future of Work: Selected Findings from Online Surveys of Business Executives and Hiring Managers," July 2018 (conducted by Hart Research), https://www.aacu.org/sites/default/files/files/LEAP/2018EmployerResearchReport.pdf.

received and the competencies required by an increasingly technical economy. The Manpower Group's annual talent shortage survey, which polls employers about difficulty filling jobs, reported in 2018 that 46 percent of US employers can't find the skills they need, and 21 percent say applicants lack required hard or soft skills.[34] A 2017 Business Roundtable report found that half its CEO members had "talent gaps [that] are already problematic or very problematic for their companies or industries," found shortages for workers with basic employability skills and for workers with specialized technical skills, and found that numerous jobs were going unfilled because applicants lacked adequate STEM skills.[35]

Shortages were especially problematic for emerging job areas requiring more specialized STEM skills such as in computing, cybersecurity, and data analytics. The report noted, "Many colleges and universities do not offer programs that integrate STEM skills with other disciplines that are needed in emerging occupations. Most postsecondary institutions teach traditional STEM courses such as chemistry, engineering, and math but are slow to recognize that STEM knowledge is needed for many new job categories outside of the traditional STEM fields."[36] Although some researchers counter the skills shortage argument,[37] it is clear industry believes there is a gap.

Some employers in the computer field, including Microsoft and Linux, have begun to develop their own online courses to fill the gap caused by the lack of courses in universities and colleges.[38] Colleges and universities turned out only 64,400 computer science graduates with bachelor's degrees in academic year 2015–2016, according to the National Center for Education Statistics.[39] Far fewer graduates are emerging from the pipeline than are needed according to industry projections.

Overall, however, the point remains that because the IT sector faces a particularly serious problem in finding workers with relevant skills, it has begun to respond by developing alternative approaches outside colleges and universities; other sectors have not. These IT firms are an exception; industry in general appears to have reduced its investment in workforce education in recent decades.

WHAT THIS ALL MEANS FOR UNIVERSITIES

Higher education is in a predicament. Clear trends show that upskilling and ever-higher credentials are required to succeed in the workforce. Achieving some higher education is now critical to finding a good job. Jobs for those with lesser skills are in decline. At least a two-year associate degree is now required, and the pressure, as the employment data shows, is increasingly toward the four-year degree as *critical*.

Universities never thought they'd have to face a workforce issue they always thought was only for high schools and community colleges. Their credentials—their degrees—have become the career differentiator and the de facto determinant of workforce success, but without being linked well to workforce realities. That increasingly frustrates students, employers, and the public.

The workforce education policy world has largely ignored the university. White House and federal workforce policies in the 2010s focused first on community colleges and then on new ideas for apprenticeship programs led by industry. But the workforce education tide is lapping at colleges' and universities' front doors. Public and business support, critical to maintaining these institutions, may depend on their response.

COLLEGE COMPLETION

If the workforce is upskilling, and the critical credential is increasingly a college degree, then colleges and universities need to raise their graduation rates. Peter McPherson, president of the Association of Public and Land Grant Universities (APLU), goes even further: the mantra for public universities must be "access, completion, and lifelong."[40] It's not enough to do better at reaching minority and underserved populations. Students need to graduate, and schools need to include more career and lifelong learning.

To track degree completion in our institutions, we need more than historic data covering an extended period; we need current student tracking data that can provide a fuller picture of what is happening now. The

TABLE 7.3
Postsecondary completion rates by type of institution[a]

Type of institution	Completion rate (within six years of entry, including at other institutions)	Percent of total students enrolled
Private nonprofit four-year	76%	20%
Public four-year	65%	45%
Community college (public)	39%	33%
Private for-profit four year[b]	37%	2%
Total, all higher education	58%	100%[c]

Source: Doug Shapiro, Afet Dundar, Faye Huie, Phoebe K. Wakhungu, Ayesha Bhimdiwala, and Sean E. Wilson, "Completing College: A National View of Student Completion Rates—Fall 2012 Cohort" (Signature Report No. 16). Herndon, VA: National Student Clearinghouse Research Center, December 2018, https://nscresearchcenter.org/signaturereport16/.
[a]For students entering in 2012, tracked through 2018.
[b]Private for-profits have a much higher proportion of shorter-term enrollment.
[c]Total of 2.3 million enrollees.

National Student Clearinghouse tracked students entering college in the 2012 academic year through 2018.[41] Four-year public and private nonprofit colleges and universities had the best completion rates within six years.[42] These rates have been inching up, but more progress is needed. At two-year public community colleges, the completion rate is far lower, which is much more problematic. For more than two million total enrolled students, the overall completion rate within six years for all these higher education institutions is below 60 percent. Table 7.3 sets out the completion data.

Completion rates for African Americans and Hispanics are even more problematic. For African Americans, the six-year completion rate at all of the four kinds of institutions listed in table 7.3 is only 41 percent. For Hispanics, it is 49.6 percent. Although these numbers have been improving, a major completion gap remains between white and Asian students on one hand and African American and Hispanic students on the other.[43]

In *Making College Work*, Harry Holzer and Sandy Baum highlight problems disadvantaged US college students have completing college credentials and from earning degrees or certificates with little value in labor markets.[44] For those with family incomes below $32,000, only 26 percent that enroll earn a bachelor's degree and 9 percent an associate degree.[45] They cite several causes: weak academic preparation; financial pressure, including having to work to support families; and a lack of information and "social capital" both before and after enrolling. Low-income students also tend to attend underfunded schools that provide limited student support, and they accumulate heavy debt loads. The authors find that students need more than money: they need guidance systems for selecting majors and institutions, reform in remedial programs, and financial and systems for academic and career counseling.[46] They also found that a number of relatively simple and inexpensive interventions can improve success rates. For example, a personalized text-messaging campaign reminding high school graduates of tasks to be completed in the summer after acceptance resulted in higher numbers of disadvantaged students actually enrolling, and confidence-building readings about how peers adjusted to college significantly raised African American students' course grade levels.[47] Because colleges have long recognized their role in enabling social mobility,[48] a key obligation of higher education institutions then is to get the completion numbers up for minorities and the disadvantaged. Obviously, this is related to the workforce education problem, which is also a top priority.

THE APLU'S "READY FOR JOBS" REPORT

The Association of Public and Land Grant Universities is one higher education group that has begun to see the workforce education dilemma more clearly. Its public college and university members are critical because they award more 60 percent of all bachelor's degrees in the United States.[49] In its 2017 report, "Ready for Jobs, Careers, and a Lifetime,"[50] the APLU noted that a college degree matters more now than ever: in the postrecession economy, good jobs increasingly depend on that degree. And it acknowledged that employers and the public increasingly feel universities are not doing enough to prepare students for employment.[51] While universities generally contend that a degree must involve a broad, foundational education, it found that public universities, with their long land grant heritage of practical education ideas, are especially well positioned to prepare students for employment. The report made an important argument: that broader education goals and employment preparation are not mutually exclusive goals. In effect, it says this is not either/or, that universities can walk and chew gum at the same time.

The report echoes a number of the findings set out earlier. Building on researcher estimates, it found that, from 2010 levels, by 2020 the United States will add fifty-five million new job openings: twenty-four million new jobs and thirty-one million openings created by baby boomer retirements—65 percent of which will require education and training beyond high school, based on long-standing upskilling trends.[52] Many millions of those new jobs will require college degrees. Citing BLS data, the report also noted that the 2017 unemployment rate for college graduates—2.5 percent—was half that of individuals with just a high school credential and one-third the rate for those without a high school diploma.[53] This number is similar to the "frictional" unemployment rate—that is, the normal rate of unemployment due to job transitions (approximately 2 to 2.5 percent)—suggesting that the unemployment rate for college graduates as of 2017 cannot go lower.

The report acknowledged that policymakers and the public are increasingly skeptical about the value of a degree in terms of preparation of graduates for jobs and careers, and that "some employers point to a widening skills gap, a disconnect between the degrees graduates earned, the competencies they developed, and the knowledge, skills, and abilities demanded by the innovation economy for a 21st century workforce."[54] While noting the debate over skills shortages, the APLU found an "engagement gap." To close it, much better coordination between labor market actors, including community colleges, research universities, employers, trade associations, government agencies, and workforce development and training organizations, has become critical.[55] Disconnects, then, between the actors in the labor market, including universities, exacerbated the ability of students to find solid career paths and of employers to find the talent they need.

One example concerns internships: many college students seek them out on their own or are encouraged through employer on-campus recruiting, and they can help smooth the school-to-work transition. Internships should be matched to academic preparation and student career interests, set student learning goals and assesses progress, provide support to students and employers during the internship, provide employers value, reach low-income students, and be paid.[56] Without these characteristics, internships fail to achieve their potential value. But relatively few college programs are organized to match these recognized criteria for optimal internship opportunities.

The APLU report found that underemployment data and the number of unfilled positions in a number of sectors suggest there is more coordination work to be done. A 2016 Pew Charitable Trust report found that job categories with the highest growth are more likely to require a higher level of social, analytical, and technical skills,[57] which may necessitate greater connectivity—including by universities. This is complicated by postcollege job mobility patterns among millennials, who are likely to change jobs an average of four times in their first decade after college—nearly double the rate of the previous generation. Data also show they will face increasing career-long mobility, with job changes and even shifts to very different job sectors over the working years. While information on the "gig economy" of contracted work and freelance jobs indicates it is still of modest dimensions, this is an additional sign of employment churn. The report found that these workforce and economy changes require institutions consider not only how to prepare students for entry into initial jobs but how to prepare them longer term.

A 2018 survey of college graduates found less than one-quarter received frequent career advice from a career services office, and almost half said career advice from faculty or staff was more helpful.[58] Clearly, career offices need more emphasis, and colleges should consider giving faculty and involved staff more background in career-related training. The APLU study found that while existing university career services and advising generally aim at the first job within a single career field, the realities of multiple jobs and career changes compel higher education to broaden this approach. Career advising is also designed largely for traditional students entering college from high school at age eighteen without significant job experience. The reality is that today's universities serve broader populations, including adults returning to college for courses, certificates, or degrees, and veterans often already managing a career.

Future student bodies of universities will also be affected by significant demographic changes. The number of students from traditionally underserved groups (minorities, first generation, low income, adult learners, etc.) will grow, which will also require changes. Career services along with educational offerings and course delivery will have to respond to these shifts in student populations and needs. The public now expects better career preparation.[59] For universities, "Academic excellence is not enough. The public expects more; you must demonstrate real-world impact, both personal and societal, to change your reputation."[60]

In summary, the APLU report found that universities need to do a better job enabling the pathway from degree to job to career, not only in the short term but for life, and a better job supporting not only traditional students but the rising number of adult learners, altering career services and curriculum to accommodate these shifts. The report acknowledged university reluctance to incorporate new aims of job and longer-term career preparation in addition to traditional goals of foundational knowledge and preparing educated citizens. Although there was tension between the two, it found that these aims were not mutually exclusive. Liberal arts and foundations will remain important to the society, and businesses value the skills that can be acquired through these studies—close analysis, thought organization, advocacy, written and oral communication.[61] Universities can offer credentials that clarify foundational capabilities *and* more career-oriented skills that matter for individuals and that connect to both personal economic and societal needs.

WHY IS WORK CHANGING? WHY IS MORE EDUCATION INPUT REQUIRED?

If there is a growing role for the university in developing and supporting the workforce education system, what will that role look like? If the rising tide of demand for workforce education has now reached the doors of colleges and universities, and high school and even community college education is not enough, what do colleges and universities have to confront? If universities and colleges are now moving into the pole position for workforce education, what does that new racetrack look like? Let's look initially at some manufacturing examples, since the manufacturing sector has always led other sectors in adopting productivity gains and thus we are most likely to see the oncoming changes in education demands there.

Since the advent of the industrial revolution, the organizing system for manufacturing has been ever-greater economies of scale. But there is now a change brewing in a number of industries. The old regime was a high volume and low mix of varieties of goods. The new regime is beginning to be more high mix and low volume, with much shorter production cycles. This shift to the manufacturing of more customized goods to meet more personalized consumer needs is only starting to come over the horizon.

ABB Robotics, a leading producer of robotic arms, argues that this will mean the workforce in new factories will need to work much more frequently with robots in intermittent ways that are not scheduled and less predictable.[62] The era of massive, multiton industrial robots that perform one task and are kept in cages to protect workers from harm will change, and more personalized robots—"cobots" voice-commanded by workers to take on new varieties of tasks—will be needed. ABB Robotics argues that low-volume, high-mix production will require more costly engineering time and factory floor disruptions as workers shift their robots and computer-controlled equipment to new production lines. Shorter product cycles will increase the cost of downtime, particularly unanticipated downtime to solve problems. Rather than a production line that can run for days without alterations, a production line that runs for hours or less will put pressure on the ability to shift to a new line effectively and efficiently. This means a growing need for workers with new, flexible sets of skills and a drop in the need for less skilled assembly workers performing repetitive tasks. We are already seeing this in the employment data cited in chapter 2.

This change will place a premium on new kinds of workforce education. Colleges and universities will not be the only entities affected, of course. Community colleges and employers will be tasked with educating new kinds of technicians and providing them with many of the needed technical skills. But the overall operation, design, and implementation of such systems, including a move to more customization, will affect technical education at the college level as well, including in supporting services positions.

A 2018 Brookings study puts this snapshot of what may happen on the factory floor into a broader skills context.[63] The story is a compelling one of occupational change, directly relevant to higher education's role. The study identified 545 occupations, accounting for 91 percent of the US labor force and created two broad categories of digitization data: (1) knowledge of computers and electronics and (2) interactions with computers. It ranked occupations by how digitized the occupation had become and applied a score for each—ranging from 94 percent for software developers and 55 percent for construction supervisors to 17 percent for construction laborers and 14 percent for personal care aides. What does the digital skill occupation landscape overall look like? Table 7.4 shows ranges of digital fluency required in different occupations.

Overall, the share of jobs requiring high and medium digital skills has grown sharply. Between 2000 and 2016, employment requiring high digital skills went up from 5 percent to 23 percent, employment requiring medium skills went up from 40 percent to 48 percent, and employment requiring low skills went down from 56 percent to 30 percent. Yet one in six working-age Americans are unable to use email, web search, or other basic online tools. Digital skill requirements vary widely by industry. Table 7.5 shows estimated scores for jobs requiring high or medium skills in several industry sectors.

Digital job content, of course, tends to drive productivity growth. Because manufacturing tends to lead productivity growth over other sectors, these skill trends tend to be more pronounced in that sector. Digital technologies and the business models that accompany them are increasingly entering into manufacturing firms. These technologies include virtual design, Internet of Things (IoT), enterprise resource planning (ERP) and business process software, manufacturing as a service (the shared use of

TABLE 7.4
Digital fluency required in a range of occupations

Occupation	Required digital fluency score
Software developer Financial manager Computer system analyst Market research analyst	*High:* greater than 60%
Lawyer Registered nurse Automotive services Technician Mechanic Office clerk	*Medium:* 33% to 60%
Security guard Restaurant cook Construction laborer Personal care aide	*Low:* less than 33%

Source: Mark Muro, Sifan Liu, Jacob Whiton, and Siddarth Kulkami, "Digitalization and the American Workforce," Brookings Institution, November 15, 2017, https://www.brookings.edu/wp-content/uploads/2017/11/mpp_2017nov15_digitalization_full_report.pdf.

TABLE 7.5
Range of digital skills in different job sectors

Skill requirements by industry	Percentage of high digital skills	Percentage of medium digital skills
Information and communication technology	70%	25%
Advanced manufacturing	35%	50%
Education services	30%	55%
Transportation and warehousing	15%	25%
Nursing and residential care	5%	35%

Source: Mark Muro, Sifan Liu, Jacob Whiton, and Siddarth Kulkami, "Digitalization and the American Workforce," Brookings Institution, November 15, 2017, https://www.brookings.edu/wp-content/uploads/2017/11/mpp_2017nov15_digitalization_full_report.pdf.

networked manufacturing infrastructure), and big data and analytics. An increasing strategy of newer manufacturing firms is to transform business operations with productivity advances to create new value.

Brookings paid particular attention to *advanced manufacturing*, defining this as the portion of the sector that has higher R&D spending and higher rates of employing STEM-educated workers. It found digitalization was a defining trend in this sector (about half of the overall manufacturing sector). The sector went from 15 percent high digital skill employment in 2002 to 34 percent in 2016. Advanced manufacturing occupations are changing: Tech-oriented occupations are increasing their share of manufacturing employment, with a corresponding loss of routine jobs. Entry requirements for middle-class careers in advanced manufacturing are systematically upskilling in terms of required digital content. Manufacturing is a bellwether for what will be evolving in other sectors.

Firms will require additional skills that complement digital skills. Deloitte, the Council on Competitiveness, and Singularity University released a report in 2018 listing technologies that a group of business leaders believed could enable transformational growth in production: 3-D printing (additive manufacturing); advanced analytics; advanced materials; advanced robotics; AI and machine learning; biofabrication and biomanufacturing; blockchain; cybersecurity; digital design, simulation, and modeling; integration of energy storage; high-performance computing; Interface of Things (AR/VR/mixed reality, wearables, gesture recognition); and IoT.[64] Innovative firms will increasingly require operational skills in these fields, and many are nondigital. In another growing area, Paul Lewis notes that biotechnology firms will increasingly automate the production of cell therapies, which require operation of complex bioreactors rather than manual methods for production.[65] When these techniques are developed for such emerging areas as regenerative medicine, the education required for new technicians will be quite sophisticated. Again, these will require changes to fields that higher education has dominated.

This rise in digital content skills and a wide range of other skills in a host of increasingly complex areas sends a message to higher education. Territories that colleges thought were the domain of modest numbers of professionals or of technicians will increasingly be the working domain of many industrial and employment sectors. Since higher education plays an important role in providing education for many of these kinds of higher-end skills—particularly where design, systems, and implementation are involved—it is going to need to find a way to scale its education offerings in these sorts of areas.

UNIVERSITY ROLES IN WORKFORCE EDUCATION

As we build a new workforce education system in which colleges and universities need to play a larger role, one size of education will not fit all. There are numerous roles and tasks: some will fit best with universities, some with four-year colleges, some with community colleges, some with industry, and some with individuals. Most will require a mix of these actors.

For example, *development of education content for higher-end technical and engineering skills* will likely best fit universities, whereas technician-level content development will likely continue to be the role of community colleges. The actual delivery of technician content will similarly fall more to community colleges, while teaching higher-end technical skills will be a four-year college or university role. However, colleges and universities can play an organizing and supporting role with industry and community colleges, which could help with technician-level content and delivery. And in new technology areas, such as advanced manufacturing or machine learning, the lines between technician and engineering content overlap, so university-developed content may be particularly needed. All these institutions will increasingly be offering certificates to supplement their degree programs and scale up to meet growing needs, in part through online materials.

Colleges and universities are already deeply involved in *developing online offerings*. Leading platforms include Coursera, which as of 2020 offered some 4,500 courses from more than 200 educational institutions, and edX, with 3,000 courses from more than 145 institutions. Enrollment in massive open online courses (MOOCs) grew 910 percent between 2011 and 2018, with more than one hundred million students enrolled worldwide and nine hundred universities offering courses among the four major offering platforms (Coursera, edX, Udacity and Udemy).[66] These totals are still growing.

Online education has received a massive boost during the coronavirus pandemic. The internet, originally built as an emergency communications system, has enabled colleges and universities, forced to close their classrooms suddenly, to continue their education tasks online. Without it, as well as the accompanying videoconferencing platforms, learning management systems, and experience with MOOCs, higher education would have been in the same state of collapse as hotels and restaurants when the pandemic erupted, with students dismissed and faculty laid off. While not necessarily optimally used (as discussed in chapter 8), online education technology kept schools "open." While many colleges and universities had been reluctant adopters of online education, the pandemic-induced switch to online learning created a new learning world from which there is probably no turning back. This means, too, that its utility as a workforce education option can be accelerated.

Online systems may require a university lead, but will also need to be tied to community colleges and industry for workforce education. Organizing a delivery framework across institutions and skill areas could be a university role. In the National Science Foundation's Advanced Technological Education program, for example, program funds go predominantly to community colleges, but universities often assist with coordination, curriculum, and online offerings. Community colleges that offer online courses generally lack resources to develop them or ensure they optimize learning science in their delivery.

With ongoing technical change in the workplace, *lifelong learning* will increasingly be required; organizing this into a system could also be largely a university task, as discussed ahead. Researching and testing optimal teaching models and applying lessons from *learning science*, particularly as online education grows and creates blended learning opportunities, could also be a university task.

Figure 7.1 shows where universities could play a constructive role and areas that will be more outside their capacities. The chart is simply illustrative; the lines on the chart don't indicate, for example, the percent of a task universities should dominate, but where a university could generally play a greater or lesser lead role.

What might these university roles actually look like? We use two case studies to flesh out some details.

Clemson's Center for Workforce Development

The mission of Clemson University's Center for Workforce Development is to be "a new national model that engages universities, two-year colleges, K-12 institutions, statewide industry and federal agencies to deliver workforce education tools that have the power to transform the economy of our state and region."[67] It works particularly to connect Clemson with the two-year technical colleges in the area.

The center began by developing a visual inspection training system using virtual reality for aircraft cargo bays for the aviation industry. VR has since been the center's core focus, and it has produced seventy-two VR modules overall, with twenty used in courses, following up with published research studies. Typically, the modules are incorporated into curriculum codeveloped with instructors from South Carolina's system of technical colleges, which also use the simulations in their existing courses. In 2009, the

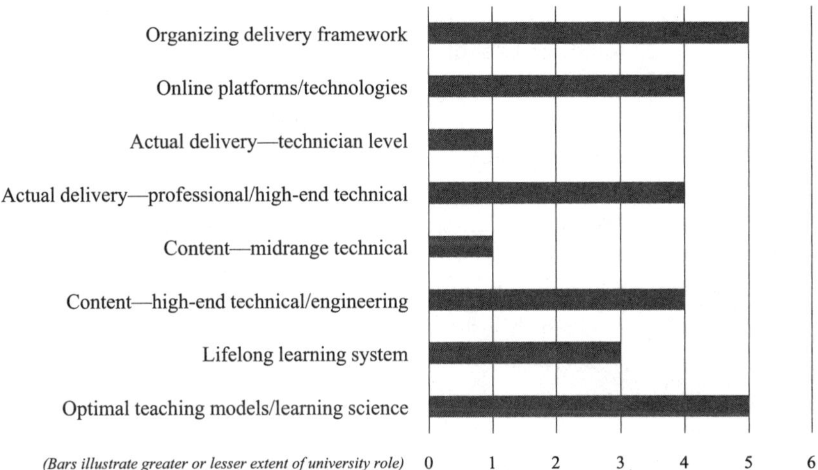

FIGURE 7.1
Potential university workforce education role.

center became an NSF Advanced Technological Education regional center for automotive and aviation education, developing VR and AR material for technical and community colleges.

As part of its ATE efforts, the center has been developing VR/AR training modules that can support certifications for manufacturing skills developed by the Manufacturing Skill Standards Council, introduced in chapter 1. Technical and community colleges nationwide can insert these simulations in their own manufacturing skills courses. By developing VR/AR modules tied to MSSC skills, the center is performing a potentially major service for manufacturing, for students, and for technical and community colleges. It is an important step, and the kind of step that probably only a university could tackle.

The center has developed an online portal to disseminate its simulations and modules; technical colleges can easily access them through the portal and readily insert them into their own learning management systems for their own courses.[68] Thus, materials the center develops can be used by technical and community college instructors, who can scaffold the VR and AR content with their face-to-face instruction and lectures, their own online courses, and their own learning management systems. Some six thousand technical college students are now using the center's modules through the ATE program.

The center is also working on career pathways, providing certificates of completion when students complete its modules. Previously, it worked with an area Chamber of Commerce on certifications for MSSC skills for high schools and for technical colleges. The students earned certificates of completion to increase employer awareness that students had gone beyond just earning a high school diploma. It also partners with South Carolina's Department of Employment and Workforce to offer a course on soft skills, with online lectures, assessments, and a completion certificate. This soft skills element is a subset of the MSSC curriculum on workforce fundamentals for manufacturing employees.

The center is engaged in research, advocacy, and networking on many levels. For example, it partners with K–12 schools on STEM summer camps for students and with high schools to educate students and parents about modern clean and technical manufacturing.

The center has also been part of the Advanced Robotics for Manufacturing (ARM) Institute, which is funded by the Department of Defense and one of the fourteen federally cost-shared advanced manufacturing institutes. Working with another manufacturing institute for integrated photonics, it is now developing advanced manufacturing courses and modules for technician training in robotics and photonics.

Clemson's Center for Workforce Development provides an interesting and significant model for how a research university can become deeply engaged in workforce education across technical and community colleges, secondary schools, and K–12 schools, using support from NSF's ATE program and state government.

Clemson also provides us with a second example of an engaged university in its new undergraduate manufacturing program, which is also linked to another South Carolina institution of higher education.

Clemson University's Undergraduate Manufacturing Engineering Program and Greenville Tech's Center for Manufacturing Innovation

Greenville Technical College sits in the center of a historic manufacturing area. Long a center for textiles, that sector left for Asia more than fifteen years ago. But unlike so many manufacturing centers, Greenville has been able to replace what it lost, including with major automakers and suppliers, from BMW to Bosch and Michelin. It is now a thriving manufacturing region, served by a major research university, Clemson (a forty-minute drive from Greenville), and by two-year technical colleges with solid apprenticeship programs. In 2016, Greenville Tech built its 100,000 sq. ft. Center for Manufacturing Innovation (CMI)[69] as its home for manufacturing skills education, using strong area industry funding along with state support. The facility is packed with the latest factory equipment, from CNC to robotics to 3-D printers, as well as classrooms, a business incubator, and research labs.

Some six hundred Greenville Tech students study manufacturing skills in a two-year academic program to earn associate degrees, including 380 in mechatronics, 120 in welding, and 120 in machining. Of these, some 250 take their courses at CMI, with most in US Labor Department–registered apprenticeships or very similar "technical scholar" programs, both involving part-time work with area manufacturers. The school also offers specialized programs, such as a fifteen-week CNC operator certificate and basic manufacturing skill certificate programs. There is a "bridge" program for students in area vocational education/CTE career centers.[70]

Greenville Tech leases 10,000 sq. ft. of CMI to Clemson for a carbon fiber facility with a thirty-ton machine for auto and aerospace industry training and research, as well as research on vehicle assembly and digital and robotics production.[71] Researchers there include grad students and undergrads, interacting with Greenville Tech students—so Clemson and Greenville Tech are now sharing CMI facilities. Beyond that, as part of its efforts, Clemson is using state funding for a new program in which undergraduates entering their senior year in mechanical engineering (one of Clemson's biggest majors) can take on an intense two-year program in manufacturing and emerge with a bachelor's degree in mechanical engineering and a master's in manufacturing. This new undergraduate manufacturing program, which began in fall 2019, also systematically connects with students in the two-year Greenville Technical College's CMI.

The new Clemson undergraduate manufacturing program aims to use CMI and its remarkable facilities to integrate Greenville Tech's CMI with the Clemson program. Clemson has built a Greenville campus on a Clemson-owned research park just outside the city, next to where CMI is located. This is Clemson's International Center for Automotive Research (ICAR), a graduate applied manufacturing education and research program, with more than seven hundred faculty, graduate students, researchers, and research technicians on site.[72] ICAR and Greenville Tech's manufacturing center are sharing programs with each other, led by Clemson's new 2019 undergraduate program.[73] Across the street is BMW's North American IT research department, with three hundred technical employees. Collaborative work with industry prevails in all these facilities. They constitute a very unusual cluster of manufacturing research, education, and technology.

The undergraduate program is centered around project-based learning, with a focus on assembly—which Professor Joshua Summers, who developed the undergraduate program, says "is 80 percent of the manufacturing cost but only a tiny part of the research investment."[74] Clemson's new manufacturing cluster[75] also has projects around composites, metals, cellular metamaterials, and polymer manufacturing, along with robotics and applied computer programs. The program is also planning "white goods" assembly work with Samsung's new 2018 appliances plant nearby, so the research will not only center on automotive manufacturing.

The undergrad program, as noted, will bring senior-year undergrads off the more traditional Clemson campus to Greenville with its ICAR and CMI facilities for a two-year program. It will have much more organizational flexibility than the on-campus program. For example, program designers are considering having BMW engineering experts come to ICAR to do a one-week class for a portion of a course credit. There will be short, application-oriented courses with direct contact with industry. Each of the four semesters in the program will have separate capstone R&D projects, applied and hands-on, which will make it more experience oriented. There will also be more use of just-in-time online materials inserted into courses—for example, using the federal Manufacturing Extension Partnership's new course modules for training in robotics. Summers also says, "Engineers don't know how to teach collaboration—they think it's just doing something with a group. So there's a real gap here where collaborative processes could be taught." He believes this is one of the only practical manufacturing programs like this evolving in US engineering schools.

The new Clemson program also aims to integrate new education technologies into production education. VR and AR have a role in the program, but it is evolving. Summers notes that "seeing is not doing or, more importantly, understanding what's behind doing." AR will work well for installation or inspection work, but more complex problems, he finds, will also need to be tied to gaming in virtual environments. VR/AR should be used if there is a spatial aspect, but if a manufacturing process in involved, more is needed. He asks, "How can you teach a mechanical engineer about injection molding? You need to teach flow rate, and what forces are generating flow. The actual process is not only visual. So, VR/AR is an important new tool—but has limits."

Integrating the Greenville Tech and Clemson students will be crucial. The former will need to develop confidence as they work with engineers and are asked to provide feedback on the processes they undertake in the context of the designs given them by the engineering students. And engineering students are divorced from the production process and the production line and need to connect. Summers argues, "They do design, but they don't learn how to do design for production. It's not in their curriculum. Teaming the two sides builds confidence in both. They need each other."

The new manufacturing undergraduate program is trying a different approach. In step one, Greenville Tech students try to build a Clemson student engineering design. These apprentices, who know their production equipment, won't be able to make it efficiently because it will not be adequately designed for production. Next is an exchange between the two sides and a learning experience for both. In the third step, the Greenville Tech apprentices will team with the Clemson engineering students to work out better design and production solutions together, collaboratively educating each other. Summers says, "This process will help make engineers humble; they need to be able to work with workforce—it is key to engineering success yet it is not now taught." In summary, this joint program is for collaborations, exposing apprentices to design and engineers to production.

The joint program is trying to mend a historic problem with American engineering education. Beginning in the nineteenth century, engineers focused on design and have been largely separated from the workforce on the factory floor ever since. Japan launched its quality manufacturing revolution in the 1970s through deep integration between engineers and the factory workforce—a lesson the United States is still learning. Clemson's new program is requiring this integration beginning with undergraduate education.

The initial size of the program, as the faculty team shapes its content and direction, is twelve undergraduates—with the plan to grow to around fifty seniors from multiple engineering majors. The program has classroom and research space for the program, across the street from CMI and ICAR, with team-oriented cubicle clusters. The faculty is aiming for a company-like working environment and an emphasis on project learning, such as applying data analytics for Internet of Things implementation, learning object-oriented programming to lay out a whole work system, and project cost estimation using engineering economics.

The Greenville Tech apprentices participate in each semester-long project with the undergraduates as part of the team, and the new program will offer joint workshops on communication, interviewing, and other job skills. The Greenville Tech students have time at and are able to use Clemson's career center fully to learn about job and career opportunities. And

Greenville Tech students can be integrated into seminars and field trips at companies aligned with project content. The joint experiences help socialize the two groups. As Summers notes, "There is a deep 'classism' challenge in manufacturing that needs to be overcome to take on new technology challenges."

The ultimate goal is to create a manufacturing program built into undergraduate engineering education overall. "American engineers are not now strong in production; they tend to disregard it," Summers argues. "American manufacturing needs pride and professionalism—to see it as craftsmanship, and to develop the psychology of the maker. The introduction of new advanced technologies will only increase the need for human capabilities."

Summers believes his own field of engineering design has to be tied to manufacturing processes. "An engineer either develops an idea or makes an idea. We need design *and* manufacturing. Many engineering programs have no manufacturing class—they have shifted manufacturing and therefore design to the fringe." He argues, "Engineering in the United States has been trying to be more a science, but that is not the only answer. It is a failure to confront manufacturing that stratifies our society today."

The new Clemson program aims to rebuild the design-production bridge, with a university linking with a two-year technical college. It could be a useful prototype for a new kind of workforce education, true to engineering discipline but much more connected to the production workplace and production design at the undergraduate level, linking the line workforce and the engineering workforce in common endeavor. It is an example of what a university can do at the workforce level.

CONNECTING THE COLLEGE-LEVEL EDUCATION TO THE WORKFORCE

We have seen how a high school education in the twenty-first century no longer ensures a good workforce career. College is increasingly important to career success, but not enough. How can colleges be better connected, while maintaining what makes a four-year college education special?

Colleges and universities, along with the state and federal governments that support them, need to develop systems to help students, families, and employers unpack credentials and access job markets. A Georgetown Center on Education and the Workforce study[76] advocates integrating education and workforce data to help students navigate complex college and career paths. This would also benefit employers by helping them better identify talented workers. Without better information on results, colleges and universities cannot effectively restructure programs to improve student outcomes, and policymakers cannot adequately allocate resources to improve their regional talent bases and economies. The report called for colleges and universities to develop an information exchange system that will better connect postsecondary education to learning and earning on the job. Similar points were made in chapter 6 on the information system challenge but deserve brief reiteration here. Colleges and universities need to do the following:

- *Develop better data* on education, skill supply, and demand projections, on business expansion, and on overall workforce quality and needs.
- Align education programs to *match identified labor market demands*, following from these data. That doesn't mean scrapping the classics, as discussed earlier, but opening education options for students based on fields with career opportunities.
- Significantly improve *counseling about career pathways*, taking a more sophisticated approach than holding job fairs to serve out-of-town employers and instead supporting students in their education and career decisions and helping to identify those who need additional assistance.

To summarize, the report argued that colleges need *a better information system showing common, measurable outcomes that will help students find and meet workplace demands.*

These issues of information and counseling need improvement not only at the college and university level; these institutions are part of a larger system. The Pathways to Prosperity Project backed by Harvard's Graduate School of Education and Jobs for the Future found that if high school career-focused pathways were more securely linked to community colleges, more students would be likely to stay the course to associate degrees.[77] There is also a need to *provide high school students and college students with far better career guidance.* Many adults over the age of twenty-five have discovered that community colleges offer programs leading to well-paying jobs in healthcare, technology, and other fields, but recent high school graduates are often poorly represented in such programs due in part to lack of information. These counseling and information systems, in turn, need to be better linked to companion systems at the college level.

The Association for Public and Land Grant Colleges has reached complementary conclusions about specific steps its colleges and university members need to undertake.[78] Rather than focusing career services at the end of a student's college experience, it proposed *career services embedded within a student's entire undergraduate pathway.* Because faculty are students' closest advisors, there should be better linkages between career services and faculty. The association called for *improved use of data by career services* to better connect student interests with career and skills development opportunities. And it found that faculty and other student advisors need to understand "career pathways" approaches and alternative credentialing so they can help *match students with career opportunities*.

Students also need more help in the transition process to careers. APLU embraced students' *participation in work-and-learn opportunities*, including internships, externships, co-ops, problem-based learning, and capstone projects situated in business and community contexts. It supported *flexible delivery mechanisms*—including courses in the evenings, on weekends, online, in hybrid formats, and in shorter terms for nontraditional students. It advocated development of alternative credentialing programs in needed job skill areas—such as certificates, badges, and competency-based programs, including those that incorporate assessments for prior learning. Finally, it supported *adaptive learning approaches—allowing students to learn on custom pathways tailored to their abilities and needed competencies*.

HIGHER EDUCATION AND LIFELONG LEARNING

There is one more piece of the higher education puzzle worth noting here: *lifelong learning*. The continuing pace of technological change demands better and ongoing ties between education and employment. In the United States, the connection between education and economic well-being has been simple: pile up as much formal education as you can early on, then cash in on the rewards for the rest of your life. As reported in "Special Report on Lifelong Learning" in the *Economist*, research suggests that each additional year of schooling leads to an 8 to 13 percent rise in hourly earnings.[79] Since the Great Recession, the cost of not completing some higher education has been made even clearer: the unemployment rate keeps dropping as you go higher up the educational ladder.

The *Economist* report did note that the relationship between degrees and income is no longer on autopilot.[80] And shifting job content suggests that a college degree acquired in the beginning of a career cannot answer the need for the continuous acquisition of new skills over the course of a career. Thus, *lifelong learning is going to require better connections and handoffs among the actors in the higher education system* because each will be a playing role. Traditionally, most colleges and universities behave like independent and disconnected actors from community colleges. However, many states are moving to better connect them. More than thirty states have required some level of transferability between their community colleges and state universities.[81] This is not easy, but a number appear to be making it work. Overall, lifelong learning will require a more uniform system. The different institutional actors, including employers, need to understand and then to complement each other's roles if lifelong learning is to work efficiently.

Universities will need more *varied delivery mechanisms*, including courses during evenings, on weekends, online, in *hybrid formats*, and of varying lengths to meet the needs of nontraditional students. These will be critical for lifelong learning. A great deal of attention will be required on developing *alternative credentialing programs*, including certificates, badges, and competency-based programs. *Adaptive learning* approaches will also be needed, including assessments for prior learning and allowing students to learn on their own pathways that meet their career needs while satisfying needed competencies.

Online education offers a unique opportunity space for lifelong learning and is a particularly important lifelong learning role for colleges and universities. It is a highly flexible new toolset, so students can study at the levels and on the timelines they choose, pacing themselves to accommodate outside pressures of work or family and to meet their own individualized learning speeds. This can also get students outside the box of needing prior credentials and grade levels.

Finally, lifelong learning offers a *major new economic opportunity for colleges and universities* if they seize it. The demographics of higher education are changing: there will be significantly fewer students of traditional college age, which means a declining tuition base.[82] If they stay the same, many schools will simply have to close, and we can already see these trends evolving. Of course, the effects will not be uniform on all schools: elite schools will face growing demand, and some growing metropolitan areas in states with declining student bases will buck the trend. But overall, enrollment throughout the system will decline unless something changes, and lifelong learning, which is increasingly required by the economy, could be that opportunity.

This series of steps colleges and universities must take to enable lifelong education parallels, as set out previously, much of what they must do for workforce education in general. Overall, what this chapter has shown is that higher education faces a big societal challenge—and a big societal opportunity.

8 THE NEW EDUCATIONAL TECHNOLOGIES

An increasingly agile workforce deserves an equally agile system for learning. This is placing new demands on our existing systems for workforce training and education in general. Online education, which has been accelerated by the coronavirus pandemic, is already assuming a growing role in workforce education, although this new role has not been adequately evaluated. While its growth makes it a moving target, we still need to see it in the context of overall education. And education is a complex field; for purposes of this discussion, we focus on three aspects: content, the pedagogical approach, and the modality by which that content is delivered—each of which has undergone changes due to advances in technology generally. This has spurred interest in new *educational technology*, also called *edtech*.

These three aspects are strongly linked in many ways. Different content requires different pedagogies and, often, different delivery modalities: for example, teaching machine learning involves algorithms and data, whereas teaching a nurse how to use a new ultrasound machine requires equipment and hands-on learning. Yet good pedagogical practice—applying what we know about how people learn and how to be effective in education—has often taken a back seat in the development of our education systems, in the United States and worldwide. In light of workforce education needs and new technologies we need for learning, a significant redesign of existing education systems is required. We posit that the optimal system would be more agile and therefore more in tune with today's labor market than the systems in place today.

So, with this view of its importance, we begin our exploration of edtech with a discussion of pedagogy.

BETTER PEDAGOGICAL PRACTICES

Insights about how the human brain gathers and stores information and develops facility with new material have been accumulating for more than a hundred years, beginning with the seminal work of Hermann Ebbinghaus.[1] Unfortunately, our systems were well in place by that time, and the runaway train could not be rerouted. Since then, we have learned a great deal more, and the subject has been widely studied.[2] For example, it appears we are more likely to learn when we are curious, because curiosity triggers a dopaminergic circuit. As Socrates presciently said, "Wonder is the beginning of wisdom."[3]

So material that inspires a student to become curious about a topic is well worth the effort. Unfortunately, this is hard to achieve in a standard classroom setting without exceptional educators—the ones many of us remember from our own experiences. But while they may have a great grasp of the material, not every teacher can be inspiring. Yet our one-size-fits-all model limits our efficacy at a time of great need for a revolution in learning. This is where technology can play, and is playing, a part.

Bite-Sized Chunks

We can learn in about ten-minute chunks. This appears to be related to the way we form short-term memories in the brain. Exceed that time and we seem to enter a mind-wandering state. Therefore, lectures need to be extremely short to be effective—a lesson parents probably recognize instantly about their children, although the insight applies equally to adults. Courses, then, should use ten minutes of a lecture, switch to another learning mode (e.g., an interactive group discussion, a demonstration, or an assessment), then return to a ten-minute lecture segment, and so on.

Impact of Educational Technology on the Lecture

Distance education has been around for many decades, delivered by correspondence, radio, or cassette. But it should not be confused with modern online education. *Online, on-demand video* has unquestionably had a massive impact on learning. Content creators such as Khan Academy, MinutePhysics, and MIT OpenCourseWare have millions of subscribers on platforms such as YouTube. Content creators and learners have naturally gravitated toward shorter videos. The ability to pause, rewind, and speed up video has made for very adaptable and vibrant content. Transcripts can be generated to make videos accessible and give viewers search options. YouTube is probably the most important edtech platform out there.

In the 2010s, Massive Open Online Courses became widespread and have since become a major force in education. They combine the short video format with computer grading (discussed ahead) and forums in which students can help each other and get help from teaching assistants. As of this writing, the three largest MOOC platforms—Coursera, edX, and Udacity—collectively count more than one hundred fifty million enrollees.[4]

Another edtech platform, *automatic lecture capture*, allows for tracking and recording traditional lectures, generating videos with very little operator effort that can then be made available for asynchronous viewing with the full pause or rewind capabilities of the videos described earlier.

These online, on-demand technologies hold great promise for education and for workforce education in particular. Unlike a classroom, they can operate at great scale and offer new education opportunities for workforce education, which is inherently more about learning by doing. Online learning, with its capability for repetitive and visual engagement, can fit this style better than a classroom.

Desirable Difficulties

Students often reread material, thinking it helps them learn. But that is illusory. A surprisingly consistent result from learning research is learners' overconfidence about their own learning and the importance of a realistic sense of one's personal competence.[5] A series of findings shows that *effortful* approaches—those in which the learner struggles with the material a bit—lead to better, more durable learning. What have been called *desirable difficulties* lead to better learning by increasing processing of the material rather than being distracting.[6]

First, when a learner is tested frequently about the material she has just been taught, learning is better.[7] Using this *testing effect* as a learning technique is referred to as *retrieval practice*—which is affected positively by effortful retrieval. So, for example, a learner given weaker cues for a test and who therefore struggles more will learn better than one given stronger cues.

Second, *testing should be spaced*.[8] This *spaced practice* concept, related to the findings of Hermann Ebbinghaus, flies in the face of *mass practice*—an expedient, prevalent approach in education today in which students might address a number of problems at the end of a chapter in a short span of time (rather than spacing them out over days, weeks, and months). Spaced practice also applies to sports and motor learning. Ironically, learners feel they have learned better with blocked practice (rehearsing a skill over and over), although they may have learned less effectively—recalling the theme of illusory learning.[9] A key aspect of spaced learning is that relearning material is most effective just before the learner forgets the material. This requires sensing when a learner is getting rusty about the material—a level of attention that a teacher in a classroom cannot achieve at any scale.

Third, *content is best interleaved.*[10] A common, and understandable, practice in education is to practice topics in blocks: multiplication, say, followed by division. Extensive research, though, points to the benefits of interleaving practice: multiplication problems alternated with division. This is, again, inconvenient in a large classroom in which students are on a march along a complex curriculum. However, the benefits have been replicated in a range of subject areas, including mathematics and art. We are just beginning to understand the neuroscientific mechanisms of this desirable difficulty, which results in so-called cognitive interference while learning.[11]

Fourth, the act of assessing a student's performance in any interaction, with a view to giving feedback, is important. *When and how to give feedback* are obviously essential in learning. Depending on context, delayed feedback may be a desirable difficulty. But feedback takes time, and succinct feedback may be generally (but not always) more efficient in terms of the allocation of total time in a learning task.[12]

These four aspects of learning—spacing, testing, interleaved content, and assessment/feedback loops—have direct application to workforce education. All can be fitted into a backdrop of desirable difficulty to keep students engaged and challenged. Unlike established classroom approaches, each can be incorporated directly into how online education instruction is organized. Online education's potential for interactive learning can make it much more sensitive than a classroom setting to the best timing for introducing spacing and feedback features to, for example, attain the right level of desirable difficulty.

The 2020 coronavirus pandemic has forced a massive education experiment in which nearly all of American higher education has been forced to shift from classrooms to online. This created a massive learning laboratory. The story of the three little pigs is relevant. The pig that built a house with bricks withstood the wolf at the door. Here, online teaching experts are finding that faculty who have already created or worked on a MOOC that embodied lessons from learning science for online education can draw on that MOOC for online course content. The wolf cannot blow that brick house down. But faculty without a MOOC or MOOC development experience have often found themselves floundering in a new education medium—they are in houses of straw and sticks.

We know, for example, that an hour-long video of a lecture with no interspersed content for assessments, participatory discussions, or feedback loops promotes mind wandering and provides quite limited learning value for students. It violates the rules of bite-sized chunks, desirable difficulties, spacing, testing, interleaved content, and assessment/feedback loops. But many faculty that suddenly have had to go online with their class lectures because of the pandemic did not know or understand this.

So while the coronavirus has forced an online shift, those who were prepared—as is the story with so many other facets of the pandemic—are proving to be better performers. They already have a house of bricks. While the fact that schools can continue providing education online is miraculous, an unthinkable technological advance from a decade ago, there has been backlash in some quarters against online education as a result of the coronavirus. Some students have faced mediocre material because too many faculty were unprepared and unaware of the lessons for online learning. But online education has been shown to be our resilient system—there is no substitute now for it. The coronavirus has given us an opportunity to optimize.

Educational Technology and Cognitive Science

Traditional lectures with large classrooms are hard-pressed to leverage cognitive science. Technologies such as classroom clickers that electronically register a class's response to a teacher's questions can engage students, make learning more active, and mimic the testing effect, but the full use of the cognitive science described here requires personalization. For example, since spaced practice would ideally detect when the learner is becoming rusty in the material, a few probing assessments are necessary to fine-tune the spacing for each student.

A series of new software learning apps provide examples of how these principles of learning can be applied. The SuperMemo software application is truly a pioneer in the use of spaced repetition.[13] Language-learning apps such as Duolingo also use a number of cognitive science principles.[14] Flashcard software such as Quizlet leverages the testing effect and can be used to apply spaced repetition and interleaving. MOOC platforms already leverage the testing effect and have a significant opportunity to incorporate spacing and interleaving. Research is ongoing.[15]

MOOCs have really changed the state of the art in assessments. For example, the edX platform today offers dozens of assessment types, including assessing the correctness of software code, circuits, mathematical expressions, and diagrams. As for essays, there is already software in word-processing systems for assessing spelling, grammar, and sentence structure and for detecting plagiarism. MOOC providers such as edX go further with peer grading—students grading each other's assignments.[16] MOOCs typically reach numbers of students beyond the ability of a single faculty member to evaluate individually, yet writing requires individual assessment. But thanks to peer grading, learning occurs for both student writers and evaluators, and results have proven quite constructive. MOOC providers have a surprisingly rich slate of courses in the humanities, arts, and the social sciences in which writing is required, and peer grading can help fill the evaluation gap.

But the ultimate challenge is *AI-based grading of subjective responses* such as essays, which has proven controversial for reasons both philosophical and pragmatic.[17] Nevertheless, because AI can enable much greater scaling, areas such as AI-based assessment will remain fertile ground for innovation in the years ahead. Systems such as edX and its open-source software corpus Open edX enable third-party software to plug in, ensuring that innovation in AI can continue in parallel and be incorporated at the discretion of the instructor.

Rich feedback is a grading problem that remains relatively unsolved. An automatic grading system such as one in a MOOC may be able to determine whether a program or derived mathematical expression is correct or incorrect, but it cannot provide constructive feedback about where the student went wrong or provide insights about the student's mental model.

Similarly, lessons from cognitive science can migrate from traditional education to workforce education. The needs for feedback and testing are profound in skill training, and online technologies can help optimize their delivery significantly. Because subjective responses and essays are less relevant to much of workforce training, current developments in AI-based assessment can already enhance fit workforce applications.

Scaffolding and Tutoring

In psychology, the concept of a *zone of proximal development* helps clarify an optimal difference between a learner and a "more knowledgeable other" who can lead the learner to greater achievement.[18] Too large a difference, and the learner cannot keep up; too small, and the learner doesn't learn. More generally, scaffolding is a way to provide learners support as they gain mastery over the material. The art lies in calibrating the challenge of the learning to the student's abilities. Anyone who has played tennis with a slightly better player can probably relate to this balance. Good tutors and coaches are able to calibrate themselves, while an expert who does not possess good coaching skills may suffer from an expert blind spot.[19]

A careful performance of tasks under the observation and tutelage of a *coaching-inclined expert* that can provide guidance to enable continuous improvement can lead to significant performance improvements. This idea underlies a technique called *deliberate practice*, which has shown significant benefits in a range of learning activities, from sports to physics education.[20]

In 1985, the noted educational psychologist Benjamin Bloom captured the benefits of good tutoring in a seminal paper in which he showed a tremendous improvement over traditional teaching.[21] But, he wondered, how can we improve scalable education to achieve similar results, given that tutoring is expensive? More recently, the *cognitive load theory*, presented in a paper, has helped put more flesh on the scaffolding theory. Novices, the authors argue, have fewer predefined schema to digest new information and so suffer from high cognitive load because the working memory available is limited.[22] Novices therefore require more fill-in-the-blank problems. But as novices becomes experts and develop the schema to absorb information, they can be exposed effectively to more open-ended problems.[23] Either way, the key appears to be expending cognitive load on germane, not distracting, tasks. Cognitive load theory and desirable difficulties seem to agree on the importance of avoiding undesirable difficulties.

Education Technology: Tutoring, Games, Simulation, and Collaborative Tools

Intelligent tutoring systems (ITSs) are computational systems that teach students a subject by modeling the student, the domain being taught, and a scheme for instruction and feedback. In many ways, ITSs have been the holy grail of automated education going all the way back to Alan Turing, the early developer of theoretical computer science, and B. F. Skinner, the pioneer of behavioral psychology. Modern ITSs model the most recent understanding of the working of the human brain.[24] They remain a key focus for edtech and capture many of the aspirations described in this section. In their ultimate form, they are also the pinnacle of personalized learning.

Games are another important area of edtech related to motivation and scaffolding. So-called serious games are those developed for purposes other than entertainment, including those for game-based learning, whereas in edutainment—the value of which has been questioned[25]—gaming is combined with entertainment. A third approach focuses on *playfulness*, such as in the Scratch system, an extraordinarily successful example in which students focus on creativity with a graphical programming language—playing to learn rather than learning to play—and thus learn programming in the process.[26]

Games can lead a student through a series of tasks and create an environment in which learning occurs naturally—such as in the case of the much-acclaimed game World Without Oil, which forces students to think about the implications of an oil shock as it leads them through a postoil world.[27]

Other games have been used for education about subjects as varied as the environment, gender discrimination, and STEM topics.[28] Designing a game to ensure well-balanced learning and participation, though, is difficult.[29] Finally, the word *gamification* has been used somewhat loosely but should really be interpreted as a fourth category. The idea of gamification is to tap into a social and potentially socially competitive network and replicate motivation factors from games generally. In some sense, any educational environment can be gamified, but the effectiveness of doing so needs to be carefully assessed.[30]

Simulations are a powerful technique similar to games, but wholly focused on modeling realistic situations and teaching real skills. Simulations provide real-time feedback and use that to scaffold the progress of the learning because of the potential to increase difficulty for the learner as the training progresses. Simulations are an old and well-established educational tool. Mechanical flight simulators, for example, long played a major part in training pilots, enabling rapid training scale-up.[31] During World War II, the military used some ten thousand automated Link Trainers to train half a million pilots.[32] As discussed in chapter 1, the military is using virtual and augmented reality tools (VR and AR) for the latest generation of simulators applied to a wide range of training needs, from operating aircraft turbines to submarines. Simulators have also been used to teach everything from business strategy to environmental dynamics.[33]

Using *collaborative tools to enable coaching* is an emerging trend in online platforms, such as with MOOCs. These include case-based collaboration tools for online learners and applications that enable, among other things, coaches to work with novices as they use a software tool. Finally, group annotation tools help students and teachers annotate the same, or versions of the same, document and provide coaching.

Intelligent tutors, games, simulations, and collaborative tools are all highly relevant technologies for workforce education. Each offers new learning capabilities by applying advances in tutoring and scaffolding approaches to learning, delivered from the new technologies that can enhance them. The ongoing education experiments with these technologies need to be incorporated into workforce education.

MENS ET MANUS

"Mind and hand" reads the seal of MIT, in Latin: *mens et manus*. This reflects MIT's early emphasis on the connection between knowledge and practice. MIT's role in creating lab-based learning[34] and its continuing strong preference for learning by doing came from this emphasis. It is a credo captured well by the more current phrase *hands-on learning*, which is embedded in a related series of educational approaches. Tactile experience, in which a student physically feels angular momentum or gestures to capture a phenomenon, have been shown to improve learning.[35]

Similarly, *generative learning theory* posits that learning is better when the agency of the learner is engaged in the generation of new information based on prior concepts.[36] More generally, *active learning* is any instructional approach that engages the student in the learning process—as opposed to passive listening.[37] *Blended learning* is an approach that mixes online with face-to-face education. The online component is focused on the information content, which frees up increasing face-to-face time between students and teachers so that the class can be more active and more opportunities for coaching arise.[38] The term *flipped classroom*[39] describes the use of online courses to leave time in the classroom to do more hands-on, blended activities. *Project-based learning, problem-based learning,* and *task-oriented learning* are all techniques to give students more agency and purpose. *Integration* is another important aspect of learning, which projects and tasks can help enable. Learning through discipline-aligned courses can lead to siloed knowledge, and integration connects topics across silos.[40] *Teamwork* is another important element of learning that also can be helped by projects and group activities.

Edtech for Hands-On Learning

There is a small fleet of prototyping technologies that are a form of edtech that enables hands-on learning, including 3-D printing, Lego Mindstorms, Arduino, Raspberry Pi, App Inventor, and even the programming language Python. They put unprecedented power at students' fingertips to actualize their ideas, learn from real creation, seek feedback, and enjoy the pleasure of achievement. They will increase with time. Competitions, led by FIRST Robotics, have leveraged such technologies to increase even further the reach and power of scaffolded mentoring and coaching. All this could be characterized as learning by creating.

When prototyping on a benchtop is not possible, there is simulation. Virtual reality is another step in the direction of creating realistic situations, physical access to which would be difficult. VR can be used, for example, to perform a hands-on, team-oriented task in an undersea environment. Augmented reality can be used for on-the-job training. An engineer performing a maintenance task may have an expert view the task in real time over an AR headset and provide subtle feedback.

Hands-on learning is clearly critical to workforce education, since so much of it requires training for physical tasks. Related kinds of learning, from tactile to active to blended, are all highly relevant to workforce education. The prototyping technologies for learning by creating are further enablers when applied to a range of skill areas, such as manufacturing. Blended learning and VR and AR technologies are particularly important for workforce education. Blended learning can shift more of the rote learning online, freeing expert instructors for coaching and personal and small-group problem solving and instructing. Because displaced and older workers may be less ready for online courses, blended learning appears critical to reaching these groups. VR and AR enable true learning by doing in immersive environments that will be ideal for many aspects of workforce education. Chapter 1 highlighted the navy's work using these technologies for training.

NEW DELIVERY MODALITIES

Clearly, as discussed earlier, the internet and computers enable an entirely new paradigm for education that will enable us to implement lessons from learning science in dramatic new ways. However, there is an important aspect we have not discussed: access.

In 2001, MIT launched OpenCourseWare, making its curriculum free to the world.[41] By 2019, the number of downloads was approaching three hundred million.[42] This spurred a major online revolution that resulted in the launch of MOOCs. Today, the top three MOOC providers, edX, Coursera, and Udacity, boast nearly one hundred fifty million enrollments.[43]

The benefits of online programs are many, but perhaps the most important is the ability of working people to learn on their own without interrupting work and careers. This is particularly helpful to individuals with obligations to families or who have other circumstances that make traditional place-based education difficult. New microcredentials enable job-friendly academic accomplishments without the need to attend college. These kinds of online offerings multiply education access.

The edX software is also open sourced, through Open edX, enabling any member institution to download and run its own MOOCs. Universities, companies, and entire nations have taken advantage of this facility to create local education ecosystems. They can create a MOOC and take advantage of the latest technologies and the broadband access edX has created. In addition, learning management system (LMS) vendors have adopted many MOOC-like features that can support university-size user bases, even if they are not necessarily scalable (like the MOOC platforms) to hundreds of thousands of users.

Online education, even if some researchers have found serious limitations,[44] seems for the most part to work when done right.[45] However, there are clearly many lessons on online delivery still to be learned.

Access is a deep problem for workforce education. With a workforce of more than 150 million people requiring systematic upskilling and lifelong learning, and a problematic existing delivery system, it is difficult to envision how provide this access without extensive use of the scaling possibilities of online education. New delivery modalities have evolved to expand the reach of online education, from MOOCs to online certificate programs. Clearly online education, and the suite of technologies and learning approaches that can enhance it, will be important to workforce education. However, much work needs to be done to adjust online training for the kinds of learning challenges different workforce groups face, including incumbent, displaced, and new entrant workers. One size clearly won't fit all: online training will have to be adjusted to worker needs.

There are three types of content for the working learner of the future: formal, informal, and professional. The technology for each will be different.

Formal, typically academic, education is still very relevant to the workforce. We have already described the pedagogy, the modalities, and the technologies that affect it, and we have stated that there is a cognitive benefit to having learners receive some in-person education. This leads to the opportunity for technologies that support the deeper insights in-person modalities enable, such as virtual lab equipment. In addition, collaboration software can serve as a middle ground that achieves some aspects of in-person education without physical copresence.[46]

Informal education has flourished over the past two decades. Informal education occurs outside formal institutions and either helps students do better in school or prepare for standardized tests and certifications such as bar exams. A significant amount of educational technology innovation has occurred in this sphere, and there is a rich ecosystem of downloadable and web-based testing software. Some companies, mostly focused on highly defined topics such as mathematics, claim to have personalized software using AI tools, creating student models as students learn.[47] This may be a new generation of intelligent tutors. Can such technologies be used to teach a student how to write G-codes for a CNC machine tool?

Professional education is another market in which edtech tools have flourished. It occurs inside companies or in fields that require continuing education that can be rewarded with continuing education units (CEUs). A number of specialized corporate learning management systems enable corporate learning libraries, which allow integration with HR systems.[48] There is even an emerging category of recognizing and rewarding informal education in the professional category.[49]

These technology developments in all three types of education are potentially relevant to workforce training. Clearly, professional education enhanced by these new technologies allows firms to provide their own training systems in new ways. But new technologies entering both informal and academic education clearly can carry over to workforce education delivery.

EDTECH AND WORKFORCE EDUCATION: ADDITIONAL TECHNOLOGY STRANDS

Our presentation of edtech in the context of pedagogy, modality, and content leaves out a few capabilities that are best presented holistically. Each offers significant promise for workforce education.

Artificial Intelligence in Education

The idea of using AI in education, and eventually the personalization of education, is very attractive in an era of rapid workforce training. The idea is that smart systems might be able to adapt to and personally guide individual students, at scale, through a learning journey that ensures better outcomes. However, it is useful to separate what it means to personalize.

- Asynchronous video-based courses let students slow down or speed up delivery, and in this sense enables what we refer to as *self-personalization*.
- The logistics of education can be made smoother using AI and natural language programming (NLP). This includes chatbots to address student questions and requests and to answer frequently asked questions. The much-reported Jill Watson experiment, a virtual teaching assistant used at Georgia Tech to advise students, is a good example.[50]
- The ultimate AI-based personalized system might well be the intelligent tutor we described earlier. Some systems, though, offer adaptive guidance to students using Bayesian and other learning algorithms, but in the end involve a human teacher who can provide personal attention. This helps manage the load of the human. Perhaps one day AI systems will be able to truly coach the student by understanding their deeply embedded misconceptions. But that may be a few years away.

Sensors

There is much research about the human body's response to learning. This ranges from EEG responses to eye tracking.[51] In the future, galvanic skin reflex, expression tracking, and heart rate variability may also become key measures. These high-technology systems may become valuable in understanding whether a student is comfortable with the learning, but they will take time to be refined, accepted, and adopted.

Digital Certificates and Badging

As we've discussed, new credential systems will be needed for workforce education and lifelong learning. There has been much work done with digital badging to recognize learning achievements.[52] But there are unresolved issues about what credentials mean and their validity.

In early 2019, nine universities around the world launched an effort to make digital badging more scalable and prevalent for use in online courses.[53] Digital credentialing, using strong cryptography, can create fraud-resistant, readily verifiable certificates (under the control of the credential holder rather than the education institution) that can be much more detailed with respect to the skill content that is their basis. This can help assure the rapid transportability of credentials and help employers understand what they represent, as chapter 11 discusses in more detail.

Online education, coupled with a swarm of complementary new technologies and learning approaches, offers a new tool for workforce education. Given the scale of the workforce education task—a workforce that requires ongoing upskilling and lifelong learning—online education's ability to scale rapidly will be important. It provides a dramatic new tool to open up access to workforce education. While online education so far is better when combined with face-to-face education for blended learning, it should become a critical element of workforce education delivery.

Complementary technologies will increasingly enhance it. These include MOOCs, intelligent tutoring systems, computer games, simulations, collaborative IT tools, VR and AR, AI, digital credentialing, and, potentially, sensors. This bundle of new education tools can also further learning. We are beginning to absorb lessons about improving the learning process through new pedagogy tools: bite-size chunks (short, focused segments), desirable difficulties (through testing, spacing, interleaved content, and assessment/feedback loops), and hands-on learning (through tactile, active, and blended approaches). These learning lessons can be boosted in an online context by the new technologies available to help with delivery. New systems and modalities for delivery are also evolving, from MOOCs to the platform systems that support them and to new companies and digital certificate systems.

To apply this new toolset, we will have to overcome barriers. Current MOOCs primarily serve better-educated users who are already employed and seeking career and education benefits.[54] Online is only beginning to be seen as a medium for teaching technical skills used in the workplace, and we lack a solid system for implementation. However, workforce education, with learning by doing and hands-on requirements, is a direct beneficiary of this mix of new technologies with what we've learned about learning. It can also benefit from the new delivery modalities and systems that online education has spurred. There is much promise here, along with many challenges.

9 THE EDUCATIONAL CONTENT

So far, this work has focused on workforce skill acquisition and the role of the education system. Just what skills are needed and what specific content will be required in workforce education to ensure workers have those skills are, of course, obvious questions to address. To make the answers as actionable as possible, it's worth first reviewing two particular movements in education—competency-based education and the development of shorter-term programs with certificates—because of the promise they hold for dramatically assisting the ways in which skills can be acquired as part of workforce education. These movements complement and enhance the utility of each other, and each can also be enhanced by the possibilities of new online, digital technologies.

COMPETENCY-BASED EDUCATION

The first movement is competency-based education, a concept that originated in apprenticeship, technical, and military training and then moved into K–12 education, with a focus on outcomes that lead to student demonstration of proficiency in using relevant information, ideas, and tools.[1] Along the way, a number of education theorists spelled out early concepts.[2] The demonstration of particular skills and knowledge followed by ongoing assessments was the organizing key to modifying instruction practices around demonstrated outcomes. By 2015, the US Department of Education found the movement had reached into higher education, with perhaps as many as six hundred colleges and universities adopting the approach for some classes or larger programs,[3] although that still represented only a fraction of college offerings.

Competency-based education means measurable learning targets in specific areas of competency that are made clear to students at the outset, with students receiving instruction until they fully grasp these concepts and skills.[4] *Competencies* can be defined as observable and measurable standards for an area of skills, knowledge, and personal abilities. A *skill* is narrower, related to the ability to perform a particular task with determinable results. Continual assessments measure whether students demonstrate mastery of the area; once they do, they move to the next topic. The approach not only aims for the ability to recognize and repeat a concept after it has been taught, but also promotes cognitive *mastery* of a concept—the ability to evaluate it, comparing it to related concepts, and extend it in new directions. The competency approach divides an education area into bite-size, manageable pieces that complement each other and, when combined, enable mastery of a group of topics that amounts to understanding an overall field.

This approach requires additional instruction support that differs depending on students' individual learning needs. The continual assessments are embedded throughout the learning cycle along students' individualized learning pathways as they move at their own paces toward specific learning outcomes. Monitoring how students are performing all along their pathways is important to the model.[5]

The differences between traditional education and the competency-based approach are significant. The former is tied to fixed time periods, and students move on regardless of whether they have fully acquired the necessary concepts and skills. Learning targets are organized around grade levels set by age, not an individual's learning capacity and development. Students who aren't meeting academic or behavior standards can receive occasional targeted assistance, whereas they receive differentiated support all along, based on their learning needs, in the competency model. Traditional education assessments are used at set times, typically near the end of one of the fixed periods and to summarize content acquisition. Grades reflect completion of assignments and content-based test scores with corresponding student ranking; in competency learning, grades are used primarily to orient students and inform them of their position along their learning pathways.

Competency-based education is by nature instructor- and labor intensive, but with the addition of online features it can be less costly.[6] Reflecting its training origins, this approach also appears significantly better fitted to educating for workforce skills than traditional education; in fact, workforce training has long used a variety of competency-type approaches implicitly. Workforce education requires a major dose of hands-on learning by doing, which by its nature matches competency learning patterns. It can be better shaped into modular units of varying length and knowledge intensity, with frequent skill demonstration and assessment to assure skill proficiency.

Stated more explicitly, a competency approach for trainees allows them to advance as they demonstrate fluency with each skill element. Learning targets are organized and paced to better fit the individual's learning capacity and development, and trainees receive monitoring and support throughout based on their learning needs—and if they aren't meeting skill standards, then they receive targeted help. Assessments are embedded throughout the training program, and performance evaluations are used to orient students to their progress along the training pathway.

COMPACT, CREDENTIAL-BASED EDUCATION PROGRAMS

Soaring student debt is making the expense of higher education increasingly difficult to manage (as noted in chapter 7), and traditional higher education schedules don't fit work patterns well.[7] Most students who leave degree programs do so because they have to earn money.[8] These factors, along with the availability of online offerings, have spurred a significant shift toward nontraditional credentialing.[9] In 2016, some 6 percent of adults had work-relevant, nondegree certificate credentials, and 21 percent had licenses.[10] The number of *learning workers*—adults over eighteen that are both working twenty plus hours a week and participating in education programs—has now passed the number of traditional learners ("full-time" students), particularly after age twenty-four.[11] Some 60 percent of certificate holders surveyed say their certificate was "very useful" in finding a job,[12] and a 2019 report found that adults without a postsecondary degree who hold a certificate or certification have higher levels of full-time employment than their peers (85 percent vs. 78 percent) and have a median annual income of $45,000 versus $30,000 for those without a certificate.[13] Those who attended a vocational or technical school are the most likely (77 percent) to have a certificate or certification.

We need to define some terms here. A *credential* or *certificate* is generally offered by education or training institutions for skills or competencies. A *certification* attempts to validate a credential or certificate. It often involves a third party independent of the credential provider that confirms or accredits a demonstrated skill or competency. This is often through a testing or verification process and can be for a limited period—after which a recertification is required. A license is granted through a government-approved process and has legal status: a person can't practice a particular skill, competency, or profession without it.

So-called nanodegrees and microcredentials are also evolving.[14] Udacity, for example, offers a series of related online courses on data science, programming, and other areas for technicians that it argues can move a student from beginner to job-ready in seven to twelve months.[15] MITx, MIT's online course system, now offers MicroMasters certificates on the edX platform that are open to anyone, for completion of six to eight related courses in a growing series fields, from advanced manufacturing to supply chain management.[16] MOOC courses offered by colleges and universities now include courses from some nine hundred schools; enrollment has grown over 900 percent since the first MOOCs in 2011.[17] The Labor Department's CareerOneStop, a job search site, offers 5,700 certification tests to users, from restaurant food preparation to childcare to wiring. Workers can take these tests to demonstrate their skills, presenting the test results as validation and thus side-stepping degree requirements. All these short, more bite-size courses and programs sit firmly within competency-based education. They amount to a new prehire certification mechanism.[18]

Academic institutions are increasingly offering digital credentials and badges (which are visual symbols of the credential), and the numbers are proliferating. This is making it difficult for both employers and employees to understand what they mean. Key lessons are emerging.[19] For example, if schools offer only manual processes (websites and email) to collect credential assessment information from students, this in turn dictates that the credentials must be issued manually, so they can't scale. Instead, assessment management and credential and badge issuance need to be integrated. Issuing credentials and badges not backed by academic rigor, including assessed evidence, frustrates employers and undermines their credibility. Tying them to established industry standards, when available, is important. Issuing credentials and badges that don't match well to actual performance for work or internships is also detrimental to their value. Credentials need to cross-link to the evidence behind them, and this information must be easy for employers to access, not buried in learning management systems. Certificates are most valuable when subject to certification from an independent third party, such as an industry association or standards-setting entity, and when there is rigor in that process through an exam and periodic recertification to ensure continuing competency. While self-certifications and voluntary certifications can still be useful, third-party certification is an important step to help employers make sense of the accelerating numbers of certificates.

Despite these challenges, digital credentials, and the badges that often go with them, can play an important role in demonstrating workplace skills and competencies. They can be aimed at particular skills, offered on a timetable that helps working adults, and stacked with related credentials to show broader skill and career capabilities to employers. People without college degrees are the most interested in pursuing additional education and training,[20] and graduates of both nondegree and graduate vocational and technical programs are those most likely to agree that their education has made them strong job candidates.[21] The demand, then, for these kinds of programs appears to be in place.

NEW ONLINE DELIVERY TOOLS CAN ASSIST

These competency-based and compact credential program movements in education have each been supported by development of online digital tools. For example, the Labor Department has supported several online delivery tools to assist in the adoption of new workforce approaches and worker access to them. For instance, through a grant from the department's Trade Adjustment Assistance Community College and Career Training (TAACCCT) program,[22] some seven hundred community colleges created a free and open online library called SkillsCommons that offers support materials for workforce development; it's a major collection of workforce-related online resources, revised and adapted by individual institutions and industries.[23]

Three other Labor Department efforts, all developed by the Employment and Training Administration, should be mentioned. The first, mySkills myFuture, an attempt at a one-stop job search navigation system, has a number of features to help workers assess their skills and search for careers in areas that fit their skills.[24] Next, WorkforceGPS collects resources on workforce education for a wide range of groups and organizations, such as workforce development boards, career education or rural services providers, employers, and state programs. The resources include materials on apprenticeships and skills training.[25] Finally, there's CareerOneStop, a website that includes a job search toolkit with information on occupational profiles, a personal interest assessment, a targeting system for seeking occupations, local training and apprenticeship finders, and information on growing job sectors. It also provides access to job certification tests. Users can create their own job search plans. It also contains focused information for older and displaced workers and other worker categories.[26]

The value of online education programs can be seen in the example of Western Governors University (WGU), which has a competency-based education approach in all of its courses.[27] Formed in 1997 by nineteen states, its enrollment in 2019 was more than 110,000 students—older (average age thirty-seven; mean age forty-three) and mostly (61 percent) first-generation college students[28]—studying in sixty undergraduate and graduate degree programs. Nearly 80 percent of WGU students are employed full time, a significantly higher rate than for similar programs for nontraditional students; mentoring and having a job or internship are key to the success of the program.[29] WGU demonstrates that online degree and credential content can work, particularly with work and mentoring scaffolding.

The private sector has also been creating a series of online delivery tools to assist in workforce education and career development. For example, HoloPundits in Ohio provides virtual and augmented reality training materials for manufacturing and healthcare sectors, using guided feedback to users that fits competency education approaches.[30] In software design and development, LinkedIn Learning (formerly Lynda), also now owned by Microsoft, offers some 1,500 courses as part of the LinkedIn system.[31] There are many efforts ongoing; other examples of digital projects are noted ahead.

But how do we better alert workers to the kinds of training (and therefore jobs) that could be within their grasp? Academic research is beginning to yield these kinds of career-enabling online elements; two examples follow. For example, researchers from Arizona State University and LinkedIn have developed a system called NEMO[32] to help with career move prediction, and a group at the MIT Media Lab has developed a prototype called Skillscape that creates clusters of skills using Labor Department data.[33] These kinds of systems are important potential enablers to place optimal workforce education into the hands of workers.

Finally, new blockchain technology—just emerging—is helping address the major difficulty workers and students face when it comes to explaining their certificates and degrees to employers, who need to know whether they are valid, what they mean, and what their value is. This new technology allows workers and students to own and control their own secure records in ways that enable them to answer these questions. Institutions are beginning to authorize this blockchain approach,[34] which also helps make credentials transportable.

SKILLS REQUIREMENTS

We now come to the skills needed and the specific content (often called taxonomies) that will be required in workforce education to ensure workers have those skills. The US Department of Labor has created a series of training competency categories as part of articulating needed workplace education content:[35]

- *Personal skills*—interpersonal skills and lifelong learning
- *Academic competencies*—basic academic skills such as reading, writing, and mathematics, as well as more advanced knowledge relevant to a particular occupation
- *Workplace competencies*—understanding the role of the company and industry, such as inputs, throughputs, and outputs, and teamwork and collaboration
- *Industry-wide technical competencies*—the knowledge, skills, and abilities associated with a particular industry, such as manufacturing or healthcare
- *Occupation-specific technical competencies*—the skills and abilities associated with particular occupations, such as manufacturing technicians

In the early 1990s, the Labor Department empaneled the Secretary's Commission on Achieving Necessary Skills (SCANS), which identified the following competencies and foundation skills: *basic skills* (reading, writing, arithmetic, mathematics, listening and speaking), *thinking skills* (creative thinking, decision-making, problem solving, seeing things in the mind's eye, knowing how to learn, and reasoning), and *personal qualities* (responsibility, self-esteem, social, self-management, and integrity/honesty).[36] Since then, the research behind the SCANS list has become ever more detailed.[37]

Industry has developed detailed general skill requirements as well. The common employability skills across sectors from the National Network of Business and Industry (NNBI) include *personal skills* (integrity, initiative, dependability and reliability, adaptability, and professionalism), *people skills* (teamwork, communication, and respect), *applied knowledge* (reading, writing, mathematics, science, technology, and critical thinking), and general *workplace skills* (planning and organizing, problem solving, decision-making, business fundamentals, customer focus and working with tools and technology).[38] Each skill category (such as personal skills) is further defined with descriptions of each competency (such as initiative) being sought. The NNBI provides services to the company members that belong to the twenty-six major industry associations that make up the network, with materials advising them on how to create their own standards-based credentials and about industry-recognized credentialing systems they can rely on in areas such as advanced manufacturing.[39]

SCANS and NNBI list general skills needed for employment. Individual industry sectors have articulated their own sets of skills. For example, the Manufacturing Skills Standards Council developed a detailed set of skills for certified production technicians that covers the following areas: safety, quality practices and measurement, manufacturing processes and production, maintenance awareness, and "green" production.[40] The MSSC provides both courses and assessments for employers and their employees, and the certificates are backed by the National Association of Manufacturers.

For our purposes, we have identified three critical areas in which content is required in workforce education systems: foundational academic skills, personal and interpersonal skills, and occupational skills. Let's address each in turn.

FOUNDATIONAL ACADEMIC SKILLS

Basic academic skills, in our context, are those that should be acquired in the K–12 education system but also that serve as a foundation for the follow-on stages of personal and interpersonal skills and required technical skills. In their now classic 1996 book *Teaching the New Basic Skills*, Frank Levy and Richard Murmane suggested that the traditional academic skills taught in the K–12 system at the time were insufficient for high school graduates in a period of technological change in the workplace and proposed a mix of general education skills and soft skills as foundational for nearly all occupations.[41] What they called *new basic skills* would have high school students graduating with the ability to

- read at the ninth-grade level or higher;
- do math at the ninth-grade level or higher;
- solve semistructured problems for which hypotheses must be tested;
- communicate effectively, both orally and in writing; and
- use computers to carry out simple tasks, such as word processing.

They argued that students could acquire these basic skills if their education followed a group of principles that are also characteristic of good training management practices in strong companies: reach agreement on the problem; provide the right incentives and opportunities; train the frontline workers; measure progress regularly; and learn from mistakes.

There are a number of programs in the United States that mix basic academic skills into technical, occupational education. Some of these are highlighted ahead.

ACT WorkKeys

The widely used American College Testing (ACT) WorkKeys system of curriculum and related assessments for basic academic and personal workplace skills exemplifies many of the Levy and Murmane concepts.[42] Its *applied math* course builds ability to apply math principles to problems faced in the workplace; its *graphic literacy* course includes the ability to find, understand, present, and use information needed in the workplace; and its *workplace documents* course builds the ability to apply written information. Problem solving, using actual workplace problems, is built into all three. The courses also measure soft skills relevant to most jobs.

ACT's web-based KeyTrain interactive training program builds on the content, progressions, and assessments of the WorkKeys system.[43] KeyTrain courses move to the next applied level in areas such as electricity, mechanics, and business writing, and also addresses personal characteristics such as dependability and emotional stability. There is also a classroom training element users can apply. ACT's courses can lead to its National Career Readiness Certificate (NCRC) for essential workplace skills, which is recognized by thousands of employers.

ACT also offers a service in which licensed job profilers meet with employers to get background on jobs to be profiled and help set out job elements that correspond to WorkKeys assessment scores, creating a standard for the job. This creates target scores for applicants to meet to qualify for the job. These profilers also collect training manuals, annual reports, newsletters, and other information about the company, as well as information on the job itself and how it serves the company. These are built into the job profile and tied to the WorkKeys elements. Some fourteen states have participated in ACT's job credentialing system, using WorkKeys as part of their involvement.

ACT has used experts from a range of fields to develop its assessments and then field test them to assure their validity, particularly their ability to predict success in a range of occupations.[44] It has a monitoring and evaluation process to help ensure their ongoing effectiveness. Based on its program evaluations, ACT has found that individuals who complete the WorkKeys certification are more likely to possess job-related cognitive skills and successfully complete training programs, leading to better job performance.[45]

The application of WorkKeys at Phifer in Tuscoloosa, Alabama, offers an example of how employers use and view the WorkKeys program.[46] Phifer, which manufacturers aluminum and fiberglass screens and designs fabrics for outdoor use, faces significant competition in finding qualified employees in North Alabama with its growing manufacturing sector. In addition, its job profiles need continual updating because of changes in production technology and processes. So the company worked with ACT WorkKeys to develop job profiles with skills that were measurable and then, working with a local community college, developed the training to fit these profiles. This resulted in a five-week program in which participants earned the WorkKeys NCRC.

Phifer has also faced relatively high turnover and has needed higher-level employees to meet the technology advances. Using ACT WorkKeys improved hiring, identifying high turnover positions to focus on. The job profiles enabled much better assessment of applicants, so the right employee tended to be matched to the right job. That cut turnover from 17 to 5 percent annually—a major cost-saving move that more than paid for the program. The company believes it now has a validated hiring model, with predictable outcomes thanks to hiring candidates with the WorkKeys credential.

The company also uses ACT's KeyTrain for applicants, with its scoring system, and applicants have to score high enough to match the job profile; if they don't, they can retake the assessment and get targeted instruction on skills where they need to score higher. In effect, then, applicants can train to become qualified applicants. Because half the firm's workforce is approaching retirement, the company also needs to develop and move up current employees to fill openings. So the company also uses WorkKeys to identify promotable employees.

All told, Phifer's return on its workforce training investment has been a $2 million reduction in training costs, a 25 percent cut in training time (through improved retention), a 40 percent improvement in the quality of applicants, a 33 percent reduction in orientation time, and a 15 percent increase in workforce punctuality.

Phifer adopted an approach of getting buy-in from managers and employees across the company for the new system, and it has led to implementation of a number of Levy and Murmane's recommendations for basic skills. As part of this effort, the company participated in organizing a manufacturing network with fourteen area companies that also leverage ACT WorkKeys solutions and use a "community" approach to building employee talent. The result is one of the ACT WorkReady Communities, which use ACT WorkKeys and the NCRC system. The company also serves on the area's Labor Department–supported workforce investment board.

Other examples of WorkKeys being used come from colleges in Alabama and Tennessee. Alabama's Community College System is adopting WorkKeys and ACT's NCRC system statewide to address employers' need for a stronger employee pipeline.[47] The state's community colleges are also adopting the MSSC standards as the accepted regional system for evaluating manufacturing skills. And the state and its community colleges are pushing ACT-type foundational skill training preparation down into the early stages of high school, as well as looking at it for use in prisoner education.

In Tennessee, the state's twenty-seven Tennessee Colleges for Applied Technology (TCATs, formerly known as Technology Centers) are also demonstrating the utility of ACT's WorkKeys and KeyTrain programs. TCATs provide rigorous one- to two-year technical education programs with high completion (for a range of diplomas or certificates) and job placement rates, yielding relatively high wages.

The TCATs began as the state's vocational/career technical education high schools, evolved into a postsecondary education system, and became part of the state's higher education institutions. They have overcome the common problem that faced community colleges nationwide—poor preparation of students coming from high schools and the pressing need for remedial programs. They have achieved program completion rates that range from 61 to 87 percent across schools, and job placement rates from 76 to 92 percent.[48] Overall completion rates, according to Tennessee Reconnect in 2020, were 81 percent and job placement rates into positions in the student's field of study were 86 percent.[49]

All entering TCAT students participate in an ACT WorkKeys/KeyTrain Techology Foundations program, which includes applied math, reading, locating information, writing, problem solving, and teamwork. Instructors set up an individualized learning plan with each student, who pursues the WorkKey/KeyTrain curricula at her or his own individual pace. The learning lab is open five days and some evenings each week for students to work on their programs and consult with foundations instructors. Lectures and group activities supplement the program, in a highly blended education model. It is competency-based learning with students mastering a series of stages and skills.

The great majority of students complete Technology Foundations a little after their first trimester; only a handful have not done so by the third trimester.[50] They then take ACT's online NCRC assessment. The TCAT goal is for all students to have certificates at a silver and gold level, the two highest. In 2010, of the 4,250 TCAT students completing the certificate, 30 percent were gold and 57 percent were silver.

The Technology Foundations competencies are fully integrated into the occupational and technical training programs students are undertaking in parallel. It is a self-paced, competency-based program geared to individual students, which helps those who have not done well in the past in classroom settings. Foundations instructors build relationships with students and communicate with them frequently, building learning communities that match the online curriculum.

The high completion rate for these developmental and basic technical skills and the high job placement rate are testaments to how well it works and to employer satisfaction with graduates.[51]

Washington State's I-BEST

Washington State's Integrated Basic Skills and Training (I-BEST) is another program that mixes basic academic skills into technical, occupational education.[52] It has come to be recognized nationally as a model for offering foundational skills.

Initiated by the state's community and technical colleges, I-BEST uses a team approach to teach community college students basic literacy, employability, and college-readiness skills so they can move through school and into jobs faster. I-BEST rejects the traditional community college notion that students with learning gaps must get through a sequence of precollege basic education and remedial courses before they can start working on certificates or associate degrees.

Rather than having to postpone their career and work goals until they catch up on academic basics, I-BEST students get the academic help they need while studying in the career field they choose. Each I-BEST course has two teachers: one provides technical job training; the other teaches basic and complementary reading, math, and English language skills. These catch-up studies make more sense to students because they can be seen in a career-enhancing context.

Compared to students who first enroll in remedial courses, I-BEST students are three times more likely to earn college credit and nine times more likely to earn a certificate or degree.[53]

Programs for Improving Math Skills

The US Department of Education has identified postsecondary math as a major barrier to degree completion. Nationally, 60 percent of incoming community college students are placed into at least one developmental math course annually, and yet only one-third complete the developmental math sequence and only 20 percent complete a college-level math course over three years.[54] Men, older students, African American students, part-time students, and students in vocational/CTE programs are less likely to progress. The issue affects four-year colleges as well. Thus there are many specific efforts underway to address foundational math skills—including these innovative programs:

- *Statway and Quantway* began in 2011 and assist students with college-level introductory math courses. The highly affordable programs (as low as thirty-five dollars per student) combine a college-level math course with remedial and developmental math "corequisites" and feature innovative curricula, research-based pedagogy, and relevant analytics to help educators provide targeted support for students. Students work together in small groups observed by the instructor. Participating faculty are trained online and in one-on-one mentoring. Some twenty-seven thousand students across eighteen states have enrolled in Statway and Quantway since 2011, and they have completed the courses at triple the rate (65 percent) of their peers.[55] Studies show that participating students at six community colleges went on to transfer to four-year schools and complete their programs at significantly higher levels than students taking other math programs.[56]
- *Mathematics Pathways*, a program of the University of Texas at Austin's Charles A. Dana Center, identifies underprepared students for an accelerated one-semester approach with modernized math instruction.[57] It was launched in nine Texas community colleges in 2013,[58] and by 2015 more than 7,600 students with a developmental need had used the program and completed a college-level math course within a year. The program has been rapidly scaling into higher education institutions across Texas and is also available nationally.
- *Math Start* provides a semester of remedial education before students begin a program in one of the City University of New York (CUNY) system's ten community colleges. It is an intensive and directed program for students with significant preparedness gaps. CUNY's Math Start students make more progress and enroll in for-credit courses in their second semesters at their colleges at a higher rate than their peers who did not participate in the program.[59]

These promising programs, along with the ACT programs noted earlier, offer new routes to tackling foundational academic skills. While these math programs offer significant curriculum reforms to help clear a critical bottleneck in higher ed, the ACT program takes more advantage of online and blended features. Blended learning can enhance foundational skill efforts. A Joyce Foundation evaluation, for example, found that while online programs alone were not that helpful in teaching foundational skills to adult learners, a blended model offered real benefits.[60] Online tools for basic reading, writing, and math augmented face-to-face instruction, with adult students improving over time in their ability to work independently using online tools. Online programs were best used to supplement and enhance the classroom for this group, which was not experienced with online learning, and also assisted instructors in evaluating and supporting different student capabilities

The Rise of Digital Skills

Even before personal computing and the internet were pervasive, Levy and Murmanes identified "the ability to use computers to carry out simple tasks such as word processing" as a basic skill. Since 1996, when their book came out, the need for digital skills has grown substantially—as the 2017 Brookings study cited in chapter 7 showed.[61]

Based on a survey of two thousand employers, LinkedIn has identified twenty-five digital skills companies increasingly want, from cloud and distributed computing and web architecture to software control systems, user interface design, and data presentation.[62] A 2018 UK government report offers an "essential digital framework" that matches specific digital skills to broader areas of work tasks, including communication, handling information, transactions, problem solving, and so on.[63]

The education system has not adjusted to the scale of the challenge in teaching these skills. Larger-scale use of new online technologies offers a way out of this dilemma. For example, in 2014 Georgia Tech was the first university to offer an online master's program in computer science; this well-reviewed program had more than 8,600 paid enrollees in 2019.[64] IT company certificates and university online computer science MOOC courses now abound.

PERSONAL AND INTERPERSONAL SKILLS

In addition to basic foundational skills, a number of personal and interpersonal skills are critical. These are the kinds of common "soft" and social skills relevant to employability across sectors, as identified by the National Network of Business and Industry (as discussed earlier): personal skills, including integrity, initiative, dependability and reliability, adaptability, and professionalism; and people skills, which we call *interpersonal skills*, such as teamwork, communication, and respect. Others have added to or altered that list. LinkedIn asked two thousand companies about the soft skills they need most; employers identified leadership, communication, collaboration, and time management as their top four.[65] Surveys by the Center for Third Space Thinking at the University of Southern California have identified five core soft skills—adaptability, cultural competency, empathy, intellectual curiosity, and 360-degree thinking; the center then developed programs to teach these skills.[66] And as we already mentioned, the Labor Department's SCANS foundational skills include both personal and interpersonal skills.

SOCIAL SKILLS AND THE LABOR MARKET

According to Harvard University Professor David Deming, an expert in social and education policy, the labor market increasingly rewards social skills; with more and more jobs requiring high levels of social interaction as team production expands, workers rely on each other, and employers need workers that can adapt flexibly to workplace changes, including the ability to trade jobs and tasks.[a] All occupations are becoming less routine over time, reports Deming, as information and communication technologies shift job tasks away from rigid categorization and toward more job rotation and worker multitasking. These social, nonroutine interactions are at the core of human advantages over machines.

Deming found evidence of strong relative employment and wage growth for social-skill-intensive occupations between 1980 and 2012. Jobs that require high levels of cognitive skill *and* social skills fared particularly well, while jobs requiring high math but not high social skills (including in many STEM occupations) did not.

[a]David J. Deming, "The Growing Importance of Social Skills in the Labor Market," NBER Working Paper 21473, June 2017 (revised), https://www.nber.org/papers/w21473.

However, there is a deep problem in assessing such personal and interpersonal skills: while the sought-after skill can be identified by surveys and analysis, the education interventions to teach it often cannot be or haven't been adequately tested and therefore cannot be fully validated. For example, a 2017 National Academies study, "Supporting Students' College Success," pursued a topic related to workforce skills, the soft skills students need to succeed in college.[67] These soft skills overlap with those sought by employers. However, of the eight skills identified, the report found research substantiating effective interventions for only two. The report called for more research on the needed assessments.

This same challenge of testing affects the personal and interpersonal skills employers seek: assessing and testing are necessary to enable sound training interventions to evolve. While testing has developed in concrete skill areas such as visual literacy and visual data needed in the performance of many jobs—ACT has been a leader in creating job-related testing in these areas—more personal competencies have been harder to correlate.

Merrilea Mayo, author of numerous workforce education studies, has summarized key personal and interpersonal skills set out by employers:[68]

- *Critical thinking*, which employers characterize as problem-solving approaches, from gathering relevant information to generating effective, ranked solutions from diverse perspectives and using trial and error.[69] This general, procedural approach is not subject matter specific; it can be used across problem classes and involves breaking a problem into solvable pieces, not just relying on context. A related problem is *collaborative* problem solving.[70]
- *Works independently*, which for employers is related to problem-solving ability. Employees that work independently don't keep coming back with problems someone else has to handle; they can solve the problems on their own.
- *Collaboration and teamwork*, which employers see as somewhat different personal skills. Collaboration typically happens between people viewed as equals who operate interchangeably; teamwork can have leaders. Some models have associated upwards of 180 different skills with teamwork.[71] When employers seek teamwork, for example, they also tend to seek *emotional stability*, which they see as a key part of teamwork. Employers want employees who, when working with others, can accept criticism graciously, take responsibility for their actions and not blame others, and stay calm, clearheaded, and unflappable under stress.[72] Energy and enthusiasm for the task are also viewed as contributing to teamwork,[73] and diversity and personality can also play a role.[74] Still, there are very real limits on how to teach teamwork as a workplace skill, although there have been advances in ideas for categories to measure.[75]
- *Grit* and *mindset* are personal skills often identified by employers. Angela Duckworth characterizes grit as the "power and passion of perseverance" and has developed questions that can be asked about it.[76] Grit appears to be is a strong predictor of job performance and is related to *persistence*. It is also related to *conscientiousness*, which—while not malleable—could potentially be enhanced with time management (discussed later) and goal-setting techniques. Carol Dweck has done for mindset what Duckworth has done for grit.[77] Some studies show a relationship between growth mindset (an understanding that intelligence and ability can be developed) and academic task persistence, and in some cases with

learning gains,[78] but there are not yet studies that show a direct correlation between mindset and work performance.

- *Time management* includes getting things done on time (meeting deadlines) and showing up on time. These skills can be encouraged by teaching workers to negotiate with supervisors to set timetables and goals for job performance.
- *Curiosity* appears to be a predictor of intellectual skills and how people perform in life. It can be encouraged by getting people to ask questions and then follow-on questions. Those with curiosity tend have higher job satisfaction but not necessarily better job performance. Not all jobs require curiosity; it can, however, help tedious jobs seem more interesting and can also encourage people to expand their job roles to seek new experiences or connections that will improve performance. In education, fostering curiosity works best with younger students, so if curiosity is valued in work, it may need to be fostered early.
- *Creativity* is a skill that has been subject to testing. Idea fluency appears to be a component, and can be measured through queries such as "name five adjectives that start with the letter A." But employers often express a desire for creativity when what they really mean is *expertise*, which is different. For instance, an employer may seek a "creative" worker with engineering-type skills who can solve problems, but it's the expertise that comes with those sorts of skills—as opposed to broad creativity—that might be what leads to innovative solutions.
- *Openness* is another personal skill noted by employers and is one of the "big five" positive personality traits.[79] For employers, openness is straightforward: it simply means being open—not closed to ideas, which would limit the range of problem solutions.
- *Motivation* is a priority personal skill for employers. Research on what motivates people goes back seven decades.[80] Employers are keen to have delivery mechanisms and interventions for building this skill.

Overall, there is an evolving story of measuring and training for the personal and interpersonal skills employers often cite as priorities for their employees. While progress has been made in identifying sought-after skills, the ability to test and therefore train for them remains a mixed story. This problem makes it difficult to prioritize among them for training. That, in some sense, brings us back to whether the college graduates employers hire are prepared in these soft skills. The effectiveness of colleges at soft skill education is the subject of an ongoing debate.

While liberal arts colleges have argued they prepare their students effectively in the kinds of skills just discussed, an Association of American Colleges and Universities survey suggests there are problems.[81] Of 501 business executives and 500 hiring managers from companies in a range of sizes, regions, and sectors, 63 percent had overall confidence in colleges and universities, and 70 percent of expressed broad satisfaction with the ability of recent college hires to apply skills and knowledge they acquired in college. But the survey revealed significant gaps between key personal and interpersonal skills these executives and managers prioritized and their views about the preparedness of recent graduates in these skills. For example, while 78 percent identified analytical reasoning as a very important skill, they considered only 34 percent of recent college graduates well prepared in that area. There were significant gaps in many other areas as well, including self-motivation, the ability to work independently and to work in teams, and complex problem solving. These results suggest that educational institutions have some distance to go in conveying the soft skills employers desire.

Personal and interpersonal skills, then, are clearly important to employers in the skills training equation—but the specifics of that training are still developing. Progress on how to test for them will help with better training design.

OCCUPATIONAL SKILLS

Our third category, occupational skills, puts us back on firmer validation ground. Because occupational skills—which vary by sectors and occupations—often require significant learning by doing using the actual equipment technologies and practices required in the workplace, they are easier to test for and measure.

The Labor Department has a number of tools to help in understanding occupational skills required for particular jobs. The CareerOneStop site of the department's Education and Training Administration, mentioned earlier, provides career information on nine hundred occupations, available online through the O*NET system.[82] Its occupation profile descriptions include what employees in a particular job do, what a typical day's work is like, the outlook for jobs by area, projected employment levels, the range of typical wages, education levels of those in the field, certifications available to demonstrate the skills required, apprenticeship opportunities, knowledge and physical abilities required to perform the job, related opportunities, and links to area job openings.[83] The ETA's *building blocks* are skill pyramids that detail foundational academic skills and personal and interpersonal skills, in addition to details on occupational skills needed for different jobs, and are available online for twenty-two industry occupational areas.[84]

The Labor Department also supports a nationwide network of workforce development boards that sponsor training programs in local communities under the Workforce Investment and Opportunity Act, as discussed in chapter 3.

The *credential movement* has been particularly important to occupational skills. While two- and four-year degrees remain the most likely pathways, an influx of credentials is adding new opportunities for certificates, digital badges, occupational licenses, and employer certifications. This system can be online, blended, or in the classroom, with new learning providers, from community colleges to employers to online firms and, more recently, colleges and universities. The hold of traditional educational institutions over education is gradually changing. However, the morass of credentials has created its own problems, as noted in chapter 6. It has become very difficult for students and workers to navigate among the options they now have.

The Lumina Foundation has been working to create new systems of credentials.[85] Between 2016 and 2018, it worked with the Corporation for a Skilled Workforce (CSW) to build learning-based credentialing systems in a project called Connecting Credentials, negotiating and forming a shared space for credential providers.[86] Credential Engine runs a complementary effort aimed at making all credentials transparent, shifting credentials into a functioning, information-based market.[87] It estimates there are some 334,000 credentials in the United States alone, and its website allows anyone to search and compare types and levels of credentials, with detailed information about the content and quality indicators for each. Hundreds of organizations are on its registry, and it has support from a series of foundations and organizations, including Lumina. The plethora of certificates and credentials underscores the importance of independent, third-party certification systems, particularly in occupational skill areas.

So-called on-ramps are a new institutional element, available particularly to assist in developing occupational skills. These are new education and training intermediary organizations that can connect adults without postsecondary degrees to credentials that can be acquired quickly and lead directly to employment. Strada Institute identified nine model on-ramp programs in various regions that perform a combination of functions: finding and enrolling participants; providing intense, short-term education and training aimed at specific occupational pathways; wraparound support to ensure participant success combined with continuous mentoring; and a direct route from occupational training to actual job placement.[88]

These functions are largely separated in our current system, but are brought together in the on-ramp model. Each step is aimed at overcoming the series of uncertainties workers face about career pathways, childcare and transportation costs, and employment outcomes.

The Council for Adult and Experiential Learning (CAEL) is an organization of education providers, employers, and cities, states, and regions focused on career education for adults. It is tied to the Strada Education Network and aims to increase emphasis on adult learners, to increase opportunities and remove barriers to help working adults find and complete new work credentials, and to strengthen experiential learning and nurture new models for adult occupational education.[89] Supporting institutions that can serve as on-ramps is one of CAEL's basic approaches.

Apart from these overall efforts at credentialing and on-ramps, each occupation area has its own occupational skill sets. In *manufacturing*, for example, community colleges and states that retain vocational/CTE education institutions provide manufacturing education. There are now many online course offerings in manufacturing skills from companies such as THORS,[90] 180 Skills,[91] and Tooling U-SME.[92] NIMS, the MSSC, [93] and NIST's Manufacturing Extension Partnership, through its network of state programs, offer manufacturing skill education courses and programs as well. The new technology fields within advanced manufacturing, such as digital production, biofabrication, and advanced materials, are particularly critical because there is no established education system to train for them. Some of the new advanced manufacturing institutes are working to fill this gap.

At least some start-ups are entering the manufacturing skills landscape, as well. Tulip, of Somerville, Massachusetts, is attempting to bring the industrial Internet of Things (IoT) and supporting analytics to the manufacturing floor and its workforce.[94] Its Manufacturing App Platform combines intelligent hardware sensors, computer vision, assistive user interfaces, and applied machine learning, along with a training system, to enable its new digital production system. Its customers include large manufacturing firms worldwide; installation of its manufacturing operating system platform at a Merck plant reduced training time by 57 percent overall.[95] Tulip's technology blends human-operator-focused technology with industrial IoT technology and software, bringing data analytics on a continuous basis to employees, measuring time and efficiency at each stage of the production process and enabling improvements in human-machine interfaces. The training system was built into the process changes. While veteran employees previously had to take a break from their production jobs to train new employees, the system enabled largely self-training in the assembly process, dramatically cutting the time the experienced employees had to spend on training tasks.

Manufacturing training programs abound:

- The Department of Energy's Energy Efficiency and Renewable Energy Office has, through its Tech to Market program, developed a Build4Scale online program for bringing manufacturing know-how to start-up firms that need to manufacture their new products.[96]
- MForesight, an NSF- and NIST-supported think tank for the advanced manufacturing institutes, has studied and identified thirty promising programs across the country for manufacturing skill building.[97]
- The US Chamber of Commerce Foundation has been developing a talent pipeline project with employers that essentially enables groups of regional employers to collaborate on and develop common job education needs, and then to negotiate jointly with community colleges and other providers for development of courses and training that fit the needs set by these regional groups of employers.[98] A job registry grew out of the data being developed on job position descriptions by employers. To implement the new system, building on lessons learned, the foundation has also organized a Talent Pipeline Management (TPM) Academy focused on developing the ability of local chambers to organize employer members and support talent supply chains. The TPM Academy is supported by a curriculum and related software tools that allow staff inside the foundation's regional organizations to implement talent supply chain solutions for their employer members.
- Henry Ford College, a community college in Dearborn, Michigan, obtained a Trade Adjustment Assistance Community College and Career Training workforce skills grant from the Department of Labor in 2012 and led a consortia of thirteen community colleges with support from Ford, Toyota, Bridgestone, and other auto sector firms. The group built a series of course offerings for advanced skill competencies in manufacturing, available across the community colleges, including an apprenticeship model.[99]

The coming shift in the manufacturing sector to adopt advanced manufacturing technologies (see chapter 4) will require a host of new technical skills. A number of the advanced manufacturing institutes are working to identify these skills and beginning to develop training curricula for them, but this process remains in its early stages. A new system still has to be developed for this next level of skills. While manufacturing may be among the first sectors affected by the oncoming suite of new technologies, particularly in information technology areas, other sectors, from health to retail, will also be affected. A major content task ahead will be developing the new training curricula these new technologies will require.

As with manufacturing, programs in *other occupational areas* are growing. Daniel Bustillo, director of the Healthcare Career Advancement Program at the Service Employees International Union, has noted that although healthcare jobs are expanding, larger-scale on-the-job training is hampered because there is no fifty-state system of hospitals; hospital systems are very local and regional.[100] This decentralization makes on-the-job training more difficult to implement, and it must have a smaller scale and regional focus. Despite these problems, he noted that approximately a thousand healthcare employers now offer joint labor-management training efforts in which his union participates.

Training in healthcare is not just for young, new employees; for example, training for minority group women already in the system at lower levels to move up should be a major component of health training. The emerging system requires mentor skills, too, so mentoring is also a training need to make new on-the-job training approaches work. Bustillo noted there is still a stigma on vocational education that is solved by a collaborative effort with a community college around a degree or certificate.

Fairview Health Services in Minnesota has a program that enables working two-year-degree nurses to stay on the job and keep earning while they obtain bachelor's nursing degrees. This makes them eligible for positions with increased responsibility and compensation.[101] In nursing, this is a crucial step; the four-year degree opens up many professional opportunities. The two-year-degree nurses often have been out of school for many years but are a pool of talent to fill a significant gap in needed four-year registered nurses (RNs). The Fairview program has 125 two-year RNs that are part of an on-the-job program, and it is working with a network of Minnesota higher-ed institutions. The program has a high retention rate because it is creating new job opportunities. Fairview is now looking at extending this program to other medical training areas, including for medical assistants, surgical technologists, and nurse practitioners.

Online credential programs in the health field are evolving as well. For example, the American Health Information Management Association (AHIMA), which has long offered tested certifications in health information fields, is now offering a certificate for professionals in health informatics.[102] This reflects the advent of big data and analytics for health to enable better analysis, diagnostics, and outcomes. The online classes are self-paced to fit readily into student schedules and learning patterns. The credentials AHIMA (and other organizations) now offer enable creating what amounts to a new and much-needed allied health profession, with certified informatics professions serving a new role on medical teams.

The programs noted in the preceding discussion amount to only a tiny fraction of the occupational skill offerings from the more than 334,000 credential and degree providers. The challenge in this field, as noted, is to navigate through the system. The availability of content, of course, does not solve the content-delivery problem. While we seem to be developing a Tower of Babel of occupational skill content, corresponding reforms in institutions to deliver it have not caught up.

ORGANIZATIONAL LEARNING

Organizational learning, which is akin to teamwork but examines the organizational level above work teams, is another occupational skill that requires some attention. Linda Argote, a professor at Carnegie Mellon University who specializes in industrial and organizational psychology, has studied extensively not just how individuals learn, but also how organizations learn.[a]

Organizational learning can have a dramatic effect on cutting production and service costs and improving quality and timeliness—which makes it an important issue for businesses. Organizations vary widely in their learning rates: some learn quickly, significantly improving their productivity, while others learn more slowly. Different teams and parts of an organization can vary in their learning speed.

Argote has identified four factors that affect rates of organizational learning:

- *Individual training skills*, which can affect the combined learning of the group
- *Developing transactive memory*—that is, identifying who on a team knows how to perform the needed tasks, which allows both specialization and sharing of know-how
- *Using technology effectively*, since new technologies can speed progress on the production learning curve
- *Knowledge transfer*, through which one part or team in a company learns from another

This points to the importance for employers to consider skill development for employee teams and groups, not just individual employees, to create organizational learning.

[a]Linda Argote, Presentation, National Academy of Engineering Workshop, "Preparing the Engineering and Technical Workforce for Adaptability and Resilience to Change," November 3, 2017; National Academy of Engineering, *Adaptability of the US Engineering and Technical Workforce* (Washington, DC: National Academies of Sciences, 2018), 29–31; Linda Argote, *Organizational Learning, Creating, Retaining and Transferring Knowledge*, 2nd edition (New York: Springer, 2013).

If we are to change our workforce education system, it will be critical, of course, to get the content right. Three areas are priorities: foundational academic skills, personal and interpersonal skills, and occupational skills. The development of competency-based learning has a lot to offer. This approach divides an education area into more bite-sized, manageable pieces that can be assessed. The pieces complement each other, and when combined they enable mastery of the group of topics that represent the overall field.

The emergence of certificates and credentials fits this competency-based approach. There are now shorter education programs that better fit the time available to adults already in the workforce, who can't leave their jobs to seek a traditional degree (for whatever reasons) but need to find more promising career opportunities. New online delivery tools can be tailored to fit competency-based approaches.

Foundational academic skills are being addressed through a host of programs, and some are working well. Employers are increasingly emphasizing the importance of soft personal and interpersonal skills—which create challenges because not enough progress has been made in developing tests that show proficiency, and absent validated tests it is difficult to design an appropriate training program to convey a skill. Occupational skills represent a more established territory: because so much of workforce education is learning by doing, we can better validate training to work. The complication is that we have a plethora of content providers providing a relentlessly growing level of content, both in classes and online. We're missing a navigation system to tie the right content to individual student and employee needs (as chapter 6 discusses), and we still haven't developed the skill content for a new range of technologies that will be entering the workplace, in both production and services occupations. Finally, we need better *content-delivery* mechanisms. That is the problem confronted in the next two chapters.

10 THE APPRENTICESHIP MODEL

Apprenticeships historically have aimed at youth and new entrants to the workforce. Germany, Switzerland, and Austria run famous, multiyear apprentice programs that serve the majority of their workforce sectors and have built an envied infrastructure of skilled talent that undergirds strong manufacturing and other industries. The United States lacks this system.

Once upon a time, flagship employers in the United States hosted strong apprenticeship and incumbent employee education programs. For example, back in 1919, what became known as the Flint Institute of Technology in Flint, Michigan, was organized to teach automotive industry skills. General Motors took it over in 1926, and it became the General Motors Institute (GMI)—sometimes called the West Point of the automobile industry. GMI focused on a unique co-op model combining education and work pioneered at the University of Cincinnati in 1907. Work and school were mixed in six-week segments, with a GM division sponsoring each student and subsidizing the tuition. General Electric meanwhile had a Shop Apprenticeship System for Boys at its Schenectady, New York, production center. A 1917 pamphlet detailed the multiyear coursework for training machinists, milling cutters, and boring millers; the curriculum went from arithmetic in the first year to graphs, radicals, quadratics, and graphing in the fourth year.[1] Overall, GE's was a model apprenticeship program.[2]

In 1982, with competition in the automotive sector intensifying as Japan introduced a quality production model its US competitors hadn't mastered, General Motors severed its relations with GMI. It became a private college with engineering programs named Kettering University, after a noted former GM research head.[3] At its height, GE employed thirty thousand in Schenectady; in 2016, it employed four thousand there, primarily in healthcare and retail work. One former manufacturing site had become a casino.[4] The massive employment drop led to the end of the manufacturing apprenticeship program; there wasn't a production worker base to support it.

Newport News Shipbuilding in Virginia has one of the only great industrial apprenticeship programs still remaining.[5] The Apprentice School, founded in 1919, continues to thrive, with 725 students in multiyear programs in a wide range of occupational specialties, with sixteen academic instructors and over fifty craft instructors. It is now tied to the area community college, offering associate degrees and lifelong learning on a campus adjacent to the shipyard. It represents a model that has been largely lost.

According to US Labor Department estimates, there were only 585,000 registered apprentices in a range of fields in the United States in 2018, through programs run by labor unions or individual companies.[6] The number represents only a modest rise from the 490,000 apprentices in the early 2000s. And that's in an economy with more than 150 million jobs: the apprenticeships are less than 0.4 percent of the total US workforce.[7] Contrast that with Germany, which has 1.5 million apprentices across all sectors in a workforce of forty-four million, including in manufacturing.

One reason for the paucity of US apprenticeships, some employers argue, is clearly related to regulation. The Registered Apprenticeship Program run through the Department of Labor sets detailed standards for employers that are part of it, including quality requirements and wage progressions as apprentices become more skilled.[8] It has been dominated by skilled construction trades, where a long history of construction unions has helped sustain it. But unions have been in sharp decline in the US private sector, and so they can play only a limited role in expanding apprenticeships.

Another reason is that US labor markets are very decentralized, with relatively few regulations and safety net features compared to other developed nations.[9] Because apprenticeship and formal training programs are often viewed as requiring some regulatory framework to provide assurances to participants, this practice of limited regulation may be another factor, despite employer views. Also, companies often aren't willing to invest in worker skills because competitor companies can poach these trained employees, avoiding their own workforce training investments. This prevents the first company from recapturing its training investment, discouraging it from investing in the first place.[10] If employers in a region cooperate and share an apprenticeship program—if they all jump into the swimming pool together—this creates peer pressure that can offset the poaching problem. But a tradition of collaboration between employers is not well established in the United States. Exacerbating the problem, federal funding for employment training has fallen by half as a share of GDP since the mid-1980s.[11]

National data on apprenticeship programs are limited. Some studies, however, show statistically quite significant gains for apprentices' earnings, exceeding other options, and some also indicate significant benefits to companies.[12]

To the extent it has them, however, US apprenticeships involve adults, not youth, and typically require three to four years of work-based learning and classroom teaching.[13] Only a few states have youth apprenticeships: for instance, school systems in Georgia participate in apprenticeships involving more than 6,700 students; Wisconsin high school students can spend one or two years in an apprenticeship beginning in their junior year; and Charleston, South Carolina, has an interesting youth apprenticeship program detailed later in this chapter.

But apprenticeships for *youth* are critically important, especially given the challenges of transitioning American youth into productive work.

YOUTH EMPLOYMENT AND UNEMPLOYMENT

The United States has long had a problem with a high youth unemployment rate, which is a signal of a major underlying problem. During the Great Recession and its early years of recovery, the youth unemployment rate exacerbated the social disruption of the period, scarring that generation. In 2007, youth unemployment was at 13 percent; by 2010 it reached just under 21 percent,[14] with many remaining unemployed after more than a year of searching for jobs. Even with the gradual recovery, this number (for those aged sixteen to twenty-four actively looking for work and not in school) was still at 9.2 percent in July 2018.[15] Unemployment was higher among young men (9.8 percent) compared to women (8.6 percent), and higher among African Americans (16.5 percent) and Hispanics (10.8 percent) compared to young whites (7.6 percent). These rates compare to an overall US unemployment rate of 3.9 percent at that time.

Germany, by contrast, had a youth unemployment rate of 6.3 percent in July 2018.[16] We will return to Germany as an example later in this chapter.

Education and the Youth Labor Market

A 2018 report from the Pathways to Prosperity Project provides some insight into the youth labor market.[17] It reveals that between 2000 and 2010, there was an uptick in high school graduation rates in the United States overall, from 77 percent to 84 percent, with corresponding increases for whites, Blacks, and Hispanics. But the United States—the inventor of mass higher education and long the leader—is only eleventh among developed (OECD) nations in degree attainment among young adults, and the problems are exacerbated the lower on the economic ladder a student's family may be (see chapter 7 for a discussion of college completion rates).

Projections show that 35 percent of the US workforce will have a bachelor's degree or higher in 2020; 30 percent will have an associate degree *or* a postsecondary certificate; and 35 percent will have a high school diploma or less. A very large number of students lack any postsecondary education, despite its growing importance in obtaining solid jobs. But occupations, not just degrees, matter; some 43 percent of young workers with certificates and licenses earn more than those with associate degrees; some 27 percent of young workers with certificates and licenses earn more than those with bachelor's degrees; and 31 percent of young workers with an associate degree earn more than those with bachelor's degrees. The message here is that young people who get licenses and certificates for particular technical skills, primarily through community colleges, can still do well—even compared to better-educated peers.

Half of all STEM jobs in the "hidden STEM economy" (see chapter 2) are available to workers without four-year college degrees, and they pay good wages. This means there are routes to well-paying jobs for those not on a four-year college degree path.[18] But technically skilled young people without four-year college degrees need to be better connected to these quality jobs. What about the significant number of young people outside the postsecondary education system?

A "college for all" goal seems doomed to failure.[19] Instead, a much stronger focus on career-oriented programs that lead to occupational credentials for middle-income jobs appears to be required. Unfortunately, the completion rate for career technical education programs is low.[20] Could apprenticeships, which involve active employment with education, be part of turning that around?

FEDERAL SUPPORT FOR APPRENTICESHIP PROGRAMS

Both the Obama and Trump administrations have supported apprenticeship programs. In October 2014, under the Obama administration, the Advanced Manufacturing Partnership (AMP), a group of leading companies and technical universities, issued recommendations for building the skilled production workforce needed for advanced manufacturing, including a new apprenticeship approach.[21] Specifically, the AMP 2.0 report proposed a new model through a coalition of companies partnered with community colleges and labor market intermediaries,[22] and AMP participants developed a pilot project led by three major production companies and two community colleges to develop a workable, validated, and replicable model for workforce education shared between companies and community colleges that could be implemented on a more widespread basis. It required completion of an associate degree at a connected community college and parallel completion of a Department of Labor skill certification in a two-year program. The pilot also included a *playbook*—a detailed how-to instruction manual for employers and colleges on how to implement and develop this approach.[23]

AMP also promoted the Live, Work, Earn model developed by a statewide consortium of Minnesota community colleges, employment centers, and more than twenty-five manufacturers, to match training with available jobs.[24] The model included "employer-driven competency-based apprenticeships, curricula alignment with national [skills] credentialing systems and bridging modules for veterans and other underrepresented populations."[25] AMP thought the model could be developed nationwide and build on and coordinate with existing union apprenticeship programs.

Apprenticeship, as AMP 2.0 understood, was an ambitious approach in the United States, but it argued that the skills required for advanced manufacturing would encourage employers increasingly to turn to it. So it worked to develop model approaches, shared between community colleges (with public investments) and employers. Could the 250,000 small manufacturing firms participate? Did they have the financial resources? AMP leaders saw that US implementation of apprenticeships at a larger scale would require regional supply chains of small and large firms, including competitors, to engage together along with publicly supported community colleges, to avoid labor market disincentives for training. It would initially be particularly difficult because many small employers are not prepared to manage the additional costs of training. There could also be a major *state role* in encouraging and enabling the apprenticeship model. State programs could be tailored regionally within the state to particular company and sector needs.

AMP 2.0 also called for investment and implementation of *nationally recognized, portable, and stackable skill certifications* that employers can use in hiring and promotion decisions, to complement apprenticeships.[26] Such a system could be very useful in enabling employee mobility by providing transferable credentials. This could also encourage training programs because recognized credentials would more clearly signal training's value and so help employers and employees alike in meeting skill needs. They could raise wages for skills, reduce hiring costs, enable a more flexible labor market through increased worker mobility, and encourage a better-trained and higher-quality workforce.

As a model, AMP considered efforts by the Manufacturing Skill Standards Council to develop new credentialing programs for manufacturing, including identifying key work-based learning elements within different skills. The AMP 2.0 report stated that successful credentialing approaches should ensure easy entrance, exit, and reentry throughout a manufacturing career; certificate training that is organized in modules and can be acquired over time and stacked to help working adults keep building their skills; and credentials aligned with community college for-credit education programs and correspondingly with education grant programs (such as Pell and Workforce Investment Act programs).[27] AMP recommended systematic efforts to increase awareness among employers and in education institutions of credentialing systems, demonstrate successful credentialing programs based on supporting evidence and data, and provide funding to support credentialing programs to get over roadblocks to adoption in statewide systems.[28]

The report also called for *career pathways*, a workforce development approach aimed at transitioning workers from education programs into the workforce and offering services that tie academic competency and credentials to technical skills, particularly those in increasing demand. It requires partnerships between community colleges, secondary schools, workforce and economic development agencies, and employers and labor organizations. There are already programs working on this. (Florida's FLATE program, discussed in chapter 1, has had a particularly noted program that forms these partnerships.[29])

Linking community colleges to teaching skills needed by regional employers is particularly important, although coordination is needed at all education levels. The report noted a particular opportunity to create online programs to help in these career pathways, including making them eligible to receive federal support through federal job training programs.

Following on the efforts of the Obama administration, the subsequent Trump administration also strongly backed apprenticeships. A presidential executive order established a task force of industry and labor leaders to advise the secretaries of the Labor and Education Departments; the task force met beginning in November 2017, issuing a report in May 2018.[30]

The task force found that "apprenticeship programs, when implemented effectively, provide workers with a career path featuring paid on-the-job training, skills development, and mentorship, while at the same time providing employers with a steady source of highly trained and productive workers. These programs have the potential to grow into a critical and successful component of America's workforce strategy, but are currently underutilized."[31] Meanwhile, though, the report continued, taking a swipe at colleges and universities, "the American higher education system is churning out a pool of in-debt job seekers who are not equipped to meet the skills needs of many employers in the modern American economy."

The task force's various subcommittees made several specific recommendations:

- The *Education and Credentialing* subcommittee recommended new Industry-Recognized Apprenticeship programs built onto "traditional work-and-learn models to achieve higher levels of employer engagement and better outcomes" and to "include work-based learning and performance assessments."[32] It also called for nationally recognized and portable "standards-based, industry-recognized credentials," to be developed and disseminated by the public and private sector partners implementing the programs. The federal agencies involved were asked to make technical instruction affordable for apprentices and, in partnership with employers, to provide resources for certifying organizations, institutions of higher education, and other participating education providers.
- The *Attracting Business to Apprenticeship* subcommittee recommended updating federal funding criteria, streamlining state grant access, and exploring sector-led financial options.[33] It asked the Department of Labor to identify existing skills shortages and quantify the benefits of apprenticeships in meeting labor market challenges, and also to compile apprenticeship information in one centralized website.
- The *Expanding Access, Equity, and Career Awareness* subcommittee proposed that federal agencies should fund a public outreach campaign for apprenticeships and actively promote an "earn-and-learn" model for employers and apprentices.[34] Clearer guidelines and funding from the Labor Department were recommended for regional organizing efforts and for certifiers and sponsors to form outreach strategies. The Department of Labor was also asked to make changes to its existing Registered Apprenticeship system.
- The *Administrative and Regulatory Strategies to Expand Apprenticeship* subcommittee recommended a pilot project in an industry without well-established Department of Labor Registered Apprenticeship programs (i.e., outside the construction sector);[35] an education focus on mastery and competency, not simply seat-time or training hours, with implementation guidelines that spelled out corresponding quality standards; and that programs not be required to follow specific wage-progression rules but instead make clear to apprentices at the outset what wages they

will be paid and when their wages will increase.[36] It also identified additional regulatory changes that required attention for apprenticeships to expand.

The task force argued that implementing its recommendations could "begin to break down the silos that currently exist between traditional education and workforce learning" through a major expansion of apprenticeship programs.[37]

Following up on the task force proposals, the Labor Department issued regulations in 2020 to allow a new form of apprenticeship, supplementing its registered apprenticeship program and aimed at industries such as healthcare that haven't used apprenticeships.[38] Called Industry-Recognized Apprenticeship Programs (IRAPs), it allows third-party groups such as community colleges, trade associations, and nonprofits to develop apprenticeships in their own industries that include paid work, an industry-recognized credential, and credit for competency-based education. The Labor Department delegates oversight of quality to third parties called standards recognition entities. The changes were supported by community colleges, which hope to use them in cooperation with employers, but were opposed by labor unions, which argued they dropped needed worker and quality protections.

As we consider these and other recommendations for the United States, it is important to put them into the context of what may be the most successful national apprenticeship model in the world—the German one.

THE GERMAN APPRENTICESHIP MODEL

Vocational education and training are the norm in northern and central Europe. It supports young people in the shift from adolescence to productive work and adulthood. Between 40 and 70 percent of young people in Austria, Denmark, Finland, Germany, the Netherlands, Norway, and Switzerland opt after grades nine or ten for educational programs that typically combine classroom and workplace learning over the following three years, culminating in a diploma or certificate.[39]

The German apprenticeship model has long been the gold standard for workforce education, so any evaluation of apprenticeship models must consider it. German-based firms doing business in the United States[40] have identified job skills as a key to their future success here, and the German embassy in the United States has begun its own skills initiative to share German best practices in workforce development with US employers.[41] German-American Chambers of Commerce in a number of regions have been making a similar effort.[42]

The German apprenticeship program has several key characteristics:[43]

- *Skill development,* primarily through firm-based training complemented by mandatory school-based education
- *Strong reliance on the private sector,* with widespread firm-based participation (even though participation is not compulsory) and financing
- *Collective approach,* with firms training to standards that are set jointly by firms, educators, government, and unions, and with firms held accountable for the quality of their training based on their apprentice's exam performance

The program ensures a low level of youth unemployment, and enjoys support from political parties across the political spectrum. And the program remains attractive to Germany's young people. Although there has been a modest shift to more university education, there is now a popular hybrid approach of a university degree from Germany's technical colleges and work-based certification, so apprenticeships are extending to postsecondary education as well as secondary.

A 2015 Brookings study argued that Germany's apprenticeships are a significant contributor to its innovation in manufacturing. Three statistical comparisons were particularly telling: the United States that year ran a $668 billion trade deficit in goods, while Germany ran a $425 billion surplus; the US youth unemployment rate was nearly twice Germany's; and the OECD's ranking of the share of graduates in STEM fields in thirty-six developed nations ranked Germany third and the United States thirty-third.[44] The Brookings researchers set out three benchmarks to guide US stakeholders if they were to consider adapting and using the German apprenticeship program:

- Regional collaborations among public, private, and civic actors
- Institutional intermediaries that can address market and coordination failures
- Incentives to support small and medium-sized firms[45]

The Brookings study noted further that the national credentialing system that accompanies the German apprenticeship program and is frequently updated to reflect occupation changes provides both transparency and certainty for both employers and graduates. Each element achieves potential benefits for "students, who have reasonable confidence that their education investment will be recognized and rewarded by employers; educators, who better ensure that the education they are providing is economically relevant; and employers, who more clearly understand how prospective employees' education, competencies, and skills match the needs of their open positions."[46]

Of course, a centralized skills certification system may have limits. It can be inflexible and create barriers to entry. To offset these potential problems, pathways have been created that can lead workers to obtain other occupational credentials. However, the German system is limited in its ability to provide continuing and lifelong education because it is aimed at new entrant workers. It is also, therefore, difficult to switch occupational fields. Overall, however, the system has created a highly skilled workforce that is a significant enhancement for its industrial leadership. This strong base of skilled technical workers particularly helps Germany's highly respected *Mittelstand* of small and midsize firms keep current with productivity and technology advances. Of course, the German system extends to many occupational areas beyond manufacturing, with comparable benefits.

Could the German apprenticeship system transfer to the United States? The German secondary and postsecondary education system is clearly very different, and there are important economic differences between the two countries. It should come as no surprise, therefore, that there are opposing views about the answer to this question. Some researchers argue that Germany's quite different social, educational, economic, and cultural attitudes mean its apprenticeship model simply will simply not fit US circumstances.[47] The different varieties of capitalism between the two countries are a problem. The liberal market economy in the United States is oriented to technology breakthroughs and has limited state intervention and limited protections for workers, whereas Germany has a coordinated market economy with negotiated collaborations among government, labor, and employers oriented toward more incremental advances, particularly in manufacturing. The close collaboration in a well-established system among companies, chambers of commerce, unions, and state and federal government that is embedded in the German economic system and at the heart of its dual education and apprenticeship system simply does not exist in the United States. The stakeholder collaboration that is foundational to German apprenticeships is missing in the United States, as is an underlying social commitment to the workforce.

On top of that, Germany's heavily tracked education system locks students into permanent employment paths and class status by ages ten to twelve. That tracking guarantees the pool of apprentices and thus is also foundational. In contrast, the US system has more limited tracking and offers students a chance to redirect their employment options at a number of stages. Without the tracking, goes the argument, the necessary committed labor pool for an apprentice system cannot be assured. Furthermore, German workers, used to tracking, are much more accepting of careers with single firms, enabling the costs of apprenticeships to be accepted by firms, while workers in the United States switch jobs and even careers much more frequently, complicating the apprenticeship economic equation for employers.

An opposing argument acknowledges that the German system cannot be exported wholesale to other nations because the underlying social systems will be different, but contends that essential components can be adapted.[48] Many core features of Germany's dual education system could apply to any successful education program anywhere: broad objectives that achieve a mix of social, economic, and individual goals, including producing skilled workers with flexible qualifications ready to work in their selected field; using a combination of classroom and on-the-job training; partnership across government and business, jointly funded; quality standards and qualifications for teachers and trainers; a balance between standardization and flexibility reflected in an established program design; and ensuring acceptance of respect for the program by businesses, educators, and the area's society. Looked at this way, the German apprenticeship system appears more adaptable.

Germany certainly offers some lessons. The country's dual education and apprenticeship program has been able to solve problems that remain unsolved in the United States. It has created a direct connection between secondary education and good-paying, quality jobs, largely avoiding the social disruption from a high youth unemployment rate. Germany has also obtained economic benefits, particularly for its strong manufacturing sector, from the productivity gains available from a skilled technical workforce; workforce productivity gains have tended to be ignored in US company workforce policies.

The German model requires close collaboration among employers, educators, and state and federal governments. If education and work opportunities are to be better connected in the United States, these stakeholders—who have considerably less history of working together—would need to engage in collaboration that seems a prerequisite. Joint funding participation by these actors also seems necessary. The dual education, work and learn combination appears central and ensures a practical focus. Program certification and standards—including quality standards for teachers and trainers and for student assessment—likewise seem critical if a program is to meet employer needs. These basic lessons from the German model appear transportable.

Germany's emerging dual study program combining apprenticeships and its applied technical universities offers an additional interesting model.

APPRENTICESHIPS IN GREAT BRITAIN

The United Kingdom offers additional lessons for scaling-up US apprenticeships. Like many economies, Britain faces shortages in skilled technicians, especially in emerging industries. The biotech sector, for example, has many young firms that need small talent pools, but firms in the sector have reported losing orders because of a lack of skilled technicians. They have attempted to fill the gap by using college science graduates in technician roles, but these graduates are "overqualified and underskilled"; they have difficulty applying their theoretical knowledge (such as in cell biology) to practical needs (such as cell cultivation), and were never taught technical skills. Too often, they have a "graduate-level attitude"; they want "do science," not highly skilled but more routine work, and lack the perspective to be craftsmen.[49]

Apprenticeship training could fill this gap. Such programs, long-established in Britain's manufacturing sector, typically have involved a day or two a week of off-the-job education coupled with on-the-job training. Britain has been making a major effort to expand its apprenticeship programs, shifting more control to companies by limiting government-imposed standards and requirements, to enable more rapid expansion. In recent years, formal certifications for apprenticeships have been established in new fields, and they've been found to work for information technology skills, manufacturing skills, and lab technicians.

However, Britain is now dropping its apprenticeship program in retail and comparable services areas, which has not worked well. For example, a nine-month certificate in customer service tried to serve firms ranging from Harrods, a high-end department store, to small convenience stores with very different cultures and needs. It backfired.

Apprentices in front-line retail too often found their training a waste of time; there wasn't enough difference between skilled and unskilled workers in this sector to justify the time investment in an apprentice program. Successful apprenticeship programs offer a *layered* pathway to continuing success: skill acquisition is rewarded with higher pay and status as a worker advances. These kinds of continuing skill pathways exist in manufacturing, for example. However, in retail there wasn't really much of a pathway to advancement, with corresponding status and pay rewards for new layers of skills; there were only basic skills that in many cases required limited expertise. There is limited justification for an apprenticeship program that fails to offer a clear pathway to continuing employment advances.[50]

Retail, hospitality, and some other service-sector apprenticeships may offer limited prospects for advancement, with many positions on the bottom but few jobs at higher levels and few pathways up. Ways need to be found to professionalize apprenticeship jobs and increase their status; apprenticeships for everything is likely not the answer. If American apprenticeship programs grow, they should consider carefully what occupational fields should be included, and this lesson from the UK could be useful.

The 2012 Richard Report[51] to the UK Department for Business, Innovation, and Skills and the Department for Education took a hard look at refining Britain's apprenticeship program and made several recommendations:

- Apprenticeships should be targeted at those who are new to jobs or at roles that require sustained and substantial training.
- The training program should focus on apprenticeship outcomes—that is, what apprentices can do when they complete their training. Trusted, independent assessment is key to an outcome focus.
- Apprenticeship training should be organized around recognized and established industry standards for skills.
- All apprentices should reach a sound level in communication and math skills before they can complete their apprenticeship.
- Government funding must create the right incentives for employers and educators to participate in apprenticeship training. The bulk of the investment in apprenticeship training should lie with the employer.
- Greater diversity and innovation in training is needed, with employers and the government safeguarding quality.

When the report was released, its author had this to say:

> We need to make sure that apprenticeships are the success story they deserve to be. With the myriad of learning experiences which are currently labeled as apprenticeships, we risk losing sight of the core features of what makes apprenticeships work, so my conclusion is that we need to look again at what it means to be an apprentice and what it means to offer an apprenticeship as an employer. Apprenticeships need to be high-quality training with serious kudos and tangible value both to the apprentice and the employer. I want to hear about an 18-year-old who looked at their options and turned down a place at Oxbridge to take up an apprenticeship if that is the right path for them. And I want to hear that their parents were thrilled.[52]

AMERICAN EXPERIMENTS WITH VOCATIONAL EDUCATION

In the United States, racial and ethnic minorities and lower-income students once tended to be tracked into vocational education, as noted in chapter 3, while the track to college was for middle-class and upper-middle-class students. But in the aftermath of the civil rights movement of the 1960s, some of the attention to racial discrimination focused on the secondary education system and the heavy use of tracking in American high schools. Much of the vocational track was shut down, and most high school students were pushed onto a college pathway. But by the 1970s, that wasn't working, and college graduation rates were stagnating.

Today, a number of education reformers are calling for a departure from the single pathway of college education in favor of developing and delineating multiple paths that would give youth a better-connected route from school into solid jobs and careers. Employers would need to play a greatly expanded role supporting these new paths.

The Pathways to Prosperity Project identified the elements of a new system.[53] First, pathways to all major occupations would be clearly delineated at the outset of high school so that students and families could see what courses and experiences would help them gain access to their sought-after fields. This would maintain a unique and positive feature of the US education system: keeping a number of doors open, and being forgiving, so that students can keep trying even if they want to change their minds and shift to different career options.

Second, relevant work experience would be built into the new system. A workplace is the best place to experiment with career choices and is the best place to learn and practice the twenty-first-century skills that will be vital to success in the emerging economy. Learning that is connected to work can also be critical in engaging students who are frustrated or bored with traditional high school.

Third, new learning systems to help teach new technology skills, tied to the proper foundational skills, would be part of a new system—replacing the many old vocational education programs that were largely dumping grounds for students who couldn't cope with the college-preparation route.

Fourth, improved career counseling would be required. The current system in both secondary schools and higher education is inadequate, and many young people are adrift. Pathways to Prosperity estimates that the average ratio of students to counselors in middle and high schools is nearly five hundred to one, creating a workload under continuous strain.[54] Many counselors must focus on students' more immediate personal, psychological, and social problems, and lack expertise in quality career advising. The broken labor market information system discussed in chapter 6 only exacerbates the problems. Overall, students would need individualized plans that include career objectives, a program of study, degree and/or certificate objectives, and work-linked learning experiences.

A fifth point—in addition to those raised by Pathways to Prosperity—is the need for "good governance" policies at the state or federal level to ensure that apprenticeships are not synonymous with cheap labor.[55] Legislation can provide guideposts for setting up high-quality apprenticeship systems within a legal framework that establishes clear rights and responsibilities of the apprenticeship partners and protections for apprentices themselves, while leaving the content, testing, and certification to agreements between employers and their apprentices or their representatives. The Labor Department's registered apprenticeship system helps assure this.

There are numerous experiments now underway in the United States on new workforce education systems for young people that fit within the Pathways to Prosperity concepts of creating multiple pathways from high school to work and careers. For instance, Washington State's Integrated Basic Education and Skills Training (I-BEST) program (detailed in chapter 9) integrates remedial English and math skills training into college-level technology education programs in fields ranging from auto repair to nursing using a dual-instructor approach.[56] Project Lead the Way promotes STEM education through structured programs and rigorous curriculum provided to thousands of high schools in all fifty states through a four-year sequence of courses.[57] The Career Academy, which began in Philadelphia in 1969, now has seven thousand academies (California alone has more than five hundred) that reach one million high school students using a "school within a school" approach.[58] The Linked Learning Initiative emphasizes career technical education and work-based learning with support systems; it operates in more than one hundred school districts with learning certifications and analytics to provide pathway data to educators to raise graduation rates, increase college enrollments for low-income students, and enable them to earn more college-relevant high school credits.[59]

Pathways to Prosperity itself, supported by the Harvard Graduate School of Education and Jobs for the Future, is now connected to more than twelve states providing a working framework for its approach.[60] The Tennessee program in particular is worth exploring in some detail.

Tennessee Pathways

The Pathways to Prosperity program in Tennessee provides an interesting example of an energized state program attempting to merge education and work.[61] Two governors from different political parties drove significant education system reforms, primarily in response to requests from employers for more skilled and better-trained workers. The state's political, business, and education leaders saw a need to better connect high school students to both postsecondary learning and employer needs. They also sought to make it easier for students to find efficient routes to good careers. The state adopted a slogan, Drive to 55, indicating the goal to increase the percentage of state students with postsecondary degrees or certificates.

The state became an early adherent to the Pathways to Prosperity approach, adopting Tennessee Pathways statewide to give students, beginning in high school, access to solid academic and career pathways matched to local and state economic and labor market needs. Students take academic- and career-focused courses in high school and participate in work-based learning experiences that include internships and job shadowing at companies, which smooth transitions to both college education and the workforce. The overall aim is to support more high-wage, high-skill jobs.

In the current, disconnected national system, students complete high school and college without actual workforce skills and career information. But apprenticeships can be complex and expensive for employers, so Tennessee is attempting a kind of *apprenticeship lite*.[62] The state is building an alternate, more connected approach. Programs at high schools and the state's community and technical colleges and four-year universities are articulated and aligned so students can acquire credit for courses taken and degrees earned across the system. To match local labor market needs, employers contribute work-based learning opportunities and curriculum support. Intermediary organizations, such as chambers of commerce, link employers and education institutions. There is career information and awareness building early on for students. The commitment of state leaders is reflected in a positive policy environment.

To help enable these connections, the state in 2014 created the Tennessee Promise Scholarship program, thorough which the state funds students with the "last dollars" for tuition costs not covered through state and federal scholarship and grant programs. Since then, some sixteen other states have formed similar programs.[63] The state supplemented this program with Tennessee Reconnect, aimed at incumbent workers without degrees and giving them the opportunity to attend the state's community and technical colleges tuition-free. The state has also integrated the efforts of its Departments of Education, Labor, and Economic and Community Development, along with its college and university governing agencies and the Business Roundtable.

An important part of Tennessee's approach is its statewide network of twenty-seven colleges of applied technology, discussed in chapter 9, which provide technical training leading to certificates and diplomas in more than fifty occupational fields.[64] These centers have achieved a graduation rate exceeding 75 percent, more than three times the rate of the state's separate community college system.

What does this program look like on the ground? In Rutherford County, a fast-growing, urbanizing county near Nashville, the area chamber of commerce was a key convener in creating five industry councils behind Rutherford Works. By 2017, dozens of employers were participating in the programs, which included paid four-week summer internships for high school students, a hiring fair for high school seniors, a career awareness fair for eighth graders, an externship for CTE teachers with local employers, and a program in which students received a notation on their high school diplomas of their level of career readiness. In 2019, there were forty-three students from the county in four-day-a-week internships, as well as a standard CTE program in mechatronics across all county high schools that connects to follow-on two- and four-year college programs.[65]

In a rural four-county area known as the Highlands in the Upper Cumberland region, the area chamber of commerce again provided leadership. In 2017, the area's Highlands Economic Partnership programs included company tours, a twelfth-grade job fair, an externship for teachers, and a "work-based learning" capstone program that allowed high school students to intern at an employer for four days per week, 1.5 hours per day, for a semester.

These Tennessee career pathways programs were delivered across networks of educators and employers with area chambers of commerce programs (Rutherford Works and the Highlands Economic Partnership) working as intermediaries sitting at the center. The chambers created the communication space for educators and employers, including in different industries. They also provided resources that reduced the participation burden of both schools and employers.[66]

The results coming out of Tennessee's overall program, reported in 2017, are noteworthy:[67]

- The percentage of high schools offering dual-enrollment programs to students, wherein they can enroll in both high school and community college courses, was 77 percent.
- Dual-enrollment participation was significant: more than 40 percent of 2015 Tennessee graduates were enrolled in one of eight early

postsecondary opportunities, and nearly 20 percent of these were in dual-enrollment courses.

- Almost 50 percent of 2016 high school graduates—some forty thousand students—were career technical education concentrators (taking three or more courses in a career cluster).
- CTE teachers reported that 2,116 Tennessee students in the state's high schools (7 percent of the total) earned an industry certification.
- Some 83 percent of Tennessee high school students had access in 2016 to *high-priority career clusters* (in advanced manufacturing, health care, and IT), and eight hundred students completed work-based capstone concentrations in these clusters.
- Pilot projects on work-based learning were underway, with 3,480 students seeking matches with 1,600 employers.

AMERICAN EXPERIMENTS WITH APPRENTICESHIPS

There are also examples of *apprenticeship programs* evolving at the state level in different parts of the country.

Kentucky Federation for Advanced Manufacturing Education

The automotive industry constitutes the largest sector in Kentucky's manufacturing economy, employing sixty-five thousand workers at more than four hundred plants. The state is home to Toyota's largest plant worldwide, the Georgetown plant, with seven thousand workers manufacturing some of the company's top car lines.

Facing an aging workforce and pending skilled worker retirements, Toyota partnered in 2009 with Bluegrass Community and Technical College (BCTC) in the Lexington area to create the Advanced Manufacturing Technician (AMT) program, which offers a multidisciplinary associate degree focused on electricity, fluid power, mechanics, and fabrication. The program, which has significantly strengthened the supply of young manufacturing workers in the area, has expanded to more than fifteen companies and now has a regional consortium with some two hundred companies—the Kentucky Federation of Advanced Manufacturing Education (KY FAME).[68]

The AMT and FAME programs resemble the German approach to dual education.[69] Participating companies recruit from a pool of high school students who must meet significant threshold requirements to qualify, including graduating from a high school that has adopted Project Lead the Way STEM education, having an ACT score of twenty-five, and achieving a 3.0

grade point average (GPA). They then participate in a two-year apprenticeship at Toyota for three days a week, earning from twelve to sixteen dollars an hour, and take classes two days a week at BCTC. Toyota has even built a BCTC campus on its site that affords students experience with robotics, computers, and advanced equipment, and BCTC has also built a new advanced manufacturing training center at another campus. AMT program graduates can continue into four-year engineering programs at Northwood University and the University of Kentucky.

KY FAME, which began with fifteen students, was employer-generated but closely allied with a technical college. Toyota next helped organize other regional manufacturers with similar talent needs, including those in its supply chain, growing the program from four companies. KY FAME has since grown significantly to six regions in the state. As of 2017, 232 students had earned AMT degrees, 650 students were enrolled in FAME programs that fall, and the graduation rate that year was 89 percent.[70]

Michigan Advanced Technician Training Program

Michigan, with its automotive manufacturing sector hit hard, had a particularly disastrous Great Recession. Since then, the state's recovery has been one the nation's strongest. Nevertheless, like other areas, Michigan has an aging workforce and needs younger workers in its manufacturing system. Skills in mechatronics, a design process that requires mechanical engineering, electronics, and computer science, are a particular need.

After a trade mission visit to Germany, Michigan's then governor concluded that Germany's dual-education apprenticeship model could assist in meeting the state's manufacturing skill needs. He tasked the Michigan Economic Development Corporation (MEDC) to solve the collective action problems the pilot workforce development efforts face. Michigan community colleges had to be convinced they could enroll at least fifteen students needed to make a capital-intensive mechatronics program cost-effective; employers had to be convinced the program would be worth the investment of some $20,000 annually to cover apprentices' tuition and wages; and students and parents, with the memory of the state's terrible job losses in the Great Recession still fresh, needed to be convinced that a manufacturing training program was a sound path to a well-paid career with advancement opportunities.[71]

In 2013, MEDC launched the Michigan Advanced Technician Training Program (MAT^2), along with Henry Ford Community College and Oakland Community College and eleven southeast Michigan manufacturers. The first cohort of thirty-one students focused only on mechatronics, but by the beginning of 2015 MAT^2 had expanded to include twenty-nine employers, ninety-eight students, and four community colleges, and also offered programs in CNC machining.[72] The program is tuition-free for students, who also earn wages, an associate degree, and a national Department of Labor credential, as well as an internationally recognized German industry credential. Over a three-year period, employers must invest a total of $68,040: $20,000 to support the student's community college tuition; a school stipend of $14,400 ($200/week); and wages that grow from ten to thirteen dollars an hour—totaling $34,080 over the three years.[73]

Each community college program costs about $300,000 to launch. MAT^2 has an annual budget of $1 million supported by the state of Michigan.[74] MEDC, a quasi-public agency, has been the coordinating body during the program's ramp up, with support from an advisory committee that includes representatives from industry, community colleges, the state's Department of Labor, and the area German-American Chamber of Commerce. Manufacturing firms work with the participating community colleges to design the curriculum and core competencies. Graduating high school seniors can choose an alternative route to a four-year university, acquiring theory, practice, and work experience over the three-year apprentice program. Most important, graduates have a skilled technician job with good pay and benefits waiting for them.

North Carolina Youth Apprenticeship

North Carolina offers an apprenticeship program that begins in high school, run through its community college system in collaboration with area companies.[75] Many of the state's many European-based firms have encouraged the program. The apprenticeships are registered with the US Department of Labor and offered in building trades, utilities, healthcare, information technology, logistics, and manufacturing.

The four-year program in North Carolina's Research Triangle area is illustrative of other programs in the state.[76] In their junior year, interested high school students and their parents tour facilities of participating area companies, and then students participate in fifteen hours of orientation and undertake an initial project. In the summer before their senior year, students take on a six-week paid preapprenticeship at an area company to test out the program and reach a decision about participating.

Students who choose to continue become full-time paid employees in their senior year, working for four days each week at a company and spending one day at the local high school. The following year, that one day shifts to the area community college.

The program focuses on manufacturing, with students undertaking 6,400 hours of learning manufacturing skills and 1,600 hours of college-level education. At the end of the four years, apprentices obtain an associate degree in mechanical or mechatronics engineering technology from one of the two participating area community colleges. In addition to the degree, graduates obtain a journeyman certificate from the US Department of Labor and the state's community college system.

The Research Triangle program is not large; in 2019, there were fifty-four apprentices in the pending five years of apprentice classes working at area manufacturing companies. Participants are paid a wage that increases as they complete each program stage, beginning at up to twelve dollars per hour in the first year of the apprenticeship and rising to eighteen dollars per hour in the fourth year. Tuition at the community college is free, and students are earning while learning. The program provides a guaranteed job such as a machinist or electrician and assures a two-year college degree. Transferability to a four-year state college is also guaranteed for interested apprentices.

It's notable that most of the Research Triangle partner businesses were founded by former program apprentices who understand the value of the program.

Wisconsin Youth Apprenticeship

Wisconsin has built a large youth apprenticeship program combining state leadership and regional partnerships with industry and education institutions.[77] At the state level, the Bureau of Apprenticeship Standards in the state's Department of Workforce Development provides oversight, and a network of thirty-three regional consortia throughout the state operates the program. The consortia are led by a variety of stakeholders: regional education organizations or technical colleges or area chambers of commerce or nonprofit entities or local workforce development boards. Each consortium has a steering committee of local employers, high school districts, state technical colleges, and workforce organizations. The state sets the standards regional consortia must meet for enrollment, completion rates, diploma rates, and apprentice certificate content.

It is a business-driven model, with employers identifying skill standards, interviewing and selecting students, providing students with paying jobs, and assigning them skilled mentors. School-based youth apprentice (YA) coordinators at high schools work closely with area employers to ensure the program is working for them. These YA coordinators also manage outreach to parents and students, advise students on careers, and set up interviews with employers. Apprenticeships are in a variety of fields, including health services, manufacturing, finance, transportation and logistics, and hospitality.

Students may work before, during, or after school hours, as well as during summers and holiday breaks. Students in the YA program therefore obtain on-the-job skills as paid employees, and the job becomes an extension of the classroom. Skilled mentors supervise and train students in the skills identified for the career cluster. On-the-job learning is reinforced by related classroom instruction that may be provided at the high school, the local technical college, online, or at the employer's worksite, depending on the program model adopted by the regional consortium. The coursework must comply with state guidelines. Students must pass their classes and demonstrate proficiency in state-defined competencies through ratings from their worksite supervisors on a standardized skills checklist.

Students can change their career clusters or employers during the program. Through their coursework, they may also receive advanced standing toward an associate degree at any of the state's technical colleges or credits toward a technical college's program of study in a related field.

Some 2,500 employers and 3,500 students from 342 high schools participated in the YA program in the 2016–2017 school year. The previous school year, the program completion rate was 84 percent and the students' average wage in the program was $9.93 an hour.

The US Department of Labor identified several keys to the success of Wisconsin's YA program:[78]

- The state has a strong set of online tools and resources available through a comprehensive state website, including a detailed YA guide for companies and for curriculum standards.[79]
- Through the Department of Workforce Development, the Department of Public Instruction, and the Wisconsin technical college system, the YA program has a strong framework of support and program standards for businesses, school systems, students, and parents.
- At the regional and local levels, each regional consortium has a lead organization that manages the program, as well as dedicated high school YA coordinators who oversee the day-to-day operations.
- Wisconsin's YA program works to engage all partners and strengthen these relationships at the regional level. YA programs meet the needs of businesses and effectively engage community organizations and resources, with attention to regional differences.

- Wisconsin provides state funding, at $900 per student in 2018, to the regional consortia through a competitive grant process. This funding supports the YA coordinator and costs associated with classroom instruction, student materials and supplies, and recruiting businesses and students, along with school-based coordination and supervision. The partners absorb other program costs, including wages paid by employers.

The Kentucky, North Carolina, and Wisconsin programs have all incorporated core elements of the German apprenticeship model.

CASE STUDY: CHARLESTON, SOUTH CAROLINA, YOUTH APPRENTICESHIP MODEL

More than twenty-eight thousand workers are employed at German-owned manufacturing facilities in South Carolina. According to one survey, South Carolina ranks first among states in terms of jobs available through foreign investment.[80] German companies in the state—BMW, Mercedes-Benz, Bosch, and others—understand the value of apprenticeship programs and have promoted the model.

Apprenticeship Carolina—named a national model by the US Department of Labor—assists companies in using apprentices by providing free apprenticeship consultants who link them to state resources, assist them in developing standards and training programs, connect them to programs in area technical colleges, and manage the paperwork to register apprenticeships with the US Department of Labor. These consultants also advise on the state's employer tax credit. The program was formed in 2007; there were 33,528 apprentices in 2019, forty times the number in 2007, in 1,031 company-registered programs that operate in all forty-six South Carolina counties and with all sixteen of the state's two-year technical colleges participating.[81] The state provides employers with a $1,000 tax credit for each apprentice.

The program has become a crucial intermediary between its sponsor, the state's technical college system, and employers. It complements readySC, formed in 1961 as part of the state's technical college system, which works with technical colleges to design workforce training systems for state employers. Both Apprenticeship Carolina and readySC are housed in the Division of Economic Development, which underscores their economic role for the state.

South Carolina's technical college system itself was established by Ernest Hollings, the state's innovative governor, in the early 1960s. One of the original "New South" governors, Hollings sought to bridge the historic poverty and racial divides in his state by multiplying economic opportunity for all sides. He made a determined effort to bring international manufacturing companies to his state and to create the education infrastructure he foresaw they would need. In his subsequent thirty-six years as one of South Carolina's US senators, he helped create the federal Manufacturing Extension Partnership and other manufacturing programs.

Many states compete by trying to lure firms to relocate, offering tax benefits and other financial incentives. South Carolina instead works to attract companies by offering them a well-trained workforce. This now includes the most successful apprenticeship program in the nation. Because the workforce is a critical contributor to productivity, it has become an increasingly effective strategy.

Apprenticeships in South Carolina start after high school. They typically consist of the two "work-and-learn" components we've discussed before: on-the-job training at the workplace and job-related technical instruction at the local state technical college.[82] As apprentices' skills progress, their pay increases under a set formula. This is a way for employers, who set the wage levels, to offset costs when investing in employees who are not immediately fully productive and to retain employees when investing in their training. Both sides, then, have incentives to improve skills—the apprentice, who can gain higher pay and status, and the company as the apprentice becomes more productive. For example, the BMW Scholars program offers full-time students at three local technical colleges the opportunity to work up to twenty hours per week at BMW's Spartanburg auto plant while they complete their two-year associate degrees.

Within this state framework, which has focused on technical college students earning associate degrees and incumbent workers taking additional courses, Trident Technical College and Charleston-area employers have come up with a particularly interesting youth apprenticeship program that begins in area high schools.

The Charleston area, part of the state's "low country" plantation and agricultural region, is a relative newcomer to high-end manufacturing. The upstate areas were home to much of the nation's textile production before it moved to Asia, and later the upstate region acquired international manufacturing firms like BMW and its suppliers. Charleston did acquire a major US Navy shipyard in 1901, but that large employer closed in 1996, after the Cold War ended. The local economy reverted largely to tourism. Later, an increasing number of manufacturers were attracted to a major industrial park in North Charleston, which now concentrates Boeing, Mercedes-Benz,

Volvo, and a large network of suppliers. But Charleston didn't have a base of industrial workers like the upstate region. It had to start largely from scratch.

In 2013, IFA Rotarian, a German auto supply manufacturing firm making drive shafts and joints at a plant just northeast of Charleston, approached Trident Tech, the local technical college. The company, used to working with youth apprentices in secondary schools in Germany, was having trouble finding skilled workers in the area.[83] IFA Rotarian wanted to hire sixteen-year-olds to start a similar program and teamed up with five other area manufacturing firms with similar problems. These companies were having trouble competing for workers with brand-name area companies like Boeing and Mercedes and thought that the loyalty a strong youth apprenticeship program could create would help them compete for talent.

Trident Tech's president tasked two experienced administrators, Mitchell Harp and Melissa Stowasser, to work on developing the new youth apprenticeship program.[84] The companies and Trident were joined at the table by the Charleston Metro Chamber of Commerce, which had undertaken a project it called Accelerate Greater Charleston in 2012–2013 to improve the area's talent base and help employers.[85]

The chamber took up the challenge. High school students enrolled in college for six credit hours receive state lottery–funded tuition assistance that covers about half the cost; the chamber has paid the difference, as well as paid for books, paid wages for mentors, and paid for supplies. Employers pay their apprentices' wages.

The initial parents' night at Trident to explain the new apprenticeship was a critical moment. Many parents were skeptical about manufacturing; they wanted their children to go to college, not into a technical college apprentice program. But when a representative stood up and said his company would pay the four-year college tuition for students who do well in the program at his facility, the tide turned. Now these nights are packed with parents who generally understand the program's value.

SIGNING DAY

Each fall, Trident Tech sponsors a Signing Day event for new youth apprentices. Tia Marie Vice, who has written about the program, described this event: "Modeled after signing days for sporting evenings, students publicly sign on with companies they will be working with as apprentices. Family members, media, and local leaders are all present. Students feel honored to be chosen, and the crowd cheers them on. All of these are deliberate attempts to show manufacturing, advanced manufacturing, and careers in STEM as desirable career paths."[a]

[a]Tia Maria Vice, "Can Apprenticeships Alleviate a Regional Skills Gap?: A Case Study of Programs at Trident Technical College in Charleston, SC," thesis, Department of Urban Studies and Planning, MIT, February 2019, 62. See also Charleston Regional Youth Apprenticeship Signing Day 2018, October 30, 2018, https://www.youtube.com/watch?v=tIjRiPt0ZBA (YouTube video).

In the first year, there were six companies and thirteen students. Harp and Stowasser state that by fall 2018, there were 130 companies with Department of Labor–registered apprenticeships and ninety-four students (not all companies take apprentices every year). As of fall 2018, in total, there have been 232 apprentices hired from out of the program. Of these, 42 percent are from minorities, 66 percent are male, and 34 percent are female. Although Trident students overall are two-thirds women, historically fewer females have enrolled in technical apprenticeships. Along with more women students, Trident especially has been trying to reach African American and Hispanic males, who face significant youth unemployment problems.

One of the most notable aspects of the program is the participation by *small companies*. Policymakers have long viewed apprenticeship programs as not necessarily workable for smaller firms that lack the deeper pockets of larger employers. It was smaller employers in need of talent, though, that initiated the Charleston Youth Apprenticeship program, and it created an attractive cost equation for companies. Today, the significant majority of companies in the Trident program are smaller companies with small employment bases. These are often the best apprenticeships for students: small and midsize companies can offer the most varied and in-depth work experiences, and their size allows them to focus on individuals in ways larger companies cannot.

Now, Trident gets calls every week from companies wanting to participate, but demand is outrunning the scholarship fundraising. A number of states now fund dual-enrollment programs in which high school students can attend two-year college courses without paying tuition, but South Carolina is not yet one of them. Harp and Stowasser believe that if that changed, the program would now have three hundred employers involved, which reflects the rising level of company interest. They believe something in the education funding system may have to change to solve this Trident tuition support mechanism issue. Stowasser states, "If you want to reach the poor, the under-resourced, you have to fund dual enrollment."

Apprenticeship Carolina, the state intermediary organization, is especially useful in helping employers with the US Department of Labor. It handles the Department of Labor registration paper processes at no charge to employers. Intermediaries of this sort—both state and local—are important for apprenticeships to work. Some type of registration for both employer and apprentice roles establishes a formal agreement that allocates responsibilities, so students, parents, and employers clearly understand their roles. The Department of Labor registration provides this and also is important because it enables apprentices to obtain the national Department of Labor journeyman credential.

As for where the apprentices come from, companies today can hire rising high school juniors in area high schools, generally reaching out to them first as tenth graders or rising seniors. South Carolina now requires students to prepare individual graduation and career plans when in middle school, so companies also now visit those schools to explain job and career possibilities. Companies make hiring/apprentice decisions, not Trident.

While the Charleston program began with area manufacturing firms, it now has sixteen career pathways available, including industrial mechanics (engineering CAD, machine tool, and CNC technicians), culinary arts, nursing assistant, emergency medical technician, hotel operations, and various computing skills.[86] Apprentices can start at ages sixteen to eighteen. They typically attend high school in the morning, where their employers often insist they take math and science classes; spend early afternoons in more technical work-related classes at Trident; and work part time in afternoons and summers at their employers. They receive Trident credit through the program, accumulating approximately one year (thirty credits) toward a two-year associate degree. Most apprentices continue on their jobs at their companies after high school graduation, but most also continue until they've earned their associate degrees. Some have continued on to earn four-year degrees, including four-year engineering degrees. The completion rate for all students who have been in the program reflects national levels—about 80 percent for whites but less than 60 percent for minorities.

It is an attractive package for many high school students, who get out of what might be a boring or frustrating high school experience and into college-level work and a job that pays around ten dollars per hour—a nice sum for kids from poorer backgrounds in particular. They interact in much more mature social settings at the community college and at their workplaces. They get work experience, validation of their career interests, an opportunity to develop professional relationships, college completion credit, and career readiness.[87]

To get a company perspective on the Charleston Youth Apprenticeship program, we spoke with Vincent Lombardy, training and employee development manager for VTL Precision.[88] VTL, a US division of a UK-based transmission company, was one of the original six small companies participating in the Trident Technical College program for youth apprentices. VTL really needed skilled employees for its sophisticated, high-precision drivetrain and engine parts. The company has new mechatronics, CNC, and robotics that require upskilled employees and is using a number of employee training programs, both internally and in training schools operated by its robotics supplier.

VTL is now using the youth apprenticeship route as a key source for employees; apprentices now make up 8 percent of its workforce. When we spoke with Lombardy, VTL had three Trident-enrolled apprentices—one in the combined high school-Trident program and two earning their Trident associate degrees—and six Trident apprentices in total had been through VTL since the 2014 start of the program.

VTL and other employers decide who to hire and at what level. For example, they have a graduated senior who now works a forty-hour week and also attends Trident classes; he must get good grades or VTL will cut the work hours. Trident and VTL together plan for each apprentice's needs and program with the apprentice. "This program," Lombardy told us, "is strengthening VTL's workforce pipeline. There is historically low unemployment in the area and it's hard getting good employees, so this pipeline helps solve the problem. We've had much success with the program."

Lombardy told us about one apprentice who "alone justifies the investment": the daughter of an African American preacher who went on to Clemson's undergraduate engineering program after the Trident apprentice program and who still works at VTL over holidays and summers. "She's helping redesign the CAD software system to link with our robots and is a now a critical employee." He also told us about VTL's first apprentice, who also has gone on to get an engineering degree and has become a key employee. His work at VTL is helping him pay for school. "He came in an average student, but a hard worker, not well founded in math, and not straight As. But now he can troubleshoot a line and home in on key tasks; he really learned problem solving here. He has been here four and a half years—a great value for him and for VTL. He earned his apprenticeship journeyman certificate in 2016, is now full time at VTL, and is also doing well in the Citadel's engineering degree program."

These apprentices each provide twenty to forty hours of productive work each week. They earn starting pay of ten dollars per hour and are doing actual work; full-time workers from outside would cost more (including for benefits). VTL has offered a full-time job to every apprentice it's had come through the program. "We get active, producing employees at the end of the program." It has been a big part of competing for employees with the larger companies in the area.

VTL tweaks the apprenticeship program every year. It rotates apprentices through all of the plant functions—production, safety, maintenance, and finance—so they learn many roles and how the entire facility works. Each apprentice has a mentor. And there is a specific task for starting apprentices on fluid inputs for machine-cutting processes, which is a critical step in production. Clearly, VTL has had a positive experience with the program, using it to help solve its skilled workforce problems and obtain employees important to the company. The US Department of Labor evaluated the Charleston Youth Apprenticeship program and identified four major reasons for the program's success:[89]

- *Business champions:* Business has been the real driving force behind the Charleston program, initiated by one manufacturer and now involving 130 firms in the region offering sixteen career pathways.
- *Strong leadership and partners:* Trident Tech, with some visionary administrators, is the managing partner, but other partners play critical parts, including the area chamber of commerce, Apprenticeship Carolina, area high schools, and the participating employers. Trident provides support to participating businesses, school systems, and local youth apprentice coordinators to ensure the program is working.
- *Engaged area high schools:* Trident administrative and technical education staff work closely with high school guidance counselors, principals, and teachers to help ensure student participation and positive outcomes for both students and companies. Parents are also key because they support students and help with worksite transportation.
- *Tuition support:* Financial support from the Charleston Metro Chamber of Commerce has been critical in offsetting tuition and other costs.

Despite the growing importance of postsecondary education in obtaining good jobs, young people who get licenses and certificates for solid technical skills, primarily through community colleges, can still do well. The key issue is how to get more young people into this technical education track; youth unemployment and the social disruption it causes remain too high.

There has been progress on policies and programs that better connect the long-separated silos of education and work. For high schools and community college students, apprenticeships may be an option. Apprenticeships create a direct line between the silos of education and work. They don't assist with upskilling incumbent or displaced workers, but they could be an important option for young people entering the workforce.

If apprenticeships could be made to work in the United States (and they may be affected by the coronavirus downturn), they appear to have promise as a way to erase the divide in the United States between education and work for young workers seeking to enter the workforce. Because the current route from high school into both postsecondary education and the job market is not serving as it should, a work-and-learn approach seems well worth experimentation.

11 THE NEW CONTENT-DELIVERY MODELS

Despite all the problems and challenges discussed in previous chapters, we are seeing solutions emerge in areas such as apprenticeships, new education technologies, and improving information systems. These solutions need to reach three groups of workers: *new entrants* to the workforce, *incumbent* workers who have jobs but need to upgrade their skills, and *displaced or underemployed* workers who have lost jobs or are stuck in low-end positions and need to find new skills to reenter the workforce or advance to better jobs.

In this chapter, we review nine models for new approaches to content delivery. Most concern educational institutions, some concern industry, and others concern broader system problems such as developing new education technologies. They apply to the different groups of workers in different ways.

Community or technical colleges play a leading role in the first four models, but partners from industry and/or government are also vital.

MODEL 1: THE TRIFECTA: THE SYNERGISTIC REACH OF ASNUNTUCK COMMUNITY COLLEGE

Frank Gulluni, in his eighties and semiretired, has seen it all.[1] He began in workforce education in 1965 in Springfield, Massachusetts, an old industrial city in the Connecticut River valley, starting with what was then the relatively new Manpower program. The evening program "tore up too many families," Frank says, because "trainees couldn't both work during the day and leave their families at night." So he developed instead the Massachusetts Career Development Institute, a day and evening program with a four-part approach: thorough vocational and academic assessment of students; changing attitudes and building a sense of self-worth and confidence; working on math, reading, and writing skills; and creating real opportunities for getting jobs by training in specific skills in machining, welding, health-related careers, and other areas. He found the students needed to "change their attitudes for the training to work, they needed foundations to build the training on." In 1981, he testified about this Sequential Training and Employment Progression System (STEPS) system before Congress.[2]

Gulluni later moved his general approach to Enfield, Connecticut, another old industrial town, establishing a vocational education program in manufacturing at Asnuntuck Community College. He started with a program for dislocated workers who were jobless and in need of retraining and developed a for-credit certificate program in machine technology. Pratt and Whitney and a large segment of the American aerospace industry supply system were located in central Connecticut, so there were employment opportunities. To build in-depth, lasting career skills, he found these students needed "one thousand hours over a two-semester timeframe, thirty to thirty-five hours a week—not just the typical twelve to fifteen hours a week, community college schedule."

When a Connecticut governor came to tour the program and saw students working on CNC machines, Gulluni could tell that the politician had not been convinced that manufacturing was part of a "real" college program or even integral to the state's economic development strategy. So he had the governor sit down in a conference room with some twenty area manufacturers. The first employer told the governor he was cutting the sales and marketing efforts of his midsize aerospace supply firm because without skilled workers he couldn't produce his products in the state. "You could hear a pin drop," Gulluni recalls. "Nobody told that to a governor."

Representatives from company after company, though, chimed in with the same message about the lack of skilled workers. By meeting's end, the governor was convinced there were hundreds of skilled jobs that couldn't be filled just from the employers in that room. Within a month, he proposed a $500 million program for state manufacturing training, equipment, and facilities. Four community colleges in different parts of the state, including Asnuntuck, were selected to become manufacturing centers, essentially replicating the Asnuntuck model. With a $25 million grant, Asnuntuck built a fifty thousand sq. ft. Advanced Manufacturing Technology Center, fitted out with the most advanced computer-driven production technologies. It opened in 2017.

Asnuntuck now offers three programs in advanced manufacturing technology skills for community college students, high school students, and incumbent workers. It's rare to serve all these in a synergistic way. Frank Gulluni and colleagues are, in a way, attempting a trifecta by pursuing all three. These programs reach all the categories of workers identified earlier: new entrant, incumbent, and underemployed. Each program is reviewed in the following sections.

The "Regular" Community College Program

Asnuntuck offers a two-semester certificate program in manufacturing that can also lead to an associate degree in manufacturing. It accepts all those interested in the program; there are typically three hundred to four hundred students enrolled either full or part time and ranging in age from eighteen to sixty-five—including middle-aged career changers and many inner-city minority youth from the Hartford area. They are typically at the program six to seven hours a day for thirty-two weeks, participating for thirty to thirty-five hours a week. Asnuntuck is also in the third year of providing some three hundred prisoners approaching release with certificate and degree programs in a range of disciplines, including several dozen who spend approximately twenty-five hours a week on campus in the manufacturing program.

Regular students spend a quarter of their time in classrooms, a quarter in the computer lab, and the remaining half is hands-on learning in a major technical area—machining, welding and fabrication, electromechanical. They learn using state-of-the-art machine tools and other high-tech equipment and can extend the program by taking a third semester with even more specialized courses and equipment. There is a major need for technicians in the area, and graduates are often starting jobs at $40,000 to $65,000 per year. The manufacturing program has a 95 percent job placement rate.

Total tuition at this writing was $8,300 for Connecticut students and those who come from neighboring Massachusetts and Rhode Island; the Asnuntuck student population can afford the program because 85 percent are Pell Grant eligible and receive up to $6,000 toward their two-year degree program. The school stretches out payment periods for the balance. Eight- to nine-week internships in the second semester, which pay about one hundred dollars per day, bring in some of the additional tuition funding. Unemployed workers are covered by Workforce Investment and Opportunity Act (WIOA) funding from area workforce boards, which adds an additional $5,000 as needed on top of Pell grants. So the program is reaching both new entrants and the under- or unemployed.

The College Connection Program for High School Students

Connecticut helps cover Asnuntuck's costs for a program free to high school students, and a number of high school districts pay for their students to participate. It reaches into as many as ten school systems in the greater Hartford-Enfield area. Machining, welding, and fabrication are the skill focus areas.

High school students spend ninety minutes or more each weekday at Asnuntuck in a college-level program, completing six to eight community college credits annually, giving them a big boost toward completing associate degrees and certificates. To reduce transportation time and accommodate more students, other regional community colleges are also adopting the program. With additional sites, students can break into sections and rotate all day in different time periods for better efficiency in the use of facilities. Ultimately, Gulluni would like to see a thousand or more high school students a day in a web of high schools and community colleges modeled on what Asnuntuck is doing. There is a special need to reach inner-city students from Bridgeport and Hartford.

Reaching parents and area high school staff is an important component of making the high school program successful. Asnuntuck's leadership is well aware that the job losses of the 2000s have given parents a negative image of manufacturing and that high school guidance counselors and principals have an outdated image of manufacturing. To address this, the college has a special one- or two-week program in basic manufacturing technology skills specifically for high school administrators and guidance counselors. They come out understanding that high-tech modern manufacturing has become a meaningful career pathway. Asnuntuck President James Lombella also wants to launch a major "train the trainers" program—a certificate program, or at least a special two-week bootcamp, that would update all the tech trainers in Connecticut high schools on career and technical education in advanced manufacturing.[3]

Incumbent Workers Program

Asnuntuck has built a strong program for incumbent workers that includes the software and high-level skills area employers want. Annually, some 750 to 800 of these workers participate in an Asnuntuck course of study at the college or a company site. Pratt & Whitney, for example, hosts a one hundred plus–hour core skills program for more than 350 workers every two to three weeks, as many as twenty times each year. Companies in the area's aerospace manufacturing association, as well as Sikorsky Aircraft sixty miles away, all use this program. More than two-thirds of all instruction (math, CNC, blueprinting reading, and metrology) happens at company sites, with time at Asnuntuck devoted to high-end machining or electromechanical course material on its advanced equipment.

Instructors from Asnuntuck faculty and smaller companies can come together to form a training consortium, sharing the program and its costs between firms. The area aerospace association arranges the courses and contracting for its 125 member companies. The incumbent worker program is also a way for Asnuntuck to market its regular college students for potential employment, and it works: local manufacturers participating in the incumbent worker program routinely hire from the regular college program.

Put simply, Asnuntuck's three programs are mutually reinforcing, and with Asnuntuck's tuition for its regular community college program covering only half of the college's actual costs, the large incumbent worker program makes up much of the difference.

Gulluni argues that a key to the success of the three manufacturing programs at Asnuntuck is an understanding of the responsibility to educate for actual workforce needs. Too often in community colleges, he feels, instructors are not current with the latest developments and the equipment is antiquated. But at Asnuntuck, the private sector gives support at every stage, providing equipment and advice and helping develop curricula on the latest skills. For twenty years, the manufacturing program has had a close working alliance with the region's aerospace companies and its area association, which keep the college's offerings up to date; they want the students they are hiring to be fully prepared for their jobs on day one.

ASNUNTUCK'S STRONG LINK TO EMPLOYERS

Eppendorf is a life science company based in Hamburg, Germany, that develops and sells instruments for liquid, sample, and cell handling in laboratories worldwide. It offers a good illustration of how Asnuntuck Community College's incumbent worker program operates.

As Eppendorf moved in highly automated production equipment to its midsized Enfield, Connecticut, branch, the company's leadership recognized that its workforce wasn't ready. They worked with Asnuntuck to develop a company-specific curriculum in circuit theory, robotics, math, math for electricity and electronics, programmable logic controllers, industrial motor controls, hydraulics, industrial maintenance, troubleshooting, conveyors, pneumatics, and process controls, drawn from Asnuntuck's manufacturing course offerings. The company wanted its employees not only to learn how to operate the new technologies, but also to understand the foundations and theory behind those technologies so they could fully understand the new processes.

In 2015, the curriculum was launched as a two-year, four-hundred-hour program for a group of twelve Eppendorf workers in Enfield, who one day each week would spend six hours in the program, overlapping the first and second shifts. Eppendorf's managers credit the on-site training with enabling a much more efficient production system that has allowed the company to expand its markets significantly.

Now the company routinely hires Asnuntuck-trained students from both the regular program and the manufacturing internship program, which an Eppendorf senior manager describes as "a great way to identify and drive talent" to the company.[a]

As we write, Eppendorf is exploring training another group of six employees, as well as instituting a "train the trainer" program to teach a group of its workers to teach other workers to operate some new automation equipment at the plant.

[a]Meeting with Dr. Axel Cramer, vice president of manufacturing, Eppendorf, Enfield, Connecticut, May 30, 2019.

Quality Instructors

Another key to the success of the Asnuntuck programs is the instructors. "We want career people from manufacturing," Gulluni says, "who love manufacturing. Asnuntuck then can get them to a level where they can impart skills very well." Asnuntuck has long been training its own manufacturing instructors, coordinating with Central Connecticut State University for help in teacher credentialing and training, and a number continue on there to get their teaching degrees. Two-thirds of the instructors are graduates of the Asnuntuck manufacturing program itself; they go to work for companies, where they can practice the most current skills, and then return to teach.

The school tries to bring back its very best students to teach, and also has retirees with specialty skills in the most advanced areas but who do not want to work forty hours a week. "At Asnuntuck," Gulluni explains, "they can work ten to fifteen hours and really contribute and play a key role in the latest areas the companies are developing."

Instructor Jose Marcelino's story is typical.[4] A printer when online entry was killing that business, he needed something else and came to Asnuntuck for retraining in the advanced machine technology program—using his savings and displaced worker benefits. That training enabled him to move quickly to earn $100,000 per year at an area manufacturer. But he wanted to help students, and so he came back to teach when he was invited to join the manufacturing faculty.

Community colleges can operate day and night for fifty-two weeks a year, with a program flexibility that is often outside the range of other kinds of schools. Asnuntuck uses that flexibility to go beyond the community college itself to run high school and incumbent worker programs that reach a wide range of people and ages with advanced skills and lead directly to high-paying jobs. It has already moved many thousands through these programs. This is a model that others could emulate.

MODEL 2: REACHING NEW ENTRANT WORKERS THROUGH YOUTH APPRENTICESHIPS

Trident Tech, the technical college in South Carolina that developed a new youth apprenticeship program detailed in chapter 10, provides a model for how to reach new entrant workers. It tears down the wall between learning and work, deeply integrating the two by linking high schools, the community college, and area companies. Along with other programs in chapter 10—including Tennessee's Career Pathways, Kentucky's FAME, Michigan's MAT^2, and North Carolina's and Wisconsin's youth apprenticeships—Trident Tech's program offers a number of lessons about organizing apprenticeships.

Effective youth apprenticeships connect community or technical colleges with employer groups, high schools, and state or local government, with one or more serving as critical intermediaries between high schools and employers. They can begin in a student's junior year with courses in high school that emphasize science and math, technical courses at the community college, and part-time work at an area company during the school year and even full time during summers and holidays. Wages generally start at around ten dollars an hour and increase as apprentices build experience.

Apprenticeships of this sort shift students from the high school environment alone and add maturing aspects by putting them in new social and age contexts, studying with adults at the community college and working with adults at their companies. The programs can lead them directly into solid jobs and careers that can fund further higher education. They graduate high school with a diploma, credits that take them to near completion of a year of community or technical college, and a Department of Labor or other skill certification. If programs like this could scale, they could make a real difference in closing America's notorious work/learn gap and shrinking the country's high youth unemployment rate.

There are several key enablers of program success. The impetus often comes from area employers, small as well as large, driven by the high demand for skilled workers. Small employers in particular feel a skills pinch because they cannot always compete with "big brand" firms and lack the resources and ability to field their own programs for training. These apprenticeship programs generally enable employers to interview and select apprentices that would best fit their needs. Industry groups can help organize employer interest. Community colleges provide the glue, making and maintaining the day-to-day connections between business and high school actors, as well as forming the technical education programs. Industry groups can also help fund the community college's tuition costs,[5] as well as work with state or local governments to help with the paperwork that comes with being registered with the Labor Department (and the benefits that come with that).

Experience suggests that while youth apprenticeships may work for major companies, they are too expensive for small companies. The mix of shared costs and organizing among the employers, industry associations, high schools, and community or technical colleges shows that a working partnership can help resolve this issue. While challenges remain—particularly solving transportation for students among high schools, community colleges, and employers—the overall emerging models could be workable in many communities.

MODEL 3: FIXING THE TWO-YEAR COLLEGE COMPLETION RATE IN TENNESSEE

Tennessee is another state that didn't abandon its vocational schools, but instead repurposed them into affordable one- to two-year technical schools offering certificates and associates degrees. As detailed in chapter 9, there is a network of twenty-seven Tennessee Colleges for Applied Technology (TCATs), spread across the entire state, offering seventy career programs leading to certificates and associate degrees and also offering specialized training for larger area employers.[6] The Tennessee Lottery helps fund skills grants that can help pay for tuition. Other state programs for new entrant and older workers provide scholarships to supplement other state and federal aid, making it possible for students to attend TCATs tuition-free.[7]

The twenty-seven TCATs combined have had remarkable success, far surpassing—at 81 percent—the state's community colleges in terms of completion rates for certificates or degrees.[8] Some 86 percent of TCAT graduates find jobs in their field of study. In surveys, nearly 100 percent of TCAT alumni and their employers rate the programs as "satisfactory" or higher. One particularly impressive feature of the TCATs is the system used to address the problem community colleges face nationwide: the high number of unprepared students needing remedial courses. Most schools first put inadequately prepared students into separate remedial programs in which they often they get bogged down, never moving on to college-level courses, which is a leading cause of the low community college completion rate. TCAT's approach is to have all students take courses that prepare them for college-level work so that no one gets singled out as needing remedial help. At the same time, students start their technology CTE courses. All students therefore get right into their chosen career courses so they can see their career opportunities from the outset. Coupled with the known high job placement rate, this makes the career opportunity very real real—not some dim light at the end of a long remedial tunnel.

The TCATs call this the Technology Foundations approach. For the remedial work, all entering students participate in ACT's WorkKeys/WorkTrain program (discussed in chapter 9), focusing on applied math, reading, locating information, writing, problem solving, and teamwork. Students have individualized learning plans and based on these have a mix of classes, online exercises, and access to mentoring at a learning lab. Each student pursues the foundations program at his or her own pace. This is a highly blended education model combining online and personal instruction; it's competency-based learning, with students mastering a series of stages and skills.

The great majority of students complete their foundations programs shortly after their first trimester, and only a handful have not done so by the third trimester.[9] When they complete it they take ACT's online Career Readiness Certificate Assessment; the goal of the TCATs is to have all students with certificates at a silver and gold level.

The Technology Foundations approach, along with tuition assistance from the state, results in high certificate and degree completion rates across the twenty-seven TCAT colleges. With completion rates one of the most serious barriers to occupational education, it's an approach worthy of emulation.

MODEL 4: REACHING DISPLACED AND UNDEREMPLOYED WORKERS WITH A SHORT PROGRAM

Valencia College, previewed in chapter 1, set out to reach some of the approximately three hundred thousand people in poor families in the Orlando, Florida, area, often Black or Hispanic immigrants. They were generally working but typically at lower-end, minimum-wage service jobs, in less than full-time jobs without benefits, and often holding down two or even three of these jobs to meet family needs. The two-year timetable for an associate degree or one year for a certificate simply did not work for this group. Night classes didn't fit with family demands. These people had been left outside the education pipeline and without a path to the middle class.

The *short program*—Valencia's response to the aforementioned issues—is an intensive ten- to twenty-two-week course, five days per week for eight hours, that offers industry-standard certificates in advanced manufacturing, construction, heavy equipment, logistics, and healthcare fields. Certificates in specific skills can be stacked for multiple certified complementary skills. The program also provides credits toward a Valencia associate degree; these credits are also transferable to the four-year degree program at the University of Central Florida. As this program scales up, it could start to make a real dent in area poverty and create new lives for many.

Key to the program is putting students rapidly into a hands-on learning environment, then into the workplace, with skills that promptly command a good wage. Valencia has built ties with area employers to ensure jobs for its trainees on the first rung of a solid employment ladder, with wages at twenty dollars per hour or more with benefits. After a service job at Florida's $8.46 minimum wage doing seasonal work, this can bring families to a new level.

This accelerated workforce program doesn't fit US Labor or Education Department financial assistance program requirements, but Valencia offers tuition subsidies. Area employers provide the training equipment for the manufacturing program, which is housed in a small repossessed factory.

How can promising short programs evolve? We need to open up a number of experiments to discover what kinds work best. Poor quality could undermine the whole effort.

There are numerous experiments. Project Quest, for example, has been successful in reaching poor and undereducated workers in San Antonio with training and job placement targeted to expanding area job sectors. One factor has been its funding support and services to students to help them meet family obligations while they train at the nearby community college.[10]

Legislation was introduced in Congress in 2019 to make short programs like these eligible for federal Pell Grant funding,[11] which in effect would divert funding from associate and bachelor's programs open to both nonprofits and for-profit education providers. However, the legislation needs accountability over these providers to assure students actually obtain employment in the fields they trained in.[12] To a significant extent, education quality is assured when educators, students, and businesses work as equal partners, each with a clear stake in the outcome.[13] Without the participation of companies that *need* trained workers and therefore have a stake in the quality of the program, students may be subject to poor but expensive programs. Experiments with short programs should definitely be undertaken to settle on the best approaches, and solid employer participation should be required.

We also need to ensure that programs lead not just to single jobs but toward careers. Valencia, for example, is careful to tie its short program to community college credit, make the credentials stackable, and make them possible routes to associate degrees. It has built into its short program an access path to longer-term and more in-depth skill training and a potential degree. Asnuntuck Community College, as another example, focuses on one- to two-year manufacturing technology programs that build lifetime skills, including an understanding of the underlying theory behind the skills for when equipment changes, as well as enduring foundational skills in reading, writing, and math. These kinds of approaches can ensure strong short programs.

MODEL 5: REACHING NEW ENTRANT WORKERS IN MASSACHUSETTS TECHNICAL HIGH SCHOOLS

Beyond community and technical colleges, technical or comprehensive high schools could also play a role. At Diman Regional Vocational Technical High School in Fall River, Massachusetts, students complete five semesters of technical and academic high school courses in one of eighteen fields and then are considered ready to start skilled jobs in their selected career areas as part of a co-op work program that begins in the second semester of their junior year. Some 80 percent are placed into co-op jobs; juniors and seniors alternate between working full time for their employers for two weeks, doing homework online at night, and spending two weeks in school completing their academic and specialized technical courses. There's a 90 percent retention rate for co-op jobs.

In effect, Diman is running an apprenticeship program comparable to Charleston's Trident Tech. At Diman's ninth annual job fair in April 2019, seventy-nine companies and organizations packed the school gymnasium. Hundreds of students jostled about. In the bustle, employers were clearly vying to employ co-op students, who they pay, on average, $412 weekly.[14]

Some 70 percent of Diman's graduates go on to community college and/or four-year college. Nearby Bristol Community College certifies Diman technical courses for college credit; dual enrollment means Diman students graduate with a high school diploma, a year of community college credits, and skill certifications in a career area. Students often continue after graduation with their co-op employers at $50,000 or more a year, complete community college at night, and move on to Bridgewater State University or UMass Dartmouth, where they have guaranteed transferability to pursue four-year degrees—working at high-paying jobs all the way through and avoiding piling up student debt for an uncertain career path.

Diman has a large business advisory council of area employers and sub-councils that advise the eighteen program tracks and drive the curriculum. Let's look at three of these tracks:

- *Business technology* students emerge with a full suite of business IT skills, including Microsoft and Intuit QuickBooks certificates that have widespread industry recognition. They do a practical project, such as designing an actual website and logos, mostly for area nonprofits. Most students go on to college business education programs; many have good full- or part-time jobs while attending college to offset costs. In some cases, these employers pay students' college tuition.
- *Advanced manufacturing technology* students train first on traditional, person-controlled machine tools and move gradually to the most modern CNC machines, laser-cutting equipment, and 3-D printers (thanks to a state capital equipment program), arrayed on a 9,000 sq. ft. industrial floor with special closed-off spaces for computing and programming equipment and some of the newest "clean" equipment. Students in this co-op track earn up to sixteen dollars per hour; they've achieved strong competency on the advanced equipment by the time they enter their co-ops. Most go directly into highly paid production jobs at more than twenty dollars per hour after graduation, although a number enter engineering and technical college programs.
- The *drafting* program trains students in the latest computer design equipment and software, as well as on a suite of mid- to high-range 3-D printers. Each year, drafting students design and assist in building a home for a needy area family; a significant number of these students go on to architecture programs.

Diman students run a high-end restaurant, as well as the daily school lunch program. Landscape architecture students run the school's campus and have teamed up with other programs to build a new stone outdoor terrace for the restaurant. The auto mechanics program is continually repairing a fleet of cars. Students trained as FAA-rated commercial drone pilots are operating drones. There are also major good deed projects: various building programs recently rebuilt the Fall River Water Department's ancient hot-water heating plant with modern boilers, new piping, and an energy-efficiency system; others raised a new roof on Fall River's Rowing Center; and the Diman health and dental assistant program provided dental advice and treatment for 140 Head Start students.[15]

Among the dedicated faculty, 70 percent are Diman graduates. Demand for admission is high, and the process is rigorous: for the 2016–2017 school year, the acceptance rate was 47 percent. Some 98 percent of students graduate.

Diman demonstrates that there's a place for vocational or career and technical education in the American education system—and that it doesn't have to reinforce the former view that such education is a dead end for poor and minority students (as discussed in chapter 3).[16] While many states gave up on this kind of education,[17] Massachusetts did not: the state rebuilt it and has thirty-eight schools across the state that vary in size and programs. "What we wanted to do was create a student who was able to go out and get a job but also able to get accepted into a four-year college or university," explains David Ferreira, executive director in 2014 of the Massachusetts Association of Vocational Administrators. "The idea was to make sure all students were both career *and* college ready."[18]

This approach has largely succeeded; the academic quality of Massachusetts vocational high schools is now on par with its traditional academic high schools. In 2016, the graduation rate was 9 points higher than other high schools, the dropout rate was one-third of other schools, and two-thirds of vocational education (voc ed)/CTE graduates were going on to postsecondary education. Some 4,400 students were on voc ed school admission waitlists.[19] Studies have shown higher incomes accrue to graduates of CTE programs, and a 2015 study of Massachusetts regional vocational schools showed that low-income students were 32 percent more likely to graduate than students in traditional high schools.[20] Graduates of the Massachusetts technical schools are far more career-ready than other students.

There are other lessons from Diman: emphasis on academic performance must be kept high and made to complement technical skills; instructors and equipment must be kept current with developments at the cutting edge of industries; business advisors must be involved in developing the curriculum; and the curriculum should be coordinated with community colleges for joint credit to ease entry to postsecondary education. Diman provides a good example of how these kinds of schools can erase the historic barriers between learning and work and enable both good careers and higher education entry.

How useful, though, is the vocational/CTE school model if many states have dropped it? It seems unlikely, but not impossible, that at a time when most states have been cutting back their education commitments, these states would actually start funding and creating new secondary CTE schools, which require not only classrooms but extensive technology and equipment. But as many areas, particularly urban areas, continue to create a plethora of new schools through charter school programs, perhaps they can explore new technical schools as well—particularly given the pressing need for skilled workers. States throughout the country are showing renewed interest in technical schools.[21] Organizing a political base among parents and employers to advocate for this might be necessary.

Massachusetts offers a possible middle way. The state has been creating "comprehensive high schools," an old model being renewed,[22] to address the long waiting lists for existing vocational high schools and the fact that fifty-two municipalities don't have access to those schools. These new schools focus on both traditional academic subjects, such as English, science, math, languages, and social studies, and on technical skills. They expand their electives to reach a wider range of students seeking vocational education, offering business technology and finance, machining, information technology skills, early childhood education, and so on. These schools can also offer vocational programs operating as a school within a school.

Chicopee Comprehensive High School, for example, offers vocational programs in twelve areas, including business and IT, culinary arts, design and visual communications, electrical, machining and metal fabrication, joining, and others. The machine tool program has a fleet of advanced machining equipment housed in a large, new floorspace; it offers a range of hands-on courses that move students from simple milling and grinding machines to computer-aided manufacturing, computer drafting, and advanced CNC machining. Seniors do co-ops at area manufacturers and earn community college–level credits. After the regular school day ends, underemployed and displaced workers use the facility, working with skilled instructors in a cooperative effort with the area workforce development board, which offers machining courses to these workers.

While it can't offer quite as rich a program as Diman, Chicopee Comprehensive represents an alternative approach.

MODEL 6: EMPLOYER PROGRAMS FOR NEW ENTRANT AND INCUMBENT WORKERS

Some companies and industry associations have been taking the lead in developing new training or skill certification programs. Model 6 highlights some examples.

The IBM Apprenticeship

Ginni Rometty, the first woman to serve as IBM's CEO, passionately pushed her major corporation toward workforce education for new entrants during her 2012 to 2020 tenure. Some of this may stem from her own background. She attended Northwestern University on a scholarship funded by General Motors; her single working mother couldn't afford college tuition. She interned at companies in her junior and senior years.

IBM's interest in apprenticeships came in significant part from its 2011 participation in Pathways in Technology (P-TECH), a program from ninth grade through community college that connects high school directly with college and aims at putting technology at the forefront of the student experience.[23] It began in Brooklyn, New York, in a P-TECH school of one hundred students within a larger city high school, and now includes some two hundred schools in eleven states.[24] The underlying idea was to fill a gap in the education ladder between high school and college, with a *school within a school* approach that is more financially manageable and flexible than creating separate, new institutions.

P-TECH students focus on STEM and information technology courses while in high school, take classes at New York City College of Technology (City Tech) and other campuses, and then can earn an associate degree there at no cost. They have the option to go on to complete four-year undergraduate degrees or move into work. Students also undertake internships at IBM and at other P-TECH partner companies, which also provide mentors. The only entry requirement is an interest in IT and a willingness to attend additional classes to complete both regular high school and IT requirements.

Soft skills—leadership and teamwork—are taught from the outset through group learning; the program's hard skills courses are directly relevant to real problems students are tackling. Students start going to college classes early on in their high school career, easing the transition.

With the number of four-year graduates holding computer science degrees far below the market demand, IBM has begun hiring at the associate degree level, which is why the company is hiring P-TECH graduates. The program is providing comparable talent.

Drawing from its experience with the P-TECH program, IBM has been developing an apprenticeship program. It has developed fifteen different apprenticeship tracks for careers in growing fields, including software engineering, data science and analytics, cybersecurity, mainframe system administration, creative design, and IT program management. It began at IBM's mainframe (servers) business unit, which had an aging workforce and needed new talent; since then, IBM apprenticeships have grown at twice the expected rate.

The website for those interested in an IBM apprenticeship boldly states: "No degree? No problem!"[25] The company is seeking to create "new collar workers" with solid technical skills. IBM went through the process of using the Department of Labor's registered apprenticeship system; it used some Department of Labor funding to create the required learning plan and objectives, and the education is competency-based. It's allied with collaborating community colleges for associate degrees and certifications, but all the training is internal to IBM. Several hundred apprentices work with IBM employees on the job in three locations around the country (with more planned); they are paid less than full-time employees but have jobs and are both taking courses and working. The apprentices commit to at least two thousand hours in competency-based training that they can complete in less time.

IBM apprentices join a cohort of apprentices from a number of business units in an IBM locality. In the opening weeks, they learn about the company and are introduced to the skills they will learn in the apprenticeship. With managers and mentors, they develop a personal skills roadmap to learning, demonstrating new knowledge and competencies, hands-on applications, and working within project teams. Digital credentials validate skills at milestones. The retention rate for apprentices is very high.

A CONSORTIUM OF COMPANIES COMMITTED TO APPRENTICESHIPS

In early 2019, IBM brought together a group of eight companies for a joint announcement of a new commitment to apprenticeships through the Consumer Technology Association (CTA).[a] The other companies include Ford Motor Company, Phone2Action, Postmates, SoftBank Robotics, Sprint, Toyota, and Walmart. Each company made a pledge to hire apprentices; IBM pledged to create four hundred to five hundred apprentices a year for five years.

The other companies are modeling their apprenticeships in large part on IBM's apprenticeship program. IBM has shared all of its apprenticeship course materials and software with the coalition. Why are the other firms participating? Walmart, for example, needs skilled employees in its rural locations to run its extensive IT systems; it has trouble recruiting them but believes trained apprentices from the area could be retained.

The announcement was made at the massive annual Consumer Electronics Show in Las Vegas and featured four IBM apprentices. One was a Latino "dreamer" who had gone through the P-TECH program and had become an IBM apprentice. His talk about what the apprenticeship meant to him brought down the house, receiving a standing ovation.

[a]Computer and Electronics Show (CES) Press Release, "CTA and IBM Announce Apprenticeship Coalition to Help Close U.S. Skills Gap," January 8, 2019, https://www.ces.tech/News/Press-Releases/CES-Press-Release.aspx?NodeID=20769cf6-315a-435f-a70e-ba05c7ce76c4; Cat Zakrzewski, "Technology Companies Turn to Apprenticeships in Tight Labor Market," *Washington Post*, January 8, 2019.

IBM's is not the only new employer-led apprenticeship program, but it is an example of what could evolve in the tech sector. It's particularly interesting because it's an employer's attempt to move non-college-degree students into a field—computer and information technologies—dominated by college degrees, where there is now high employer demand and a major talent shortfall.

Apprenticeships now reach less than 1 percent of the workforce; for this effort to scale, we need more than one-off efforts by single companies. Much more industry collaboration is required for sharing best practices and content. IBM's example with a group of companies is a positive and instructive step (see "Consortium" box).

Manufacturing Skills Standards Council

Developing skill standards is a critical step for educating and hiring the manufacturing workforce needed in the coming decade.[26] The process of taking a technical occupation area and identifying component skills and systems to teach them, developing effective assessments, and providing corresponding certifications, plus making these into living systems that incorporate ongoing developments, is a massive one. But it's crucial to education and training. The lack of standards certification in a given occupation area can be frustrating: educators don't know what to teach, employers don't know how to evaluate potential employees and current employees, and employees don't know how to qualify for jobs and can't transfer their qualifications to other firms or areas.

The Manufacturing Skills Standards Council (MSSC) has become the leading certifying body for the nation's frontline manufacturing production and supply chain logistics technicians.[27] It offers a nonprofit, industry-led certification, training, and assessment system based on industry-defined and federally endorsed standards. It's the only certification organization in the manufacturing industry accredited under the international ISO system and has had the support of the National Association of Manufacturers, the leading industry association.[28] Its certifications enable both new entrant and incumbent workers to demonstrate they have the required skills for increasingly technical manufacturing tasks.

MSSC has two broad certification programs. Its Certified Production Technician program incorporates a host of tasks within five modules: safety, quality practices and measurement, manufacturing processes and production, maintenance practices, and green production. The Certified Logistics Technician program has two levels and includes tasks such as global supply chain logistics lifecycles, material handling equipment, quality control principles, computing skills, packaging and shipment handling, inventory control, and safe handling of hazmat materials. Both certifications have systems for online assessments, support online and blended learning courses, and include a supporting system of certified instruction organizations and trainers. MSSC has begun a skills development effort centered on the suite of advanced manufacturing technologies now beginning to enter manufacturing firms, including practices in artificial intelligence, robotics, data analytics, and computer control programming.

The IT sector has been able to develop skill certifications for key occupation areas, the automotive repair sector certifies qualified mechanics, and the medical sector has long had certifications for doctors and nurses. The ongoing MSSC project in manufacturing could be critical for meeting that sector's expected workforce skill demands. Without an educated workforce, and standards to meet for educating that workforce, new technology areas simply can't grow.

Chamber of Commerce Foundation

The US Chamber of Commerce Foundation, the nation's largest business organization, has the ability to reach companies of all sizes and sectors in every region. Its Talent Pipeline Management (TPM) Initiative, introduced in chapter 9, is designed to enable business-led efforts allied with other stakeholders to implement new training systems and curricula.[29] The program reaches both new and incumbent workers to help upskill the workforces at two hundred partner employers in twenty-six states.[30]

The training side, called TPM Academy, offers both in-person and online training for workforce leaders to learn the TPM approach. It's backed by a customized curriculum that serves as a toolkit for participants. A web-based tool activates the six TPM strategies embedded in the program to streamline the data collection and visualization needed for sound program construction. It provides a framework for employers that can be customized to their particular needs in building high-performing talent pipelines.

The TPM Academy works through five steps:

1. Create a collaboration that organizes employer groups to identify shared workforce needs and the best opportunities for engagement.
2. Develop projections for job openings to predict actual job needs and their accompanying skill areas accurately.
3. Establish competency and credential requirements and communicate them across employer and stakeholder groups.
4. Examine current talent flows and their capacity to meet demand; identify possible new sources.
5. Form new talent supply chains to ensure a return on commitments.

Once the new system has been implemented, the talent supply data system provides continuing information to allow improvements and adjustments. Overall, the TPM program offers constructive help to employers of all sizes trying to formulate workforce solutions.

Joint Programs with Unions

Another workforce coordination space available to some employers is working with unions. While unions currently make up only 6 percent of the overall private-sector workforce, some significant sectors remain unionized, including construction, manufacturing, aerospace, utilities, and healthcare. Industry-union workforce education collaborations can bring in groups of employers. For example, the Wisconsin Regional Training Partnership is an industry-led and worker-focused effort, with state, federal, and community participation and foundation support, that provides short-term training for skilled manufacturing, construction and healthcare jobs in the Milwaukee area.[31] The program's construction element, Big Step, works with the construction trades' joint apprenticeship programs in the region and has significantly increased the entry of minorities and women into skilled construction jobs in the area and helped meet overall needs for skilled workers.[32] Another example is the Culinary Academy of Las Vegas, which had trained some 42,000 workers for skilled jobs in that area's hospitality sector, from professional cook to baker to wine server. A collaboration between the area's numerous hotel and casino employers and the culinary and bartenders union locals, it has emphasized reaching large numbers of minorities, youth, and displaced workers through small classes of fifteen or fewer and expert instructors from industry, using a large, specialized training facility that also operates a "hands-on" restaurant and catering service.

An underlying feature of the employer-led efforts described above—creating apprenticeships, establishing industry skill standards, and helping employer groups form training programs or coordinating training with unions—is that they are collaborative. Employers face a strong disincentive to work with other employers because they compete with each other for talent. This barrier to collective efforts amounts to a market failure. Yet shared programs can significantly lower training costs and risks. The solution is for groups of employers to coordinate their workforce efforts, and each of these programs provides an example. This will be crucial in scaling employer efforts.

The economic fallout from the coronavirus will make companies, particularly small companies, less willing or able to adopt a workforce education role, although pressures to upskill the workforce will still be ongoing. This will propel more of a workforce support role for government. Yet efficient and well-designed workforce education requires companies to be involved in the content and its delivery to ensure that it fits actual workplace needs. So the collaboration model discussed here, involving government (particularly local and state, with federal support), with strong company input and involvement, will become even more central to workforce education efforts. Employers, smaller employers in particular, will be less likely to undertake them on their own.

MODEL 7: THE STATE'S ROLE IN UNIFYING WORKFORCE PROGRAMS

One of the deeper problems in workforce education is that the major federal programs supported by the Departments of Education and Labor are not well connected and don't reach incumbent workers easily. But because the federal programs are the major source of funding for state workforce programs, they drive how states organize their own programs: state implementation follows federal patterns. The result is a disconnect at both levels.

States, though, are essential workforce actors. The ongoing effort in Florida to bring together manufacturing and workforce programs and community colleges (see chapter 1) is a good working model for how these federal programs could be better linked. Another is in Massachusetts, where the state government has tried to connect this range of programs at the state level in response to employer concerns about the lack of a trained workforce.[33]

In 2015, the governor of Massachusetts created a "skills cabinet" with the secretaries of the three departments involved in workforce matters. The Department of Education covers all public education in the state, which includes vocational technical high schools, community colleges, and the state university system. The Executive Office of Labor and Workforce Development focuses on unemployed and underemployed workers, managing workforce boards and MassHire, the state's unemployment and job placement employment service; it also supports the state's apprenticeship program and its new intern program.[34] The Department of Housing and Economic Development is the state's economic development agency; it encourages firms to locate in the state and supports a range of programs, including ones in entrepreneurship and R&D, and also supports the MassTech Collaborative, which focuses on innovation infrastructure and talent for the state, including an innovative advanced manufacturing initiative.[35]

The skills cabinet meets biweekly and makes program decisions jointly; all three member departments must approve any new workforce-related program from the constituent departments. The focus is on advanced manufacturing, healthcare, and information technology, which the state sees as the critical future job sectors for Massachusetts. Between 2015 and 2018, the cabinet awarded $52 million in Workforce Skills Capital Grants to 188 vocational technical high schools, community colleges, traditional public high schools, and companies to bring the latest technology and equipment to each to expand skills training programs.[36] A major initiative has been to develop workforce strategic plans in the state's seven economic regions.[37] Each involves a planning group of regional stakeholders—state agencies, community colleges, vocational technical high schools, workforce boards, and industry leaders—with each region's workforce board serving as a lead organizer.

Massachusetts has committed $100 million in cost sharing with the federal government and industry to fund five of the nation's fourteen advanced manufacturing institutes, each of which is located in or has program elements in the state. No other state has such a broad commitment to these institutes. The Massachusetts Manufacturing Innovation Initiative (M2I2) program, a part of the MassTech Collaborative, supports these institute efforts and helps provide advanced manufacturing equipment and training through regional partnerships involving universities, community colleges, and companies.[38]

The M2I2 program is also coordinating an effort by the three state agencies to develop a new state plan for a system of advanced manufacturing education, coordinated across state education and workforce institutions and the manufacturing institutes and aided by a 2020 Defense Department ManTech grant. It is a pathbreaking example of Massachusetts's commitment to meeting future skill needs.[39] It will require a new curriculum centered on new technologies such as robotics and photonics, aided by online delivery, to be implemented in the state's community colleges, technical high schools, state universities, and manufacturing employers. There is no existing system for educating for the new advanced technologies entering the workplace, so this example may well be the first systematic attempt. This program, which will reach incumbent as well as new entrant workers, could be a critical state model for what the nation needs to undertake.

AIM Photonics Academy, a manufacturing institute workforce program that has already developed online education courses and modules for educating engineers and technicians in photonics, is assisting in developing these plans. Because it cost-shared their programs, the state is involving four other manufacturing institutes as well; they can contribute know-how on their new technologies and how to educate workers to use them. Overall, this new effort seeks to lead the state's production industries into a position of competitive leadership. An education system for new advanced manufacturing technologies that includes curricula, courses, and modules to be used in education institutions and industry will be another first, and a potentially important new national model.

Massachusetts has strengthened its vocational technical high schools, is bringing new technical skills programs into traditional high schools to create comprehensive high school programs, and has used its MassMEP manufacturing partnership program—which brings new technologies and processes to area manufacturing—as a coordinator for training programs for small manufacturers. The state's Workforce Training Fund offers grants to employers to upskill their incumbent workforces. In other words, Massachusetts has developed a suite of new organizational and program elements that integrate education, workforce, and economic development at the state level, making up for the disconnects in these programs at the federal level.

The state does all this by bringing together employers, education institutions, and state resources—a key three-way connection. Employers need to be involved in designing and funding workforce programs and in finding jobs for graduates. Classroom education must be integrated with opportunities to apply new skills in real or simulated settings, and training must focus on career pathways, not just skills for a particular job.[40]

The Massachusetts solution to the federal workforce program disconnects is to fill the gaps.[41] The state grasps that strong workforce development efforts need to be the at the heart of state economic development efforts: they will be key to growing companies and keeping them in the state, as well as attracting new ones.

MODEL 8: TOWARD NEW LABOR MARKET INFORMATION SYSTEMS

American labor markets lack a good information system, as detailed in chapter 6. We need job skill information, with supporting credentials that connect to job openings data, are tied to rich data on training and education options, and that in turn are structured to fit needed skills and job requirements linked to the training systems themselves. We need an online navigator that integrates workers, employers, and educators and helps them sort out their best options within a data-rich environment.

There are signs this missing navigator is evolving. Federal agencies, industry associations, and the private sector could play key roles. Two projects, both still works in progress, are noted here as examples for how progress could be made.

Labor Department Efforts

The 2014 Workforce Investment and Opportunity Act requires the Labor Department to build a new and much larger workforce and labor market information system and provides a full framework for organizing it.[42] A subsequent advisory council developed detailed implementation recommendations, including recommendations for better identification "of in-demand occupations and industries" and to "fill a career awareness gap" for workers. Its report recommended building new databases from unemployment wage records; expanded information collection on occupations, skills, and credentials; a new career awareness education framework; and better information on the changing nature of work. Improved data sharing, new involvement by states and other agencies, and new analytics were also recommended.[43]

Meanwhile, the US Census Bureau in 2019 created a jobkit site that compiles government job information sources and is also developing more data on postsecondary school employment outcomes.[44] NSF undertook in 2019 a new National Training, Education, and Workforce Survey.[45] And the Commerce Department and the White House, also in 2019, created an American Workforce Policy Advisory Board.[46] Income and employment data from the Social Security Administration and the Internal Revenue

Service, and other Commerce and Labor Department agencies, given appropriate data privacy protections, could also contribute to a new information system. Federal agencies could aggregate their data and allow the private sector to build specialized information systems from it in a public-private model.

The Labor Department's O*NET online system already provides workers with valuable data about occupations and their prospects nationally and by region.[47] If this new system, including data from the other agencies, can be created, the combination would be a major step toward a workable information system.

Chamber of Commerce Foundation's T3 Network and JDX Project

In 2018, the US Chamber of Commerce Foundation, with support from the Lumina Foundation, formed the T3 Network to link businesses, community colleges, technical standards organizations, employment experts, and technology firms with a data system available to all.[48] The network of 150 organizations, including federal government agencies, is organized around four tasks: developing open data standards to harmonize and enable interoperability for skill competencies and worker and student records; identifying gaps in the standards for employment, earnings, and student records; developing tools for shared competency and skill statements for participants in labor markets; and developing protocols for workers and learners to access and use their skills data and competencies through blockchain and distributed ledgers. The project is taking on complex data gathering and organization tasks across public and private sectors. It could enable a better labor market information system.

The US Chamber of Commerce Foundation also began its Job Data Exchange (JDX) project in 2018.[49] The idea was that if employers provided much clearer job information, labor markets could better connect worker skills and qualifications with job openings. The National Association of Manufacturers and the US Labor and Education Departments participate in JDX, as do state organizations and some major employers, including Walmart and Microsoft. They are working on pilot projects in six states to develop standardized, structured data for web posting of jobs and create human resource systems for transferring job data.

Sound information systems will require public and private sector collaboration; these programs attempt to do this. Neither T3 nor JDX are likely to grab headlines. But like the Labor Department's information efforts, they are undertaking the difficult, complex work with data, standards, and systems needed for progress on a job navigation system.

MODEL 9: INTRODUCING NEW EDUCATION TECHNOLOGIES

Developing and implementing new education technologies will be important to scaling new workforce education efforts. The US military provides an example of what is possible, and universities could play a significant development and dissemination role.

Naval Air Warfare Center Training Systems Division

Chapter 1 details work by the Naval Air Warfare Center Training Systems Division on training programs using virtual and augmented reality (VR and AR) in online gaming simulations and run on high-end gaming computers and touch screens. The navy is now shifting a substantial amount of its training for advanced equipment on ships, on submarines, and at air bases into these online systems, and they are increasingly in place at navy training centers and are moving into the fleet, beginning with aircraft carriers. The systems require that software be developed for each type of equipment, but the online hardware platforms are commercially available and the costs have become quite manageable—in the $10,000 to $15,000 range.

The new VR/AR technology enables realistic training without risks to the actual equipment and while ensuring the safety of new operators. It enables significant learning by doing, which makes it a major step forward in training. Preliminary findings by the navy indicate that the level of skill that can be acquired through these VR/AR simulations is quite close to actual hands-on learning. The other US service branches are moving rapidly to shift their training to these technologies.

Industry is further behind. While industry is beginning to use VR/AR for tasks such as inspections, it's still a long distance away from introducing it at scale for training—in part a reflection of industry's still limited commitment to training. This shifts responsibility for obtaining training to individuals and publicly funded community colleges. While the online equipment could make training much less costly for community colleges—they wouldn't have to acquire full factory floors of advanced manufacturing equipment—they do not have the resources or capabilities to develop the required software. But once the software is developed, it could disseminate rapidly online.

Online videos themselves are a powerful new tool for education now coming into increasing use, but they can be further enhanced. Who is in a position to develop the VR/AR and gaming software for the learning-by-doing aspect of training? Industry could do it for equipment now in use but will have trouble developing training for advanced technologies that are not yet widespread because there isn't yet a market. Technology and equipment providers might fill the gap, but only for their own products. VR companies such as Oculus are only beginning to offer consumer games, much less education programs. Universities, many of which have now implemented extensive online courses, might take on this role. Clemson and MIT are two examples of universities adopting online technologies; chapter 8 detailed the emerging education technologies and their potential importance.

Clemson's Center for Workforce Development

Clemson University's Center for Workforce Development, discussed in chapter 7, has worked with South Carolina's system of technical colleges, with support from NSF's Advanced Technological Education (ATE) program, and developed a system of online courses in high-end manufacturing skills.[50] These modular courses can be readily adopted in classes at technical and community colleges, enhancing rather than replacing face-to-face learning. The course materials fit the MSSC skill standards (discussed earlier) and can lead to MSSC certifications.

Notably, VR/AR features are also being built into course modules.

MIT Open Learning

Our colleagues at MIT Open Learning have a growing list of accomplishments.[51] Working with MIT faculty, they have now produced more than 170 MOOCs available online around the world and involving millions of learners. Because Open Learning believes blended learning is best—it can optimize both online and face-to-face learning—it has also been running boot camps to match up with a series of its MOOC courses. Students who complete MOOCs are eligible to participate for a fee in boot camps that often consist of a week of intense group learning. Boot camps allow face-to-face and learning-by-doing features to be added to online education.

MIT's long-standing OpenCourseWare system posts course materials and a growing number of lecture videos for nearly all MIT courses; more than three hundred million learners worldwide have used it. MIT and Harvard partnered to lead the creation of edX, a major online course platform that hosts MOOCs from more than 130 universities around the world, with many millions of learners. MITx, the institute's online course system, is also developing new certificate programs. Its low-cost MicroMasters programs group sequences of courses, including in manufacturing and supply chain management, and reach 850,000 total enrollees. Students can qualify to come to MIT or more than three dozen other cooperating universities to complete a full master's degree in supply chain management on an accelerated schedule, with full credit for the MicroMasters courses.

MIT also now has an xPro suite of online courses developed for particular companies that want to train their technical and engineering staff. Boeing, for example, wanted to develop a common understanding of systems engineering across its workforce of thousands of systems engineers in many countries educated in different concepts. So it supported Open Learning to develop foundational systems engineering courses. These courses are also available to non-Boeing students. And Open Learning has already worked with a number of community colleges that use its MOOCs as modules in their courses. It aims to start including VR/AR simulations in its courses, and the MIT Game Lab has already developed a group of educational online games.[52] MIT Open Learning is also working with nine other large universities to develop a digital credentialing system for both online course certificates and university degrees.[53] The schools are working to create the standards for a trusted, distributed, but shared infrastructure for issuing, storing, displaying, and verifying academic credentials. Using blockchain and strong cryptography to prevent fraud, credentials can now be owned and displayed by the credential holder—representing a democratization of transcripts. It will also enable much richer and detailed credentials, potentially reflecting particular competencies the student has learned and making the system much more useful to employers trying to understand the skills and competencies that are actually behind a degree or certificate. It could help open new pathways for individuals to become what they want to be, as well as a serve as a protected validation system underpinning online credentials.

In addition, MIT is home to the AIM Photonics institute's education and training programs. AIM has already developed MOOCs posted on the MITx and edX platforms for photonics and optics skills at the engineering and technician level and is working on more. It is also working with the state of Massachusetts and in cooperation with MIT Open Learning on the statewide advanced manufacturing education system noted earlier; online courses will be an important feature. It recently received a grant to develop VR/AR training modules for photonics.

The work at Clemson, MIT, and other institutions suggests university models that could play a role in supporting entry of new online technologies into education and training, particularly for advanced technologies still in development and on which universities are working. Because online learning can scale quickly, a small number of schools can take leading roles. That's how MOOC platforms developed. The work at the Naval Training

TABLE 11.1
New workforce education delivery models

Delivery model	Stakeholder roles	Examples	Groups of workers reached		
			New entrants	Displaced/ underemployed	Incumbents
1: Synergistic "trifecta" for high schools, community colleges, and incumbent workers	Community/ technical college (lead); employers, high schools, state (supporting)	Asnuntuck Community College (Enfield, CT)	✓	✓	✓
2: Youth apprenticeships	As above	Trident Tech (Charleston, SC)	✓		
3: Fixing the two-year college completion rate	As above	Tennessee Colleges for Applied Technology	✓	✓	✓
4: Intensive short program for skills and certification	As above	Valencia College (Orlando, FL)		✓	✓
5: Technical and comprehensive high schools	State (lead)	Massachusetts	✓		
6: Employer workforce programs	Employers (lead); industry associations (supporting)	IBM, MSSC, US Chamber of Commerce Foundation	✓		✓
7: Unifying workforce programs across a state	State (lead)	Massachusetts	✓	✓	✓
8: New labor market information systems	Federal agencies, industry associations, private sector (lead)	US Department of Labor; US Chamber of Commerce Foundation	✓	✓	✓
9: Introducing new education technologies	Universities and employers (lead)	US Navy; Clemson University (SC); MIT (MA)	✓	✓	✓

Center and other military training centers provides examples of what the new technologies can accomplish in training.

The nine models for workforce education delivery explored in this chapter reach the full range of affected workers—new entrants, underemployed and displaced, and incumbents. The models require different institutional leads. Table 11.1 summarizes the models.

Together, the models amount to approaches that states, education institutions, and employers could adopt, filling significant gaps in the current workforce education system. They are complementary: no single model is adequate for the full range of workforce challenges, but a combination could have a significant effect. There are also implications from each program for federal education and labor programs. These policy implications are explored further in the final chapter.

12 A ROADMAP TO NEW WORKFORCE SYSTEMS

Workforce education is a complex system. There are many tasks to perform, actors involved, and categories of workers and industry sectors to reach. It's also a legacy system, locked into existing routines that make change difficult. Even with improvements to the system, the complexity will remain, and a range of different policy initiators will be needed.

We have a disconnected workforce education system now, poorly linked to jobs and careers and with critical gaps. As this work has shown, the various federal programs are not complementary; we lack an integrated approach to this major education challenge. The workforce is upskilling and will require significant additional education to adapt to a new suite of advanced technologies. Automation is being implemented gradually; the robots won't take all our jobs tomorrow, if ever. The economy's low productivity and capital plant, equipment, and IT investment rates suggest we have some time to get ready, and the economic effects of the coronavirus will push that back further. The workplace is not standing still, but it won't change overnight. It will create and change jobs, as well as ending them. We have skilled workforce demand, not a surplus.

The problems, though, won't go away without a way to reach incumbent workers systematically and ways to help new entrant workers lower barriers between school and work. Current programs don't effectively reach either of these groups. The curricula for the new skills required by technology advances has yet to be formed, and new delivery systems are needed.

Where we are and where we need to get as quickly as possible can be summed up in five points:

- The system is under-resourced.
- There are major system gaps, particularly around upskilling incumbent workers and better connecting the worlds of working and learning for new entrant workers.

- Significant new technologies, particularly IT, are moving into major economic sectors, but there is not a sound work education system for bringing the skills required to the workforce.
- Our labor markets require the sound information system we now lack that will assist workers, employers, and educators in meeting workforce needs.
- New education technologies could create new scaling opportunities for workforce education to help us meet these problems, with a blended approach and much learning by doing incorporated.

Social policy generally evolves through the identification of demonstrated, replicable models that can be scaled up to achieve social impact. Models themselves are not policy; they can guide policy, but they require implementation. From the new models discussed in this work, we review in the following sections ways these needs might be met, including specific policy interventions. But first we need to review our findings to understand the challenges and the foundations upon which we must build.

THE SYSTEM IS BROKEN

Growing the number of quality jobs is now a central societal task in a period of growing economic inequality; workforce education is a critical means to that end. The first part of this work detailed the challenges faced by the US working class and a workforce education "system" that has not been working well. The coronavirus has dramatically highlighted the inequality problem by disproportionately striking the poor, the working class, and minorities, underscoring the need for new workforce education to remedy it.

A catalog of *social disruption* begins with the decline in the manufacturing sector, which has led to so many of the problems the working class now faces. Manufacturing had long been a key route into the middle class for those with high school educations or less, including for minorities, but it was significantly curtailed by the end of the first decade of the 2000s. The nation lost one-third of its manufacturing jobs between 2000 and 2010, and only some 18 percent of these jobs had come back by 2018. Because manufacturing is the largest job multiplier—manufacturing jobs create many more jobs throughout the economy than service jobs—these effects rolled through other sectors of the economy. Manufacturing decline has been a leading cause of precipitous drops in the median income of men without high school diplomas, men with high school diplomas and some college, and women without high school diplomas. As an overall result, the workforce has been increasingly polarized, with income inequality growing and middle-class numbers in decline.

Meanwhile, the requirements in workforce are for more and more skills. Higher-skilled jobs, defined as requiring some college education, now make up a growing part of the workforce, and lower-skill jobs have declined, with expanding low-pay services jobs at the bottom.

The upper middle class has been thriving throughout the period just described. A significant portion of the middle class has lost its place, shunted toward jobs in a growing lower-paid, lower-end services sector. Despite a long American history of geographic mobility, the working class has been largely stuck in place, unable to capture job opportunities because they lack the necessary skills. Overall, the country has been experiencing its highest labor nonparticipation rate: 33 percent of prime-age workers were not working and not seeking work over much of this period. The quality jobs have been going to the college educated, while those with only a high school education or less face declining opportunities. The downturn from the coronavirus has exacerbated these problems.

The workforce education system *could* help pull us out of this social disruption, but not in its current state. There are too many holes, too many breakdowns in the current workforce education system. At a time of growing need, resources devoted to training workers, both from the federal government and employers, have been stagnant or in decline. US Labor Department programs haven't focused on incumbent workers and the higher technical skills they need. There is also a gap for young, new entrant workers: US Education Department programs focus on two- and four-year college education, not on the needs of the rest of the workforce. Neither department's programs are complementary.

Meanwhile, the vocational education/career and technical education system in US high schools has been largely dismantled; publicly supported community colleges are seriously underfunded and lack the resources to provide advanced training in emerging fields; and four-year colleges and universities are disconnected from workforce education and the other participants in the system, particularly from community colleges. There is a general disconnect between the still separate worlds of work and learning and a missing lifelong learning link. The scale of creative attempts to address these problems remains too small.

New challenges to the workforce system will come from the *entry of new technologies*. These technologies, led by information technologies, artificial intelligence, robotics, simulations, digital production, new sensor platforms, and data and analytics, will eliminate some jobs, particularly lower-end rote jobs, but at the same time will create complementary jobs for operating and applying the new technologies and new jobs for building the new technology systems. IT-related fields are not the only ones that will change; advanced composites, new materials, power electronics, photonics, and new bioprocessing advances will also change work with similar effects. So the jobs story will be a mixed story of gain and loss.

What seems clear is that a suite of new skills will be required. These will include significant new technical skills, but there will also be a premium on jobs that emphasize creativity and adaptability in managing the new technologies. There will be new tasks and new occupations we are only beginning to anticipate. To adapt, the workforce education system will need to change. We are not currently educating for these new technologies—in most cases, the curriculum does not yet exist—and a massive effort will be required to train the trainers if we are to achieve the new education levels required. The existing system is simply not ready yet.

To understand workplace developments best, we have drilled down from the economy-wide level to explore three major economic sectors that tell a particularly salient story: manufacturing, healthcare, and retail. Together they amount to approximately one-third of American jobs.

Manufacturing decline and the accompanying loss of jobs has been a major cause of social disruption, as noted earlier. But because manufacturing has an aging worker demographic, there likely will be more than two million manufacturing job openings in the coming decade, so it will be a significant job opportunity space. The sector is already upskilling: the jobs lost were predominantly in lower-end assembly work, and the education level of manufacturing workers is rising. Because manufacturing generally leads other sectors in productivity advances, the new technologies will likely enter this sector first, accelerating the need for need for new manufacturing workforce education.

Healthcare is quite different. It's an expanding sector, driven by the demographics of aging. New technologies are entering the sector and will create many new job categories as medical assistantships evolve to include operating new technologies and performing complex tests. Although existing health professions have sought to create barriers to their entry, this sector overall will be both expanding and upskilling.

Retail, in contrast, continues to experience economic shocks. Retail was thoroughly overbuilt in the United States, and with the economic shock of 2008, older retail malls began to close and retailers went for a discount approach, cutting workforce costs and building up a base of lower-level service workers. The coronavirus downturn is deepening these economic problems. Now, online ordering and warehousing, while still less than 10 percent of retail sales, are creating another shock. Retail is emphasizing *omnichanneling*—seeking to make online and face-to-face customer links seamless and connected. Notably, retail is finding that physical stores work when salesclerks are highly informed and can be guides to customers, building personal relationships and steering them through the maze of competing products. Checkout and reshelving can be automated, but the "guide" role likely cannot. This workforce, therefore, will also likely be upskilling, becoming fluent with online technologies and educated in product lines and sales.

All three of these sectors, despite being quite different, illustrate the need for new workforce education.

Lurking behind the workforce problems we face is a broken labor market information system. Efficient markets are backed by efficient information systems so that market participants can act, not guess, based on sound data and information. The United States, though, has the most decentralized labor market of any developed nation, lacking information about work at every stage. Market participants are largely flying blind: workers don't know what skills are needed for what careers or how to get them; employers lack good information on applicant skills and the skills they need; and educators don't know what skills are needed and what to train for. Most sectors lack recognized certifications to demonstrate skills, so workers can't readily transport their skills to other areas and jobs.

A work navigation system could be an answer. Online-delivered interventions could help workers in mediocre or dead-end jobs find opportunities requiring skills adjacent to their own that they could master. The navigator could be an online guardian that collects and scans occupation shifts and alerts employees, finds relevant job openings, and identifies the skills needed for new jobs—from soft teamwork skills to basic education skills to technical skills. This tool could be organized around jobs, skills, and openings. Information on government job training support could also be delivered. The navigator could also link workers to training interventions, including training opportunities from colleges and community colleges. Employers could use the navigator to post job opportunities, describe the skills they seek, and assess job applicants' skills. Educators could use the navigator to understand employer skill demands and better educate for sought-after skills. Such a navigation system could play a transformative role in adding sound information to our broken labor markets.

Here are the big challenges, then: social disruption and growing economic inequality; a workforce education system with major gaps in educating incumbent and new entrant workers and for emerging skills; agency programs that pull in different directions; the entry of new technologies that could make this social disruption worse unless we prepare for them; a need for different strategies for different sectors (manufacturing, healthcare, and retail are different and require different kinds of workforce education); and a failed labor market information system that does not help its worker, employer, and educator participants.

There is an additional important point we need to consider: Just how does workforce education contribute to growing the economy? Where does the technical workforce fit in? The power of innovation-based growth has long been recognized in economics. Nobel Prize–winning economist Robert Solow found that technological and related innovation led to 60 percent or more of historical U.S. economic growth—it was the dominant growth factor.[1] Paul Romer, also a Nobel Prize winner, added a talent factor to Solow's concept, arguing that technological knowledge (human capital engaged in research) was the foundation behind Solow's technology development.[2] But neither offered a full look at the innovation system, presenting innovation as largely R&D-based. Obviously, the workforce contributes significantly to productivity, but there is an additional element.

Economist Richard Nelson's suggestions about the important role of innovation actors—from firms to university research to government support—allow us to see innovation as a system,[3] and arguably give us a third direct innovation factor: innovation organization.[4] It's not enough to have researchers and R&D; these need to be well connected to other actors in the system for innovation to be implemented. Because this broader innovation organization concept embraces firms, this helps us see that economic growth must include the technical workforce. As discussed in chapter 5, technological innovation needs to stretch beyond R&D to production, particularly production of new and complex technologies, because so much innovation is involved in development, testing, demonstrating, designing for production, and actual production.[5] Much engineering innovation and often a redo of the underlying science are required to get through to the production stage. A similar argument can be made for innovation in the services sector. Because the technical workforce is integral to those development and implementation phases, it is integral to the innovation process. A theory of growth that fails to account for a skilled technical workforce underestimates its role. It is an important one.

A NEW WORKFORCE EDUCATION FRAMEWORK IS CRITICAL

Given these challenges, chapters 7–11 of the book examined what a new framework for workforce education could look like.

What is the *role of four-year colleges and universities*? They have generally regarded workforce education as someone else's problem—a task for high schools and community colleges. Yet the tide has moved up the beach and is now lapping at the front doors of these institutions because the college degree has become the critical credential for workforce success—even if it's largely a "default" credential given that it's not clear what workforce skills it actually represents. But in the absence of other effective nationwide credentials, it has become the coin of the realm.

One key task for colleges and universities is to do a better job preparing their students for careers. Computing, for example, is becoming a foundational skill for many fields, and colleges could do a much better job readying their students. Better career information and guidance are also needed. This does not mean abandoning the traditional liberal arts, but expanding the focus to help students also be more career-ready. This does not mean specific training for the first job after school, but longer-term career education.

Universities can also play an important role in filling gaps in the broader workforce education system, working in concert with other actors. Community colleges, for example, will continue to lead on developing content and content delivery for mid-range technical skills; universities are not going to become the premier places to learn welding, but they could help develop content for high-end technical skills, particularly for emerging new technologies. They could also help develop, test, and apply new education technologies. Unlike high schools and community colleges, they could organize online education content, developing online platforms and optimal teaching models and the learning science behind it all. They could also help develop new delivery frameworks that connect businesses, government, and education institutions in ways individual actors cannot.

In other words, there are some things four-year colleges and universities can do that community colleges cannot and vice versa. Each side needs to optimize what it can do best.

New education technologies could also enhance workforce education, as demonstrated during the coronavirus. A major advantage of online education over providing new classrooms is that it can scale. While initial production costs are sizable for online courses, the per-student cost becomes quite advantageous as they disseminate across large groups of learners. And new technologies—gaming and simulations, virtual and augmented reality, digital credentialing and digital tutors—could greatly improve online workforce education applications, moving them closer to learning-by-doing capabilities.

Online learning, however, will work better for some workers than others: younger new entrant workers may be more comfortable with online learning, and incumbent workers are often already working with computers at their worksites, but displaced workers or underemployed workers often have morale and technology fluency issues and will likely need to be in supportive communities first before online features are introduced. Overall, blended learning is best, wherein face-to-face teachers can be mentors and classroom communities can hone face-to-face communication skills. Online learning can then do what it does best: communicate content and information. New experiments are in order that combine online with face-to-face learning, such as through boot camps.

Improving workforce education requires getting the *education content* right. Content falls into three broad categories: foundational academic skills (reading, writing, mathematics), personal and interpersonal skills (so-called soft skills), and occupational skills (technical skills that vary by occupation). Competency-based education—dividing learning fields into specific topic areas with measurable targets that can lead to mastery—provides an education approach well suited to workforce education. This sort of instruction can vary based on an individual student's learning needs, and it can be supplemented with new certifications and credentials tied to specific topic areas. We have been multiplying non-degree-based certificates at a dizzying rate, usually without tying them to a credentialing system accepted by employers. Too often, this undermines their effectiveness for both workers and employers. But if this gap can be closed, the growing credentialing movement, linked to specific skill sets recognized by employers, could be a new force for workforce education.

While there are new approaches to teaching foundational skills (such as through ACT's WorkKeys, the twenty-seven Tennessee Colleges for Applied Technology, and Washington State's I-BEST program), soft skills are very difficult to measure and test for, and accordingly we have limited workable educational approaches. Yet these are clearly important, and ongoing efforts should be continued. Occupational skills—a major focus of this work—are easier to validate because they translate directly into work performance. But we need to solve three problems: we need to tie the right content to individual student and employer needs; we need to develop the skill content for the new range of technologies that will be entering the workplace in both production and services occupations; and we need better content-delivery mechanisms.

New apprenticeship approaches could also play a role in content delivery. Unlike European nations with more developed workforce education systems, the United States never developed an apprenticeship system for its youth. Many argue it won't work here because apprenticeship programs require long-term training commitments from companies, and U.Ss employers tend to focus on short-term needs. Perhaps apprenticeships won't work for all employers, but they may work for some. Because larger companies in more stable economic sectors are facing aging worker demographics, many appear interested, although the economic effects of the coronavirus may have to be worked through first.

The examples of Trident Tech in Charleston, South Carolina, and in some other states show that youth apprenticeships can work for even small and midsize employers in competition for skilled workers. A sound youth apprenticeship program appears to build employee loyalty and retention. Apprenticeships tackle the disconnect between working and learning environments, one of the deepest problems in the workforce system—and so they have appeal from a student perspective. If apprenticeships lead to community college credit and can tie to college programs, they appear to offer a road ahead for students. Alternative forms of youth apprenticeships are being experimented with in Tennessee, Kentucky, Michigan, and Wisconsin, as detailed in chapter 10.

Finally, because the current workforce education system has major gaps, *new content delivery models* are needed. We detailed nine models in chapter 11 that could be the basis for driving change in the system:

- Turn community and technical colleges into platforms that can deliver workforce education to serve not only community college students but also area incumbent workers and high school students.
- Use community colleges along with high schools and area employers to create youth apprenticeships that begin in high school.
- Reverse low community college completion rates across states by reorganizing remedial and developmental education and connecting studies better to occupation opportunities.
- Create short technical training programs at community colleges for underemployed workers that can also lead to certificates and degrees.
- Revive career and technical education through technical high schools or programs in comprehensive high schools.

- Expand employer workforce roles through enhanced training, apprenticeships, industry certifications, and employer collaborations.
- Bring together state government leaders to work toward unifying a state's labor, education, and economic development programs to support complementary program delivery, and create statewide plans and efforts to bring education in advanced technologies to the workforce.
- Develop new labor market information systems to guide employees, employers, and educators.
- Develop online, virtual, and augmented reality learning, digital tutoring, and other education technologies that can scale to meet workforce education needs and move toward more learning-by-doing approaches.

Implementing new models like these across the country could change the workforce landscape. Where they are already in place, they are helping in every way implied by the preceding bullet points. These nine models speak to the major problems in the workforce system, and to ways to resolve them.

TRANSLATING NEW DELIVERY MODELS INTO POLICY RECOMMENDATIONS

The current system faces a deep resourcing problem at nearly every level, which poses the question of how the models could scale to have an impact. Federal programs are inadequately funded, which affects the state role because federal funds support so many state efforts. There is not going to be a single implementation approach: different states and regions will have different strengths, and the actors, including educators and companies that step forward to lead them, can vary by area. All the models will require collaboration among government, businesses, and educators.

We already have many of the institutional elements needed for a renewed workforce education system; we aren't going to start again from scratch. The task ahead is repurposing existing approaches. We need policies that crosscut worker categories (new entrant, displaced or underemployed, and incumbent workers) and industrial sectors (including manufacturing, retail, and healthcare).

We first examine policy at the *provider* level and consider the state and federal role, the role of educational institutions (community colleges, technical high schools, and universities), and the role of employers. Each of our recommendations is tied to the policy models listed earlier or to the relevant chapter in which that model is discussed.

Recommendations for States

We've already detailed the deep involvement of many states in workforce education through their roles supporting community and technical colleges, secondary education (especially specialized high schools), state universities, and workforce development boards. Many of the models discussed in chapter 11 have vital roles for states to play. Going forward, our recommendations for states are as follows:

- Use community and technical colleges to deliver workforce education not only to community college students, but also to incumbent workers and high school students (model 1).
- Use community colleges along with high schools and area employers to create youth apprentices that begin in high school (model 2).
- Reverse low community college completion rates by reorganizing remedial and developmental education (model 3).
- Create short technical training programs at community colleges for underemployed workers and create credits for these that can lead to degrees and broader certificates (model 4).
- Revive career and technical education through technical high schools or programs in comprehensive high schools (model 5).
- Create lifelong learning programs at higher education institutions (chapter 7).
- Require stronger career advising and workforce skill education in higher education (chapter 7).
- Work to unify state labor, education, and economic development programs to support complementary program delivery (model 7).
- Create statewide plans and efforts to bring education in advanced technologies to the workforce (model 7).

These tasks will require *more resources*, but efforts at the state level have shown that there is public support for workforce programs and that initiating new efforts in this area, efforts which are not partisan, can work well politically regardless of party. Still, this won't be simple. States have been disinvesting in higher education; community colleges in particular have been underfunded (see chapter 3). This will need to be reversed.

Also, states shouldn't wait for the federal government. While the federal government has historically provided support for state workforce programs, a number of states are already making progress on new approaches and must keep moving ahead regardless of whether additional federal support is forthcoming. It is also important to remember that states can't implement these models alone; industry and educators must be close collaborators and must be fully engaged with the states in these efforts.

States also can apply other policy levers. Because the college degree has become the critical workforce credential, states can assure that programs in secondary schools can give community college credit and that *credentials from community colleges can transfer to state colleges*. For example, *short programs* can help underemployed workers get onto the first rung of solid employment, but do not provide for longer-term career preparation; ensuring that they are connected with other programs, with credits that can lead to associate degrees or broader certificates, is important. States can assist with this. Overall, workers will keep needing higher levels of skills, so certificates that keep building toward degrees and enable continuing learning will be key to avoiding education dead ends for the workforce.

States can also work to ensure that their state universities are moving toward stronger *career education and preparation* programs—including in information technology fields—in addition to traditional foundational knowledge and liberal arts education. These need not be opposing forces. They should be complementary parts of higher education. *Lifelong learning* will be important to all workers. As part of a reorientation of higher education to include more career education, states can ensure lifelong learning programs at state universities and at community colleges.

Recommendations for the Federal Government

The federal government, of course, has long played an important funding role in workforce development and education, particularly in providing critical support for state programs. But there are important gaps in federal programs. While Labor Department programs for displaced and underemployed workers are offered through workforce development boards in every state, the Education Department focuses on student aid for college students. Funding for the former is stagnating and funding for the latter has been increasing, but neither address training for incumbent and young, new entrant workers and for emerging advanced technology skills.

Our recommendations for the federal government are as follows:

- Put adequate resources into the key Labor Department programs, the Workforce Investment and Opportunities Act (WIOA) and the Trade Adjustment Assistance Act (TIAA), as well as the Education Department's Perkins Act (chapter 3).

- Restructure these programs so they better reach new entrant and incumbent workers who need upskilling, as well as displaced and underemployed workers (chapter 3).
- Experiment by supporting student aid pilot projects for nondegree workforce education in which education quality is ensured through partnerships among educators, students, and businesses (chapter 11).
- Coordinate across the federal agencies involved, with consolidated budgeting for workforce development and shared criteria for evaluating programs and dispersing funds (chapter 3).
- Expand federal support for apprenticeships and career technical education (chapters 3 and 10; models 2 and 5).
- Undertake a concerted effort across agencies and with employers and educators to build a robust workforce information system (model 8).
- Expand the National Science Foundation's Advanced Technological Education (ATE) program to reach more community colleges (with collaborating universities) with advanced technology skill development (chapter 3).
- Strengthen the advanced manufacturing institutes' workforce education programs and encourage them to enter into development efforts with states for new advanced manufacturing curricula and delivery (chapter 3; model 7).

The Perkins Act is the major tool for career and technical education, and the Workforce Investment and Opportunities Act program is the major tool for reaching underemployed and displaced workers. Funding for both, as well as for displaced workers under the Trade Adjustment Assistance Act, has been stagnant. Broadened Perkins funding should be available to states so they can experiment with and expand on the kinds of new models identified in this book. Congress should structure and fund WIOA to better reach incumbent and new entrant workers. The Labor Department's apprenticeship programs should be expanded, including into youth apprenticeships, with protections for workers and students assured.

Beyond direct federal funding for these sorts of programs, there is the issue of *federal student aid* to help cover tuition. There are significant quality-related risks in simply making the Education Department's aid programs readily available for non-college-degree certificate programs. Protections need to be built in so that students don't run into the same problems of poor performance and completion rates associated with so many for-profit providers. Education quality can be ensured when educators, students, and businesses work as partners and each has a clear stake in the outcome and can push the other stakeholders to ensure quality. For example, employers cannot settle for poorly trained workers, so ensuring they are involved with education providers in designing and using new education programs can be an important quality assurance step.

All these elements could help us make significant progress in filling the gaps in current federal Labor and Education Department programs, making disconnected efforts much more integrated.

The federal government has another important role—helping fix America's broken *information system* behind our labor markets (see chapter 6). Markets fail without good information.

We need an online navigator that integrates workers, employers, and educators and helps them sort out their best options within a data-rich environment. A sound information system would fill in what is largely missing in our system and provide job skill information, with information on supporting credentials that is connected to job opening data and is tied to rich data on training and education options. The information would be structured to fit needed skills and jobs, which, in turn, would link to the training systems themselves.

A host of federal agencies—the Bureau of Labor Statistics, the Census Bureau, the Bureau of Economic Analysis, the Social Security Administration, the Internal Revenue Service, and others—have vital data that could be the basis for such a system (with privacy protections in place, of course). The Labor Department's O*NET system already provides valuable data online about occupations and the prospects for job growth both regionally and nationally, and the DOL has already been directed by Congress to build a much more far-reaching system. But more progress is needed.

Federal data could be shared with the private sector so companies can combine it with industry data to meet specialized functions for different occupations and sectors. The US Chamber of Commerce Foundation, for example, could be an early beneficiary: the foundation is building a job data exchange for employers to standardize job qualifications and searches and an accompanying job data system. Companies such LinkedIn, which is building employment information systems for employers and professionals, could also benefit.

Two additional areas deserve federal agency attention. The National Science Foundation's Advanced Technological Education program is a key mechanism to link community colleges and universities for joint development of curriculum and online education in new technologies in a wide range of technical fields. ATE's limited budget and its efforts need to be increased substantially given the scope of the workforce challenges ahead. There is a corresponding role for developing education content for new technologies by the fourteen advanced manufacturing institutes. These institutes also need to work with states, universities, and community colleges on development of advanced manufacturing content and its delivery. ATE and the institutes are already collaborating on both content and delivery.

Recommendations for Education Institutions

While *universities* continue to treat workforce education as a problem for high schools and community colleges (see chapter 7), the college degree has become the dividing line for workforce success. But four-year colleges and universities need to change their mindsets. They must do better at preparing their students for careers, for example, by imparting to students the computing skills now key to many fields. They need to provide better career information and guidance to students. They must offer lifelong learning opportunities so workers at all career stages can update their skills to keep up with technology advances. State colleges in particular should improve transferability with community colleges. Universities could also play an important role by organizing broader workforce education systems, working in concert with other educational institutions and employers.

Our specific recommendations for universities are as follows:

- Use their relationships with other actors, including states, industry, and, potentially, community colleges, to help organize new delivery frameworks for workforce education, particularly for higher-end skills (chapter 7).
- Develop online delivery systems for workforce education, including development and implementation of new education technologies—virtual and augmented reality, application of computer gaming and simulations, and use of artificial intelligence and digital tutors—and create blended learning approaches, such as through boot camps (chapter 8; model 9).
- Prepare content and delivery for higher-end workforce skills, including for new information and other technologies in which universities have expertise that will be needed in the workplace (chapter 7; model 7).
- Develop lifelong learning curricula and offerings, particularly for higher-end skills and new advanced technologies (chapter 7).

- Develop the learning science for optimal teaching approaches that can be incorporated in both online and classroom education and applied to workforce education (chapter 7).

Not every university will be ready to pursue these tasks, of course. But given that many are already implementing online education at scale and developing the new technologies that will enter the workplace, they are better positioned to be involved on the education side than are other actors.

Community colleges are already central to workforce education efforts; they were largely designed for this task. A number have already developed the new models we've discussed in this and earlier chapters. Asnuntuck Community College in Connecticut has developed, in cooperation with area companies, the trifecta model that reaches incumbent workers and high school students, as well community college students, with high-skill manufacturing courses and certificates. Trident Technical College in South Carolina has developed an innovative youth apprenticeship program with area high schools and businesses. The system of twenty-seven Tennessee Colleges of Applied Technology has developed ways to improve student completion rates dramatically, as well as to place the vast majority of its students into jobs in the fields of their training. Valencia College in Florida has created innovative short programs to move underemployed workers into well-paid jobs with benefits in ten to twenty-two weeks. These are only some of the innovations coming out of community colleges.

Additional efforts are needed. Our recommendations for community colleges are as follows:

- Significantly increase completion rates for degrees and certificates, with particular attention to the major barriers of remedial and developmental education courses, as well as cost (model 3).
- Work to mitigate the social and economic life circumstances that cause students to drop out, including through expanded mentoring and career advising for students (model 3).
- Expand connections with high schools for youth apprenticeships, internships, and other programs for workforce education that open community colleges to new entrant workers (models 1 and 2).
- Implement short skill programs and create credits for them that tie to degrees and broader certificates (model 4).
- Reach incumbent workers and closely link on an ongoing basis to employers to ensure that courses are relevant to meeting employer needs (model 1).

- Link to universities and NSF's ATE program and the advanced manufacturing institutes for support in developing materials for workforce education, particularly to obtain access to online courses and modules on high-level technical and advanced skills for emerging new technologies (chapters 3 and 7).

Because of long-standing barriers between school and work, there is a particular need for *technical and comprehensive high schools* to ease the transition of new entrant workers from school into good workforce jobs—and, as a by-product, cut youth unemployment. Unfortunately, there are simply too few high-quality examples of these technical institutions nationwide (chapter 11 explored the successful Massachusetts model).

Local school districts and states should encourage growth of this model through either technical high schools or comprehensive high schools—that is, technical education programs located within existing academic high schools. Close ties with area employers are also needed for internships at companies that would typically begin in the junior year; support from states, especially for the special equipment training often requires, may be needed. Additional federal Perkins Act CTE funding and alliances with community colleges with strong workforce programs are also needed.

Our recommendations for technical and comprehensive high schools, states, and school districts are as follows:

- Form comprehensive high schools by altering existing academic high schools to develop workforce education programs in cooperation with area community colleges and employers (model 5).
- Create new technical high schools with high-quality workforce education programs developed in cooperation with employers and community colleges (model 5).

Recommendations for Employers

While all the models require collaborations among employers, educators, and governments, employer involvement is particularly important.

Employers historically provided on-the-job training for many workers, but data in chapter 3 suggest this support has been declining. Global competition has put cost pressure on employers to cut training costs, and those that do invest in training feel they lose the benefits of their investment when workers change employers. But an aging workforce and shortages in needed higher skills may be leading some employers to reconsider training.

Some large employers have provided *apprenticeships* for young employees in the past (see chapter 10); nearly all of these are gone. Apprenticeships involve long-term commitments from employers that typically act to fill short-term needs. Federal support for new apprenticeship efforts has grown since 2008, however, and some large employers, including a group led by IBM, have begun to run their own apprenticeship projects.

Programs in which employers share education costs for apprenticeships and internships for new entrant workers may be an option for some. Employers in several states, including South Carolina and Wisconsin, have supported apprenticeship programs in which both small and large employers pay apprentice wages while educational institutions, government, and industry associations share the costs for the education side. These programs put employers in a collaborative relationship with community colleges and state government.

Cost sharing of training among regional groups of employers may also be possible. The US Chamber of Commerce Foundation's Talent Pipeline Management program reaches both new and incumbent workers to help employers in upskilling their workforces, providing both online and in-person programs customized to area employer needs. At this writing, the program had two hundred partnerships reaching thousands of employers in twenty-six states.

Employer associations have also sponsored *skill certification efforts and standards*. The Manufacturing Skills Standards Council (MSSC) has created an industry-led certification, training, and assessment system for some sixty manufacturing skills that are industry defined and federally endorsed. This still evolving common certification system helps employers understand applicants' qualifications, enables workers to show transportable skills, and allows educators to design programs.

In general, as each of these examples illustrates, employers need to *collaborate with educators and area governments*. The workforce development boards that manage regional training efforts with Labor Department funding have long been employer led. If board programs can be structured to reach incumbent workers better, the employer role will grow. Collaborative training efforts shared among area employers and efforts by industry groups to establish much-needed skill certification systems for sector skills appear to be workable training approaches for employers. In some regions, businesses can provide leadership for workforce efforts; in others, they will be active participants. Workforce training is a team activity and must involve education institutions, area governments, and industry working together.

Our recommendations for employers are as follows:

- Collaborate with educators and state and local governments, as well as labor organizations, in developing workforce education systems, including apprenticeships and internships at the high school and community college levels, as well as upskilling for incumbent workers (models 1, 2, 4, and 6).

- Collaborate with other employers, including small and medium-size employers, on workforce development to break the pattern of one-off, nonreplicable programs by single employers (model 6).
- Use industry associations and work with educators to develop skill standards and certification systems (such as the MSSC system) for existing and new technical tasks and occupations (model 6).
- Support new labor market information systems (model 8).

The nine models for specific delivery programs offer concrete ways these recommendations can be implemented.

APPLICATION TO WORKER CATEGORIES

Given the widespread disruption to the American working class we've described, led by a decline in the manufacturing sector but expanding into large areas of less skilled work, any workforce education recommendations must address the three different worker categories we've been using throughout this book:

- *Incumbent workers* need to raise their skill levels to meet the demands of new technologies. They could be helped by community college programs at workforce sites; improving completion rates for community college certificate and degree programs; expanded employer training roles; short programs at community colleges for upgrading and changing skills; collaborative efforts by states, educators, and industry to develop education for advanced skills required for oncoming technologies; new labor market information systems; and scalable new education technologies.
- *New entrant workers* need better routes from school to work. Skill education programs at community colleges, youth apprenticeships, and technical and comprehensive high schools, as well as most of the other approaches noted for incumbent workers, would help.
- *Underemployed or displaced workers* have morale problems from job loss or are stuck in lower-end, lower-paid jobs inadequate for supporting themselves and their families. They could benefit particularly from short programs, improved completion rates, more unified state labor and education programs, and new labor market information systems, as well as the other approaches noted earlier in this list.

The new models and our recommendations based on them, then, speak directly to these categories.

IMPLEMENTATION IN SECTORS

Workforce education cannot be understood in the abstract. Workforce needs must be seen in the context of particular industry sectors that differ widely. We've examined three sectors closely—manufacturing, retail, and healthcare delivery—that together account for about one-third of the nation's workforce. The new delivery models and our recommendations noted earlier fit these sectors.

Manufacturing

Manufacturing is important to the nation's overall economic performance, despite the major decline in employment and output between 2000 and 2010. Prior to the COVID-19 outbreak, output levels had only recently recovered, but jobs remained well below year 2000 levels.

Nevertheless, manufacturing faces significant employment needs in the coming decade because of an aging workforce. And as new technologies enter the sector—typically the first to adopt new productivity opportunities—new levels of skills will be required of the workforce. There is no workforce education system yet for advanced manufacturing, which will include new digital and information technologies, advanced materials, photonics, composites, 3-D printing, and robotics. Both content and content-delivery approaches need development. There are big stakes here: becoming an early mover on advanced manufacturing will play a significant part in America's future economic well-being.

This sector will require new content, new certification systems, and improved means of delivery. Existing skill shortages will be compounded by shortages in new sets of required skills. These present major challenges. All nine new delivery models detailed in chapter 11 and listed earlier will be relevant, requiring new programs in manufacturing education. They can be adapted to fit advanced manufacturing workforce needs, as detailed in table 12.1.

Manufacturing employers, preferably acting through area industry consortia, will need to create new training and apprenticeship roles and apply new certification systems for the new production technologies. In addition, states that want to retain their manufacturing sectors will need to form statewide plans for developing and delivering training to workers in the new advanced manufacturing technologies, as Massachusetts has done.

TABLE 12.1
Workforce education policies for advanced manufacturing

Policy approach	Policy model #
Use community colleges to deliver skills training for incumbent manufacturing workers, high school students, and community college students in state-supported advanced manufacturing centers	1
Form apprenticeship and youth apprenticeship programs in cooperation with manufacturing employers, community colleges and high schools, and government	2 6
Increase community college completion rates, including in manufacturing skills	3
Develop short training programs in manufacturing skills at community colleges	4
Form technical or comprehensive high schools with advanced manufacturing programs	5
Unify education, workforce development, and economic development programs for delivery of advanced manufacturing skills at the state level	7
Support new information systems to help workers, employers, and educators navigate job searches, job qualifications, skills certifications, and skills acquisition	8
Use new education technologies delivered online to scale up the advanced manufacturing content-delivery process	9

This will require strong involvement from industry, as well education institutions and government agencies, all playing their roles, as discussed earlier.

Retail

Employment in the retail sector has been in decline at brick-and-mortar stores, which have suffered shocks from the Great Recession and the coronavirus, but growing for online ordering and warehousing. As retailers move to omnichanneling—making connections between online ordering and physical stores seamless—they will also need to change to well-trained, highly informed sales clerks who become customer guides, helping them through the maze of product options and using online capabilities to create personalized products and solutions for customers. Apple's sleek stores, which have created the highest retail returns ever, exemplify this approach with their expert trained staff and Genius Bars.

Training in retail has historically been minimal. Stores and chains locked into older retail models with poorly trained staff now face a major upskilling task to be competitive. If an expert staff is now the key to in-person retail, staff members must be trained in product lines, business services, and online skills. Many of the models we've discussed are relevant, including short programs and certificates in computing and business services at community colleges. The trifecta community college approach to reach incumbent workers at existing worksites, as well as new skills certifications, will be needed. Retail workers in an increasingly disrupted sector will be in particular need of new workforce information systems.

Large retailers with large numbers of employees face a daunting training task. They likely need to supplement new face-to-face training efforts with online education that can scale far more rapidly than classroom training, including applying new online technologies. They can also consider online strategies to "train the trainers," using the first level of managers to train retail staff.

Healthcare

Healthcare is an expanding sector because of patient need, but the established physician and nurse professions face shortages in primary care, drug treatment, treatment of the elderly, and other important areas. At the same time, new technologies rapidly entering the sector require experts trained in their use. New varieties of medical assistants, as well as physician assistants and nurse practitioners, are growing in parallel to the rising demand. These forces are creating a training task of great magnitude. Yet these new fields face barriers to entry because of the long-established roles of the existing professions. Nearly all nine models we've discussed could prove relevant to meet the education needs in these new healthcare fields.

America's social fabric is being torn by the social disruption and growing economic inequality driven by declines in the manufacturing sector and lower-skill jobs. Too many people are falling behind, lacking the skills needed to keep up—let alone get ahead. We need a renewed workforce education system. It's a societal imperative.

We have a disconnected workforce education system, with critical gaps for incumbent and new entrant workers. We have quality jobs we aren't filling, a situation that will pick up again as we recover from the coronavirus downturn. We have a host of new advanced technologies beginning to enter the economy and no system for educating workers to understand and use them. We have a massive gap between school and the workplace, and an unacceptable youth unemployment rate as a result. We have a dysfunctional labor market information system that leaves workers, employers, and educators adrift. We have new education technologies evolving to scale our training, but we have failed to deploy them adequately to meet our needs. We have not applied the resources—funding, talent, and new approaches—we need to fix these problems.

We see the need for expanding the community college role to reach not only community college students but also incumbent workers and high school students. We need apprenticeships where they fit employer needs. We must dramatically increase the completion rate for community college certificates and degrees. We need short programs that are also connected to certificates and degrees and that can reach displaced and underemployed workers.

It's time for new technical and comprehensive high school programs, expanded employer training roles, and for universities to assist in developing advanced content, online delivery, and new education technologies. We need unified state program delivery for education and workforce development, and state efforts with educators and industry to develop new education content and delivery for the oncoming advanced technologies. We must have new information systems that can help workers, employers, and educators navigate complex labor markets. And we need new education technologies to help these workforce education programs to scale. Collaboration between employers, educators, and government will be a critical criterion for all these efforts.

This is a tall order—but one we can fill.

In the early twentieth century, the demands of a rapidly industrializing economy created a need for high schools nationwide. Within three decades, a new secondary education system was built in every state and school district. If our nation could accomplish that, the workforce education challenge we face now is not a "mission impossible." Many of the institutions we need are already in place. The models for a renewed workforce education system are not abstract ideas; they are already being tested. We can build this.

The stakes are too high to ignore. The American workforce is the key to our economy and our democracy.

NOTES

1 INTRODUCTION

1. Dr. Sanford C. Shugart, conversation with author, Kissimmee, FL, June 26, 2018.

2. Dr. Kathleen Plinske, conversation with author, Kissimmee, FL, June 26, 2018.

3. Wesley Naylor, conversation with author, Orlando, FL, June 25, 2018.

4. Capt. Erik Etz, conversation with author, Orlando, FL, June 25, 2018.

5. Careersource Florida, https://careersourceflorida.com/about-us/.

6. FLATE, regional and statewide impacts, http://fl-ate.org/about-us/impact/.

7. Kevin Carr, conversation with author, Orlando, FL, June 26, 2018.

8. Careersource Florida, "Florida Summit Aims to Help Shape the Future of Apprenticeships as a Vital Career Pathway," June 18, 2018, https://careersourceflorida.com/apprenticeshipflasummit/.

9. William B. Bonvillian, "Donald Trump's Voters and the Decline of American Manufacturing," *Issues in Science and Technology* 32, no. 4 (Summer 2016), http://issues.org/32-4/donald-trumps-voters-and-the-decline-of-american-manufacturing/.

10. William B. Bonvillian and Peter L. Singer, *Advanced Manufacturing: The New American Innovation Policies* (Cambridge, MA: MIT Press, 2018), 1; Federal Reserve Bank of St. Louis, Federal Reserve Economic Data, All Employees: Manufacturing, https://fred.stlouisfed.org/series/MANEMP.

11. David Autor, David Dorn, and Gordon Hanson, "The China Shock: Learning from Labor-Market Adjustment to Large Changes in Trade," *Annual Review of Economics* 8 (2016): 205–240.

12. Bonvillian and Singer, *Advanced Manufacturing*, 53–55, 265.

13. Bonvillian and Singer, 245–254.

14. Melissa S. Kearney, Brad Hershbein, and Elisa Jacome, "Profiles of Change: Employment, Earnings and Occupations from 1990–2013," Hamilton Project report, April 20, 2015, http://www.hamiltonproject.org/assets/legacy/files/downloads_and_links/Employment_Earnings_Occupations_Changes_1990-2013_FINAL_1.pdf.

15. Kearney, Hershbein, and Jacome, "Profiles of Change." See also Gregory Mankiw, "Why Aren't More Men Working?," *New York Times*, June 15, 2018.

16. Bureau of Labor Statistics, "Occupational Employment Statistics, 51-0000 Production Occupations," May 2015, http://www.bls.gov/oes/current/oesstru.htm#510000. See Bureau of Labor Statistics, "Concepts and Methodology," http://www.bls.gov/cps/documentation.htm#concepts.

17. Alicia Sasser Modestino, "The Importance of Middle-Skill Jobs," *Issues in Science and Technology* 33, no. 1 (Fall 2016), https://issues.org/the-importance-of-middle-skill-jobs/.

18. Vernon Bundage Jr., "Profile of the Labor Force by Education Attainment," Bureau of Labor Statistics, August 2017, https://www.bls.gov/spotlight/2017/educational-attainment-of-the-labor-force/pdf/educational-attainment-of-the-labor-force.pdf. See also Modestino, "The Importance of Middle-Skill Jobs," 42. If high-skill jobs are defined to include some college education, the report found that by 2016 two-thirds of the labor force had achieved this level of education. Of the remaining one-third, between 1992 and 2016 the number of jobs held by workers without a high school diploma fell by 5 percent and the number of jobs for workers with a high school diploma but no college education fell by 10 percent.

19. Facundo Alvaredo, Anthony B. Atkinson, Thomas Piketty, Emmanuel Saez, and Gabriel Zucman, "The World Wealth and Income Database," http://www.wid.world/.

20. Claudia Goldin and Lawrence F. Katz, *The Race Between Education and Technology* (Cambridge, MA: Harvard University Press, 2008).

21. David H. Autor, "Polanyi's Paradox and the Shape of Employment Growth," *Proceedings of the Federal Reserve of Kansas City*, August 2014, 139–142. See also David H. Autor and David Dorn, "The Growth of Low-Skill Service Jobs and the Polarization of the US Labor Market," *American Economic Review* 103, no. 5 (2013): 1553–1597.

22. Gary S. Becker, *Human Capital: A Theoretical and Empirical Analysis, with Special Reference to Education* (New York: National Bureau of Economic Research, 1975).

23. Council of Economic Advisors, "Active Labor Market Policies: Theory and Evidence of What Works," issue brief, White House, December 2016, 4, https://obamawhitehouse.archives.gov/sites/default/files/page/files/20161220_active_labor_market_policies_issue_brief_cea.pdf.

24. Council of Economic Advisors, "Active Labor Market Policies," 1–2.

25. Martin Ford, *Rise of the Robots: Technology and the Threat of a Jobless Future* (New York: Basic Books, 2015); Tyler Cowen, *Average Is Over: Powering America Beyond the Age of the Great Stagnation* (New York: Dutton Penguin Group, 2013); Carl Benedikt Frey and Michael A. Osbourne, *The Future of Employment: How Susceptible Are Jobs to Computerisation?* (Oxford, UK: Oxford Martin School, University of Oxford, Oxford, September 17, 2013), http://www.oxfordmartin.ox.ac.uk/downloads/academic/The_Future_of_Employment.pdf.

26. Shawn Sprague, "Below Trend: The U.S. Productivity Slowdown since the Great Recession," *Beyond the Numbers*, 6, no. 2 (January 2017), https://www.bls.gov/opub/btn/volume-6/below-trend-the-us-productivity-slowdown-since-the-great-recession.htm. See also Adams Nager, "Trade vs. Productivity: What Caused U.S. Manufacturing's Decline and How to Revive It," Information Technology and Innovation Foundation report, February 13, 2017, https://itif.org/publications/2017/02/13/trade-vs-productivity-what-caused-us-manufacturings-decline-and-how-revive.

27. Robert D. Atkinson, "How to Reform Worker-Training and Adjustment Policies for an Era of Technological Change," Information Technology and Innovation Foundation report, February 2018, 7, http://www2.itif.org/2018-innovation-employment-workforce-policies.pdf?_ga=2.110161607.390165303.1536533172-1797272473.1536533172.

28. MIT Work of the Future Task Force, The Work of the Future: Shaping Technology and Institutions, Fall 2019, https://workofthefuture.mit.edu/sites/default/files/2019-09/WorkoftheFuture_Report_Shaping_Technology_and_Institutions.pdf.

29. Dani Rodrik, presentation on Building a Good Jobs Economy, MIT Future of Work Task Force, April 2, 2020.

30. Strengthening Career and Technical Education for the 21st Century Act, Public Law 115-224, H.R. 2353, passed with Senate Amendment 3408 (passed Senate July 23, 2018), enacted July 31, 2018.

31. Presidential Executive Order on Expanding Apprenticeships in America, June 15, 2017, https://www.whitehouse.gov/presidential-actions/3245/. See also Task Force on Apprenticeship Expansion, Final Report to the President of the United States, submitted by Secretary of Labor R. Alexander Acosta and Secretary of Education Betsy DeVos, May 10, 2018, https://www.dol.gov/apprenticeship/docs/task-force-apprenticeship-expansion-report.pdf.

32. US Chamber of Commerce Foundation, Center for Education and Workforce, Workforce Development initiatives, https://www.uschamberfoundation.org/workforce-development.

33. Workforce Information Advisory Council, "Recommendations to Improve the Nation's Workforce and Labor Market Information System," submitted to Alexander

Acosta, Secretary of Labor, January 25, 2018, https://www.doleta.gov/wioa/wiac/docs/Second_Draft_of_the_WIAC_Final_Report.pdf.

34. Michelle Weise, Andrew Hanson, Allison Salisbury, and Kathy Qu (Strada Institute), "On Ramps to Good Jobs" (report), Strada Institute, January 31, 2019, 2, 37, https://go.stradaeducation.org/on-ramps.

35. Pew Research Center, "The Rising Cost of Not Going to College," report, 2014, http://www.pewsocialtrends.org/2014/02/11/the-rising-cost-of-not-going-to-college/.

36. Margaret Cahalan, L. W. Perna, M. Yamashita, J. Wright, and S. Santillan, "Indicators of Higher Education Equity in the United States," Historical Trend Report, Pell Institute for the Study of Opportunity in Higher Education, Council for Opportunity in Education and Alliance for Higher Education and Democracy of the University of Pennsylvania, 2018, 96, http://pellinstitute.org/downloads/publications-Indicators_of_Higher_Education_Equity_in_the_US_2018_Historical_Trend_Report.pdf.

37. Raj Chetty, Nathaniel Hendren, Patrick Kline, and Emmanuel Saez, "Where Is the Land of Opportunity? The Geography of Intergenerational Mobility in the United States," *Quarterly Journal of Economics* 129, no. 4 (November 2014): 1553–1623.

2 THE AMERICAN WORKING CLASS

1. Christine Walley and Chris Boebel, *Exit Zero*, http://www.exitzeroproject.org.

2. Amy Goldstein, *Janesville, An American Story* (New York: Simon and Schuster, 2017).

3. William Julius Wilson, *The Truly Disadvantaged: The Inner City, the Underclass, and Public Policy* (Chicago: University of Chicago Press, 1987).

4. Anthony P. Carnevale, Neil Ridley, Ban Cheah, Jeff Strohl, and Kathryn P. Campbell, "Upskilling and Downsizing in American Manufacturing," Georgetown Center on Education and the Workforce, June 2019, 26–27, https://1gyhoq479ufd3yna29x7ubjn-wpengine.netdna-ssl.com/wp-content/uploads/Manufacturing_FR.pdf; Andew Stettner, Joel S. Yuken, and Michael McCormack, "Why Manufacturing Jobs Are Worth Saving," The Century Foundation, report, June 2017, 3, https://tcf.org/content/report/manufacturing-jobs-worth-saving/.

5. Gregory Tassey, "Make America Great Again: Investing in Research, Technology Development, Worker Training, and Modern Technological Infrastructure Is the Only Prescription That Will Maintain the Health of the US Economy," *Issues in Science and Technology,* Winter 2018.

6. Robert M. Solow, *Growth Theory: An Exposition*, 2nd ed. (New York: Oxford University Press, 2000); William B. Bonvillian and Peter L. Singer, *Advanced Manufacturing, The New American Innovation Policies* (Cambridge, MA: MIT Press, 2018), 65–99.

7. Stephen A. Merrill, "Righting the Research Imbalance," Center for Innovation Policy at Duke University Law School, report, June 2018; Tassey, "Make America Great Again."

8. Tassey, "Make America Great Again."

9. Andres Ortega, "U.S.: Massaging Unemployment Numbers," *The Globalist*, October 25, 2018, https://www.theglobalist.com/united-states-unemployment-republicans-donald-trump/. See also "Macrotrends, U6 Unemployment Rate (compared to U3 official unemployment rate 1995–2018)," https://www.macrotrends.net/1377/u6-unemployment-rate.

10. David H. Autor, "Polanyi's Paradox and the Shape of Employment Growth," *Proceedings of the Federal Reserve of Kansas City*, August 2014, 142.

11. Mike Stobbe, "U.S. Life Expectancy Will Likely Decline for the Third Straight Year," *Bloomberg Business*, May 23, 2018, https://www.bloomberg.com/news/articles/2018-05-23/with-death-rate-up-us-life-expectancy-is-likely-down-again (based on Centers for Disease Control data); Anne Case and Sir Angus Deaton, "Mortality and Morbidity in the 21st Century," Brookings Institution, March 23, 2017, https://www.brookings.edu/bpea-articles/mortality-and-morbidity-in-the-21st-century/.

12. Autor, "Polanyi's Paradox," 139–142. See also David H. Autor and David Dorn, "The Growth of Low-Skill Service Jobs and the Polarization of the US Labor Market," *American Economic Review* 103, no. 5 (2013): 1553–1597.

13. Paul Osterman and Beth Shulman, Good *Jobs America: Making Work Better for Everyone* (New York: Russell Sage Foundation, 2011).

14. Jay Shambaugh, Ryan Nunn, Patrick Liu, and Greg Nantz, "Thirteen Facts about Wage Growth," Hamilton Project report, September 24, 2017, https://www.hamiltonproject.org/assets/files/thirteen_facts_wage_growth.pdf.

15. Thomas Piketty, Emmanuel Saez, and Gabriel Zucman, "Distributional National Accounts: Methods and Estimates for the United States," National Bureau of Economic Research, NBER Working Paper 22945, December 2016.

16. Shambaugh et al., "Thirteen Facts about Wage Growth."

17. Steven J. Davis and Till M. von Wachter, "Recessions and the Cost of Job Loss," National Bureau of Economic Research, NBER Working Paper 17638, December 2011 (revised March 2017).

18. Shambaugh et al., "Thirteen Facts about Wage Growth."

19. Brad Hershbein, Melissa Kearney, and Lawrence Summers, "Increasing Education: What It Will and Will Not Do for Earnings and Earnings Inequality," Brookings Institution, 2015, https://www.brookings.edu/blog/up-front/2015/03/31/increasing-education-what-it-will-and-will-not-do-for-earnings-and-earnings-inequality/.

20. Jonathan Haskel, Robert Z. Lawrence, Edward E. Leamer, and Matthew J. Slaughter, "Globalizaton and U.S. Wages: Modifying Classic Theory to Explain Recent Facts," *Journal of Economic Perspectives* 26, no. 2 (Spring 2012); Michael Spence, "The Impact of Globalization on Income and Employment: The Downside of Integrating Markets," *Foreign Affairs* 90, no. 4 (July–August 2011): 40.

21. David Autor, David Dorn, and Gordon Hanson, "The China Shock: Learning from Labor-Market Adjustment to Large Changes in Trade," *Annual Review of Economics* 8 (2016): 205–240. See also J. Bernard Andrew, Bradford Jensen, and Peter Schott, "Survival of the Best Fit: Exposure to Low-Wage Countries and the (Uneven) Growth of U.S. Manufacturing Plants," *Journal of International Economics* 68, no. 1 (2006): 219–237 (imports from low-income countries led by China led to reductions in US employment rates during the period 1977 to 1997); Justin R Pierce and Peter K. Schott, "The Surprisingly Swift Decline of US Manufacturing Employment," *American Economic Review* 106, no. 7 (2016): 1632–1662 (the major decline in US manufacturing employment after 2000 tied to the trade recognition of China, to its entry into the WTO, and to US trade policy that granted Permanent Normal Trade Relations [PNTR] to China); Daron Acemoglu, David Autor, David Dorn, Gordon H. Hanson, and Brendan Price, "Import Competition and the Great US Employment Sag of the 2000s," *Journal of Labor Economics* 34, np. S1 (2016): S141–S198 (Chinese imports account for a significant part of US manufacturing unemployment). See, generally, Dani Rodrik, *Straight Talk on Trade: Ideas for a Sane World Economy* (Princeton, NJ: Princeton University Press, 2017). The other side of the regional nature of the recovery was also underscored in *The China Shock*. For example, when China entered the WTO in 2001, there were nearly four hundred thousand jobs in American textile mills. While a small portion of the overall US workforce, these jobs accounted for more than 15 percent of all jobs in fifty-seven counties in the US Southeast. The impact of Chinese production competition in these communities was "like a mini economic bomb going off over downtown." In other words, beyond an education differential, the largest force pulling down the availability of good, middle-skill jobs was globalization, particularly China's rise.

22. Harry J. Holzer, "Job Market Polarization and U.S. Worker Skills," Brookings, Economic Studies, April 2015, 2–3, https://www.brookings.edu/wp-content/uploads/2016/06/polarization_jobs_policy_holzer.pdf.

23. Shambaugh et al., "Thirteen Facts about Wage Growth."

24. Jay Shambaugh and Patrick Ryan, "Introduction," in *Revitalizing Wage Growth: Policies to Get American Workers a Raise*, ed. Jay Shambaugh and Patrick Ryan (Washington, DC: Brookings Institution, 2018), 3–7.

25. David Card, "The Effect of Unions on Wage Inequality in the U.S.," *Industrial and Labor Relations Review* 54, no. 2 (January 2001): 301; Jake Rosenfeld, *What Unions No Longer Do* (Cambridge, MA: Harvard University Press, 2014), 68–83.

26. Council of Economic Advisors, "Labor Market Monopsony: Trends, Consequences and Policy Responses," issue brief, October 2016, https://obamawhitehouse.archives.gov/sites/default/files/page/files/20161025_monopsony_labor_mrkt_cea.pdf; David Autor, Alan Manning, and Christopher Smith, "The Contribution of the Minimum Wage to U.S. Wage Inequality over Three Decades: A Reassessment," *American Economic Journal: Applied Economics* 8, no. 1 (January 2016): 58–99.

27. Shawn Sprague, "Below Trend: The U.S. Productivity Slowdown since the Great Recession," *Beyond the Numbers* 6, no. 2 (January 2017), https://www.bls.gov/opub/btn/volume-6/below-trend-the-us-productivity-slowdown-since-the-great-recession.htm.

28. John Fernald, "Productivity and Potential Output Before, During, and After the Great Recession," *NBER Macroeconomics Annual* 29 (1) (2015): 1–51.

29. Jason Furman (chair, Council of Economic Advisors), "Business Investment in the United States: Facts, Explanations, Puzzles and Policies," remarks, Progressive Policy Institute, September 30, 2015, https://obamawhitehouse.archives.gov/sites/default/files/page/files/20150930_business_investment_in_the_united_states.pdf.

30. Shambaugh and Ryan, "Introduction."

31. Furman, "Business Investment in the United States"; Ana Paula Cusolito and William F. Maloney, *Productivity Revisited, Shifting Paradigms in Analysis and Policy—Overview* (Washington, DC: The World Bank Group 2018), 2.

32. See, for example, Robert Gordon, *The Rise and Fall of American Growth* (Princeton, NJ: Princeton University Press, 2016); Cusolito and Maloney, *Productivity Revisited,* 2–6; Mathilde Pak and Cyrille Schwellnus, "Labour Share Developments Over the Past Two Decades: The Role of Public Labor Poliices," OECD Economics Department Working Papers No. 1541, February 14, 2019; Jason Furman and Peter Orszag, "A Firm-Level Perspective on the Role of Rents in the Rise in Inequality," presentation at Columbia University's "A Just Society" Centennial Event in Honor of Joseph Stiglitz, New York, October 16, 2015. Effective decline in federal R&D has been a problem (American Association for the Advancement of Science [AAAS], "Federal R&D as a Percent of GDP," 1976–2018, https://www.aaas.org/sites/default/files/s3fs-public/RDGDP%253B.jpg), and so has manufacturing decline, as this sector historically leads productivity advance (Bonvillian and Singer, *Advanced Manufacturing*, 75–76).

33. Kearney, Hershbein, and Jacome, "Profiles of Change."

34. Gregory Mankiw, "Why Aren't More Men Working?," *New York Times*, June 15, 2018. See also Council of Economic Advisors, "Active Labor Market Policies: Theory and Evidence of What Works," issue brief, White House, December 2016.

35. Diane Whitmore Schanzenbach, Lauren Bauer, Ryan Nunn, Megan Mumford, "Who Is Out of the Labor Force," Hamilton Project report, August 17, 2017, https://www.hamiltonproject.org/papers/who_is_out_of_the_labor_force.

36. Katherine G. Abraham and Melissa S. Kearney, "Explaining the Decline in the U.S. Employment-to-Population Ratio: A Review of the Evidence," paper, University of Maryland, February 8, 2018. See also Martha Ross, "The Labor Market: Who Is In and Who Is Out?," Brookings Institution, August 30, 2017, https://www.brookings.edu/blog/the-avenue/2017/08/30/the-labor-market-who-is-in-and-who-is-out/; Martha Ross and Natalie Holmes, "Meet the Out-of-Work: Local Profiles of Jobless Adults and Strategies to Connect them to Employment," Brookings Institution, June 22, 2017, https://www.brookings.edu/research/meet-the-out-of-work/.

37. Alex Hollingsworth, Christopher J. Ruhm, and Kosali Simon, "Macroeconomic Conditions and Opioid Abuse," NBER Working Paper No. 23192, February 2017 (revised March 2017).

38. Kerwin K. Charles, Erik Hurst, and Mariel Schwartz, "Transformation of Manufacturing and the Decline in U.S. Employment," National Bureau of Economic Research, NBER Working Paper 24468, March 2018, 48.

39. Council of Economic Advisors, "Active Labor Market Policies."

40. Council of Economic Advisors, "The Long-Term Decline in Prime-Age Male Labor Participation," June 2016, 27.

41. Schanzenbach et al., "Who Is Out of the Labor Force?"

42. See, for example, Katherine G. Abraham, John C. Haltiwanger, Kristin Sandusky and James R. Spltzer, "The Rise of the Gig Economy: Fact or Fiction?," *American Economic Association Papers and Proceedings* 109 (May 2019): 357–361, https://www.aeaweb.org/articles?id=10.1257/pandp.20191039.

43. Jay Shambaugh, Ryan Nunn, and Lauren Bauer, "Independent Workers and the Modern Labor Market," Brookings Institution, June 7, 2018, https://www.brookings.edu/blog/up-front/2018/06/07/independent-workers-and-the-modern-labor-market/; BLS, The Economic Daily, Independent contractors made up 6.9 percent of employment, June 21, 2018, https://www.bls.gov/opub/ted/2018/independent-contractors-made-up-6-point-9-percent-of-employment-in-may-2017.htm.

44. Lydia DePillis, "Black Unemployment Is at a Record Low—But There Is a Lot More to the Story," CNN Money, January 23, 2018, https://money.cnn.com/2018/01/23/news/economy/black-unemployment/index.html.

45. Statista, The Statistics Portal, "Unemployment Rate of Hispanic Americans in the U.S., 1990–2017," https://www.statista.com/statistics/194154/unemployment-rate-of-hispanic-americans-in-the-us-since-1990/.

46. Stephen Greenhouse, *The Big Squeeze* (New York: Alfred Knopf, 2008), 38; Bureau of the Census, *Income, Poverty and Health Insurance Coverage in the United States 2006* (Washington, DC: Bureau of the Census, 2007), 6.

47. Greenhouse, *The Big Squeeze*, 38–39.

48. Greenhouse, *The Big Squeeze*, 39.

49. Economic Innovation Group, "Millions Mired in Poverty as U.S. Upturn Passes Them By," September 2017.

50. Clara Hendrickson, Mark Muro, and William A. Galston, "Countering the Geography of Discontent: Strategies for Left-Behind Places," Brookings Institution, November 2018, https://www.brookings.edu/research/countering-the-geography-of-discontent-strategies-for-left-behind-places/.

51. Third Way, Report: "The Opportunity Index: Ranking Opportunity in Metropolitan America," October 30, 2018, https://www.thirdway.org/report/the-opportunity-index-ranking-opportunity-in-metropolitan-america.

52. Hendrickson, Muro, and Galston, "Countering the Geography of Discontent."

53. Charles et al., "Transformation of Manufacturing and the Decline in U.S. Employment," 2, 62.

54. Harry J. Holzer, *Where Are All the Good Jobs Going?* (New York: Russell Sage Foundation, 2011).

55. Jeffrey Lin, "Technological Adaptation, Cities, and New Work," *Review of Economics and Statistics* 93, no. 2 (May 2011): 554–574.

56. David H. Autor, "Work of the Past, Work of the Future," Ely lecture, American Economic Association annual meeting, Atlanta, GA, January 4, 2019, 21–23, 35, https://www.aeaweb.org/webcasts/2019/aea-ely-lecture-work-of-the-past-work-of-the-future (webcast version).

57. David H. Autor, presentation to Aspen Institute Work of the Future and MIT Future of Work Initiatives, forum, Washington, DC, May 20, 2019.

58. Autor, "Work of the Past, Work of the Future," 5, 13–31.

59. Economic Innovation Group, "Distressed Communities Index 2018," 2 (The Ruralization of Distress) https://eig.org/dci. See also Eduardo Porter, "The Hard Truths of Trying to 'Save' the Rural Economy," *New York Times,* December 14, 2018, https://www.nytimes.com/interactive/2018/12/14/opinion/rural-america-trumpdecline.

60. Clara Hendrickson, Mark Muro, and William A. Galston, "Strategies for Left-Behind Places," Brookings Institution, November 2018, 7–11, https://www.brookings.edu/wpcontent/uploads/2018/11/2018.11_Report_Countering-geography-ofdiscontent_Hendrickson-Muro-Galston.pdf.

61. Economic Innovation Group, "The New Map of Economic Growth and Recovery," May 2016, https://eig.org/wp-content/uploads/2016/05/recoverygrowthreport.pdf and https://eig.org/recoverymap.

62. Department of Agriculture, Economic Research Service, "Rural Poverty and Well-Being," 2018, https://www.ers.usda.gov/topics/rural-economy-population/rural-poverty-wellbeing; see also Benjamin Austin, Edward Glaeser, and Lawrence Summers, "Jobs for the Heartland: Place Based Policies in 21st Century America," Brookings Papers on Economic Activity, Spring 2018, 166–172, https://www.brookings.edu/wp-content/uploads/2018/03/AustinEtAl_Text.pdf. Austin, Glaeser, and Summers of Harvard examined the "eastern heartland," the largely rural area between the Mississippi River and the Atlantic coast states, and found it a region of particular distress indicated by rates of those not working (unemployment plus not in the workforce), mortality rates, opioid consumption, and life dissatisfaction rates.

63. Ryan Nunn, Jana Parsons, and Jay Shambaugh, "Americans Aren't Moving to Economic Opportunity," Brookings Institution, November 19, 2018, https://www.brookings.edu/blog/up-front/2018/11/19/americans-arent-moving-to-economic-opportunity/?utm_campaign=Economic%20Studies&utm_source=hs_email&utm_medium=email&utm_content=67840211.

64. Peter Ganong and Daniel Shoag, "Why Has Regional Income Convergence in the U.S. Declined?," *Journal of Urban Economics* 102 (November 2017): 76–90.

65. Steven J. Davis and John Haltwanger, "Labor Market Fluidity and Economic Performance," NBER Working Paper 20479, December 2014; Raven Malloy, Christopher L. Smith, and Abigail Wozniak, "Internal Migration in the United States," *Journal of Economic Perspectives* 25, no. 3 (Summer 2011).

66. Nunn, Parsons, and Shambaugh, "Americans Aren't Moving to Economic Opportunity."

67. Autor, "Work of the Past, Work of the Future," 50.

68. Autor, "Work of the Past, Work of the Future," 5, 13–31.

69. See, for example, policy recommendations in Hendrickson, Muro, and Galston, "Countering the Geography of Discontent."

70. Census Bureau, "Income and Poverty in the United States 2017, Selected Measures of Household Income," table A-2, Report P60-263, September 18, 2018, https://www.census.gov/library/publications/2018/demo/p60-263.html. See also Spence, "The Impact of Globalization on Income and Employment," 40.

71. Claudia Goldin and Lawrence F. Katz, *The Race Between Education and Technology* (Cambridge, MA: Harvard University Press, 2008). See also David Autor, "Skills, Education and the Rise of Earnings Inequality among the Other 99 Percent," *Science* 344, no. 6186 (May 23, 2014).

72. Goldin and Katz, *The Race Between Education and Technology* (Cambridge, MA: Harvard University Press, 2008). See also Autor, "Skills, Education and the Rise of Earnings Inequality among the Other 99 Percent"; David H. Autor, Lawrence F. Katz,

and Melissa S. Kearney, "Trends in US Wage Inequality: Revising the Revisionists," *Review of Economics and Statistics* 90 (2008): 300–323.

73. Anthony P. Carnevale, Tamara Jayasundera, and Artem Gulish, "America's Divided Recovery: College Haves and Have-Nots," Georgetown Center on Education and the Workforce, 2016, 1, 2, 3, 4, 15, 18, https://1gyhoq479ufd3yna29x7ubjn-wpengine.netdna-ssl.com/wp-content/uploads/Americas-Divided-Recovery-web.pdf. Other studies confirm these developments. For example, a Pew 2016 study found that the number of workers in occupations requiring average to above-average education, training, and experience increased from forty-nine million in 1980 to eighty-three million in 2015, or by 68 percent. This was more than double the increase over the same period in employment, from fifty million to sixty-five million, in jobs requiring below-average education, training, and experience. See Pew Research Center, "The State of American Jobs: How the Shifting Economic Landscape Is Reshaping Work and Society and Affecting the Way People Think about the Skills and Training They Need to Get Ahead," report, October 6, 2016, https://www.pewsocialtrends.org/2016/10/06/the-state-of-american-jobs/ (using Labor Dept. Occupational Information Network [O*NET] data; job rating is based on education, experience, and training required; the mid-level occupation rating corresponds to an associate degree).

74. Shambaugh et al., "Thirteen Facts about Wage Growth," 3. Of course, not all college degrees are equal. Data on high school versus college income success shows that the affected population that could benefit from skills upgrading is not only based among less than high school and high school degree holders; about one-quarter of college graduates earn the equivalent of higher-end high school degree recipients. Jason R. Abel and Richard Deitz, "College May Not Pay Off for Everyone," Federal Reserve Bank of New York, *Liberty Street Economics*, September 4, 2014; Jordan Weissmann, "When College Grads Earn Like High School Grads," paper, *Slate*, September 8, 2014.

75. Burning Glass Technologies and Strada Institute for the Future of Work, "The Permanent Detour: Underemployment's Long-Term Effects on Careers," report, May 2018, 8, https://www.burning-glass.com/wp-content/uploads/permanent_detour_underemployment_report.pdf.

76. Council of Economic Advisors, "Active Labor Market Policies."

77. John Alic, "Beyond Schooling: Educating for the Unknowable Future," *The Bridge*, National Academy of Engineering, Fall issue, September 2015.

78. Mitra Toossi and Elka Torpey, "Career Outlook, Older Workers: Labor Force Trends and Career Options," Bureau of Labor Statistics, May 2017, https://www.bls.gov/careeroutlook/2017/article/older-workers.htm.

79. Kevin Mahnken, "The Age of Retraining: How Employers Are Working to Upskill Employees and Stave Off the Rise of the Machines," *T74*, November 13, 2018, https://www.the74million.org/article/the-age-of-retraining-how-employers-are-working-to-upskill-employees-and-stave-off-the-rise-of-the-machines/.

80. See, for example, Peter Gosselin and Ariana Tobin, "Cutting Old Heads at IBM," *Pro Publica*, March 22, 2018, https://features.propublica.org/ibm/ibm-age-discrimination-american-workers/.

81. Tyler Cowan, "Forget New Robots, Keep Your Eye on the Old People: A Changing Workforce Will Fuel Companies That Tap Potential Workers over 55," *Bloomberg Opinion*, May 17, 2018, https://www.bloomberg.com/amp/opinion/articles/2018-05-17/older-workers-will-help-companies-thrive?__twitter_impression=true.

82. Mahnken, "The Age of Retraining."

83. Thomas Kochan, David Finegold, and Paul Osterman, "Who Can Fix the 'Middle Skills' Gap?," *Harvard Business Review*, December 2012, 2101.

84. Harry J. Holzer, "Workforce Development as an Antipoverty Strategy: What Do We Know, What Should We Do?," IZA, DP No. 3776, October 2008, 21, http://ftp.iza.org/dp3776.pdf. See also Harry J. Holzer and Robert Lerman, *America's Forgotten Middle-Skill Jobs: Education and Training Requirements for the Next Decade and Beyond* (Washington, DC: The Workforce Alliance, 2007), 3–4, https://www.urban.org/sites/default/files/publication/31566/411633-America-s-Forgotten-Middle-Skill-Jobs.PDF. A 2008 study of Maryland middle-skill jobs, for example, confirmed the pattern: in the upcoming decade, 46 percent of Maryland employment would be in middle-skill jobs, 35 percent in high-skill occupations, and 25 percent in occupations requiring no more than a high school degree. See Bronwyn Mauldin, "Maryland's Forgotten Middle-Skill Jobs," Skills2Compete and the National Skills Coalition, report, 2008, 4, https://www.nationalskillscoalition.org/resources/publications/file/marylands-forgotten-jobs.pdf.

85. National Academies of Sciences, Engineering, and Medicine, *Building America's Skilled Technical Workforce* (Washington, DC: National Academies Press, 2017), 2, https://www.nap.edu/catalog/23472/building-americas-skilled-technical-workforce.

86. Harry J. Holzer, "Job Market Polarization and U.S. Worker Skills," 2–3.

87. Jonathan Rothwell, "The Hidden STEM Economy," Brookings Institution, June 10, 2013, https://www.brookings.edu/research/the-hidden-stem-economy/.

88. Anita Balakrishnan, Berkeley Lovelace, Jr., "IBM CEO: Jobs of the Future Won't Be Blue or White Collar, They'll Be 'New collar,'" CNBC, January 17, 2017, https://www.cnbc.com/2017/01/17/ibm-ceo-says-ai-will-be-a-partnership-between-man-and-machine.html.

89. Gordon Lafer, *The Job Training Charade* (Ithaca, NY: Cornell University Press, 2002), 2.

90. Pew Research Center, "The State of American Jobs." The survey was made against a large sample base of representative adults—predominantly in the workforce, but two-fifths out.

3 BREAKDOWNS IN TODAY'S WORKFORCE EDUCATION

1. Paul Osterman, presentation to Aspen Institute Future of Work and MIT Work of the Future initiatives, forum, Washington, DC, May 20, 2019.

2. Kenneth C. Gray and Edwin L. Herr, *Workforce Education, The Basics* (New York: Pearson 1997). For a history of career education, see Howard R. D. Gordon, *The History and Growth of Career and Technical Education in America,* 4th ed. (Long Grove, IL: Waveland Press, 2014).

3. Council of Economic Advisors, "Active Labor Market Policies: Theory and Evidence of What Works," issue brief, White House, December 2016, 1–2, https://obamawhitehouse.archives.gov/sites/default/files/page/files/20161220_active_labor_market_policies_issue_brief_cea.pdf.

4. Harry J. Holzer, "Workforce Development as an Antipoverty Strategy: What Do We Know, What Should We Do?," IZA, DP No. 3776, October 2008, 1, http://ftp.iza.org/dp3776.pdf.

5. Holzer, "Workforce Development as an Antipoverty Strategy," 3.

6. Holzer, "Workforce Development as an Antipoverty Strategy," 9–17.

7. Holzer, "Workforce Development as an Antipoverty Strategy," 9.

8. Holzer, "Workforce Development as an Antipoverty Strategy," 22.

9. Paul Osterman, *Securing Prosperity, The American Labor Market: How it has Changed and What to Do about It* (Princeton, NJ: Princeton University Press, 2000). See also David Autor, Introduction, in *Studies of Labor Market Intermediation,* ed. David Autor (Chicago: University of Chicago Press, 2009), 1–26.

10. Paul Osterman, presentation to Aspen Institute Future of Work and MIT Work of the Future initiatives, forum, Washington, DC, May 20, 2019.

11. Osterman, Aspen and MIT forum.

12. Council of Economic Advisors, 2015 Economic Report of the President, "Achievements and Challenges in the U.S. Labor Market," c. 3, 2015, 146–147, https://obamawhitehouse.archives.gov/sites/default/files/docs/2015_erp_chapter_3.pdf.

13. Jeffrey Waddoups, "Did Employers in the United States Back Away from Skills Training during the Early 2000s?," *Industrial and Labor Relations Review* 69, no. 2 (December 2015), https://journals.sagepub.com/doi/10.1177/0019793915619904. See also Jeffrey Waddoups, "Has Complementarity between Employer-Sponsored Training and Education Changed during the 2000s?," *Education Economics* 26, no. 2 (August 2017): 1–16.

14. Robert I. Lerman, "Are Employers Providing Enough Training? Theory Evidence and Policy Implications," paper for the National Academy of Sciences Symposium on

the Supply Chain for Middle Skill Jobs, 2017, 3, https://sites.nationalacademies.org/cs/groups/pgasite/documents/webpage/pga_168146.pdf.

15. Use of these terms is detailed in Paul Osterman, "In Search of the High Road: Meaning and Evidence," *Industrial and Labor Relations Review* 71, no. 1 (October 23, 2017), https://iwer.mit.edu/wp-content/uploads/2018/04/In-Search-of-the-High-Road.pdf. The context of high- and low-road employer options is discussed at length in Thomas Kochan, *Shaping the Future of Work: What Future Worker, Business Government Leaders Need to Do for All to Prosper* (New York: Business Expert Press, 2015).

16. Lerman, "Are Employers Providing Enough Training?," 11, 17–21.

17. Lerman, "Are Employers Providing Enough Training?," 16–20.

18. Council of Economic Advisors, "Active Labor Market Policies," 3; Council of Economic Advisors, "The Long-Term Decline in Prime-Age Male Labor Force Participation," June 2016, 27–28, https://obamawhitehouse.archives.gov/sites/default/files/page/files/20160620_cea_primeage_male_lfp.pdf.

19. Paul Romer, "Endogenous Technological Change," *Journal of Political Economy* 98, no. 5 (1990): 72–102, http://web.stanford.edu/~klenow/Romer_1990.pdf; Eric Hanushek and Ludger Weissmann, "Universal Basic Skills: What Countries Stand to Gain," OECD Publishing, 2015, http://dx.doi.org/10.1787/9789264234833-en.

20. Census Bureau, Statistics of U.S. Businesses, Annual Datasets by Establishment Industry 1997–2012, 2012, https://www.census.gov/preograms-surveys/susb/dataset.All.html.

21. Business Roundtable, Workforce Education Committee, https://www.businessroundtable.org/about-us/committees/education-workforce-committee, https://www.businessroundtable.org/time-to-align-americas-skills-gap-and-how-to-overcome-it; US Chamber of Commerce Foundation, Center for Education and Workforce, Workforce Development, https://www.uschamberfoundation.org/workforce-development; Manufacturing Institute, Workforce Skills Certification, http://www.themanufacturinginstitute.org/Skills-Certification/Skills-Certification.aspx.

22. Niv Elis, "Union Membership Falls to Record Low of 10.3 Percent," *The Hill*, January 22, 2020 (citing BLS data), https://thehill.com/policy/finance/479400-union-membership-falls-to-record-low-of-103-percent.

23. Holzer, "Workforce Development as an Antipoverty Strategy," 3–6. The summary here is drawn from Holzer's history of these programs.

24. Holzer, "Workforce Development as an Antipoverty Strategy," 5–6.

25. Department of Labor, Employment and Training Administration, WIOA Overview, https://www.doleta.gov/wioa/Overview.cfm.

26. Council of Economic Advisors, "Active Labor Market Policies," 6–7.

27. National Skills Coalition, "America's Workforce: We Can't Compete If We Cut," August 2018, https://www.nationalskillscoalition.org/resources/publications/file/Americas-workforce-We-cant-compete-if-we-cut-1.pdf.

28. David Cruise (president, MassHires Hamden Co. Workforce Development Board, Springfield, MA), discussion, May 15, 2019.

29. Benjamin Collins, "Trade Adjustment Assistance for Workers and the TAA Reauthorization Act of 2016," Congressional Research Service, August 14, 2018, 3, https://fas.org/sgp/crs/misc/R44153.pdf.

30. Mark Muro and Joseph Parilla, "Maladjusted: It's Time to Reimagine Economic 'Adjustment' Programs," Brookings Institution, January 20, 2017, https://www.brookings.edu/blog/the-avenue/2017/01/10/maladjusted-its-time-to-reimagine-economic-adjustment-programs/.

31. David Autor, David Dorn, and Gordon Hanson, "China Shock: Learning from Labor Market Adjustment to Large Changes in Trade," *Annual Review of Economics 2016*, no. 8, 229–231, http://www.ddorn.net/papers/Autor-Dorn-Hanson-ChinaShock.pdf.

32. Department of Labor, Employment and Training Administration, Apprenticeship, Data and Statistics, Registered Apprenticeship to 9/30/18, https://doleta.gov/oa/data_statistics.cfm.

33. Department of Education, Federal Student Aid Office, Federal Pell Grants, https://studentaid.ed.gov/sa/types/grants-scholarships/pell.

34. Department of Education, Federal Student Aid Office, Gainful Employment Information, https://studentaid.gov/data-center/school/ge. Created in 2010, these regulations have been revoked effective July 2020. Federal Register, "Program Integrity: Gainful Employment, A Rule by the Department of Education, 7/1/19," https://www.federalregister.gov/documents/2019/07/01/2019-13703/program-integrity-gainful-employment.

35. College Board, "Trends in Higher Education: Total Pell Grant Expenditures and Number of Recipients over Time, 2017–18," https://trends.collegeboard.org/student-aid/figures-tables/pell-grants-total-expenditures-maximum-and-average-grant-and-number-recipients-over-time.

36. Robert Kelchen, "Examining Trends in the Pell Grant Program," July 3, 2017, https://robertkelchen.com/2017/07/03/examining-trends-in-pell-grant-program/. See also Department of Education, Pell Grant Annual Data Report, "Statistics by Type and Control of Institution for Award Year 2017–2018," table 18, https://www2.ed.gov/finaid/prof/resources/data/pell-data.html; Sung-Woo Cho, James Jacobs, and Christine Zhang, Community College Research Center, Columbia Teacher's College, "Demographic and Academic Characteristics of Pell Grant Recipients at Community

Colleges," CCRC Working Paper no. 65, November 2013, 3, https://ccrc.tc.columbia.edu/media/k2/attachments/demographic-academic-characteristics-pell-grant.pdf.

37. Senate Committee on Health Education and Pensions, Report on For Profit Higher Education: "The Failure to Safeguard the Federal Investment and Ensure Student Success," July 30, 2012, https://www.help.senate.gov/imo/media/for_profit_report/PartI-PartIII-SelectedAppendixes.pdf. The committee found that while for-profit two-year programs have low completion rates comparable to low rates at community colleges, the much higher cost of the for-profit programs made them a much higher risk for students and for the federal taxpayers funding student loans. It found that while 96 percent of students attending for-profit colleges borrow to attend, only 13 percent of community college students do so.

38. These include Stafford Loans (for at least half-time students in colleges, community colleges, or certificate programs; loan rates can be subsidized or unsubsidized), Perkins Loans (for at least half-time, low-income college students), and PLUS Loans (for parents of college students).

39. College Scholarships.org, Technical School Loans, http://www.collegescholarships.org/loans/technical.htm; Department of Education, Office of Federal Student Aid, Federal student loans, https://studentaid.ed.gov/sa/types/loans.

40. Alexandre Tanzi, "U.S. Student Debt in 'Serious Delinquency' Tops $166 Billion," *Bloomberg,* February 19, 2019, https://www.bloomberg.com/news/articles/2019-02-16/u-s-student-debt-in-serious-delinquency-tops-166-billion, https://www.bloomberg.com/news/articles/2019-02-16/u-s-student-debt-in-serious-delinquency-tops-166-billion ("serious delinquency" defined as in default or unpaid for three months; data calculated from Federal Reserve Bank of New York's quarterly household-debt report).

41. Advance CTE, "Strengthening Career and Technical Education for the 21st Century Act" (Perkins V) (review of new legislation), 2018, https://www.careertech.org/perkins.

42. Zuzana Cepia, National Immigration Forum, Fact Sheet, "What Is the Perkins CTE?," July 25, 2018, https://immigrationforum.org/article/fact-sheet-perkins-cte-serve-immigrants/; Advance CTE, Perkins V.

43. An option created through the 2018 reauthorization of the Perkins Act allowed states for the first time to develop joint plans for both their Labor Department-Backed Workforce Investment and Opportunity Act (WIOA) and Education Department-Backed Perkins Act programs. Some sixteen states are pursuing this, with new plans due in 2020. Gregory Henshall, Department of Education, Office of Career Technical and Occupational Education, presentation to Manufacturing Innovation Institute Workforce Education Directors, ManTech, Alexandria, VA, February 5, 2020.

44. Jeannie Oakes, *Keeping Track, How Schools Structure Inequality*, 2nd ed. (New Haven, CT: Yale University Press, 2005).

45. The Alliance for Vocational Technical Education, "High Quality Career Technical Education in Massachusetts," March 2, 2018, https://skillworks.files.wordpress.com/2018/03/avte-white-paper_final-2-8-18-1.pdf.

46. Susan Frey, "Los Angeles Unified Cuts Adult School by Half—and That's the Good News," *Ed Source*, July 5, 2012.

47. David J. Deming, Claudia Goldin, and Lawrence F. Katz, "The For-Profit Postsecondary School Sector: Nimble Critters or Agile Predators?," *Journal of Economic Perspectives* 26, no. 1 (Winter 2012): 149, https://pubs.aeaweb.org/doi/pdfplus/10.1257/jep.26.1.139.

48. Deming, Goldin, and Katz, "For-Profit Postsecondary School Sector," 139.

49. Department of Education, National Center for Education Statistics, table 303.25, Total Fall Enrollment in Degree-Granting Post-Secondary Institutions by Control of Institutions, 1970–2015," https://nces.ed.gov/programs/digest/d16/tables/dt16_303.25.asp. See also Deming, Goldin, and Katz, "For-Profit Postsecondary School Sector," 139–140.

50. Deming, Goldin, and Katz, "For-Profit Postsecondary School Sector," 146–147.

51. Meghan Perdue, "Work Training Centers: A New Model for Workforce Training," dissertation, Harvard University, May 14, 2018, 16–19.

52. Industrial Training International, https://www.iti.com/about.

53. Perdue, "Work Training Centers."

54. Perdue, "Work Training Centers," 17.

55. David Deming, Claudia Goldin, and Lawrence Katz, "For-Profit Colleges," *Future of Children* 23, no. 1 (Spring 2013): 150.

56. Deming, Goldin, and Katz, "For-Profit Colleges," 154–157.

57. Deming, Goldin, and Katz, "For-Profit Colleges," 153–154.

58. US Government Accountability Office, "For-Profit Colleges: Undercover Testing Finds Colleges Encouraged Fraud and Engaged in Deceptive and Questionable Marketing Practices," GAO-10-948T, August 4, 2010, http://www.gao.gov/products/GAO-10-948T; Deming, Goldin, and Katz, "The For-Profit Postsecondary School Sector," 154.

59. Stastica, US College Enrollment Statistics for Public and Private Colleges, 2016, https://www.statista.com/statistics/183995/us-college-enrollment-and-projections-in-public-and-private-institutions/. Compared to private colleges, public college enrollment in 2016 was 74 percent of total enrollment.

60. Bridget Terry Long, "State Support for Higher Education: How Changing the Distribution of Funds Could Improve College Completion Rates," Miller Center,

University of Virginia, December 2016, http://web1.millercenter.org/commissions/higher-ed/Long_No9.pdf.

61. Richard D. Kahlenberg, "How Higher Education Funding Shortchanges Community Colleges," Century Foundation, May 28, 2015, https://tcf.org/content/report/how-higher-education-funding-shortchanges-community-colleges/.

62. Kahlenberg, "How Higher Education Funding Shortchanges Community Colleges."

63. Kahlenberg, "How Higher Education Funding Shortchanges Community Colleges"; Natasha Ushomirsky and David Williams, "Funding Gaps 2015: Too Many States Still Spend Less on Education Students Who Need the Most," The Education Trust, March 2015, 5.

64. Education Commission of the States, "50-State Comparison: Transfer and Articulation Policies," June 2018, https://www.ecs.org/transfer-and-articulation-policies-db/.

65. Ellie Ashford, "A Smoother Path for Computer Science," American Association of Community Colleges, *Community College Daily,* October 27, 2017, http://www.ccdaily.com/2017/10/smoother-transfer-path-computer-science/ (citing studies from the Community College Research Center at Columbia Teacher's College and the Association for Computing Machinery).

66. Committee on Appropriations, Subcommittee on Energy and Water Development, House of Representatives, Hearing on Energy Workforce Development Opportunities and Challenges, March 7, 2019, Testimony of Noel Bakhtian and Sloane Evans, https://appropriations.house.gov/legislation/hearings/energy-workforce-opportunities-and-challenges.

67. ATE Central, "Supporting Advanced Technological Education," https://atecentral.net/index.php?P=Home.

68. National Science Foundation, FY2020 Budget Request to Congress, "Education and Human Resources Funding by Division and Program, Advanced Technological Education (ATE)," summary table, 2019 19, https://www.nsf.gov/about/budget/fy2020/pdf/14_fy2020.pdf.

69. National Science Foundation, FY2018 Budget Request, "Education and Human Resources Funding by Division and Program," summary tables 17, May 23, 2017, https://www.nsf.gov/about/budget/fy2018/pdf/fy2018budget.pdf; Statista, Community Colleges in the United States—Statistics and Facts, https://www.statista.com/topics/3468/community-colleges-in-the-united-states/.

70. Manufacturing USA, Program Details, https://www.manufacturingusa.com/pages/program-details.

71. William B. Bonvillian and Peter L. Singer, *Advanced Manufacturing: The New American Innovation Policies* (Cambridge, MA: MIT Press, 2018), 217–242.

72. Michael Britt-Crane, Mantech, and Julie Diop, AIM Photonics Academy, presentation to Manufacturing Innovation Institute Workforce Education Directors, ManTech, Alexandria, VA, February 5, 2020.

73. Bureau of Economic Analysis, "Underlying Detail of Industry Economic Accounts Data: GDP by Industry, Value Added by Industry," November 1, 2018, https://apps.bea.gov/iTable/iTable.cfm?reqid=56&step=2&isuri=1#reqid=56&step=2&isuri=1.

74. Manufacturing USA and NIST, 2018 Annual Report, 14–15.

75. Credential Engine, "Counting U.S. Secondary and Postsecondary Credential—April 2018 Report," April 5, 2018, 3, https://www.credentialengine.org/articles/ba957e1e-8aef-45ec-8bb4-237ae3902e75/Counting_U_S__Secondary_and_Postsecondary_Credentials___April_2018_Report.

76. William B. Bonvillian and Charles Weiss, *Technological Innovation in Legacy Sectors* (Oxford, UK: Oxford University Press, 2015).

4 TECHNOLOGY VERSUS JOBS

1. Toyota Research Institute, "Toyota Research Institute Bets Big in Vegas on Toyota Guardian Autonomy," press release, January 7, 2019, https://www.prnewswire.com/news-releases/toyota-research-institute-bets-big-in-vegas-on-toyota-guardian-autonomy-300774048.html.

2. Toyota Research Institute, "Toyota Research Institute Bets Big."

3. Toyota Research Institute, "Toyota Research Institute Bets Big."

4. Toyota Research Institute; John Leonard, "Autonomous Vehicles Have a Long Road Ahead," MIT Initiative on the Digital Economy, September 27, 2013 (also, video of seminar), http://ide.mit.edu/news-blog/blog/john-leonard-autonomous-vehicles-have-long-road-ahead; MIT Work of the Future Task Force, "The Work of the Future: Shaping Technology and Institutions," October 2019, 33–34. See, generally, David Mindell, *Our Robots Ourselves, Robotics and the Myths of Autonomy* (New York: Penguin Random House, 2015); Erica Groshen, John Macduffie, Susan Helper, Charles Carson, Richard Mudge, and David Montgomery, "America's Workforce and The Self-Driving Future: Securing America's Energy Future," report, June 2018, https://avworkforce.secureenergy.org.

5. "The Automation Jobless, Not Hired, Just Fired," *Time*, February 24, 1961.

6. Robert D. Atkinson, "How to Reform Worker-Training and Adjustment Policies for an Era of Technological Change," Information Technology and Innovation Foundation, February 2018, 5–6, http://www2.itif.org/2018-innovation-employment-workforce-policies.pdf?_ga=2.243519110.224871682.1519243251-1005716061.1518706968.

7. Nils J. Nilsson, "Artificial Intelligence and Income," *The AI Magazine*, Summer 1984, 5, http://ai.stanford.edu/users/nilsson/OnlinePubs-Nils/General%20Essays/AIMag05-02-002.pdf (citing Gail G. Schwartz); Wasily Leontief, "The New New Age That's Coming Is Already Here," *Bottom Lane/Personal* 4, no. 8 (April 1983): 1–2; Wasily Leontief and Faye Duchin, "The Impacts of Automation on Employment, 1963–2000," *New York Institute for Economic Analysis* (April 1984), http://eric.ed.gov/?id=ED241743.

8. Ray Kurzweil, *The Singularity Is Near: When Humans Transcend Biology* (New York: Viking Press, 2005).

9. Erik Brynjolfsson and Andrew McAfee, *The Second Machine Age: Work, Progress, and Prosperity in a Time of Brilliant Technologies* (New York: W. W. Norton & Company, 2014); Martin Ford, *Rise of the Robots: Technology and the Threat of a Jobless Future* (New York: Basic Books, 2015).

10. Klaus Schwab, "The Fourth Industrial Revolution: What It Means, How to Respond," World Economic Forum, January 14, 2016, https://www.weforum.org/agenda/2016/01/the-fourth-industrial-revolution-what-it-means-and-how-to-respond/.

11. Carl Benedikt Frey and Michael A. Osborne, "The Future of Employment: How Susceptible are Jobs to Computerization?," University of Oxford, September 17, 2013, 44, https://www.oxfordmartin.ox.ac.uk/downloads/academic/The_Future_of_Employment.pdf.

12. Erik Brynjolfsson and Andrew McAfee, *The Second Machine Age*, 41, 49; Ford, *Rise of the Robots*, 77, 113, 194–198; Tyler Cowen, *Average Is Over: Powering America Beyond the Age of the Great Stagnation* (New York: Plume, 2014), 39–40.

13. A "Pigovian Tax," named for the British economist Arthur C. Pigou (a leading early contributor to externality theory), is a fee imposed on private individuals or businesses for engaging in specific activities that create negative externalities (e.g., pollution). The aim is to bring those activities in line with private and social costs.

14. Robert D. Atkinson, "'It's Going to Kill Us!' and Other Myths About the Future of Artificial Intelligence," Information Technology and Innovation Foundation report, June 2016, 13–15, http://www2.itif.org/2016-myths-machine-learning.pdf?_ga=2.253897032.1145278909.1597430162-1555696460.1597430162.

15. Atkinson, "'It's Going to Kill Us!," 14–15.

16. James Manyika, Susan Lund, Michael Chui, Jacques Bughin, Jonathan Woetzel, Parul Batra, Ryan Ko, and Saurabh Saurabhvi, "What the Future of Work Will Mean for Jobs, Skills and Wages," McKinsey Global Institute (December 2017), Sec. 3, https://www.mckinsey.com/global-themes/future-of-organizations-and-work/what-the-future-of-work-will-mean-for-jobs-skills-and-wages.

17. Melanie Arntz, Terry Gregory, Ulrich Zierahn, "Risk of Automation for Jobs in OECD Countries, a Comparative Analysis," OECD Social, Employment and Migration Working Paper No. 189 (Paris, OECD, June 16, 2016); David Autor and Michael

Handel, "Putting Tasks to the Test: Human Capital, Job Tasks, and Wages," *Journal of Labor Economics* 31, no. 2 (2013): S59–S96.

18. Mark Muro, Robert Maxim, and Jacob Whiton, "Automation and Artificial Intelligence: How Machines Are Affecting People and Places," Brookings Institution, January 2019, 5, 6, 11, https://www.brookings.edu/wp-content/uploads/2019/01/2019.01_BrookingsMetro_Automation-AI_Report_Muro-Maxim-Whiton-FINAL-version.pdf.

19. Kelemwork Cook, Duwain Pinder, Shelley Steward III, Amaka Uchegbu, and Jason Wright, "The Future of Work in Black America," McKinsey & Co., October 2019, https://www.mckinsey.com/featured-insights/future-of-work/the-future-of-work-in-black-america?cid=eml-web.

20. David H. Autor, "What Are There Still So Many Jobs? The History and Future of Workplace Automation," *Journal of Economic Perspectives* 29, no. 3 (Summer 2015): 5; David Autor, presentation on The Future of Work, Roundtable Discussion, MIT, January 9, 2016.

21. MIT Work of the Future Task Force, "The Work of the Future: Shaping Technology and Institutions," 10, 17–19.

22. Michael J. Handel, Northeastern University, presentation on Skills, Job Creation and Labour Market, Conference on Smart Industry: Enabling the Next Production Revolution, OECD and Sweden Ministry of Enterprise and Innovation, Stockholm, September 18, 2016.

23. Daron Acemoglu and Pascal Restrepo, "Robots and Jobs: Evidence from U.S. Labor Markets," NBER Working Paper No. 23285, March 2017 (study covered a 17-year period showing a possible range of 360,000–670,000 jobs affected); Wolfgang Dauth, Sebastian Findeisen, Jens Sudekum, and Nicole Wobner, "German Robots: The Impact of Industrial Robots on Workers," IAB Discussion Paper, Institute for Employment Research, 2017, 4, 41, http://doku.iab.de/discussionpapers/2017/dp3017.pdf (study using the same modeling approach covered 1994–2014; part of the finding could be affected by Germany's high unionization rate and corresponding job protections).

24. J. C. R. Licklider, "Man-Computer Symbiosis," *IRE Transactions on Human Factors in Electronics*, HFE-1 (March 1960): 4–11, http://memex.org/licklider.pdf. See, generally, M. Mitchell Waldrop, *The Dream Machine, J.C.R. Licklider and the Revolution that Made Computing Personal* (New York: Viking Penguin, 2001). Norbert Weiner, at the beginning of the computer era, articulated a contrary view of computing as a threat. See Norbert Weiner, *Cybernetics: Or Control and Communication in the Animal and Machine* (Cambridge, MIT: MIT Press, 1948); Norbert Weiner, *Human Use of Human Beings* (New York: Houghton Mifflin, 1950).

25. Mindell, *Our Robots Ourselves*.

26. See also discussion in chapter 5. Manufacturers Alliance for Productivity and Innovation, MAPI Foundation (Cliff Waldman, chief economist), "U.S. Output

Recovery from the Great Recession and U.S. Manufacturing Productivity Growth—Annual Averages" (2017) (based on MAPI, BLS, and Federal Reserve data).

27. Adams Nager, "Trade vs. Productivity: What Caused U.S. Manufacturing's Decline and How to Revive It," Information Technology and Innovation Foundation report, February 13, 2017, https://itif.org/publications/2017/02/13/trade-vs-productivity-what-caused-us-manufacturings-decline-and-how-revive.

28. William B. Bonvillan and Peter L. Singer, *Advanced Manufacturing: The New American Innovation Policies* (Cambridge, MA: MIT Press, 2018).

29. David Autor, "Trade and Labor Markets: Lessons from China's Rise," *IZA World of Labor* 431 (February 2018): 2–3, https://wol.iza.org/articles/trade-and-labor-makets-lessons-from-chinas-rise/long.

30. David Autor, David Dorn, and Gordon Hanson, "The China Shock: Learning from Labor Market Adjustment to Large Changes in Trade," *Annual Review of Economics* 8, no. 1 (2016): 205–240; Daron Acemoglu, David Autor, David Dorn, Gordon Hanson, and Brendan Price, "Import Competition and the Great US Employment Sag of the 2000s," *Journal of Labor Economics* 34, no. S1 (2016): S141–S198, https://econpapers.repec.org/article/ucpjlabec/doi_3a10.1086_2f682384.htm/; Autor, "Trade and Labor Markets."

31. Computer and Electronics Show (CES) Press Release, "CTA and IBM Announce Apprenticeship Coalition to Help Close U.S. Skills Gap," January 8, 2019, https://www.ces.tech/News/Press-Releases/CES-Press-Release.aspx?NodeID=20769cf6-315a-435f-a70e-ba05c7ce76c4; Cat Zakrzewski, "Technology Companies Turn to Apprenticeships in Tight Labor Market," *Washington Post*, January 8, 2019.

32. Suzanne Berger, "Looking for Robots," presentation to the MIT Work of the Future Task Force, March 5, 2020.

33. David Autor, "Labor Market Consequences of Automation: Some Familiar Facts and Recent Insights," presentation at the MIT Work of the Future Advisory Board Meeting, October 23, 2018.

34. Sheelah Kolhatkar, "Welcoming Our New Robot Overlords," *New Yorker*, October 16, 2017, 70–81, https://www.newyorker.com/magazine/2017/10/23/welcoming-our-new-robot-overlords.

35. Thomas H. Davenport and Julia Kirby, *Only Humans Need Apply: Winners & Losers in the Age of Smart Machines* (New York: HarperBusiness, 2016).

36. Mentioned in Oren Etzioni, Allen Institute for AI, University of Washington, "Demystifying Artificial Intelligence," National Academies of Sciences' Government, University, Industry Roundtable (GUIRR), Forum on Artificial Intelligence and Machine Learning to Accelerate Translational Research, February 13–14, 2018, http://

sites.nationalacademies.org/PGA/guirr/PGA_184752?utm_source=GUIRR+Mailing+List&utm_campaign=b8f6f7bb66-EMAIL_CAMPAIGN_2018_02_21&utm_medium=email&utm_term=0_bdd65e8597-b8f6f7bb66-121960985#etzioni.

37. Erik Brynjolfsson and Tom Mitchell, "What Can Machine Learning Do? Workforce Implications," *Science* 358, no. 6370 (December 22, 2017): 1530–1534.

38. Stephen Herzenberg and John Alic, "Towards an Economy That Works for All," Keystone Research Center, Pittsburgh, February 2019, 1–2, https://www.keystoneresearch.org/sites/default/files/FOW_TowardAIEconomyForAllFinalEdit.pdf.

39. Nicolaus Henke, Jordan Levine, and Paul McInerney, "You Don't Have to Be a Data Scientist to Fill This Must-Have Analytics Role," *Harvard Business Review*, February 5, 2018.

40. McKinsey Global Institute, "The Age of Analytics: Competing in a Data-Driven World," December 2016, 5, https://www.mckinsey.com/~/media/mckinsey/business%20functions/mckinsey%20analytics/our%20insights/the%20age%20of%20analytics%20competing%20in%20a%20data%20driven%20world/mgi-the-age-of-analytics-executive-summary.ashx.

41. Digital Manufacturing and Design Innovation Institute (since renamed MxD) and the Manpower Group (Lory Antonucci, Michael Fornasciero, and Rebekah Kowalski), "Partners in Connection—The Digital Workforce Succession in Manufacturing—Digital Manufacturing and Design Job Roles Taxonomy," 2017, 16–23, http://www.uilabs.org/wp-content/uploads/2017/08/DMD-Job-Role-Taxonomy.pdf.

42. Andrew Stettner, "Mounting a Response to Technological Unemployment," The Century Foundation, April 26, 2018, https://tcf.org/content/report/mounting-response-technological-unemployment/?mc_cid=9fd7b1bc0a&mc_eid=43538a7cb1&agreed=1.

43. Bureau of Labor Statistics, Economic News Release, "Long-Tenured Displaced Workers by Occupation of Lost Job and Employment Status in January 2018" (table 5), https://www.bls.gov/news.release/disp.t05.htm.

44. Henry S. Farber, "The Great Recession and Its Aftermath: U.S. Evidence from the Displaced Worker Survey," Working Paper 21216, National Bureau of Economic Research, May 2015, 23, https://www.nber.org/papers/w21216.pdf.

45. Farber, "The Great Recession and Its Aftermath," 8–11.

46. Stettner, "Mounting a Response to Technological Unemployment"; Steven J. Davis and Till Von Wachter, "Recession and the Costs of Job Loss," Brookings Papers on Economic Activity, Fall 2011, 47, https://www.brookings.edu/wp-content/uploads/2011/09/2011b_bpea_davis.pdf.

47. Marilyn Gewax, "The Impacts of Long-Term Unemployment," National Public Radio, December 11, 2012 (based on a Kaiser Family Foundation and NPR survey), https://www.npr.org/2011/12/09/143438731/the-impacts-of-long-term-unemployment/; Gewax, "The Impacts of Long-Term Unemployment"; Daniel Sullivan and Till Von Wachter, "Job Displacement and Mortality: An Analysis Using Administrative Data," *Quarterly Journal of Economics* 124, no. 3 (August 2009): 1265.

48. Maria Heidkamp and John J. Heldrich (Center for Workforce Development, Rutgers University), "Older Workers, Rising Skill Requirements, and the Need for a Re-envisioning of the Public Workforce System," Council for Adult and Experiential Learning (CAEL), 2012, 5, http://cdn2.hubspot.net/hubfs/617695/premium_content_resources/adult_learning/pdfs/TMT_Reenvision_Public_Workforce_System.pdf. See also Richard W. Johnson and Corina Mommaerts, "Age Differences in Job Loss, Job Search, and Reemployment," The Urban Institute, January 2011, https://www.urban.org/sites/default/files/publication/27086/412284-Age-Differences-in-Job-Loss-Job-Search-and-Reemployment.PDF.

49. MIT Work of the Future, 22–23.

50. Frank Levy and Richard Mumane, *Division of Labor: How Computers Are Creating the New Job Market* (Princeton, NJ: Princeton University Press, 2004).

51. Frank Levy, "How Technology Changes Demands for Human Skills," OECD Education Working Paper No. 45, March 5, 2010, 4, http://www.oecd.org/education/skills-beyond-school/45052661.pdf.

52. Levy, "How Technology Changes Demands," 6–10.

53. Levy, "How Technology Changes Demands," 10–11.

54. Levy, "How Technology Changes Demands," 12–13.

55. David Autor, "Polyani's Paradox and the Shape of Employment Growth," NBER Working Paper, No. 20485, September 2014, 39, https://www.nber.org/papers/w20485.pdf.

56. Autor, "Polyani's Paradox," 40.

57. National Academies of Sciences, Committee on Information Technology, Automation and the U.S. Workforce, "Information Technology and the U.S. Workforce," 2017, 3, https://www.nap.edu/catalog/24649/information-technology-and-the-us-workforce-where-are-we-and?utm_source=GUIRR+Mailing+List&utm_campaign=74b72f778d-EMAIL_CAMPAIGN_2018_02_15&utm_medium=email&utm_term=0_bdd65e8597-74b72f778d-121960985.

58. National Academies of Sciences, "Information Technology and the U.S. Workforce," 9.

59. See, for example, Pablo Illanes, Susan Lund, Mona Mourshed, Scott Rutherford, and Mannus Tyreman, "Retraining and Reskilling Workers in the Age of Automation," McKinsey, January 2018, https://www.mckinsey.com/global-themes/future-of-organizations-and-work/retraining-and-reskilling-workers-in-the-age-of-automation?cid=other-soc-twi-mip-mck-oth-1801&kui=ibaK9f82QZ7UgcjR8Mi5LA&utm_source=newsletters&utm_medium=email&utm_content=2018_01_26+&utm_campaign=clocking_in; Atkinson, "How to Reform Worker-Training and Adjustment Policies for an Era of Technological Change."

5 THE THREE SECTORS

1. Bureau of Labor Statistics, "Retail Trade," NAICS 44–45, https://www.bls.gov/iag/tgs/iag44-45.htm; Bureau of Labor Statistics, "Manufacturing," NAICS 31–33, https://www.bls.gov/iag/tgs/iag31-33.htm; Bureau of Labor Statistics, "Health Care (and Social Assistance)," NAICS 62 https://www.bls.gov/iag/tgs/iag62.htm. See also Bureau of Labor Statistics, "The Employment Situation," February 1, 2019, News Release, "Total Non-Farm Employment," December 2018, https://www.bls.gov/news.release/pdf/empsit.pdf (150,270,000); Statistica, "Full Time U.S. Employment," January 2019 (based on BLS data, not seasonally adjusted), https://www.statista.com/statistics/192361/unadjusted-monthly-number-of-full-time-employees-in-the-us/(full time employment 128.17 million).

2. Bureau of Labor Statistics, "Employment Projections: 2018–28," Summary, Economic News Release, USDL-19–1571, September 4, 2019, https://www.bls.gov/news.release/ecopro.nr0.htm, and related tables.

3. Bureau of Labor Statistics, "Employment Projections, 2016–26," News Release, updated January 30, 2018, 5, https://www.bls.gov/news.release/archives/ecopro_10242017.pdf.

4. Garrison Moore and Robert Bowman, *Headcount, Understanding the American Workforce* (New Hope, PA: Lonesome Association, 2018), 35–36, http://innovationamerica.us/images/PDF/Headcount3-20-2018.pdf. See also David Autor, Frank Levy, and Richard J. Murnane, "The Skill Content of Recent Technological Change: An Empirical Exploration," *Quarterly Journal of Economics* 118, no. 4 (2003): 1279–1333; Nir Jaimovich and Henry E. Siu, "Job Polarization and Jobless Recoveries," National Bureau of Economic Research, Cambridge, MA, NBER Working Paper 18334, November 2018, 9–11, https://www.nber.org/papers/w18334.pdf.

5. William B. Bonvillian, "Donald Trump Voters and the Decline of American Manufacturing," *Issues in Science and Technology* 32, no. 4 (Summer 2016), https://issues.org/donald-trumps-voters-and-the-decline-of-american-manufacturing/.

6. Material in this section authored by one of the coauthors also appeared in National Academy of Sciences, National Materials and Manufacturing Board, "Strategic Long Term Participation by DOD in Its Manufacturing USA Institutes," report on a workshop (Washington, DC: National Academies Press, 2019), 74–81. It also draws on points made in William B. Bonvillian and Peter L. Singer, *Advanced Manufacturing: The New American Innovation Policies* (Cambridge, MA: MIT Press, 2018), 15–63.

7. Alexander Hamilton, Report on Manufactures (to the House of Representatives), section II, December 5, 1791, from, Alexander Hamilton, *The Works of Alexander Hamilton,* ed. Henry Cabot Lodge (Federal Edition), Industry and Commerce, reproduced at, https://oll.libertyfund.org/titles/hamilton-the-works-of-alexander-hamilton-federal-edition-vol-4#lf0249-04_head_012.

8. Hamilton, Report on Manufactures, introduction.

9. Hamilton, at "4. Pecuniary bounties."

10. Hamilton, section "8. The encouragement of new inventions . . ."

11. Alexander Hamilton, Report Relative to the Additional Supplies for the Ensuing Year (to the Speaker of the House), Treasury Department, March 16, 1792 (from National Archives, Founders Online, https://founders.archives.gov/?q=%20industry%20Author%3A%22Hamilton%2C%20Alexander%22&s=1111311111&r=51).

12. National Park Service, Patterson Great Fall National Historic Site, Birthplace of the American Industrial Revolution, accessed February 2019, https://www.nps.gov/pagr/learn/historyculture/the-birthplace-of-the-american-industrial-revolution.htm.

13. Department of Defense, Office of the Undersecretary of Defense for Acquisition and Sustainment and office of the Deputy Assistant Secretary of Defense for Industrial Policy, "Assessing and Strengthening the Manufacturing and Defense Industrial Base and Supply Chain Resiliency of the United States," September 2018, 19, 24–31, https://media.defense.gov/2018/Oct/05/2002048904/-1/-1/1/ASSESSING-AND-STRENGTHENING-THE-MANUFACTURING-AND%20DEFENSE-INDUSTRIAL-BASE-AND-SUPPLY-CHAIN-RESILIENCY.PDF.

14. Department of Defense, "Assessing and Strengthening," 19, 34–40.

15. Department of Defense, "Assessing and Strengthening," 19, 41–45.

16. Department of Defense, "Assessing and Strengthening," 24.

17. National Security Strategy of the United States, The White House, December 2017, https://www.whitehouse.gov/wp-content/uploads/2017/12/NSS-Final-12-18-2017-0905.pdf.

18. Department of Defense, "Assessing Strengthening Manufacturing," 4–5.

19. Bonvillian and Singer, *Advanced Manufacturing*, 178–183.

20. Bonvillian and Singer, *Advanced Manufacturing*, 178–183; Fraunhofer-Gesellschaft, "About Fraunhofer," https://www.fraunhofer.de/en.html.

21. Susan N. Houseman, "Understanding the Decline of US Manufacturing Employment," Upjohn Institute Working Papers, 2018, https://research.upjohn.org/cgi/viewcontent.cgi?article=1305&context=up_workingpapers; Adams Nager, "Trade vs. Productivity: What Caused U.S. Manufacturing 's Decline and How to Revive It," Information Technology and Innovation Foundation report, February 13, 2017, https://itif.org/publications/2017/02/13/trade-vs-productivity-what-caused-us-manufacturings-decline-and-how-revive; David Autor, David Dorn, Gordon Hanson, "The China Shock: Learning from Labor Market Adjustment to Large Changes in Trade," NBER Working Paper 21906, National Bureau of Economic Research, Cambridge, MA, January 2016; Robert D. Atkinson, Luke A. Stewart, Scott M. Andes, and Stephen Ezell, "Worse Than the Great Depression: What the Experts Are Missing about American Manufacturing Decline," Information Technology and Innovation Foundation report, March 19, 2012, https://itif.org/publications/2012/03/19/worse-great-depression-what-experts-are-missing-about-american-manufacturing.

22. MAPI Foundation, Domestic Outlook Forecast, "Full Recovery in Sight," March 22, 2018, https://mapifoundation.org/economic/2018/3/22/full-recovery-in-sight-us-manufacturing-predicted-to-regain-all-output-lost-in-the-great-recession-by-april-2019.

23. Bureau of Labor Statistics, "Multifactor Productivity Slowdown in U.S. Manufacturing, *Monthly Labor Review,* July 2018, https://www.bls.gov/opub/mlr/2018/article/multifactor-productivity-slowdown-in-us-manufacturing.htm.

24. Bureau of Labor Statistics, "Productivity and Costs," News Release, February 6, 2019, 2, https://www.bls.gov/news.release/pdf/prod2.pdf. See also Susan N. Houseman, "Understanding the Decline of US Manufacturing Employment," Upjohn Institute Working Papers, 2018, https://research.upjohn.org/cgi/viewcontent.cgi?article=1305&context=up_workingpapers.

25. Statista, "Trade Deficit of Goods Manufactured in the United States, 2000–2016," https://www.statista.com/statistics/814589/manufactured-goods-trade-deficit-us/.

26. Bureau of Economic Analysis (BEA) and Census Bureau, U.S. International Trade in Goods and Services, November 2018, Exhibit 16, U.S. Trade in Advanced Technology Products, https://www.bea.gov/system/files/2019-02/trad1118_4.pdf.

27. Bureau of Labor Statistics, Databases, Tables and Calculations, Quarterly Census, Manufacturing Establishments 2001–2015, http://data.bls.gov/pdq/SurveyOutputServlet.

28. Suzanne Berger and the MIT Task Force on Production and Innovation, *Making in America* (Cambridge, MA: MIT Press, 2013).

29. Small Business Administration, Frequently Asked Questions about Small Business, Small Businesses Comprise What Share of the U.S. Economy, 2012, https://www.sba.gov/sites/default/files/FAQ_Sept_2012.pdf.

30. Susan Helper and Thomas Mahoney, "Next Generation Supply Chains," *Mforesight*, July 2017, http://mforesight.org/projects-events/supply-chains/.

31. William B. Bonvillian and Peter L. Singer, *Advanced Manufacturing: The New American Innovation Policies* (Cambridge, MA: MIT Press, 2018), 194, 185–215.

32. Bonvillian and Singer, *Advanced Manufacturing*, 57–58.

33. Fred Block, "A Strategy for Rebuilding the Manufacturing Sector in the United States," Century Foundation Report, September 20, 2017, https://tcf.org/content/report/strategy-rebuilding-manufacturing-sector-united-states/?agreed=1.

34. David Autor, David Dorn, Gordon Hanson, Gary Pisano, and Pian Shu, "Foreign Competition and Domestic Innovation: Evidence from U.S. Patents," NBER Working paper 22879, National Bureau of Economic Research, Cambridge, MA, December 2017, 2, https://www.nber.org/papers/w22879; Susan Helper, Timothy Kruger, and Howard Wial, "Why Does Manufacturing Matter, Which Manufacturing Matters?," Brookings Institution, February 2012, 6–8, https://www.brookings.edu/wp-content/uploads/2016/06/0222_manufacturing_helper_krueger_wial.pdf.

35. Sanjay E. Sarma and William B. Bonvillian, "The Quest for Quality Jobs and Fixing an Imperfect Labor Market Information System," *Issues in Science and Technology*, Fall 2018, https://issues.org/the-quest-for-quality-jobs/ and https://issues.org/fixing-an-imperfect-labor-market-information-system/.

36. Bonvillian and Singer, *Advanced Manufacturing*, 34.

37. Bonvillian and Singer, 101–186.

38. Louis Uchitelle, *Making It, Why Manufacturing Still Matters* (New York: The New Press, 2017) (citing BEA data).

39. National Academy of Sciences, "Strategic Long-Term Commitments by DOD in Its Manufacturing USA Institutes."

40. National Academy of Sciences, "Strategic Long-Term Participation by DOD in Its Manufacturing USA Institutes," table 3.3.

41. Dan Meckstroth, "China Has a Dominant Share of World Manufacturing," MAPI paper, Manufacturers Association for Productivity and Investment (MAPI) Foundation, Washington, DC, January 2014, https://www.mapi.net/blog/2014/01/china-has-dominant-share-world-manufacturing.

42. China establishes fund to invest in advanced manufacturing, *China Daily*, June 6, 2018; Yoko Kubota, "China Sets Up New $29 Billion Semiconductor Fund," *Wall Street Journal*, October 25, 2019.

43. Advanced Manufacturing Partnership (through PCAST), Report to the President on Ensuring American Leadership in Advanced Manufacturing (PCAST, White House, June 2011); Advanced Manufacturing Partnership (through PCAST), Report to the President on Accelerating Advanced (PCAST, The White House, October 2014); Gary P. Pisano and Willy Shih, *Producing Prosperity: Why American needs a Manufacturing Renaissance* (Cambridge, MA: Harvard Business School Press, 2012); Berger *Making in America;* Uchitelle, *Making It;* Bonvillian and Singer, *Advanced Manufacturing.*

44. National Academy of Engineering, "Making Value in America: Embracing the Future of Manufacturing, Technology and Work" (Washington, DC: National Academies Press, 2015), 14, https://www.nap.edu/catalog/19483/making-value-for-america-embracing-the-future-of-manufacturing-technology.

45. National Academy of Engineering, 15.

46. Makada Henry-Nickie, Kwadwo Frimpong, and Hao Sun, "Trends in the Information Technology Sector," Brookings Institution, March 29, 2019, table 1, https://www.brookings.edu/research/trends-in-the-information-technology-sector/?utm_campaign=Events%3A%20Governance%20Studies&utm_source=hs_email&utm_medium=email&utm_content=74665174.

47. National Academy of Engineering, "Making Value in America," 27.

48. Berger, *Making in America.*

49. National Association of Manufacturing, "Top 20 Facts about Manufacturing" (accessed February 2019), https://www.nam.org/Newsroom/Top-20-Facts-About-Manufacturing/.

50. Bureau of Labor Statistics, Occupational Outlook Handbook, Production Occupations, https://www.bls.gov/ooh/production/home.htm (accessed February 2019).

51. Autor et al., "Foreign Competition and Domestic Competition"; Helper et al., "Why Manufacturing Matters"; National Science Board, Science and Engineering Indicators 2016, chapter 3, Science and Engineering Labor Force, figure 3-10, https://www.nsf.gov/statistics/2016/nsb20161/#/report/chapter-3/s-e-workers-in-the-economy/employment-sectors.

52. Bureau of Labor Statistics, Commissioner's Corner, January 16, 2019, https://beta.bls.gov/labs/blogs/2019/01/16/celebrating-the-international-year-of-the-periodic-table/.

53. Bureau of Labor Statistics, Labor Force Statistics from the Current Population Survey, January 18, 2019 (2018 data by age and industry, https://www.bls.gov/cps/cpsaat18b.htm.

54. Anthony P. Carnevale, Neil Ridley, Ban Cheah, Jeff Strohl, and Kathryn P. Campbell, "Upskilling and Downsizing in American Manufacturing," Georgetown Center on Education and the Workforce, June 2019, 5, 6, 18–19, 25–26.

https://1gyhoq479ufd3yna29x7ubjn-wpengine.netdna-ssl.com/wp-content/uploads/Manufacturing_FR.pdf. See also Manufacturing Institute, Center for Manufacturing Research, updated 2014, http://www.themanufacturinginstitute.org/Research/Facts-About-Manufacturing/Workforce-and-Compensation/Workforce-by-Education/Workforce-by-Education.aspx.

55. Deloitte and the Manufacturing Institute, "Skills Gap in Manufacturing—2018," 2018 (accessed February 2019), https://operationalsolutions.nam.org/mi-skills-gap-study-18/.

56. Accenture Strategy with the Manufacturing Institute, 2014 (accessed February 2019) http://www.themanufacturinginstitute.org/~/media/A9341A4E4A3148FF8A69E98C71E14733.ashx.

57. Andrew Weaver, "The Myth of a Skills Gap," *Technology Review*, August 25, 2017, https://www.technologyreview.com/s/608707/the-myth-of-the-skills-gap/; Andrew Weaver and Paul Osterman, "Skill Demands and Mismatch in U.S. Manufacturing," *Industrial and Labor Relations Review* 70, no. 2 (2017): 275–307, http://journals.sagepub.com/doi/abs/10.1177/0019793916660067.

58. James Bessen, "Employers Aren't Just Whining—the 'Skills Gap' Is Real," *Harvard Business Review*, August 25, 2014, https://hbr.org/2014/08/employers-arent-just-whining-the-skills-gap-is-real.

59. National Association of Manufacturing, "Top 20 Facts About Manufacturing" (based on Bureau of Economic Analysis and Bureau of Labor Statistics data).

60. MAPI, manufacturing multiplier effect, April 2014, http://www.themanufacturinginstitute.org/Research/Facts-About-Manufacturing/Economy-and-Jobs/Multiplier/Multiplier.aspx.

61. National Association of Manufacturing, "Top 20 Facts About Manufacturing."

62. MAPI Foundation (Dan Meckstroth, chief economist), "The Manufacturing Value Chain Is Bigger Than You Think" (Washington, DC: MAPI Foundation report February 16, 2016), 1–2, https://www.mapi.net/forecasts-data/manufacturing-value-chain-much-bigger-you-think.

63. Fred Block, "A Strategy for Rebuilding the Manufacturing Sector."

64. Phillip Longman, "First Teach No Harm," *Washington Monthly*, July/August 2013.

65. Bruce Steinwald, Paul B. Ginsburg, Caitlin Brandt, Sobin Lee, and Kavita Patel, "We Need More Primary Care Physicians: Here's Why and How," Brookings Institution, July 8, 2019, https://www.brookings.edu/blog/usc-brookings-schaeffer-on-health-policy/2019/07/08/we-need-more-primary-care-physicians-heres-why-and-how/?utm_campaign=Economic%20Studies&utm_source=hs_email&utm_medium=email&utm_content=74692942.

66. Concerning behavioral health, see American Psychological Association (APA) Center for Workforce Studies, Datapoint: "Where Are the Highest Concentrations of Licensed Psychologists?," *Monitor on Psychology* 47, no. 3 (March 2016): 3, https://www.apa.org/monitor/2016/03/datapoint; APA Center for Workforce Studies, "How Much Debt Do Recent Doctoral Graduates Carry?," *Monitor on Psychology* 46, no. 6 (June 2015), https://www.apa.org/monitor/2015/06/datapoint; APA Center for Workforce Studies, Data Tool: "Salaries in Psychology, 2010–2017," 2018 (based on NSF data), https://www.apa.org/workforce/data-tools/2015-salaries.

67. Discussion with Dr. Judith Glassgold, Graduate School of Applied and Professional Psychology, Rutgers, the State University of New Jersey, December 2, 2017; Communications from Dr. Glassgold, December 5, 2017, and October 21, 2019.

68. Discussion with Dr. Judith Glassgold.

69. Open Minds, "39 States Cover Peer Support Services for Behavioral Health," April 26, 2018, http://www.globenewswire.com/news-release/2018/04/27/1488741/0/en/39-States-Cover-Peer-Support-Services-For-Behavioral-Health-OPEN-MINDS-Releases-Reference-Guide-On-Medicaid-Reimbursement-For-Peer-Support-Services.html.

70. Catherine Dower, Jean Moore, and Margaret Langelier, "It Is Time to Restructure Health Professions Scope-of-Practice Regulations to Remove Barriers to Care," *Health Affairs* 32, no. 11 (November 2013): 1971. The authors acknowledge, in preparing this section, the numerous articles brought together by the journal *Health Affairs* in a 2013 special issue on these healthcare workforce topics, a number of which are cited herein.

71. Thomas W. Elwood, "Patchwork of Scope-of-Practice Regulations Prevent Allied Health Professionals from Fully Participating in Patient Care," *Health Affairs* 32, no. 11 (November 2013): 1985.

72. Rob Cunningham, "On Workforce Policy, Consensus Is Hard to Find," *Health Affairs* 32, no. 11 (November 2013): 1872.

73. See, for example, the Duke Primary Care model, Jennier Craft Morgan, Janette Dill, Emmeline Chuang, Chivon Mingo, and Crystal W. Williams, "Duke Primary Care: A Care Team Redesign Case Study," case study paper, https://gcgj.mit.edu/sites/default/files/imce/resource-uploads/DPC%20Case%20Study%20Final%207%2023%2018.pdf; Tom Strong, "Care Team Redesign: Transforming Medical Assistant Roles in Primary Care," *Health Affairs*, March 12, 2015, https://www.healthaffairs.org/do/10.1377/hblog20150312.045475/full/.

74. Michael Barr and Jack Ginsburg, "The Advanced Medical Home, A Patient-Centered, Physician-Guided Model of Health Care," policy paper, American College of Physicians, 2006, https://www.acponline.org/system/files/documents/advocacy/current_policy_papers/assets/adv_med.pdf.

75. Joanne Spetz, Stephen T. Parente, Robert J. Town, and Dawn Bazarko, "Scope-of-Practice Laws for Nurse Practitioners Limit Cost Savings That Can Be Achieved in Retail Clinics," *Health Affairs* 32, no. 11 (November 2013): 1977.

76. Vimla Patel, Edward Shortliffe, Mario Steananelli, Peter Szolovits, Michael Berthold, Ricardo Bellazzi, and Ameen Abu-Hanna, "The Coming of Age of Artificial Intelligence in Medicine," *Artificial Intelligence in Medicine* 46, no. 1 (May 2009): 5–17; Julia E. Strait, "Artificial Intelligence and the Future of Medicine," Washington University School of Medicine, December 11, 2018, https://medicine.wustl.edu/news/artificial-intelligence-and-the-future-of-medicine/.

77. See, for example, an article on diagnosis and AI from 2001 by Igor Kononenko, "Machine Learning for Medical Diagnosis: History, State of the Art and Perspective," *Artificial Intelligence in Medicine*, 23, no. 1 (August 2001): 89–109.

78. David Sontag and Peter Szolovits, "Risk Stratification Using EHRs and Insurance Claims," MIT HST.956, Machine Learning for Healthcare, February 14, 2019 (course presentation).

79. Sontag and Szolovits, "Risk Stratification." See, for example, Suchi Saria, Anand Rajani, Jeffrey Gould, Daphne Koller, and Anna Penn, "Integration of Early Physiological Responses Predicts Later Illness Severity in Preterm Infants," *Science Translational Medicine* 2, no. 48 (September 9, 2010), https://www.ncbi.nlm.nih.gov/pmc/articles/PMC3564961/.

80. Cunningham, "On Workforce Policy."

81. Arthur L. Kellermann, John W. Saultz, Ateev Mehrotra, Spencer S. Jones, and Siddartha Dalal, "Primary Care Technicians: A Solution to the Primary Care Workforce Gap," *Health Affairs* 32, no. 11 (November 2013): 1893.

82. Timothy M. Dall, Paul D. Gallo, Ritasree Chakrabarti, Terry West, April P. Semilla, and Michael V. Storm, "An Aging Population and Growing Disease Burden Will Require a Large and Specialized Health Care Workforce by 2025," *Health Affairs* 32, no. 11 (November 2013): 2013.

83. Paul Osterman, "Who Will Care for Us? Long-Term Care and the Long-Term Workforce" (New York: Russell Sage Foundation, 2017).

84. Michael A. Hoge, Gail W. Stuart, John Morris, Michael T. Flaherty, Manuel Paris, Jr., and Eric Goplerud, "Mental Health and Addiction Workforce Development: Federal Leadership Is Needed to Address the Growing Crisis," *Health Affairs* 32, no. 11 (November 2013): 2005.

85. Substance Abuse and Mental Health Services Administration (SAMSHA), "Building the Behavioral Health Workforce," *SAMSHA News* 22, no. 4 (Fall 2014).

86. State programs are also evolving in this area. See, for example, Anjalee Khemiani, "Rutgers Gets $1.3M for Drug Counsellor Program," December 12, 2017, http://www

.roi-nj.com/2017/12/12/education/rutgers-gets-1-3m-for-drug-counselor-apprenticeship/ (new apprenticeship program for drug counsellors).

87. Gail Cohen, "Challenges for the Allied Health Sector: Lessons from Building America's Skilled Technical Workforce," *Journal of Interprofessional Workforce Research and Development* 1, no. 2 (2018).

88. National Academies of Sciences, Engineering, and Medicine, *Building America's Skilled Technical Workforce* (Washington, DC: National Academies Press, 2017), 174, https://www.nap.edu/catalog/23472/building-americas-skilled-technical-workforce.

89. National Student Clearinghouse, "Completing College: A National View of Student Completion Rates—2018," December 2018, figure 15, https://nscresearchcenter.org/signaturereport16/.

90. Bianca K. Frogner and Susan M. Skillman, "Pathways to Middle-Skill Allied Health Care Occupations," *Issues in Science and Technology Policy* 33, no. 1 (Fall 2016).

91. Bureau of Labor Statistics, "Employment Projections: 2018–28," Occupational Employment.

92. J. Dennis Lord, "Retail Saturation: What the Experts Say," *Southeastern Geographer* 40, no. 1 (May 2000): 106–115.

93. Mark Bain, "America's Vast Swaths of Retail Space Have Become a Burden in the age of e-Commerce," *New York Times*, July 19, 2017; Felix Richter, "How Much Retail Space Is Too Much?," *Statista*, U.S. Retail Brands, May 18, 2017, https://www.statista.com/chart/9454/retail-space-per-1000-people/; Hayley Peterson, "The Retail Apocalypse Has Officially Descended on America," *Business Insider*, March 21, 2017, https://www.businessinsider.com/the-retail-apocalypse-has-officially-descended-on-america-2017-3.

94. Ananth Raman, Nicole DeHoratius, and Zeynep Ton, "Execution: The Missing Link in Retail Operations," *California Management Review* 43, no. 3 (Spring 2001): 136–152; Nicole DeHoratius and Ananth Raman, "Building on Foundations of Sand?," *International Commerce Review: ECR Journal* 3, no. 1 (2003): 62; Thomas W. Gruen and Daniel S. Corsten, "A Comprehensive Guide to Retail Out-of-Stock Eeduction in the Fast-Moving Consumer Goods Industry," P&G Research Study, 2007, 848–866, https://pdfs.semanticscholar.org/6e51/29164f0beaa22e6f7629af116a963667a711.pdf?_ga=2.188529256.1912193440.1564240341-615807845.1564240341; Birendra K. Mishra and Ashutosh Prasad, "Minimizing Retail Shrinkage Due to Employee Theft," *International Journal of Retail & Distribution Management* 34, no. 11 (October 2006): 817–832.

95. Peter W. Hom and Angelo J. Kinicki, "Toward a Greater Understanding of How Dissatisfaction Drives Employee Turnover," *Academy of Management Journal* 44, no. 5

(October 2001): 975–987; Marshall Fisher, "To Me It's a Store. To You It's a Factory," *International Commerce Review: ECR Journal* 4, no. 2 (Winter 2004): 9.

96. Stephanie Rosenbloom, "Retail Sales Are Weakest in 35 Years," *New York Times*, December 4, 2008.

97. Parija B. Kavilanz, "US Sellers to World: Please Buy Our Leftovers," *CNN Money* December 11, 2008, https://money.cnn.com/2008/12/11/news/economy/retail_excesssupply/.

98. Kris Hudson and Vanessa O'Connell, "Recession Turns Malls into Ghost Towns," *Wall Street Journal*, May 22, 2009.

99. Michael Issa, "The Rest of the Story About the State of Brick-and-Mortar Retail," *American Bankruptcy Institute Journal* 36, no. 11 (November 2017): 36–80.

100. Federal Reserve Economic Data, Federal Reserve Bank of St. Louis, Economic Research, E-Commerce Retail Sales, May 17, 2019, https://fred.stlouisfed.org/series/ECOMSA.

101. "The Decline of Established American Retailing Threatens Jjobs, *The Economist*, May 13, 2017.

102. Census Bureau, Business and Industry, Monthly Retail Trade and Food Service, January 1992–May 2019, https://www.census.gov/econ/currentdata/dbsearch?program=MRTS&startYear=1992&endYear=2019&categories=44X72&dataType=SM&geoLevel=US&adjusted=1¬Adjusted=1&errorData=0.

103. Alastair Fitzpayne, Ethan Pollack, and Hillary Greenberg, "Industry at at Glance: The Future of Retail," Aspen Institute paper, November 27, 2017, https://www.aspeninstitute.org/blog-posts/industry-at-a-glance-the-future-of-retail/.

104. Paul Krugman, "Why Don't All Jobs Matter?," *New York Times*, Opinion, April 17, 2017.

105. Krystal Hu, "Retail Job Losses Mount, Women Impacted More Than Men," *Yahoo Finance*, March 8, 2019, https://finance.yahoo.com/news/retail-job-losses-mount-women-impacted-more-than-men-183738884.html; Thomas Franck, "Booming Jobs Market Is Leaving the Retail Industry Behind, *CNBC*, April 6, 2019, https://www.cnbc.com/2019/04/05/booming-jobs-market-is-leaving-the-retail-industry-behind.html. See also Michael Mandel, "Ecommerce Job Gains Are Much Larger Than Retail Job Losses: Here's Why," Progressive Policy Institute paper, April 7, 2017, https://www.progressivepolicy.org/blog/ecommerce-job-gains-much-larger-retail-job-losses-heres/.

106. Leslie Patton, Matt Townsend, and Bloomberg, "America's Trucker Shortage Is About to Hit Consumers Where it Hurts," *Fortune*, March 2, 2019, http://fortune.com/2019/03/02/us-trucker-shortage/.

107. Andria Cheng, "Why Amazon Go May Soon Change the Way We Shop," *Forbes*, January 13, 2019, https://www.forbes.com/sites/andriacheng/2019/01/13/why-amazon-go-may-soon-change-the-way-we-want-to-shop/#34def34a6709.

108. Steve Banker, "Walmart Expands Use of Bossa Nova's Robots from 50 to 350 Stores," *Logistics Viewpoints* April 30, 2019, https://logisticsviewpoints.com/2019/04/30/walmart-expands-use-of-bossa-novas-robots-from-50-to-350-stores/; North American Retail Hardware Federation, "Walmart and Target Have Diverging Plans for Retail Robots," *Hardware Retailing*, October 28, 2019, https://www.hardwareretailing.com/walmart-target-have-diverging-plans-for-retail-robots/.

109. Joseph Kane and Tomer Adie, "Amazon's Recent Hiring Spree Puts New Focus on Warehouse Jobs and Worker Needs," Brookings Institution, September 12, 2017, https://www.brookings.edu/blog/the-avenue/2017/09/12/amazons-recent-hiring-spree-puts-new-focus-on-warehouse-jobs-and-worker-needs/.

110. B. Joseph Pine II and James H. Gilmore, "Welcome to the Experience Economy," *Harvard Business Review*, July–August 1998, https://hbr.org/1998/07/welcome-to-the-experience-economy; Mike Wadhera, "The Information Age Is Over; Welcome to the Experience Age," *TechCrunch*, May 9, 2016, https://techcrunch.com/2016/05/09/the-information-age-is-over-welcome-to-the-experience-age/.

111. Lauren Thomas, "Bucks from Bricks: These Retailers Make the Most Money per Square Foot on Their Real Estate," CNBC, July 29, 2017, https://www.cnbc.com/2017/07/29/here-are-the-retailers-that-make-the-most-money-per-square-foot-on-their-real-estate.html.

112. Marshall Fisher, Santiago Gallino, and Serguei Netessine, "Retailers Are Squandering Their Most Potent Weapons," *Harvard Business Review* 97, no. 1 (January–February 2019): 72–73.

113. Fisher, Gallino, and Netessine, "Retailers Are Squandering."

114. Fisher, Gallino, and Netessine, "Retailers Are Squandering," 78–79.

115. Zeynep Ton, *The Good Jobs Strategy: How the Smartest Companies Invest in Employees to Lower Costs and Boost Profits* (Boston, MA: Houghton Mifflin Harcourt, 2014). See also Zeynep Ton, "Why 'Good Jobs' Are Good for Retailers, *Harvard Business Review*, January–February 2012.

116. The Starbucks College Achievement Plan (SCAP) covers employees' full tuition for Arizona State University's online program, and also includes tutoring and career counseling; see Starbucks College Achievement Plan, FAQs, https://stories.starbucks.com/press/2015/starbucks-college-achievement-plan-frequently-asked-questions/. Amazon covers 95 percent of tuition and fees for associate degrees and certificates in high-demand technical areas; see Amazon Fulfillment, Training, https://www.aboutamazon.com/amazon-fulfillment/our-fulfillment-centers/training; see also

Susan Helper, Case Western Reserve, presentation on Amazon Fulfillment Center Meetings, MIT Work of the Future Task Force, July 23, 2019. See, more generally, Geffrey M. Cox, "Can Starbucks Save the Middle Class? No. But It Might Ruin Higher Education," *Chronicle of Higher Education*, August 1, 2019.

6 THE BROKEN LABOR MARKET INFORMATION SYSTEM

1. Adam Smith, *The Wealth of Nations,* bk. 4, c. 2 (1776), reprinted and edited by R. H. Campbell and A.S. Skinner, *The Glasgow Edition of the Works and Correspondence of Adam Smith,* 2a, no. 456 (Oxford, UK: Oxford University Press, 1976).

2. Frederick Hayek, "The Use of Knowledge in Society," *American Economic Review* 35, no. 4 (1945): 519–530, https://www.econlib.org/library/Essays/hykKnw.html. This section is drawn from Sanjay E. Sarma and William B. Bonvillian, "Fixing an Imperfect Labor Market Information System," *Issues in Science and Technology*, Fall 2018; we thank the editor for permission to use this material here.

3. Richard B. Freeman, *America Works: Thoughts on an Exceptional U.S. Labor Market* (New York: Russell Sage Foundation, 2007), 3.

4. Discussion with Andrew Reamer, George Washington University, October 6, 2017.

5. Ian D. Wyatt and Daniel E. Hecker, "Occupational Changes during the 20th Century," Bureau of Labor Statistics, Monthly Labor Review, March 2006, 35; Bureau of Labor Statistics, Occupational Employment Statistics, May 2017 Occupation Profiles, All Occupations, 2017, https://www.bls.gov/oes/current/oes_stru.htm/.

6. National Association of Manufacturers, "Top 20 Facts About Manufacturing," 3, http://www.nam.org/Newsroom/Top-20-Facts-About-Manufacturing/.

7. National Center for Education Statistics, *Digest of Education Statistics 2015,* table 317.10, 596, December 2016, https://nces.ed.gov/pubs2016/2016014.pdf. See also National Center for Educational Statistics, *120 years of American Education: A Statistical Portrait,* January 1993, table 23, 75, https://nces.ed.gov/pubs93/93442.pdf; National Center for Education Statistics, 2011–12, Integrated Postsecondary Education Data System, Methodology Report, NCES 2012-293, July 2012, 3, https://nces.ed.gov/pubs2012/2012293.pdf.

8. National Center for Education Statistics, *Digest of Education Statistics 2015*, table 303.10, 460.

9. National Center for Education Statistics, Integrated Postsecondary Education Data System, Classification of Instructional Programs Resources, 1985–2010, https://nces.ed.gov/ipeds/cipcode/Default.aspx?y=55

10. Credential Engine, Counting US Secondary and Postsecondary Credentials—April 2018 Report, April 5, 2018, 3, https://www.credentialengine.org/articles/ba957e1e

-8aef-45ec-8bb4-237ae3902e75/Counting_U_S__Secondary_and_Postsecondary_Credentials___April_2018_Report.

11. National Center for Educational Statistics, *Digest of Education Statistics 2017*, table 105.50, 2018, https://nces.ed.gov/programs/digest/d17/tables/dt17_105.50.asp?current=yes.

12. Bureau of Labor Statistics, Union Members—2017, News Release, USDL 18-080, January 19, 2018, 1, https://www.bls.gov/news.release/pdf/union2.pdf.

13. Andrew Reamer, "Information Resources to Facilitate Middle Skills Workforce Development," National Academies Board on Science Technology and Economic Policy, Project on the Supply Chain for Middle-Skilled Jobs, August 21, 2015, 6, https://sites.nationalacademies.org/cs/groups/pgasite/documents/webpage/pga_169054.pdf.

14. Joseph Parilla, Jesus Leal Trujillo, and Alan Berube, "Skills and Innovation Strategy to Strengthen U.S. Manufacturing: Lessons from Germany," Brookings Institution, 2015, https://www.brookings.edu/research/skills-and-innovation-strategies-to-strengthen-manufacturing-lessons-from-germany/; Eva Rindfleisch and Felise Maennig-Fortmann, "Vocational Education and Training in Germany, Through Practice and Theory to Skilled Employee," Konrad Adenauer Siftung, 2015, http://www.kas.de/korea/en/publications/50045/; Dieter Euler, "Germany's Dual Vocational Training System: A Model for Other Countries?," Bertelsmann Stiftung, 2013, https://www.bertelsmannstiftung.de/fileadmin/files/BSt/Publikationen/Graue Publikationen/GP_Germanys_dual_vocational_training_system.pdf; USC (Michael Lanford, Tattiya Maruco, and William Tierney), "Prospects for Vocational Education in the United States—Lessons from Germany," Pullias Center for Higher Education, University of Southern California, 2015, https://pullias.usc.edu/download/prospects-for-vocational-education-in-the-united-states/.

15. LinkedIn Job Search, https://www.linkedin.com/jobs/; LinkedIn recommendation engine—content and collaborative-based filtering, https://www.linkedin.com/pulse/recommendation-engine-content-based-filtering-ashish-kumar/.

16. Liangyue Li, How Jing, Hanghang Tong, Jaewon Yang, Qi He, and Bee-Chung Chen, "NEMO: Next Career Move Prediction with Contextual Embedding," International WWW Conference Committee, WWW 2017 Companion, April 30, 2017, http://www.public.asu.edu/~liangyue/pdfs/LiJTYHC_WWW17.pdf.

17. O*NET Online, Build Your Future, https://www.onetonline.org.

18. MIT Media Lab, Skillscape, http://skillscape.mit.edu/#/skills/17.

19. Headai, Microcompetencies, https://www.microcompetencies.com.

20. Meeting with Anu Passi-Rauste of Headai, January 3, 2018; SITRA (Heli Nissinen), "Artificial intelligence Shows What Finland Can Do and 'postiveCV' Reveals

Hidden Talent of Young People," summary of what its "PositiveCV" is attempting to do for students, 2017, https://www.sitra.fi/en/news/artificial-intelligence-shows-finland-can-positive-cv-reveals-hidden-talents-young-people-winners-sitras-100-million-euro-ratkaisu-100-challenge-competition/. See also SITRA, "We Should All Have Our Own 'PositiveCV,'" 2017, https://www.sitra.fi/en/articles/we-should-all-have-our-own-positive-cv/ and https://www.youtube.com/watch?v=HrgfshEXszI.

21. Michelle R. Weise, Andrew Hanson, and Saleh Yustina, "The New Geography of Skills: Regional Skill Shapes for the New Learning Ecosystem," Strada Institute for the Future of Work, Indianapolis, IN, December 2019.

22. Reamer, "Information Resources to Facilitate Middle Skills Workforce Development," 10–15.

23. Department of Labor, Workforce Information Advisory Council, "Recommendations to Improve the Nation's Workforce and Labor Market Information System," January 25, 2018, https://www.doleta.gov/wioa/wiac/docs/Second_Draft_of_the_WIAC_Final_Report.pdf.

24. With regard to the jobkit effort, see https://www.commerce.gov/sites/default/files/2019-08/AWPAB18June2019%20MeetingMinutes_Final_s.pdf; Census Bureau, "Post-Secondary Employment Outcomes (PSEO)," https://lehd.ces.census.gov/data/pseo_beta.html.

25. National Science Foundation, National Center for Science and Engineering Statistics, "Data Sources to Measure and Understand the Science and Engineering Workforce and the Skilled Technical Workforce," May 3, 2019, https://www.dropbox.com/s/x7qdto29qm5cado/Possible%20Data%20Sources%20for%20the%20S%26E%20Workforce%20and%20STW%20%2805-03-19%29.pdf?dl=0.

26. Department of Commerce, American Workforce Policy Advisory Board, https://www.commerce.gov/americanworker/american-workforce-policy-advisory-board.

27. Anthony P. Carnevale, Tanya I. Garcia, and Artem Gulish, "Career Pathways: Five Ways to Connect College and Careers," Georgetown Center on Education and the Workforce, July 11, 2017, https://cew.georgetown.edu/cew-reports/careerpathways/. See, generally, National Academies of Sciences, Engineering, and Medicine, *Building America's Skilled Technical Workforce* (Washington, DC: National Academies Press, May 18, 2017).

28. National Science Foundation, Advanced Technological Education (ATE), "ATE Centers," https://atecenters.org; National Science Foundation, "ATE Centers" (Madeline Patton, ed.), *ATE Impact 2016–17* (2016), https://www.atecenters.org/wp-content/uploads/PDF/ATEIMPACT_2016-17.pdf.

29. For example, the Ohio MEP offers on-demand training, https://ppc.toolingu.com/ohio-mep-osu/. See also 180Skills LLC, http://www.180skills.com/wp-content/uploads/2018/06/180_Skills_Course_Catalog_2018_7th_Edition.pdf; Thors, https://

www.thors.com/academy; Tooling U-SME, https://www.toolingu.com/about/foundation; MSSC, https://www.msscusa.org/online-e-learning-courses/.

30. William B. Bonvillian and Peter L. Singer, *Advanced Manufacturing: The New American Innovation Policies* (Cambridge, MA: MIT Press, 2018), 217–241.

31. AIM Photonics Academy, Student and Educator Resources, Online Courses, https://aimphotonics.academy/education/student-resources/online-courses.

32. American Workforce Policy Advisory Board, Data Transparency Working Group, *White Paper on Interoperable Learning Records*, September 2019, https://www.in.gov/che/files/Interoperable%20Learning%20Records_FINAL.pdf.

33. American Workforce Policy Advisory Board, 4.

34. American Workforce Policy Advisory Board, 24.

35. Department of Labor, Workforce Information Advisory Council Recommendations.

36. US Chamber of Commerce Foundation, T3 Innovation Network, https://www.uschamberfoundation.org/t3-innovation.

37. US Chamber of Commerce Foundation, "Clearer Signals: Building an Employer-Led Job Registry for Talent Pipeline Management," report, September 27, 2017, https://www.uschamberfoundation.org/reports/clearer-signals-building-employer-led-job-registry-talent-pipeline-management.

38. Credential Engine, Moving Credentialing Forward, https://www.credentialengine.org.

7 THE UNIVERSITY ROLE IN WORKFORCE EDUCATION

1. This section is drawn from William B. Bonvillian and Charles Weiss, *Technological Innovation in Legacy Sectors* (Cambridge, MA.: Oxford University Press, 2015), 97–98.

2. Eliza Berman, "How the GI Bill Changed the Face of Higher Education in America," *Time*, June 22, 2015, https://time.com/3915231/student-veterans/; Keith W. Olsen, "The G.I. Bill and Higher Education: Success and Surprise," *American Quarterly* 25, no. 5 (December 1973): 596–610, https://www.jstor.org/stable/2711698?seq=1#page_scan_tab_contents.

3. National Science Foundation, *Science and Engineering Indicators 2014*, chapter 2, International S&E Higher Education, 2-37-38, appendix table 2-34, http://www.nsf.gov/statistics/seind12/c2/c2s4.htm.

4. Claudia Goldin and Lawrence Katz, *The Race Between Education and Technology* (Cambridge, MA: Harvard University Press, 2009). See also Claudia Goldin and Lawrence Katz, "The Future of Inequality," *Milken Institute Review*, July 2009 (3rd quarter), 26–33, http://assets1b.milkeninstitute.org/assets/Publication/MIReview/PDF/26-33

mr43.pdf; David H. Autor, "Skills, Education, and the Rise of Earnings Inequality among the 99 Percent," *Science* 344, no. 6186 (May 23, 2014): 843–851, http://www.sciencemag.org/content/344/6186/843.abstract.

5. Of course, a college degree is not necessarily tied to the more technical requirements of many workforce careers, and there is also a question about whether these degrees are up to date in teaching students about current and ongoing technological advances. Arguably, however, given the absence of data on other measurements, they represent a broad, useful proxy for general skill acquisition.

6. Not all experts agree. See, for example, Daron Acemoglu and David Autor, "What Does Human Capital Do? A Review of Goldin and Katz's 'The Race Between Education and Technology,'" *Journal of Economic Literature* 50, no. 2 (2012): 426–463, http://economics.mit.edu/files/7490. They argue that Goldin and Katz's work accounts for broad labor market trends but that there are richer interactions in skills and technologies than in their analysis.

7. Autor, "Skills, Education, and the Rise of Earnings Inequality." Of course, there are other factors in this income disparity, including the decline in the size of the unionized workforce compared to the total workforce, the decline in the real value of the minimum wage, international competition, and automation affecting lower skill positions. Concerning intense international competition, particularly in industrial sectors, as discussed in chapter 2, see, for example, David Autor, David Dorn, and Gordon Hansen, "The China Syndrome: Local Labor Market Effects of Import Competition in the United States," *American Economic Review* 103, no. 6 (2013): 2121–2168.

8. MIT presents a particularly vibrant innovation story. A 2015 report projects that living MIT alumni have launched 30,200 active companies employing some 4.6 million people and generating $1.9 trillion in annual revenue. Edward B. Roberts, Fiona Murray, and J. Daniel Kim, *Entrepreneurship and Innovation at MIT* (report Cambridge, MA: MIT Sloan School of Management, December 2015), http://web.mit.edu/innovate/entrepreneurship2015.pdf.

9. See, for example, Shiri M. Breznitz, *The Fountain of Knowledge: The Role of Universities in Economic Develoment* (Sanford, CA.: Stanford University Press, 2014).

10. John Austin, "Tale of Two Rustbelts: Higher Education Is Driving Rustbelt Revival but Risks Abound," Brookings Institution, December 20, 2017, https://www.brookings.edu/blog/the-avenue/2017/12/19/tale-of-two-rust-belts-higher-education-is-driving-rust-belt-revival-but-risks-abound/.

11. Anthony P. Carnevale, Tanya I. Garcia, and Artem Gulish, "Career Pathways: Five Ways to Connect College and Careers," Georgetown Center on Education and the Workforce, July 11, 2017, https://cew.georgetown.edu/cew-reports/careerpathways/.

12. Carnevale, Garcia, and Gulish, "Career Pathways," 2; Department of Education, National Center for Education Statistics, Integrated Postsecondary Education Data

System, Classification of Instructional Programs Resources, 1985–2010, https://nces.ed.gov/ipeds/cipcode/files/introduction_cip2010.pdf (full definition of postsecondary programs of instruction).

13. Carnevale, Garcia, and Gulish, "Career Pathways," 2; Department of Education, National Center for Education Statistics, *Digest of Education Statistics* tables, table 317.10, 2015, https://nces.ed.gov/pubs2016/2016014.pdf (including two-year and four-year degree-granting institutions and branch campuses.

14. Carnevale, Garcia, and Gulish, "Career Pathways," 2; Ian D. Wyatt and Daniel E. Heckler, "Occupational Changes during the 20th Century," 2006; Bureau of Labor Statistics, *Occupational Employment Statistics*, 2015, https://www.bls.gov/opub/mlr/2006/03/art3full.pdf.

15. Anthony P. Carnevale, Tamara Jayasundera, and Artem Gulish, "America's Divided Recovery: College Haves and Have-Nots," Georgetown Center on Education and the Workforce, 2016, https://1gyhoq479ufd3yna29x7ubjn-wpengine.netdna-ssl.com/wp-content/uploads/Americas-Divided-Recovery-web.pdf.

16. Carnevale, Jayasundera, and Gulish, "America's Divided Recovery."

17. William C. Symonds, Robert Schwartz, and Ronald F. Ferguson, "Pathways to Prosperity: Meeting the Challenge of Preparing Young Americans for the 21st Century," Pathways to Prosperity Project, Harvard Graduate School of Education, February 2011, 18, http://www.gse.harvard.edu/sites/default/files//documents/Pathways_to_Prosperity_Feb2011-1.pdf.

18. Association of Public and Land Grant Universities, "How Does a College Degree Improve Graduates' Employment and Earnings Potential?," APLU fact sheet (2017), http://www.aplu.org/projects-and-initiatives/college-costs-tuition-and-financial-aid/publicuvalues/employment-earnings.html.

19. Nicholas Hillman and Taylor Weichman, *Education Deserts: The Continued Significance of Place in the Twenty-First Century* (Washington, DC: American Council of Education, Center for Policy Research and Strategy 2016), https://www.acenet.edu/news-room/Documents/Education-Deserts-The-Continued-Significance-of-Place-in-the-Twenty-First-Century.pdf.

20. Jaison R. Abel and Richard Deitz, "Agglomeration and Job Matching among College Graduates," Federal Reserve Bank of New York Staff Reports, no. 587, December 2012 (revised December 2014), 8–9, https://www.newyorkfed.org/medialibrary/media/research/staff_reports/sr587.pdf. See also Clare Coffey, Rob Senz, and Yustine Saleh, "Degrees at Work: Examining the Serendipitous Outcomes of Diverse Degrees," Emsi, August 2019, 8–9, https://www.economicmodeling.com/degrees-at-work/; Alex Baumhardt and Chris Julin, "Tens of Thousands of Dollars Later, Most College Grads Say the Degree Was Worth It," APMreports, March 11, 2019, https//wwwapmreports

.org/story/2019/03/05is-college-worth-it; Strada-Gallup, Alumni Survey, "Mentoring College Students to Success," Strada Education Network, 2018, 13–15.

21. Diane Whitmore Schanzenbach, Ryan Nunn, and Greg Nantz, "Putting Your Major to Work—Career Paths after College," Hamilton Project report, May 11, 2017, http://www.hamiltonproject.org/papers/putting_your_major_to_work_career_paths_after_college.

22. David J. Deming and Kadeem Noray, "STEM Careers and Technological Change," NBER Working Paper No. 25065, September 2018, https://www.nber.org/papers/w25065.

23. Richard L. Drury, "Community Colleges in America: A Historical Perspective," *Inquiry* 8, no. 1 (Spring 2003).

24. Columbia University Teachers College, Community College Research Center, Community College FAQs (2018), https://ccrc.tc.columbia.edu/Community-College-FAQs.html.

25. The Obama administration developed an initiative in 2016, Computer Science for All, supported through the National Science Foundation. White House, "Computer Science For All," January 30, 2016, https://www.nap.edu/read/24783/chapter/1. The program announcement found that only one quarter of K–12 schools offered computer science with coding, and twenty-two states did not allow computer science courses to count toward high school graduation. There were also serious economic and social disparities in access to computer science courses: in 2015, only 22 percent of students taking the AP Computer Science exam were girls, and only 13 percent were African American or Latino students. These statistics mirrored another problem: in the well-paying and rapidly growing tech sector, in the larger and more innovative firms, women made up less than one-third of employees and African Americans less than 3 percent.

26. The arguments for including coding in the curriculum are that it leads to promising software development jobs, coding skills help differentiate job applicants because these skills are sought after, coding literacy can help in understanding other aspects of technology, it can create freelance work opportunities, and it can improve problem solving and logic skills. See, for example, "Why Everyone Should Learn to Code," Top Universities, https://www.nap.edu/read/24783/chapter/1raskol.

27. This section is drawn from Bonvillian and Weiss, *Technological Innovation in Legacy Sectors*, 99–100.

28. John Alic, "Beyond Schooling—Educating for the Unknowable Future," *The Bridge* (National Academy of Engineering journal), Fall issue, September 23, 2015, https://www.nae.edu/19582/Bridge/142833/145201.aspx.

29. Michael Spence, "Signaling in Retrospect and the Informational Structure of Markets," *American Economic Review* 92, no. 3 (June 2002): 436–437, http://citeseerx.ist.psu.edu/viewdoc/download?doi=10.1.1.308.415&rep=rep1&type=pdf.

30. Jamai Blivin and Merrilea J. Mayo, "Shift Happens 2—Finding Strong Footing: The Future of Assessment in the Learning to Employment Landscape," *Innovate+Educate*, February 2019, 10–11, https://innovate-educate.org/wp-content/uploads/2019/02/ShfitHappens2-1.pdf.

31. Accenture, Burning Glass Technologies, and Harvard Business School, "Bridge the Gap: Rebuilding America's Middle Skills," 2014, 17–18, https://www.hbs.edu/competitiveness/Documents/bridge-the-gap.pdf.

32. Pew Research Center, "Sharp Partisan Division in Views of National Institutions, Republicans Increasingly Say Colleges Have Negative Impact on U.S.," July 10, 2017, http://www.people-press.org/2017/07/10/sharp-partisan-divisions-in-views-of-national-institutions/. See also Paul Fain, "Deep Partisan Divide on Higher Education," *Inside Higher Education*, July 11, 2017, https://www.insidehighered.com/news/2017/07/11/dramatic-shift-most-republicans-now-say-colleges-have-negative-impact.

33. Fain, "Deep Partisan Divide."

34. Manpower Group, 2018 Talent Shortage Survey, Solving the Talent Shortage (2018) https://go.manpowergroup.com/hubfs/TalentShortage%202018%20(Global)%20Assets/PDFs/MG_TalentShortage2018_lo%206_25_18_FINAL.pdf?t=1540311952572.

35. Business Roundtable, "Work in Progress" (Washington, DC, June 2017), 1, https://s3.amazonaws.com/brt.org/BRT-SkillsGap201711012017(1).pdf.

36. Business Roundtable, "Work in Progress," 4.

37. Katherine G. Abraham, "Is Skill Mismatch Impeding U.S. Recovery?," *Industrial and Labor Relations Review* 68, no. 2 (2015): 291–313; Peter H. Cappelli, "Skill Gaps, Skill Shortages, and Skill Mismatches," *Industrial and Labor Relations Review* 68, no. 2 (2015): 251–290; Andrew Weaver and Paul Osterman, "Skill Demands and Mismatch in U.S. Manufacturing," *Industrial and Labor Relations Review* 70, no. 2. (2016): 275–307. See also chapter 5.

38. Jon Marcus, "Impatient with Colleges, Employers Design Their Own Courses," *Wired Business*, December 18, 2017, https://www.wired.com/story/impatient-with-colleges-employers-design-their-own-courses/.

39. Department of Education, National Center for Education Statistics, Digest of Education Statistics, bachelor's degrees conferred by postsecondary institutions by field of study, table 322.10, 2017, tables and figures, https://nces.ed.gov/programs/digest/d17/tables/dt17_322.10.asp?current=yes.

40. Peter McPherson, "Comments, Conference on Higher Education and Research as a Vehicle of Change—The Balancing Act of Modern Universities," House of Sweden, Washington, DC, February 13, 2018.

41. Doug Shapiro, Afet Dundar, Faye Huie, Phoebe K. Wakhungu, Ayesha Bhimdiwala, and Sean E. Wilson, "Completing College: A National View of Student Completion Rates—Fall 2012 Cohort" (Signature Report No. 16). Herndon, VA: National Student Clearinghouse Research Center, December 2018, https://nscresearchcenter.org/signaturereport16/.

42. Shapiro et al., "Completing College," 11–12.

43. Shapiro et al., "Completing College," 6, 13–20.

44. Harry J. Holzer and Sandy Baum, *Making College Work: Pathways to Success for Disadvantaged Students* (Washington, DC: Brookings Institution Press, 2017).

45. Harry J. Holzer and Sanday Baum, "Making College Work," presentation, Brookings Institution, October 16, 2017, 6, https://www.brookings.edu/wp-content/uploads/2016/09/making-college-work_10-16-2017.pdf.

46. Holzer and Baum, "Making College Work," 19.

47. Harry J. Holzer and Sandy Baum, "Making College Work: Nudging Student Behavior," Future Ed, Georgetown University, October 20, 2017, https://www.future-ed.org/work/making-college-work-nudging-student-behavior/.

48. See, for example, Jennet Conant, *Man of the Hour, James B. Conant Warrior Scientist* (New York: Simon and Schuster, 2017), 131–133, 277–279, 478–479.

49. Association of Public and Land Grant Universities, "How Does a College Degree Improve Graduates' Employment and Earnings," 2017.

50. Association of Public and Land Grant Universities, "Ready for Jobs, Careers, and a Lifetime: Public Research Universities and Credentials that Count," 2017, http://www.aplu.org/library/ready-for-jobs-careers-and-a-lifetime/file.

51. Only 39 percent of the public agreed that college graduates are prepared for workforce success according to a Gallup/Lumina study. Gallup and Lumina Foundation, *Americans Value Postsecondary Education: The 2015 Gallup-Lumina Foundation Study of the American Public's Opinion on Higher Education* (Washington, DC: Gallup, Inc., 2016), http://www.gallup.com/le/services/190583/Lumina_Report_2015%20Survey_of_Americans_Attitudes_Toward_Postsecondary_Education_FINAL.pdf; Doug Shapiro, Afet Dundar, Faye Huie, Phoebe Wakhungu, Ayesha Bhimdiwala, and Sean Wilson, *Completing College: A National View of Student Completion Rates—Fall 2012 Cohort* (Herndon, VA: National Student Clearinghouse Research Center December 2018), https://nscresearchcenter.org/wp-content/uploads/NSC004_Signature-Report_V9_12DEC18.pdf.

52. Anthony P. Carnevale, Nicole Smith, and Jeff Strohl, "Recovery: Job Growth and Education Requirements through 2020," Georgetown Center on Education and the Workforce, 2013, 8, https://cew.georgetown.edu/wp-content/uploads/2014/11/Recovery2020.FR_.Web_.pdf.

53. Bureau of Labor Statistics, Economic News Release: table A-4, Employment Status of the Civilian Population 25 Years and Over by Educational Attainment (Washington, DC: Division of Labor Force Statistics, 2017), https://www.bls.gov/news.release/empsit.t04.htm.

54. Association of Public and Land Grant Universities, "Ready for Jobs," 9.

55. Association of Public and Land Grant Universities, "Ready for Jobs," 10.

56. Elizabeth Z. Rutshow and Jessica Taketa, "College to Work, Findings from a Study of the Career Readiness Internship Program," MDRC, June 2019, 3, https://www.mdrc.org/sites/default/files/CRI_Final_2019.pdf.

57. Pew Research Center, "The State of American Jobs: How the Shifting Economic Landscape Is Reshaping Work and Society and Affecting the Way People Think about the Skills and Training They Need to Get Ahead" (Washington, DC: Pew Charitable Trust, October 6, 2016), http://www.pewsocialtrends.org/2016/10/06/the-state-of-american-jobs/.

58. Strada-Gallup, "2018 Strada-Gallup Alumni Survey," 1, 9–12.

59. Edelman Insights, "University Reputations and the Public, A Roadmap for Higher Education," October 2016, https://www.slideshare.net/EdelmanInsights/university-reputations-and-the-public?from_action=save. This public opinion survey found that 59 percent of the general population felt higher education was on the "wrong track," and that there is a disconnect between university academics and the public: while 71 percent of academics wanted to preserve a "well-rounded education," 56 percent of the general public wanted "tools and resources for a successful career."

60. Edelman Insights, "University Reputations," 5.

61. Daniel J. McInerney, "Becoming a Bilingual Advocate for Your Discipline and Your Graduates," *Liberal Education* 104, no. 3 (Summer 2018). A 2020 study notes that over the course of a career, the income levels of liberal arts graduates catch up to those with technical and science educations whose income initially took off. See Anthony P. Carnevale, Ban Cheah, and Martin Van Der Werf, "ROI of Liberal Arts Colleges: Value Adds Up over Time," Georgetown Center on Education and the Workforce, January 2020, figures 1 and 2, https://1gyhoq479ufd3yna29x7ubjn-wpengine.netdna-ssl.com/wp-content/uploads/Liberal-Arts-ROI.pdf. However, figure 7 in the report suggests that part of the reason may be that four-year liberal arts colleges have lower numbers of lower-income students.

62. ABB Robotics, "From Mass Production to Mass Customization," *Process Technology*, March 20, 2018, https://www.processonline.com.au/content/factory-automation/article/from-m.

63. Mark Muro, Sifan Liu, Jacob Whiton, and Siddarth Kulkami, "Digitalization and the American Workforce," Brookings Institution, November 15, 2017, https://www

.brookings.edu/wp-content/uploads/2017/11/mpp_2017nov15_digitalization_full_report.pdf.

64. Deloitte, Council on Competitiveness and Singularity University (Michelle Rodriquez, Robert Libbey, Sandeepan Mondai, Jeff Carbeck, and Joann Michalik), "Exponential Technologies in Manufacturing" (report April 2018), https://www.compete.org/storage/reports/exponential_technologies_2018_study.pdf.

65. Paul Lewis (Kings College London), "How to Create Skills for an Emerging Industry: The Case of Technician Skills and Training in Cell Therapy" (research paper), SSRN, January 25, 2017, https://papers.ssrn.com/sol3/papers.cfm?abstract_id=2903909.

66. Blivin and Mayo, "Shift Happens," 2, 30.

67. Clemson University Center for Workforce Education, vision statement, http://cecas.clemson.edu. Discussion below is based on meeting with Kapil Chalil Madathil, faculty director, and Eddie Bennett, curriculum marketing manager, Clemson Center for Workforce Education, October 30, 2018.

68. Clemson University Center for Workforce Development, https://www.educateworkforce.com.

69. Greenville Technical College Center for Manufacturing Innovation (CMI), Greenville, SC, https://www.cmigreenville.com/index.html. Information on CMI from meeting with David Clayton, former executive director, and Carolyn Watkins, dean of student services, Center for Manufacturing Education, October 31, 2018.

70. South Carolina Department of Education, Career and Technology Education (CATE), https://ed.sc.gov/instruction/career-and-technology-education/.

71. Clemson University, "Clemson Launches Advanced Manufacturing Research and Workforce Development Hub in Greenville," *The Newsstand* (release), February 15, 2018, https://newsstand.clemson.edu/mediarelations/clemson-launches-advanced-manufacturing-research-and-workforce-development-hub-in-greenville/.

72. Clemson University International Center for Automotive Research (ICAR), http://cuicar.com/about/quick-facts/; meeting with Nick Rigas, ICAR executive director, October 30, 2018.

73. Communications from Mark A. Johnson, professor of material science and engineering and director, Center for Advanced Manufacturing, and Laine Mears, professor of automotive engineering, Clemson University, October 24 and 25, 2019.

74. Meeting with Joshua Summers, professor of mechanical engineering, Clemson University, October 23, 2018, and follow-up communication of October 24, 2019. Summers was the source of information on the undergraduate engineering program discussed in this section.

75. Clemson University Center for Advanced Manufacturing (CAM), Greenville, SC, https://clemsoncam.com.

76. Carnevale, Garcia, and Gulish, "Career Pathways."

77. Symonds, Schwartz, and Ferguson, "Pathways to Prosperity: Meeting the Challenge."

78. Association of Public and Land Grant Universities, "Ready for Jobs," 2017.

79. *The Economist*, "Special Report on Lifelong Learning," January 2017, https://www.economist.com/special-report/2017/01/12/lifelong-learning-is-becoming-an-economic-imperative.

80. One study, for example, found that the initial pay premium commanded by STEM degrees declines over time as new skills not offered in the original STEM program evolve; skills simply can become dated and less in demand; see Deming and Noray, "STEM Careers."

81. Wendy Nelson, "Community Colleges and Guaranteed Transfer Programs," August 23, 2018, https://www.mykidscollegechoice.com/2018/08/23/community-colleges-and-guaranteed-transfer-programs/.

82. Nathan Grawe, an economist at Carleton College, has predicted that based on demographic trends, the college-going population will drop by 15 percent between 2025 and 2029 and continue to decline by one or two percentage points thereafter. Using population and family income data, only seven states are predicted to see an increase in the number of students attending regional four-year colleges and universities between 2012 and 2029. The rest will see declines in students, and in twenty-three states the decline in students will exceed 15 percent. Nathan D. Grawe, *Demographics and the Demand for Higher Education* (Baltimore: Johns Hopkins University Press, 2018).

8 THE NEW EDUCATIONAL TECHNOLOGIES

1. Hermann Ebbinghaus, *Memory: A Contribution to Experimental Psychology*, trans. Henry A. Ruger and Clara E. Bussenius (New York: Teachers College, Columbia University, 1913).

2. Karen Wilcox, Sanjay Sarma, and Philip Lippel, "Online Education: A Catalyst for Higher Education Reform," MIT Online Education Policy Initiative, April 2016, https://oepi.mit.edu/files/2016/09/MIT-Online-Education-Policy-Initiative-April-2016.pdf; Peter C. Brown, Henry L Roediger, and Mark A. McDaniel, *Make It Stick, The Science of Successful Learning* (Cambridge, MA: Belknap Press, 2014); Sarma, *The Boundless Mind.*

3. Plato, *Theaetetus*.

4. Today, edX and Coursera offer certificates, microcredentials, and full master's degrees. Udacity offers certificates and "nanodegrees." In the interest of full disclosure, author Sanjay Sarma serves on the edX board, and edX is 50 percent owned by MIT.

5. Justin Kruger and David Dunning, "Unskilled and Unaware of It: How Difficulties in Recognizing One's Own Incompetence Lead to Inflated Self-Assessments," *Journal of Personality and Social Psychology* 77, no. 6 (1999): 1121.

6. Elizabeth L. Bjork and Robert A. Bjork, "Making Things Hard on Yourself, but in a Good Way: Creating Desirable Difficulties to Enhance Learning," in *Psychology and the Real World: Essays Illustrating Fundamental Contributions to Society*, ed. M. A. Gernsbacher, R. W. Pew, L. M. Hough, and J. R. Pomerantz (New York: Worth Publishers, 2011), 56–64.

7. Wilcox, Sarma, and Lippel, "Online Education."

8. Wilcox, Sarma, and Lippel, "Online Education."

9. Dominic A. Simon and Robert A. Bjork, "Metacognition in Motor Learning," *Journal of Experimental Psychology: Learning, Memory, and Cognition* 27, no. 4 (2001): 907.

10. Wilcox, Sarma, and Lippel, "Online Education."

11. Chien-Ho Janice Lin, Barbara J. Knowlton, Ming-Chang Chiang, Marco Iacoboni, Parima Udompholkul, and Allan D. Wu, "Brain–Behavior Correlates of Optimizing Learning through Interleaved Practice," *Neuroimage* 56, no. 3 (2011): 1758–1772.

12. Matthew Jensen Hays, Nate Kornell, and Robert A. Bjork, "The Costs and Benefits of Providing Feedback during Learning," *Psychonomic Bulletin & Review* 17, no. 6 (2010): 797–801.

13. Gary Wolf, "Want to Remember Everything You'll Ever Learn? Surrender to This Algorithm," *Wired*, April 21, 2008, ISSN 1059-1028 (accessed January 30, 2019).

14. Brendan Tomoschuk and Jarrett Lovelett. "A Memory-Sensitive Classification Model of Errors in Early Second Language Learning," *Proceedings of the Thirteenth Workshop on Innovative Use of NLP for Building Educational Applications*, 2018, 231–239.

15. Dan Davis, René F. Kizilcec, Claudia Hauff, and Geert-Jan Houben, "Scaling Effective Learning Strategies: Retrieval Practice and Long-Term Knowledge Retention in MOOCs," *Journal of Learning Analytics* 5, no. 3 (2018): 21–41; Dillon Dumensil, "The Effects of Spaced Repetition in Online Education." MEng thesis, Department of Electrical Engineering and Computer Science, MIT, 2016.

16. There is now a rich subfield of research studying benefits of peer assessment. See, for example, Bart Huisman, Wilfried Admiraal, Olga Pilli, Maarten van de Ven, and Nadira Saab, "Peer Assessment in MOOCs: The Relationship between Peer Reviewers'

Ability and Authors' Essay Performance," *British Journal of Educational Technology* 49, no. 1 (2018): 101–110.

17. Steve Krolowich, "Writing Instructor, Skeptical of Automated Grading, Pits Machine vs. Machine," *Chronicle of Higher Education*, April 28, 2014.

18. Saul A. McLeod, "Lev Vygotsky," *Simply Psychology*, August 5, 2018, https://www.simplypsychology.org/vygotsky.html.

19. Mitchell J. Nathan, Kenneth R. Koedinger, and Martha W. Alibali, "Expert Blind Spot: When Content Knowledge Eclipses Pedagogical Content Knowledge," *Proceedings of the Third International Conference on Cognitive Science*, 2001, 644–648.

20. K. Anders Ericsson, "Deliberate Practice and Acquisition of Expert Performance: A General Overview," *Academic Emergency Medicine* 15, no. 11 (2008): 988–994; David J. Jones, Kirk W. Madison, and Carl E. Wieman, "Transforming a Fourth Year Modern Optics Course Using a Deliberate Practice Framework," *Physical Review Special Topics-Physics Education Research* 11, no. 2 (2015): 020108.

21. Benjamin S Bloom, "The 2 Sigma Problem: The Search for Methods of Group Instruction as Effective as One-to-One Tutoring," *Educational Researcher* 13, no. 6 (1984): 4–16.

22. John Sweller, "Cognitive Load Theory," in *The Psychology of Learning and Motivation: Cognition in Education*, vol. 55, ed. J. P. Mestre and B. H. Ross (San Diego, CA: Academic Press, 2011), 37–76.

23. Fred Paas and Tamara Van Gog, "Optimising Worked Example Instruction: Different Ways to Increase Germane Cognitive Load," *Learning and Instruction* 16, no. 2 (April 2006): 87–91.

24. Steven Ritter, John R. Anderson, Kenneth R. Koedinger, and Albert Corbett, "Cognitive Tutor: Applied Research in Mathematics Education," *Psychonomic Bulletin & Review* 14, no. 2 (2007): 249–255.

25. Zühal Okan, "Edutainment: Is Learning at Risk?," *British Journal of Educational Technology* 34, no. 3 (2003): 255–264.

26. Mitchel Resnick, "Edutainment? No Thanks. I Prefer Playful Learning," *Associazione Civita Report on Edutainment*, 14, 2004, 1–4; M. Resnick, J. Maloney, A. Monroy-Hernández, N. Rusk, E. Eastmond, K. Brennan, A. Millner, E. Rosenbaum, J.S. Silver, B. Silverman, and Y.B. Kafai, "Scratch: Programming for All," *Communications of the ACM* 52, no. 11 (2009): 60–67.

27. Jane McGonigal, *Reality Is Broken: Why Games Make Us Better and How They Can Change the World* (New York: Penguin, 2011).

28. Eric Klopfer and Kurt Squire, "Environmental Detectives: The Development of an Augmented Reality Platform for Environmental Simulations," *Educational Technology*

Research and Development 56, no. 2 (2008): 203–228; D. Fox Harrell, Pablo Ortiz, Peter Downs, Maya Wagoner, Elizabeth Carré, and Annie Wang, "Chimeria: Grayscale: An Interactive Narrative for Provoking Critical Reflection on Gender Discrimination," *MATLIT: Materialities of Literature* 6, no. 2 (2018): 217–221; Thomas M. Connolly, Elizabeth A. Boyle, Ewan MacArthur, Thomas Hainey, and James M. Boyle, "A Systematic Literature Review of Empirical Evidence on Computer Games and Serious Games," *Computers & Education* 59, no. 2 (2012): 661–686.

29. Nassim Jafari Naimi and Eric M. Meyers, "Collective Intelligence or Group Think? Engaging Participation Patterns in World without Oil," *Proceedings of the 18th ACM Conference on Computer Supported Cooperative Work & Social Computing*, ACM, 2015, 1872–1881.

30. Sebastian Deterding, Dan Dixon, Rilla Khaled, and Lennart Nacke, "From Game Design Elements to Gamefulness: Defining Gamification," *Proceedings of the 15th International Academic MindTrekConference: Envisioning Future Media Environments*, ACM, 2011, 9–15.

31. Robert T. Hays, John W. Jacobs, Carolyn Prince, and Eduardo Salas, "Flight Simulator Training Effectiveness: A Meta-Analysis," *Military Psychology* 4, no. 2 (1992): 63–74.

32. See, generally, National Museum of the US Air Force, Link Trainer, fact sheet, May 4, 2015, https://www.nationalmuseum.af.mil/Visit/Museum-Exhibits/Fact-Sheets/Display/Article/196852/link-trainer/ (accessed June 2019).

33. Thomas Clarke and Elizabeth Clarke, "Learning Outcomes from Business Simulation Exercises," *Education+ Training* (2009); Stephen R. Carpenter and Lance H. Gunderson, "Coping with Collapse: Ecological and Social Dynamics in Ecosystem Management: Like Flight Simulators That Train Would-Be Aviators, Simple Models Can Be Used to Evoke People's Adaptive, Forward-Thinking Behavior, Aimed in this Instance at Sustainability of Human–Natural Systems," *BioScience* 51, no. 6 (2001): 451–457.

34. A. J. Angulo, *William Barton Rogers and the Idea of MIT* (Baltimore, MD: Johns Hopkins University Press, 2009).

35. Carly Kontra, Susan Goldin-Meadow, and Sian L. Beilock, "Embodied Learning across the Life Span," *Topics in Cognitive Science* 4, no. 4 (2012): 731–739; Carly Kontra, Daniel J. Lyons, Susan M. Fischer, and Sian L. Bellock, "Physical Experience Enhances Science Learning," *Psychological Science* 26, no. 6 (April 24, 2015): 737–749.

36. Logan Fiorella and Richard E. Mayer, "Eight Ways to Promote Generative Learning," *Educational Psychology Review* 28, no. 4 (2016): 717–741.

37. Michael Prince, "Does Active Learning Work? A Review of the Research," *Journal of Engineering Education* 93, no. 3 (2004): 223–231.

38. Charles R. Graham, "Blended Learning Systems," in *The Handbook of Blended Learning*, ed. Curtis J. Bonk and Charles R. Graham (New York: Wiley Pfeiffer Publishing, 2005), 3–21.

39. The idea was popularized by online education content provider Sal Khan, "Let's Use Video to Reinvent Education," TED2011, Ted Talk, March 2011, https://www.ted.com/talks/sal_khan_let_s_use_video_to_reinvent_education.

40. M. David Merrill, "First Principles of Instruction, *Educational Technology Research and Development* 50, no. 3 (2002): 43–59.

41. Carey Goldberg, "Auditing Classes at M.I.T., on the Web and Free," *New York Times*, April 4, 2001.

42. MIT Open Courseware, Dashboard Report, January 2019, table 1, Site Publication Statistics, Total Visits, https://ocw.mit.edu/about/site-statistics/monthly-reports/MITOCW_DB_2019_01_v1.pdf.

43. For a useful summary of the advantages of access, scale, and opportunities online programs create, see the study of the Georgia Tech computer science master's program: Joshua Goodman, Julia Melkers, and Amanda Pallais, "Can Online Delivery Increase Access to Education?," *Journal of Labor Economics* 37, no. 1 (2019): 1–34.

44. Eric Bettinger and researchers at Stamford's Center for Education Policy Analysis analyzed a for-profit university and found poor results from online courses. They also found that online learning seems to work less well than a classroom for the least prepared students. See Eric Bettinger, Lindsay Fox, Susana Loeb, and Eric Taylor, Virtual Classrooms: How Online College Courses Affect Student Success, *American Economic Review* 107, no. 9 (2017): 2855–2875; see also Eric Bettinger and Susan Loeb, "Promises and Pitfalls of Online Education," *Brookings Economic Studies, Evidence Speaks Report* 2, no. 15 (June 9, 2017), https://www.brookings.edu/wp-content/uploads/2017/06/ccf_20170609_loeb_evidence_speaks1.pdf.

45. David Figlio, Mark Rush, and Lu Yin, "Is It Live or Is It Internet? Experimental Estimates of the Effects of Online Instruction on Student Learning," *Journal of Labor Economics* 31, no. 4 (2013): 763–784; William G. Bowen, Matthew M. Chingos, Kelly A. Lack, and Thomas I. Nygren, "Interactive Learning Online at Public Universities: Evidence from a Six-Campus Randomized Trial," *Journal of Policy Analysis and Management* 33, no. 1 (2014): 94–111.

46. Platforms such as Harvard Business School's HBX online and IE Business School's WoW are examples that enable an in-person experience online.

47. See Squirrel AI Learning, "How We're Revolutionizing Education," http://squirrelai.com/about.

48. Examples include Skillsoft, Cornerstone, and Pluralsight.

49. Companies such as Degreed and edCast let companies provide this informal content—such as content libraries and even magazine articles—and keep track of learner progress.

50. Ashok K. Goel and Lalith Polepeddi, "Jill Watson: A Virtual Teaching Assistant for Online Education," Georgia Institute of Technology, College of Computing Technical Reports, 2016, http://hdl.handle.net/1853/59104.

51. Xiaowei Li, Bin Hu, Tingshao Zhu, Jingzhi Yan, and Fang Zheng, "Towards Affective Learning with an EEG Feedback Approach," *Proceedings of the First ACM International Workshop on Multimedia Technologies for Distance Learning*, ACM, 2009, 33–33; Ellen M. Kok and Halszka Jarodzka, "Before Your Very Eyes: The Value and Limitations of Eye Tracking in Medical Education, *Medical Education* 51, no. 1 (2017): 114–122.

52. David Gibson, Nathaniel Ostashewski, Kim Flintoff, Sheryl Grant, and Erin Knight, "Digital Badges in Education," *Education and Information Technologies* 20, no. 2 (2015): 403–410.

53. Suzanne Day, "Nine Universities Team Up to Create Infrastructure for Digital Academic Credentials," MIT Office of Open Learning, April 23, 2019, http://news.mit.edu/2019/nine-universities-team-up-global-infrastructure-digital-academic-credentials-0423; Jeffrey R. Young, "MIT Starts University Group to Build New Digital Credential System," *EdSurge*, April 23, 2019, https://www.edsurge.com/news/2019-04-23-mit-starts-university-group-to-build-new-digital-credential-system.

54. Chen Zhenghao, Brandon Alcorn, Gayle Christensen, Nicholas Eriksson, Daphne Koller, and Ezekiel J. Emanuel, "Who's Benefiting from MOOCs, and Why," *Harvard Business Review*, September 22, 2015, https://hbr.org/2015/09/whos-benefiting-from-moocs-and-why.

9 THE EDUCATIONAL CONTENT

1. Thad R. Nodine, "How Did We Get Here? A Brief History of Competency-Based Higher Education in the United States," *Journal of Competency-Based Education*, April 27, 2016, https://onlinelibrary.wiley.com/doi/full/10.1002/cbe2.1004.

2. Nodine, "How Did We Get Here?" In the 1940s, Tyler worked on education purposes tied to learning experiences; see Ralph W. Tyler, *Basic Principles of Curriculum and Instruction* (Chicago: University of Chicago Press, 1949). Later, Bloom worked on classification of education objectives connected to mastery learning; see Benjamin S. Bloom, *Taxonomy of Educational Objectives* (Boston, MA: Allyn and Bacon, 1956).

3. Ted Mitchell, "Guidance to Competency Based Education Experimental Site Released," *Homeroom* (blog), Department of Education, September 22, 2015, https://

blog.ed.gov/2015/09/guidance-for-competency-based-education-experimental-site-released/.

4. Chris Sturgis, "How Competency-Based Education Differs from the Traditional System of Education," New Learning Models, iNACOL, November 16, 2019, https://www.inacol.org/news/how-competency-based-education-differs-from-the-traditional-system-of-education/.

5. See, generally, "Competency-Based Education Network (C-Ben), Quality Framework for Competency-Based Education Programs," September 2017, https://www.cbenetwork.org/wp-content/uploads/2018/09/1st_button_CBE17016__Quality_Framework_Update.pdf.

6. For an example of a public middle school using a competency-based approach, see Kyle Spencer, "No Grades, No Failing, No Hurry," *New York Times*, August 13, 2017 (Metropolitan section), 1, 6, https://www.nytimes.com/2017/08/11/nyregion/mastery-based-learning-no-grades.html. The approach is being adopted in over forty schools in the New York City school system, with eight of those schools serving as lab schools to guide others by developing best practices. School districts in Vermont, Maine, New Hampshire, Idaho, and Illinois are also working to implement competency approaches.

7. Jamai Blivin and Mayo, "Shift Happens 2, Finding Strong Footing: The Future of Assessment in the Learning to Employment Landscape," *Innovate+Educate,* February 2019, 13–16, https://innovate-educate.org/wp-content/uploads/2019/02/ShfitHappens2-1.pdf.

8. Jean Johnson, Jon Rochkind, Amber Ott, and Samantha Dupont, "With Their Whole Lives Ahead of Them," *Public Agenda*, 2009, 37, https://www.publicagenda.org/files/theirwholelivesaheadofthem.pdf

9. Jamie Merisotis, "Credentials Reform: How Technology and the Changing Needs of the Workforce Will Create the Higher Education System of the Future," *Educause Review*, May 2, 2016, https://er.educause.edu/articles/2016/5/credentials-reform-how-technology-and-the-changing-needs-of-the-workforce-will-create-the-higher-ed.

10. Stephanie Cronen, Meghan McQuiggan, and Emily Isenberg, "Adult Training and Education: Results from the National Household Education Surveys, First Look," Department of Education, National Center for Education Statistics (NCES), February 2018, 6 (table 1), https://nces.ed.gov/pubs2017/2017103rev.pdf.

11. Blivin and Mayo, "Shift Happens 2," 15 (citing Census Bureau, American Community Survey, 2017).

12. Cronen, McQuiggan, and Isenberg, "Adult Training," table 7.

13. Strada Education Network, Gallup, and Lumina Foundation, "Certified Value: When Do Adults Without Degrees Benefit from Earning Certificates and

Certifications?," 2019, Strada Education Network report, 5, 7, 8, https://go.stradaeducation.org/certified-value?utm_campaign=Gallup%20Report%3A%20Certified%20Value&utm_source=hs_email&utm_medium=email&utm_content=72679322&_hsenc=p2ANqtz-9EiBK-yzk8d_9mX5S-eOmxRPbSz6bN42ikvaAyMQgoGJmcjAXjHNXvQIluzavCRUqMyrFw1X9QfcsBbwJU6JhLuCnu6w&_hsmi=72679322. The wage premium depends on the occupation; for some—such as security, construction, architecture, and mining—there can be a premium of $25,000, while for office work, education support, and some others, it is not significant.

14. Blivin and Mayo, "Shift Happens 2," 30–32.

15. Udacity, "Find the Nanodegree Program That's Right for You," https://learning.udacity.com/tax-promo2019/?utm_source=google&utm_medium=ads&utm_campaign=747168232&utm_term=53391003525&utm_content=342274971539&device=c&gclid=EAIaIQobChMImPfv9crc4QIVjFmGCh3KswaFEAAYAiAAEgIAXvD_BwE.

16. MITx, "Micromasters Programs: Bringing MIT to You," https://micromasters.mit.edu. Students who do well in the online courses can use their MicroMasters performance as an admissions credential to come to MIT or other cooperating universities to earn a full master's degree on an accelerated timetable.

17. Blivin and Mayo, "Shift Happens 2," 30.

18. Blivin and Mayo, "Shift Happens 2," 18–22.

19. Troy Markowitz, "The Seven Deadly Sins of Digital Badging in Education," *Forbes*, September 16, 2018, https://www.forbes.com/sites/troymarkowitz/2018/09/16/the-seven-deadly-sins-of-digital-badging-in-education-making-badges-student-centered/#7a8498a370b8. According to the University Professional and Continuing Education Association (UPCEA), 20 percent of academic institutions now offer digital badges and 94 percent offer alternative credentials. James Fong, Peter Janzow, and Kyle Peck, "Demographic Shifts in Educational Demand and the Rise in Alternative Credentials, An UPCEA/Pearson Survey," June 2016, 2, https://upcea.edu/wp-content/uploads/2017/05/Demographic-Shifts-in-Educational-Demand-and-the-Rise-of-Alternative-Credentials.pdf.

20. Strada Education Network (with Gallup), "Back to School: What Adults without Degrees Say about Additional Education and Training," Strada Education Network report, 2019, 6.

21. Strada Education Network (with Gallup), "What Do Americans Value from Their Education?," Strada Education Network report, 2019, 5.

22. Trade Adjustment Assistance Community College and Career Training (TAACCT) Grant Program (2011–2016), Program Summary, https://www.doleta.gov/taaccct/.

23. SkillsCommons, http://support.skillscommons.org/about/. The site was designed and managed by the California State University and its MERLOT program: https://www.merlot.org/merlot/index.htm.

24. My Skills My Future, CareerOneStop, website, https://www.myskillsmyfuture.org. While it can connect to area training providers, it does not have a full training delivery feature and lacks in-depth career prediction capability, because these kinds of systems were still in development at the time of this writing.

25. WorkforceGPS, Resource Library, https://www.workforcegps.org.

26. https://www.careeronestop.org.

27. Blivin and Mayo, "Shift Happens 2," 25–26.

28. Western Governors University (WGU) and Gallup, "Great Jobs, Great Lives: Gallup Study of Recent Western Governors University Alumni," Alumni Outcomes Report, 2019, 2–3, https://www.wgu.edu/content/dam/western-governors/documents/other-reports/great-jobs-great-lives-study-2019.pdf.

29. Western Governors University and Gallup, 3. Some 72 percent of alumni, who borrow only about half the national average to complete their degrees, strongly agreed their degree was worth the cost. Having a mentor who encouraged students to pursue their goals, which two-thirds of those surveyed had, and having a job or internship while enrolled (81 percent of those surveyed had such work), were found to be key components of a WGU education.

30. HoloPundits, "Education and Training," VirtualWhiz, https://www.holopundits.com/education-training/virtuwhiz.html.

31. Lynda.com, https://www.lynda.com.

32. Liangyue Li, How Jing, Hanghang Tong, Jaewon Yang, Qi He, and Bee-Chung Chen, "NEMO: Next Career Move Prediction with Contextual Embedding," International WWW Conference Committee, WWW 2017 Companion, April 3–7, 2017, http://www.public.asu.edu/~liangyue/pdfs/LiJTYHC_WWW17.pdf.

33. Morgan Ryan Frank, "Skillscape: How Skills Affect Your Job Trajectory, and Their Implications for Automation by AI," blog, MIT Media Lab, July 18, 2018, https://www.media.mit.edu/posts/how-skills-affect-your-job-trajectory-and-their-implications-for-automation-by-ai/.

34. See, for example, Elizabeth Durant and Alison Trachy, "Digital Diploma Debuts at MIT," *MIT News*, October 15, 2017, http://news.mit.edu/2017/mit-debuts-secure-digital-diploma-using-bitcoin-blockchain-technology-1017; Suzanne Day, "Nine Universities Team Up to Create Global Infrastructure for Digital Academic Credentials," *MIT News*, April 23, 2019, https://openlearning.mit.edu/news-and-events/news/nine-universities-team-create-global-infrastructure-digital-academic.

35. Department of Labor, Employment and Training Administration Building Blocks Competency Model, https://www.careeronestop.org/CompetencyModel/competency-models/building-blocks-model.aspx. The Department of Labor has also issued much more detailed versions of these competencies, delineating each category with specific examples and thus providing a useful organizing framework. See, for example, sector-specific models such as Department of Labor, Employment and Training Administration, Geospatial Technology Competency, June 1, 2010, http://www.geotechcenter.org/uploads/2/4/8/8/24886299/gtmc_research_report.pdf; Department of Labor, Employment and Training Administration, Transportation, Distribution and Logistics Competency Model, February 2014, https://www.careeronestop.org/competencymodel/Info_Documents/TDLmodelchanges2014.pdf.

36. The Secretary's Commission on Achieving Necessary Skills (SCANS), June 1991, in Department of Labor, "What Work Requires of Skills," A SCANS Report for America 2000, June 1991, iii, https://wdr.doleta.gov/SCANS/whatwork/whatwork.pdf.

37. Department of Labor (through ACT, Inc.), "Workplace Essential Skills, Resources Related to the SCANS Competencies and Foundation Skills," for Department of Labor, Employment and Training Administration, August 2000, https://wdr.doleta.gov/opr/fulltext/00-wes.pdf.

38. National Network of Business and Industry, common employability skills, March 2015, http://www.nationalnetwork.org/wp-content/uploads/2015/05/Common_Employability_Skills-03-30-152.pdf.

39. The National Network of Business and Industry, after five years of developing and promoting skills credentialing across networks of employers, announced in December 2018 that it would be culminating its work. National Network of Business and Industry, "National Network: A Chapter Closes," December 3, 2018, http://www.nationalnetwork.org/blog/the-national-network-a-chapter-closes-but-the-work-continues/; https://www.msscusa.org/certification/production-certification-cpt/.

40. Manufacturing Skill Standards Council, "Production Standards," 2017, https://www.msscusa.org/certification/production-certification-cpt/.

41. Frank Levy and Richard Murmane, *Teaching the New Basic Skills, Principles for a Changing Economy* (New York: Free Press, 1996).

42. ACT, WorkKeys Assessments, http://www.act.org/content/act/en/products-and-services/workkeys-for-employers/assessments.html.

43. WorkKeys and KeyTrain were developed and implemented at ACT by Dane and Sheila Boyington, who were vice presidents at ACT until 2012 and then founded Thinking Media, which operates the Learning Blade system of online STEM courses: http://www.thinkingmedia.com/about.html.

44. ACT WorkKeys, "Evidence Supporting the Use of the ACT WorkKeys National Career Readiness Certificate," https://www.act.org/content/dam/act/unsecured/documents/NCRC-Validity-Evidence-06.21.17.pdf.

45. ACT WorkKeys, "Evidence."

46. Russell DuBose, human resources director, Phifer, presentation at Manufacturing Institute, Manufacturing Workforce 4.0, forum, Knight Conference Center, Newseum, Washington, DC, July 11, 2017.

47. Jeff Lynn, Workforce Education Chancellor for Alabama's Community College system, presentation at Manufacturing Institute, Manufacturing Workforce 4.0, forum, Knight Conference Center, Newseum, Washington, DC, July 11, 2017.

48. John Hoops and Complete College America, "A Working Model for Student Success: The Tennessee Technology Centers," Complete College America, Washington, DC, 2010, 11, https://files.eric.ed.gov/fulltext/ED536826.pdf.

49. TennesseeReconnect, The Tennessee Colleges of Applied Technology, https://www.tnreconnect.gov/ChooseaDegree/CollegePath/TNReconnectCollegesandUniversities/TheTennesseeCollegesofAppliedTechnology/tabid/5253/Default.aspx.

50. Hoops, "A Working Model for Student Success," 22.

51. Hoops, "A Working Model," 24.

52. I-BEST, Washington State Board for Community and Technical Colleges, https://www.sbctc.edu/colleges-staff/programs-services/i-best/.

53. I-BEST, Pathways That Work (video), https://www.sbctc.edu/colleges-staff/programs-services/i-best/.

54. Thomas Bailey, Dong Wook Jeong, and Sung-Woo Cho, "Referral, Enrollment and Completion in Developmental Education Sequences in Community Colleges, *Economics of Education Review* 29, no. 2 (2010): 255–270, http://ac.els-cdn.com/S0272775709001071/1-s2.0-S0272775709001071-main.pdf?_tid=4ca5bebe-1b83-11e6-a854-00000aacb35f&acdnat=1463416322_f73150ebb5055d18ff9eb1f01c33b36e.

55. Carnegie Math Pathways, https://carnegiemathpathways.org.

56. Jon Norman, Hiro Yamada, and Melrose Huang, "Degree Attainment and Transfer among Statway Students" (paper), Carnegie Foundation for the Advancement of Teaching, 2018, https://storage.googleapis.com/cmp-wordpress-public-uploads/1/2019/02/Degree-Attainment-and-Transfer-among-Statway-Students-2.pdf.

57. Charles Dana Center, University of Texas, "The Case for Mathematics Pathways," 2019, https://dcmathpathways.org/sites/default/files/resources/2019-03/CaseforMathPathways_20190313.pdf.

58. Charles A. Dana Center, University of Texas at Austin, "Dismantling Barriers in Math and Science Education," https://www.utdanacenter.org.

59. Susan Scrivener, Himani Gupta, Michael Weiss, Benjamin Cohen, Maria Cormier, and Jessica Braithwaite, MDRC, "Becoming College Ready, Early Findings from a CUNY Start Evaluation," MRDC, July 2018, https://www.mdrc.org/publication/becoming-college-ready.

60. Sameer Gadkaree, "Educational Technology: Can It Improve Job Prospects for Adults Who Need Stronger Math and English Skills?," Joyce Foundation, June 8, 2017, http://www.joycefdn.org/news/educational-technology-can-it-improve-job-prospects-for-adults-who-need-stronger-math-and-english-skills. This review evaluated, Robert Murphy, Marie Bienkowski, Ruchi Bhanot, Ann House, Tiffany Leone, and Jennifer Van Brunt (SRI), "Evaluating Digital Learning for Adult Basic Literacy and Numeracy," SRI, June 2017, https://www.sri.com/work/publications/evaluating-digital-learning-adult-basic-literacy-and-numeracy.

61. Mark Muro, Sifan Liu, Jacob Whiton, and Siddarth Kulkami, "Digitalization and the American Workforce," Brookings Institution, November 15, 2017, https://www.brookings.edu/wp-content/uploads/2017/11/mpp_2017nov15_digitalization_full_report.pdf.

62. LinkedIn, "The Skills Companies Need Most in 2018, and the Courses to Get Them," report, July 2018, https://learning.linkedin.com/blog/top-skills/the-skills-companies-need-most-in-2018--and-the-courses-to-get-t.

63. Essential Digital Skills, 2018 Framework, https://assets.publishing.service.gov.uk/government/uploads/system/uploads/attachment_data/file/738922/Essential_digital_skills_framework.pdf.

64. Georgia Tech, College of Computing, http://www.omscs.gatech.edu.

65. LinkedIn, "The Skills Companies Need Most in 2018."

66. University of Southern California, Center for Third Space Thinking, http://uscthirdspace.com/about/#core-attributes.

67. National Academies of Sciences, Engineering, and Medicine, "Supporting Students' College Success: The Role of Assessment of Interpersonal and Interpersonal Competencies" (Washington, DC: National Academies Press, 2017), https://www.nap.edu/catalog/24697/supporting-students-college-success-the-role-of-assessment-of-intrapersonal.

68. Merrilea Mayo, discussions, Washington, DC, July 6–8, 2018, communication of April 29, 2019, drawing on her pending studies of workforce skill assessment. Her studies relevant to this section include, Merrilea Mayo, "Video Games: A Route to Large-Scale STEM Education?," *Science* 323, no. 5910 (January 2, 2009), https://science.sciencemag.org/content/323/5910/79; Merrilea Mayo, "Bringing Game-

Based Learning to Scale: The Business Challenges of Serious Games," *Journal of International Learning and Media* 2, no. 2 (April 2010): 81–100; Robert Atkinson and Merrilea Mayo, "Refueling the U.S. Innovation Economy: Fresh Approaches to STEM Education," Information Technology and Innovation Foundation report, December 7, 2010, https://itif.org/publications/2010/12/07/refueling-us-innovation-economy-fresh-approaches-stem-education; Jamai Blivin and Merrilea Mayo, "A Nation Upside Down: A New Vision for the Future of Learning," *Educate+Innovate,* 2018, https://innovate-educate.org/publications-a-nation-upside-down/; Jamai Blijven and Merrilea Mayo, "Shift Happens: The Future of Working and Learning," *Educate+Innovate,* 2018, https://innovate-educate.org/shift-happens-pima-community-college/; Jamai Blivin and Merrilea Mayo, "Shift Happens 2, Strong Footing: The Future of Assessment in the Learning to Employment Landscape." She was also involved in the development of CoreScore, a soft skills assessment used by employers, https://corescore.jobs.

69. MHA Labs, "Skill Building Blocks, Problem Solving," http://mhalabs.org/skill-building-blocks/problem-solving/.

70. Preliminary testing work on this combination has been undertaken by researchers in Australia. See Patrick Griffin and Esther Care, "Developing Learners' Collaborative Problem Solving Skills," Assessment Research Centre, Melbourne Graduate School of Education, European Schoolnet Academy (paper), November 2014, http://vp-learningdiaries.weebly.com/uploads/9/4/9/8/9498170/developing_learners_collaborative_problem_solving_p_griffin.pdf. A form of this is now on OECD's 2015 PISA test, although it has not been firmly established that this variant is what employers are seeking. See OECD, "PISA Test, 2015 Test Questions, Collaborative Problem Solving Scoring Guide," http://www.oecd.org/pisa/test/CPS-Xandar-scoring-guide.pdf.

71. Janis A. Cannon-Bowers, Scott I. Tannenbaum, Eduardo Salas, and Catherine Volpe, "Defining Competencies and Establishing Team Training Requirements," in *Team Effectiveness and Decision Making in Organizations,* ed. Richard Guzzo and Catherine Volpe (San Francisco: Jossey Bass 1995), 333–380.

72. MHA Labs, "Working Impact," Employee/Intern Performance Review, Survey section, http://mhalabs.org/downloads/MHA_WISurveyGuide2018.pdf. Some of the "big five" positive personality traits are also relevant to these skills. See, for example, L. R. Goldberg, "Language and Individual Differences: The Search for Universals in Personality Lexicons," in *Review of Personality and Social Psychology,* ed. Ladd Wheeler (Beverly Hills, CA: Sage Publications 1981), vol. 1, 141–116; Cambridge Analytica, "About Us, OCEAN and the Big Five," https://web.archive.org/web/20160216023554/https://cambridgeanalytica.org/about.

73. MHA Labs, "Working Impact," Employee/Intern Performance Review, Survey section.

74. See, generally, Tomas Chamorro-Premuzic and David Winsborough, "Personality Tests Can Help Balance a Team," *Harvard Business Review*, March 19, 2015, https://hbr.org/2015/03/personality-tests-can-help-balance-a-team, Pearson/TalentLens, Golden Personality Profiler, http://www.talentlens.co.uk/product/golden-personality-profiler/ (arguably assists team development).

75. While cognitive skills are a component of teamwork, they are difficult to weigh. The ability to read and understand are important, but not at the core of teamwork, nor are coping skills the whole story. As Mayo put it, "Teamwork is a 50-piece puzzle and we just don't know the relative weight to assign the pieces." Mayo, discussions.

76. Angela Duckworth, *Grit: The Power and Passion of Perseverance* (New York: Scribner, 2016).

77. Carol S. Dweck, *Mindset: The New Psychology of Success* (New York: Random House, 2006).

78. See, for example, the summary at Mindset Works, "Decades of Scientific Research," https://www.mindsetworks.com/science/.

79. Cambridge Analytica, "About Us, OCEAN and the Big Five."

80. Abraham H. Maslow, *A Theory of Human Motivation* (New York: Martino Fine Books, [1943] 2013).

81. Association of American Colleges and Universities, "Fulfilling the American Dream: Liberal Education and the Future of Work," Washington, DC, July 2018, https://www.aacu.org/sites/default/files/files/LEAP/2018EmployerResearchReport.pdf.

82. O*NET OnLine, "Build Your Future with O*Net OnLine," https://www.onetonline.org.

83. Department of Labor, Employment and Training Administration, CareerOneStop. Occupation Profiles, https://www.careeronestop.org/ExploreCareers/Learn/career-profiles.aspx.

84. Department of Labor, Employment and Training Administration, Competency Model Clearinghouse, Industry Models, https://www.careeronestop.org/CompetencyModel/competency-models/industry-cluster.aspx?industry=6.

85. Lumina Foundation, "Create New Systems of Credentials," https://www.luminafoundation.org/create-new-systems-of-quality-credentials.

86. Corporation for a Skilled Workforce, "The Competency Project," http://thecompetencyproject.com.

87. Credential Engine, https://credentialengine.org.

88. Michelle Weise, Andrew Hanson, Allison Salisbury, and Kathy Qu (Strada Institute), "On Ramps to Good Jobs," Strada Institute, March 11, 2019, https://go.stradaeducation.org/on-ramps.

89. Council for Adult and Experiential Learning (CAEL), Strategic Plan, 2019–2021, https://www.cael.org/hubfs/Strategic-Plan_CAEL_2019.pdf?hsCtaTracking=45bcdca6-0dbc-4e44-9597-c2825ba279ef%7Ce448b2d1-3844-4a04-b40f-9723ebd60a5a.

90. Thors, "Digitizing Manufacturing Knowledge," https://www.thors.com.

91. 180Skills, Manufacturing Skills Training, http://www.180skills.com.

92. Tooling U-SME, Online Classes, https://www.toolingu.com/training/online?creative=248833256133&keyword=manufacturing%20training&matchtype=b&network=g&device=c&gclid=EAIaIQobChMIlpjHkumC4gIVBhgMCh0M0AR0EAAYASAAEgJ5aPD_BwE.

93. NIMS, https://www.nims-skills.org; Manufacturing Skills Standards Council (MSSC), "Our Services," https://www.msscusa.org.

94. Tulip, "The Smarter Way to Manufacture: Bring Your People, Machines, and Processes Together with Manufacturing's First Platform as a Service," https://tulip.co.

95. Eric Bender, "Tulip and Merck Partner to Accelerate Operator Training for Complex Assembly," *Startup Exchange*, MIT ILP, June 28, 2017, http://ilp.mit.edu/newsstory.jsp?id=23513&startup-exchange=Y.

96. Department of Energy, Tech to Market Program, EERE, Build4Scale, Manufacturing Training for Cleantech Entrepreneurs, July 2017, https://energy.gov/eere/technology-to-market/build4scale-manufacturing-training-cleantech-entrepreneurs. See also MForesight, "Manufacturing 101: An Education and Training Curriculum for Hardware Entrepreneurs," http://mforesight.org/projects-events/mfg-101/.

97. MForesight, "America's Next Manufacturing Workforce: Promising Practices for Education and Skills Building," July 2017, http://mforesight.org/download-reports/.

98. Jason Tyszko, executive director, US Chamber of Commerce Foundation's Center for Education and Workforce, discussion, November 7, 2017. See also US Chamber of Commerce Foundation Talent Pipeline Management Initiative, https://www.uschamberfoundation.org/talent-pipeline-management.

99. Betty Daniels, "HFCC Lead College in Manufacturing Consortium," *Mirror News*, October 22, 2012, https://mirrornews.hfcc.edu/news/2012/10-22/hfcc-lead-college-manufacturing-consortium; Ken Poole and Mark Troppe, president and vice president, Center for Regional Economic Competiveness, meeting, October 23, 2017.

100. Daniel Bustillo, director of the Healthcare Career Advancement Program, Service Employees International Union (SIEU), presentation at New America Foundation forum, December 6, 2017.

101. Keisha Powell, Workforce Development Consultant, Fairview Health Services, Minnesota, presentation at New America Foundation forum, December 6, 2017. See also Ivy Love and Alice McCarthy, "Apprenticeship and the Future of Nursing, An Equity-Based Strategy to Address the Bachelor's Degree Gap," New America Foundation,

September 2018, https://d1y8sb8igg2f8e.cloudfront.net/documents/Apprenticeship_and_the_Future_of_Nursing_2018-08-30_170634.pdf.

102. American Health Information Management Association (AHiMA), Certified Professional in Helath Informatics (CPHI), https://www.ahima.org/education/health-informatics.

10 THE APPRENTICESHIP MODEL

1. "General Electric History: The Shop Apprenticeship System for Boys—Machinist Course," The Schenectady Digital History Archive, Schenectary Co. Public Library (excerpts from 52-page pamphlet from 1917), http://www.schenectadyhistory.org/ge/sasfb/machinists.html.

2. Magnus W. Alexander, "The Apprenticeship System of the General Electric Company at West, Lynn, Massachusetts," *Annals of the American Academy of Political and Social Science* 33, no. 1, Industrial Education (January 1909): 141–150, https://www.jstor.org/stable/1011752?seq=1#metadata_info_tab_contents.

3. Kettering University, "About Us," https://www.kettering.edu/about/planning-assessment-and-accreditation/accreditation.

4. *Guardian* Weekly, "When General Electric Jobs Left Schenectady So Did a Way of Life," November 6, 2016, https://www.theguardian.com/us-news/2016/nov/06/general-electric-factory-schenectady-new-york-manufacturing-jobs.

5. Apprentice School, Newport News Shipbuilding, About, https://www.as.edu/about/index.html.

6. President's Council of Advisors on Science and Technology (PCAST), "Advanced Manufacturing Partnership, Report to the President on Accelerating Advanced Manufacturing" (Washington, DC: White House PCAST October 2014)(AMP 2.0), 34, https://www.manufacturingusa.com/sites/prod/files/amp20_report_final.pdf; Department of Labor, Employment and Training Administration, Apprenticeship, Data and Statistics, Registered Apprenticeship to 9/30/18, https://doleta.gov/oa/data_statistics.cfm.

7. Erica Smith and Ros Brennan Kemmis, "Towards a Model Apprenticeship Framework: A Comparative Analysis of National Apprenticeship Systems," International Labor Organization and The World Bank, 2013.

8. For a description of how registered apprenticeships work, see Susan Helper, Ryan Noonan, Jessica Nicholson, and David Langdon, "The Benefits and Costs of Apprenticeship: A Business Perspective," Case Western Reserve University and the Department of Commerce, November 2016, https://files.eric.ed.gov/fulltext/ED572260.pdf.

9. Richard B. Freeman, *America Works: The Exceptional U.S. Labor Market* (New York: Russell Sage Foundation, 2007), 3.

10. Gary S. Becker, *Human Capital: A Theoretical and Empirical Analysis, with Special Reference to Education* (New York: National Bureau of Economic Research, 1975).

11. Robert D. Atkinson, "Restoring Investment in America's Economy," Information Technology and Innovation Foundation report, June 2016, 8, http://www2.itif.org/2016-restoring-investment.pdf?_ga=1.113675271.1482316035.1476207219.

12. Robert Lehman, "Are Employers Providing Enough Training?," 18. See also Robert Lerman, "Do Firms Benefit from Apprenticeship?," *IZA World of Labor*, 2014, http://wol.iza.org/articles/do-firms-benefit-from-apprenticeship-investments; Robert Lerman, Lauren Eyster, and Kate Chambers, "The Benefits and Challenges of Registered Apprenticeship: The Sponsors' Perspective," The Urban Institute Center on Labor, Human Services, and Population, Washington, DC, 2009, http://www.urban.org/UploadedPDF/411907_registered_apprenticeship.pdf.

13. Robert Lehman, "Are Employers Providing Enough Training? Theory, Evidence and Policy Implications," paper, National Academy of Sciences, Symposium on the Supply Chain for Middle-Skill Jobs, 2017, 17, https://sites.nationalacademies.org/cs/groups/pgasite/documents/webpage/pga_168146.pdf. See, generally, Robert Lerman, Can the United States Expand Apprenticeship? Lessons from Experience IZA Policy Paper No. 46, 2012.

14. United Nations Statistics Division, "Youth Unemployment Rate, Aged 15–24," Millennium Development Goals, https://unstats.un.org/unsd/mdg/SeriesDetail.aspx?srid=597.

15. Bureau of Labor Statistics, "Employment and Unemployment Among Youth—Summer 2018," August 16, 2018, https://www.bls.gov/news.release/pdf/youth.pdf.

16. Trading Economics, "Germany Youth Unemployment Rate," September 2018, https://tradingeconomics.com/germany/youth-unemployment-rate.

17. Bob Schwartz and Amy Loyd, "Pathways 101: An Introduction to the Network and the Work," Pathways to Prosperity Project, October 23, 2018, https://ptopnetwork.jff.org/sites/default/files/Pathways%20101-%20Introduction%20to%20the%20Pathways%20to%20Prosperity%20Network.pdf.

18. Jonathan Rothwell, "The Hidden STEM Economy," Brookings Institution, June 10, 2013, https://www.brookings.edu/research/the-hidden-stem-economy/.

19. William C. Symonds, Robert Schwartz, and Ronald F. Ferguson, "Pathways to Prosperity: Meeting the Challenge of Preparing Young Americans for the 21st Century," Pathways to Prosperity Project, Harvard Graduate School of Education, February 2011, 7, http://www.gse.harvard.edu/sites/default/files//documents/Pathways_to_Prosperity_Feb2011-1.pdf.

20. While CTE programs in academic year 2017–2018 disproportionately reached low income and minority students, only an estimated 23 percent completed a CTE-related degree or certificate. "Higher Learning Advocates and Advance CTE, 101: Career

Technical Education," online paper, June 2019, https://ejm0i2fmf973k8c9d2n34685-wpengine.netdna-ssl.com/wp-content/uploads/2019/06/CTE-101-Career-Technical-Education-FINAL.pdf?mc_cid=8c5d3ce5bf&mc_eid=b4a13b6555.

21. AMP 2.0 report.

22. Discussion drawn from Bonvillian and Singer, *Advanced Manufacturing*, chapter 8.

23. AMP2.0, appendix 2, 71–73.

24. This consortia approach built on a framework developed by a prior NSF-supported effort, AMTEC. This was formed in 2005 because of concerns from community colleges in states with major auto manufacturing plants about a need to improve training to keep up with production advances in that sector. AMTEC includes twelve community colleges and eighteen auto companies and suppliers working across five states. See Automotive Manufacturing Technical Education Collaborative (AMTEC), http://autoworkforce.org/about-amtec/.

25. AMP2.0, 35.

26. Discussion drawn from AMP2.0, 33–34.

27. AMP2.0, 34.

28. AMP2.0, 34.

29. Florida Advanced Technological Education (FLATE), website, http://fl-ate.org/about-us/impact/. See also FLATE infographic of pathways (which are not linear), http://fl-ate.org/wp-content/uploads/2014/12/10_2016-ET-Highlights.pdf. The Florida Department of Education aos has a strong precollege through college framework for manufacturing education. See Florida Department of Education, 2015–2016 Frameworks, Manufacturing (precollege through college framework for manufacturing education), website, http://www.fldoe.org/academics/career-adult-edu/career-tech-edu/curriculum-frameworks/2015-16-frameworks/manufacturing.stml.

30. White House, Executive Order 13801, "Expanding Apprenticeships in America," June 15, 2017, https://www.whitehouse.gov/presidential-actions/3245/; Secretaries of Labor, Education and Commerce, Task Force on Apprenticeship Expansion, Final Report to the President of the United States, May 10, 2018 (Task Force on Apprenticeship Expansion), https://www.dol.gov/apprenticeship/docs/task-force-apprenticeship-expansion-report.pdf.

31. Task Force on Apprenticeship Expansion, 10.

32. Task Force on Apprenticeship Expansion, 10, 21–25.

33. Task Force on Apprenticeship Expansion, 10, 26–30.

34. Task Force on Apprenticeship Expansion, 10–11, 31–33.

35. Task Force on Apprenticeship Expansion, 11, 34–38.

36. This recommendation includes that participants in the new apprenticeship program no longer be considered as apprentices for the purpose of meeting wage requirements under the federal Davis-Bacon Act, which requires the payment of the prevailing wage rates (as determined by the Labor Department) to all laborers and mechanics on federal construction projects in excess of $2,000.

37. Task Force on Apprenticeship Expansion, 39.

38. Department of Labor, Employment and Training Administration, Final Rule, Apprenticeship Programs, 85 Federal Register 14294, 29 CFR 29, March 11, 2020.

39. Symonds, Schwartz, and Ferguson, "Pathways to Prosperity: Meeting the Challenge," 15.

40. There were some 3,400 German companies, large multinationals as well as smaller companies, with investments and operations in the United States as of 2014. Their investment level at the end of that year totaled $224 billion, which approached 8 percent of the total of foreign firms invested in the United States. See Embassy of the Federal Republic of Germany in Washington, The Skills Initiative overview, February 5, 2018, 2, https://www.germany.info/blob/922054/3800187264cdad52d44acb dfb2915ffb/skills-initiative-brochure-pdf-alt-data.pdf.

41. German Missions in the United States, Skills initiative (2015), https://www .germany.info/us-en/welcome/wirtschaft/03-Wirtschaft.

42. See, for example, German-American Chamber of Commerce—Midwest, Skills Gap and Apprentice Benefits (2018). As part of the Skills Initiative, the Illinois Consortium for Advanced Technical Training (ICATT) is working with the German-American Chamber of Commerce to encourage American companies in the region to adopt a German-style training system. See Elizabeth Schulze, "U.S. Companies Turn to German Training Model to Fill Jobs Gap: Vocational Approach Popular in Germany Helps Smaller U.S. Firms Build Skilled Workforce," *Wall Street Journal*, September 26, 2016. Organizations in several other states, specifically Michigan, Kentucky, and Georgia, are also working with the German-American Chamber of Commerce.

43. Kathleen Thelen, presentation to MIT's Work of the Future Initiative, Workforce Task Force, January 14, 2019, 1. See also Kathleen Thelen, *How Institutions Evolve: The Political Economy of Skills in Germany, Britain, the United States and Japan* (Cambridge, UK: Cambridge University Press, 2004).

44. Alan Berube, Joseph Parilla, and Jesus Leal Trujillo, "Skills and Innovation Strategy to Strengthen U.S. Manufacturing: Lessons from Germany," Brookings Institution, 2015, 7, https://www.brookings.edu/research/skills-and-innovation-strategies-to -strengthen-manufacturing-lessons-from-germany/.

45. Berube, Parilla, and Trujillo, "Skills and Innovation Strategy," 3.

46. Berube, Parilla, and Trujillo, "Skills and Innovation Strategy," 17.

47. Michael Lanford, Tattiya Maruco, and William Tierney, "Prospects for Vocational Education in the United States—Lessons from Germany," Pullias Center for Higher Education, University of Southern California, 2015, https://pullias.usc.edu/download/prospects-for-vocational-education-in-the-united-states/.

48. Dieter Euler, "Germany's Dual Vocational Training System: A Model for Other Countries?," Bertelsmann Stiftung, 2013, https://www.bertelsmann-stiftung.de/fileadmin/files/BSt/Publikationen/GrauePublikationen/GP_Germanys_dual_vocational_training_system.pdf.

49. Paul Lewis, presentation to Manufacturing USA Workforce Education Directors, workshop sponsored by the Association of Public and Land Grant Universities, Washington, DC, March 9, 2018. See also Paul Lewis (Kings College London), "Developing Technician Skills for Innovative Industries: Theory; Evidence from the UK Life Science Industry and Policy Implications," *British Journal of Industrial Relations*, March 3, 2020, 1–27 .

50. These insights are from Lewis, presentation to Manufacturing USA. See also Paul Lewis and Paul Ryan, "A Hard Sell? The Prospects for Apprenticeship in British Retailing," *Human Resource Management Journal* 18, no. 1 (2008): 3–19.

51. Doug Richard, "The Richard Review of Apprenticeships," report for the Departments of Business, Innovation and Skills, and Education, November 2012, https://dera.ioe.ac.uk/17733/1/richard-review-full.pdf; summary from https://www.gov.uk/government/news/the-richard-review-of-apprenticeships. A 2019 report known as the "Augar Review" has underscored the findings of the Richard review, Phillip Augar (chair), "Review of Post-18 Education and Funding," independent panel report presented to Parliament by the secretary of state for education, May 2019, 142–161, https://assets.publishing.service.gov.uk/government/uploads/system/uploads/attachment_data/file/805127/Review_of_post_18_education_and_funding.pdf.

52. Doug Richard, comments at Report Launch, Department of Business, Innovation and Skills, November 27, 2012, https://www.gov.uk/government/news/the-richard-review-of-apprenticeships.

53. Symonds, Schwartz, and Ferguson, "Pathways to Prosperity: Meeting the Challenge," 24–26.

54. Symonds, Schwartz, and Ferguson, "Pathways to Prosperity: Meeting the Challenge," 26.

55. Andrea Messing-Mathie, "Building Apprenticeship Systems for Middle-Skill Employment: Comparative Lessons in Innovation and Sector-Base Strategies for Apprenticeships," National Academies of Sciences, Committee on the Supply Chain for Middle-Skill Jobs: Education, Training and Certification Pathways, 2017, 10–11,

https://sites.nationalacademies.org/cs/groups/pgasite/documents/webpage/pga_170050.pdf.

56. Washington State Board for Community and Technical Colleges, Integrated Basic Education Skills and Training, https://www.sbctc.edu/colleges-staff/programs-services/i-best/.

57. Project Lead The Way (PLTW), "Bringing Real World Learning to PreK-12 Classrooms," https://www.pltw.org/about-us/our-approach.

58. Symonds, Schwartz, and Ferguson, "Pathways to Prosperity: Meeting the Challenge," 27.

59. Linked Learning, "About Linked Learning," http://www.linkedlearning.org/en/about/; Linked Learning Alliance, "At Scale, for Equity," Annual Report for 2017/2018, http://www.linkedlearning.org/wp-content/uploads/2018/10/annual-report-2018-final-1026.pdf.

60. Pathways to Prosperity, "About Us," https://ptopnetwork.jff.org/about-us.

61. Richard Kazis, "Pathways Tennessee Balances Bold State Policy and Regional Flexibility," Pathways to Prosperity and Harvard Graduate School of Education, 2017, https://jfforg-prod-prime.s3.amazonaws.com/media/documents/Tennesee-Case-Study_v5a_012918.pdf.

62. Jenna Myers of the MIT Workforce Education Project calls it an "in between way, requiring less employer commitment than apprenticeships but much better connectivity between educators and employers than in the current fragmented system." See Jenna Myers, "Employer Engagement in College and Career Pathways in Middle Tennessee," paper, Workforce Education Project, MIT Office of Open Learning, July 29, 2019, 2, https://openlearning.mit.edu/mit-open-learning-workforce-education-project.

63. Jen Mishory, "The Future of Statewide College Promise Programs," The Century Foundation, March 6, 2018, 1, https://tcf.org/content/report/future-statewide-college-promise-programs/?session=1.

64. Symonds, Schwartz, and Ferguson, "Pathways to Prosperity: Meeting the Challenge," 27.

65. Myers, "Employer Engagement in College and Career Pathways in Middle Tennessee," 6.

66. Myers, "Employer Engagement in College and Career Pathways in Middle Tennessee," 21.

67. Kazis, "Pathways Tennessee Balances Bold State Policy and Regional Flexibility," 5.

68. Kentucky FAME, "KY FAME Comes into Its Own, Sets Sights on Expanding Missions," August 2017, http://kyfame.com/ky-fame-comes-into-its-own-sets-sights-on-expanding-missions/.

69. Berube, Parilla, and Trujillo, "Skills and Innovation Strategy," 21.

70. Kentucky FAME, "KY FAME Comes into Its Own."

71. Berube, Parilla, and Trujillo, "Skills and Innovation Strategy," 23.

72. Berube, Parilla, and Trujillo, "Skills and Innovation Strategy," 23.

73. MAT2 Fact Sheet for Employers, October 27, 2017, https://www.mitalent.org/Media/Default/Files/MAT2/MAT2_EmployerFactSheet.pdf. See also Michigan Talent Connect, MAT2 Employer Information, https://www.mitalent.org/mat2-employer-information.

74. Berube, Parilla, and Trujillo, "Skills and Innovation Strategy," 23.

75. ApprenticeshipNC, North Carolina Youth Apprenticeship Guide, https://www.apprenticeshipnc.com/sites/default/files/file-uploads/nccc-printablehandbook-final-r1-print_quality.pdf.

76. North Carolina Triangle Apprenticeship Program, presentation, http://nctap.org/#about.

77. Department of Labor, Office of Apprenticeships, High School Apprenticeship Toolkit, July 2018, Wisconsin Youth Apprenticeship Case Study, 1–4, https://www.dol.gov/apprenticeship/high-school/. See also State of Wisconsin, Department of Workforce Development, Wisconsin Youth Apprenticeship, website, https://dwd.wisconsin.gov/youthapprenticeship/.

78. Department of Labor, High School Apprenticeship Toolkit, Wisconsin YA Case Study, 4.

79. State of Wisconsin, Department of Workforce Development, Wisconsin Youth Apprenticeship, https://dwd.wisconsin.gov/youthapprenticeship/.

80. Division of Economic Development, ReadySC, Rankings and Stats, https://www.readysc.org/rankings-and-stats.html.

81. Apprenticeship Carolina, "By the Numbers," https://www.apprenticeshipcarolina.com/by-the-numbers.html

82. Berube, Parilla, and Trujillo, "Skills and Innovation Strategy," 25.

83. Department of Labor, Office of Apprenticeships, High School Apprenticeship Toolkit, July 2018, Charleston Youth Apprenticeship Case Study, 2, https://www.dol.gov/apprenticeship/high-school/pdf/Charleston_SC_Youth_Case_Study-FINAL_20180830.pdf.

84. Information on the Trident Tech youth apprenticeship program in this section is from meeting with Mitchell Harp, dean of apprenticeships, and Melissa Stowasser, assistant vice president for community partnerships, Trident Technical College, North Charleston, SC, November 1, 2018 (W. Bonvillian meeting notes).

85. See Charleston Metro Chamber of Commerce, Accelerate 2, 2017–18, https://www.charlestonchamber.org/accelerate2/, an updated report.

86. Department of Labor, Charleston Youth Apprenticeship Case Study, 2.

87. Department of Labor, Charleston Youth Apprenticeship Case Study, 3.

88. Information on in this section on VTL and the Trident Tech youth apprenticeship program is from Meeting with Vincent Lobardy, Training and Employee Development Manager, VTL Precision, Inc., North Charleston, SC, November 1, 2018 (W. Bonvillian meeting notes).

89. Department of Labor, Charleston Youth Apprenticeship Case Study, 4.

11 THE NEW CONTENT DELIVERY MODELS

1. Discussions with Frank Gulluni, Manufacturing Technology Center, director emeritus, Manufacturing Program and System Development, Asnuntuck Community College, February 19, 2019, and May 30, 2019.

2. Hearing Before the Subcommittee on Employment Opportunities of the U.S. House of Representatives, Committee on Education and Labor, on CETA Reauthorization, 97th Cong., 1st Sess., November 2, 1981 (hearing chaired by Rep. James Jeffords), 29–30, https://files.eric.ed.gov/fulltext/ED219605.pdf.

3. Discussion with James Lombella (president, Asnuntuck Community College), May 30, 2019.

4. Discussion with Jose Marcelino, Academic Associate, Manufacturing Technology Center, Asnuntuck Community College, May 30, 2019.

5. Tia Marie Vice, "Can Apprenticeships Alleviate a Regional Skills Gap? A Case Study of Programs at Trident Technical College in Charleston, SC," thesis, Department of Urban Studies and Planning, MIT, February 2019, 45.

6. TennesseeReconnect, The Tennessee Colleges of Applied Technology, https://www.tnreconnect.gov/ChooseaDegree/CollegePath/TNReconnectCollegesandUniversities/TheTennesseeCollegesofAppliedTechnology/tabid/5253/Default.aspx. See, generally, Tennessee Board of Regents, The College System of Tennessee, Colleges of Applied Technlogy, https://www.tbr.edu/institutions/colleges-applied-technology.

7. The TenneessePromise program offers free community college tuition, paying the "last dollar" of tuition after other federal and state scholarships. TennesseePromise, About, https://www.tn.gov/tnpromise/about.html. See also TennesseeReconnect at https://tnreconnect.gov for tuition assistance for adult learners.

8. See chapter 9. In comparison, the state's community college graduation rate is in the 25 percent range. Tennessee Board of Regents, The College System of

Tennessee, Community College Graduate Rates, https://www.tbr.edu/cc/community-college-graduation-rates-real-story. There are other efforts emerging to help improve the community college completion rate problem. For example, systems for online "nudging"—personalized reminders to students of deadlines and encouraging them to complete assignments—has met some success. See, for example, Lisa Soricone and Barbara Endel, "Nudging to STEM Success," Jobs for the Future, Fall 2019, https://jfforg-prod-prime.s3.amazonaws.com/media/documents/Nudging_to_STEM_Success.pdf; Ross E. O'Hara and Betsey Sparrow, "A Summer Nudge Campaign to Motivate Community College STEM Students to Reenroll," *AERA Open* 5, no. 3, July–September 2019, https://journals.sagepub.com/doi/full/10.1177/2332858419875715#_i26.

9. John Hoops and Complete College America, "A Working Model for Student Success: The Tennessee Technology Centers," Complete College America, Washington, DC, 2010, 22, https://files.eric.ed.gov/fulltext/ED536826.pdf.

10. Project Quest, https://www.questsa.org/history/; Ida Rademacher, Marshall Bear and Maureen Conway, Project Quest – A Case Study of a Sectoral Employment Development Approach, Aspen Institute, August 2001, https://assets.aspeninstitute.org/content/uploads/files/content/docs/PQCASESTUDY.PDF?_ga=2.250206598.1091378394.1585852431-938139177.1585852431. Two community organizations began Project Quest in 1992, after San Antonio lost more than 14,000 manufacturing jobs, to provide support and services to low-income residents while they participated in occupation certificate as well as associate degree programs at the local community college. Working with area employers to identify both expanding fields with promising jobs and on-the training curriculum, it has served some 800 largely low-income, Hispanic students a year, moving them into well-paid jobs from nursing to offices, providing both training and job placement services, with funding support from the city, county .and state governments. It cites an 89 percent placement rate for its graduates.

11. JOBS Act of 2019, S.839, introduced by Sen. Tim Kaine (D-Va.) and 10 bipartisan cosponsors, https://www.congress.gov/bill/116th-congress/senate-bill/839/text.

12. Mary Alice McCarthy and Livia Lam, "Making the JOBS Act Work," *The Hill*, June 14, 2019, https://thehill.com/blogs/congress-blog/education/448622-making-the-jobs-act-work.

13. Livia Lam, Center for American Progress, discussion, June 24, 2019.

14. Section drawn from discussions with Diman Faculty and Administrators (Michael Valario, advanced manufacturing yechnology department head, Anne Marie Zenni, business technology department head, Mitchell Sweet, drafting faculty, Kenneth Lazarro, director, cooperative education program, and Elvio Ferreira, principal), Diman Regional Vocational and Technical High School, April 2, 2019; Diman 2018

Annual Report, https://www.dimanregional.org/cms/lib/MA01929605/Centricity/Domain/139/Official%20Annual%20Report%202018.pdf.

15. Diman Vocational Technical High School, Fall River, MA, website, https://www.dimanregional.org/domain/135.

16. See, generally, Jeannie Oakes, *Keeping Track: How Schools Structure Inequality*, 2nd ed. (New Haven, CT: Yale University Press, 2005).

17. Brian Jacob, "What We Know about Career and Technical Education in High School," Brookings Institution, October 5, 2017, https://www.brookings.edu/research/what-we-know-about-career-and-technical-education-in-high-school/.

18. Emily Hanford, American Public Media, American Radio Works, "The Troubled History of Vocational Education," September 9, 2014, http://www.americanradioworks.org/segments/the-troubled-history-of-vocational-education/.

19. Tom Birmingham, "Voc-Tech Schools Are a Massachusetts Success Story," *Commonwealth*, February 6, 2017.

20. Jacob, "What We Know About Career and Technical Education"; Shaun M. Dougherty, "The Effect of Career and Technical Education on Human Capital Accumulation: Causal Evidence from Massachusetts," University of Connecticut, Center for Education Policy Analysis Working Paper 3, March 4, 2015.

21. Jacob, "What We Know About Career and Technical Education."

22. W. Norton Grubb and Marvin Lazerson, "Is the Comprehensive Doomed?," *Education Week*, September 20, 2004, https://www.edweek.org/ew/articles/2004/09/22/04lazerson.h24.html.

23. Discussions with Ned McCullough (Global Issue Manager for Skill Development, IBM), January 17, 2019, and December 4, 2017, Washington, DC (source for points throughout subsection).

24. P-TECH, "What Is P-TECH?," http://www.ptech.org. See also Stanley S. Litow, "These Schools Are a Nationwide Answer to the Skills Crisis and High Unemployment," *Business Insider*, June 1, 2017, https://www.businessinsider.com/sc/ptech-ibm-coding-jobs-employment-2017-6.

25. IBM Apprenticeship Program, "Discover What You Can Do at IBM," https://www.ibm.com/us-en/employment/newcollar/apprenticeships.html.

26. Deloitte and the Manufacturing Institute, "Skills Gap in Manufacturing—2018," 2018, https://operationalsolutions.nam.org/mi-skills-gap-study-18/. The Manufacturing Institute has developed a detailed series of toolkits for employers to meet workforce demands, train workers, and develop apprenticeships. Manufacturing Institute, Tools We Offer, http://www.themanufacturinginstitute.org/~/media/0EC097AA93EA4953BEEC2E01E8288B61.ashx (accessed June 2019).

27. Manufacturing Skill Standards Council, https://www.msscusa.org/history/. See also John Rauschenberger (chair, Manufacturing Skill Standards Council), "The Blueprint for a Skilled Mobile Workforce," *MH&L News*, September 1, 2001, https://www.mhlnews.com/labor-management/blueprint-skilled-mobile-workforce.

28. Manufacturing Skill Standards Council, https://www.msscusa.org/about-mssc/.

29. US Chamber of Commerce Foundation Talent Pipeline Management Initiative, https://www.uschamberfoundation.org/talent-pipeline-management.

30. US Chamber of Commerce Foundation, Talent Pipeline Management, Overview and History, https://www.uschamberfoundation.org/talent-pipeline-management.

31. Wisconsin Regional Training Program, Industry Led and Worker Centered, https://wrtp.org.

32. Wisconsin Regional Training Program, Big Step Services and Center of Excellences, https://wrtp.org/about/.

33. Meghan Perdue, Massachusetts Work Training Case Study, paper, MIT Office of Open Learning Workforce Education Project, June 2019, https://openlearning.mit.edu/mit-open-learning-workforce-education-project (case study of MA workforce education).

34. MassTech Collaborative, MassTech Intern Partnership, http://www.masstech.org/intern/other-programs-and-resources.

35. Mass.gov, Department of Labor and Workforce Development, Division of Apprenticeship Standards, Apprenticeship Program for Expansion Industries (advanced manufacturing, healthcare and technology), https://www.mass.gov/guides/registering-an-apprenticeship-program-for-expansion-industries; MassTech Collaborative, About, http://www.masstech.org/masstech.

36. Mass.gov, Executive Office of Education, Massachusetts Skills Capital Grants, https://www.mass.gov/service-details/massachusetts-skills-capital-grant-program.

37. Mass.gov, Workforce Skills Cabinet, "Workforce Skills Cabinet Kicks of Regional Planning Initiative," April 5, 2017, https://www.mass.gov/news/workforce-skills-cabinet-kicks-off-new-regional-planning-initiative.

38. MassTech Collaborative, Massachusetts Manufacturing Innovation Initiative, M2I2 http://m2i2.masstech.org.

39. Planning Meeting with Ira Moskowitz, director, Advanced Manufacturing Program of the MassTech Collaborative, and officials of Massachusetts state offices of Education, Labor and Workforce, Housing and Economic Development, the Department of Defense Mantech program, and AIM Photonics Manufacturing Institute, at MIT, Cambridge, MA, May 14, 2019.

40. Thomas Kochan, David Finegold, and Paul Osterman, "Who Can Fix the 'Middle Skills' Gap?," *Harvard Business Review*, December 2012, 2103.

41. Meghan Perdue, Massachusetts Work Training Case Study, 2.

42. Andrew Reamer, "Information Resources to Facilitate Middle Skills Workforce Development," National Academies Board on Science Technology and Economic Policy, Project on the Supply Chain for Middle-Skilled Jobs, August 21, 2015, 6, 10–15, https://sites.nationalacademies.org/cs/groups/pgasite/documents/webpage/pga_169054.pdf.

43. Department of Labor, Workforce Information Advisory Council, "Recommendations to Improve the Nation's Workforce and Labor Market Information System," January 25, 2018, https://www.doleta.gov/wioa/wiac/docs/Second_Draft_of_the_WIAC_Final_Report.pdf.

44. With regard to the jobkit effort, see https://www.commerce.gov/sites/default/files/2019-08/AWPAB18June2019%20MeetingMinutes_Final_s.pdf; Census Bureau, "Post-Secondary Employment Outcomes (PSEO)," https://lehd.ces.census.gov/data/pseo_beta.html.

45. National Science Foundation, National Center for Science and Engineering Statistics (NCSES), "Data Sources to Measure and Understand the Science and Engineering Workforce and the Skilled Technical Workforce," May 3, 2019, https://www.dropbox.com/s/x7qdto29qm5cado/Possible%20Data%20Sources%20for%20the%20S%26E%20Workforce%20and%20STW%20%2805-03-19%29.pdf?dl=0.

46. Department of Commerce, American Workforce Policy Advisory Board, https://www.commerce.gov/americanworker/american-workforce-policy-advisory-board.

47. Department of Labor, Education and Training Administration, O*Net OnLine, https://www.onetonline.org.

48. US Chamber of Commerce Foundation, T3 program, https://www.uschamberfoundation.org/t3-innovation/pilot-projects.

49. US Chamber of Commerce Foundation, JDX program, https://www.uschamberfoundation.org/press-release/job-data-exchange-jdx-pilot-launches-modernize-labor-market-data.

50. Clemson University Center for Workforce Development, EducateWorkforce, https://cecas.clemson.edu/cucwd/educateworkforce/.

51. MIT Office of Open Learning, "Reinventing Education," https://openlearning.mit.edu.

52. MIT Game Lab, http://gamelab.mit.edu/about/.

53. Suzanne Day, "Nine Universities Team Up to Create Infrastructure for Digital Academic Credentials," MIT Office of Open Learning, April 23, 2019, http://news

.mit.edu/2019/nine-universities-team-up-global-infrastructure-digital-academic-credentials-0423.

12 A ROADMAP TO NEW WORKFORCE SYSTEMS

1. Robert M. Solow, *Growth Theory: An Exposition*, 2nd ed. (New York: Oxford University Press, 2000), ix–xxvi (Nobel Prize Lecture, December 8, 1987, http://nobelprize.org/nobel_prizes/economics/laureates/1987/solow-lecture.html).

2. Paul Romer, "Endogenous Technological Change," *Journal of Political Economy* 98, no. 5 (1990): 71–102, http://pages.stern.nyu.edu/~promer/Endogenous.pdf.

3. Richard R. Nelson, *National Systems of Innovation* (New York: Oxford University Press, 1993), 3–21, 505–523.

4. William B. Bonvillian, "The Connected Science Model for Innovation," in *21st Century Innovation Systems for Japan and the United States*, ed. S. Nagaoka, M. Kondo, K. Flamm, and C. Wessner (Washington, DC: National Academies Press, 2009), 171–173.

5. William B. Bonvillian and Peter L. Singer, *Advanced Manufacturing: The New American Innovation Policies* (Cambridge, MA: MIT Press, 2018), 34–35, 55–63.

INDEX

Note: Page numbers in italics indicate illustrations; those with a *t* indicate tables.